The Louisville & Nashville Railroad

The Louisville & Nashville Railroad

1850-1963

KINCAID HERR

With a Foreword by Lyle Key

First Printing - April 1943
Second Printing - August 1943
Third Printing - October 1959
Fourth Printing - December 1960
Revised Edition - March 1964

THE UNIVERSITY PRESS OF KENTUCKY

Publication of this volume was made possible in part by
grants from the E.O. Robinson Mountain Fund and
the National Endowment for the Humanities.

Copyright © 2000 by The University Press of Kentucky
Paperback edition 2009

The University Press of Kentucky
Scholarly publisher for the Commonwealth,
serving Bellarmine University, Berea College, Centre
College of Kentucky, Eastern Kentucky University,
The Filson Historical Society, Georgetown College,
Kentucky Historical Society, Kentucky State University,
Morehead State University, Murray State University,
Northern Kentucky University, Transylvania University,
University of Kentucky, University of Louisville,
and Western Kentucky University.
All rights reserved.

Editorial and Sales Offices: The University Press of Kentucky
663 South Limestone Street, Lexington, Kentucky 40508-4008
www.kentuckypress.com

Cataloging-in-Publication Data is available from
the Library of Congress.

ISBN 978-0-8131-9318-2 (pbk: acid-free paper)

This book is printed on acid-free recycled paper meeting
the requirements of the American National Standard
for Permanence in Paper for Printed Library Materials.

Manufactured in the United States of America.

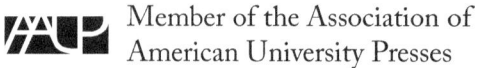

Member of the Association of
American University Presses

Contents

Foreword to the 2000 Edition vii
Author's Note ix

Chapter			
	I	An Acorn is Planted	1
	II	Behind the Blueprints	6
	III	Wresting a Passageway	11
	IV	The Course is Shaped	15
	V	First Through Train	20
	VI	Mars in the Ascendant	29
	VII	Recovery from War	39
	VIII	Southward to Coal and Iron	45
	IX	Yellow Jack and Teredos	53
	X	Coke Feeds the Furnace	62
	XI	Presidential Parade	67
	XII	Changing the Rail Gauge	76
	XIII	Growth in Mining Areas	84
	XIV	Entering the Cumberlands	91
	XV	Expanding Services	100
	XVI	Builders and Wreckers	108
	XVII	More Bluegrass Pastures	114
	XVIII	Alabama Steel	120
	XIX	Consolidation Maneuvers	127
	XX	Nashville's New Station	135
	XXI	Southward—to Georgia	144
	XXII	New Fields of Usefulness	151
	XXIII	L'Affaire Gates—Hawley	160
	XXIV	Shop Talk	164
	XXV	Y's and Otherwise	169
	XXVI	A Look at Eastern Kentucky	178
	XXVII	North Fork Extension	187
	XXVIII	Harlan County Coal	199
	XXIX	Adjustment to War	207
	XXX	Federal Control	214
	XXXI	War's Aftermath	223
	XXXII	An Era Ends	230
	XXXIII	We Mend Our "Ways"	238
	XXXIV	Belt-Tightening	247
	XXXV	Water on the Track	256
	XXXVI	War Again!	266
	XXXVII	World War II Years	274
	XXXVIII	The First Century Ends	282
	XXXIX	First Ten—Second Hundred	290
	XL	Into the Space Age	304
Appendix	I	From Wood to Steel	328
	II	"Varnish" Train Ensemble	337
	III	L. & N. Motive Power	349
	IV	L. & N. Roadway and Track	367
		Presidents of the L. & N	385
		Railroads Acquired, Leased or Constructed	388
		In Grateful Acknowledgment	389
		Indices	390

Foreword to the 2000 Edition

During my high school years in the early 1960s, I purchased a copy of the fourth edition of this book for a mere three dollars. The volume proved to be a good investment for a young railfan with a voracious appetite for information about railroads, the Louisville & Nashville in particular. Much to my delight, Kincaid Herr wrote in a light, entertaining style that made his history quite enjoyable. The book proved to be detailed enough to answer most of my questions about the L&N's origins and development, yet the line's history was sufficiently condensed and distilled to prevent the sensation that one was ploughing through a thick and tedious textbook. Thanks to the corporate background provided by Kincaid Herr, I felt quite at home in November of 1969 when I reported for my first L&N job in room 100 of Louisville Union Station.

Kincaid Herr's career with the L&N spanned over forty years, and during most of that time, he was associated with *L&N Magazine*. Thus, *The Louisville & Nashville Railroad* is an in-house corporate history that endeavors to cast the railroad's activities in a positive light. Nevertheless, it does not come across as a propaganda piece and generally may be characterized as a solid recounting of the railroad's long and notable existence.

Herr's book traces the development and expansion of the L&N system, from its beginning in 1850 to the early part of the twentieth century. After covering the railroad's era of expansion, the book then focuses on significant events involving the L&N from the early 1900s to the early 1960s. Herr also offers four appendices on special topics—such as passenger equipment and motive power—and a veritable treasure trove of photographs and drawings spanning the life of the company. The author goes to great lengths to cover the many facets of the railroad, writing about subjects such as expansion into new markets, large and small railroad stations, connections with sailing ships in Pensacola, the expansive South Louisville Shops, and the once-famous *Pan American* broadcasts over WSM radio in Nashville.

Herr also discusses Milton H. Smith, who served as the company's president for an incredible thirty-two years. During his tenure, which began in the 1880s and ended in 1921, Milton Smith shaped the destiny of the Louisville & Nashville as one of America's preeminent rail carriers. For instance, he had the foresight to establish an expansive network of rail lines throughout the Birmingham District to serve the Magic City's fledgling iron and coal industries. During my years in the L&N Law Department, one of my colleagues was Milton H. Smith II, President Smith's grandson. The younger Milton was a distinguished gentleman with the elegant bearing and independent spirit of a bygone era. His office was furnished with wicker furniture handed down from his grandfather, and the numerous historic photographs on his walls included a broadside shot of the Pullman sleeper *Milton H. Smith*.

The author also mentions two colorful non-employees who left their unusual marks on the L&N's history. The company's rail lines took on great strategic importance during the War Between the States, and Confederate general John Hunt Morgan and his raiders inflicted considerable damage on the young railroad. Further south in Alabama, the L&N suffered at the hands of railroad bandit Morris Slater, who is remembered in folk song and legend as "Railroad Bill."

No history of the L&N would be complete without mentioning its famous passenger service, and Herr does not neglect that aspect of the line's historical record. At one point, the railroad held a contest to select names for its two post–World War II streamliners. The competition attracted nearly three hundred thousand entries, and the winning names were *Humming Bird* and *Georgian*. Everyone knows that passenger trains traditionally are given distinctive names, but Herr notes that the L&N once even fielded a named fast freight train, the *Silver Bullet*.

This reprint is sure to be welcomed by both hardcore railfans and anyone who has a sense for the significant role the L&N played in the territory it served. The Old Reliable was a powerful railroad with a rich heritage, and its most ardent admirers have formed the L&N Railroad Historical Society, which boasts a membership of around twelve hundred. As the Kentucky Historical Society recently discovered, however, the fascination with the L&N extends far beyond the LNHS.

In 1999, CSX gave the Kentucky Railway Museum a substantial grant to cover the cost of creating a traveling L&N history exhibit. The museum created the exhibit in concert with the Kentucky Historical Society, whose curator was pleasantly surprised when, after only two weeks, the exhibit was fully booked for one year in advance. That had never happened before during the twelve-year history of the society's traveling exhibits program.

Some might question why there was no attempt to update this reprint of the fifth and final edition, which was published in March of 1964. Charlie Castner and Ron Flanary come to mind as L&N aficionados who would have been more than capable for that task. On balance, however, it seemed preferable to reprint this "pure" version of Herr's work, which concluded with the L&N still headquartered in Louisville and still very much in the passenger business. Agents were still deployed around the railroad in small town depots, and most of the system's rail lines remained in place and in service.

The Louisville & Nashville Railroad has been out of print for many years, and I think it is safe to say that all alumni and friends of the line are delighted that the University Press of Kentucky has reprinted it for the next generation of L&N admirers. The decision to reprint the book is especially gratifying as we celebrate the 150th anniversary of the Louisville & Nashville Railroad's corporate charter. I hope that everyone will enjoy this volume as much as I have enjoyed the one I purchased almost forty years ago.

Lyle Key
Regional Vice President
CSX Corporation
Nashville, Tennessee

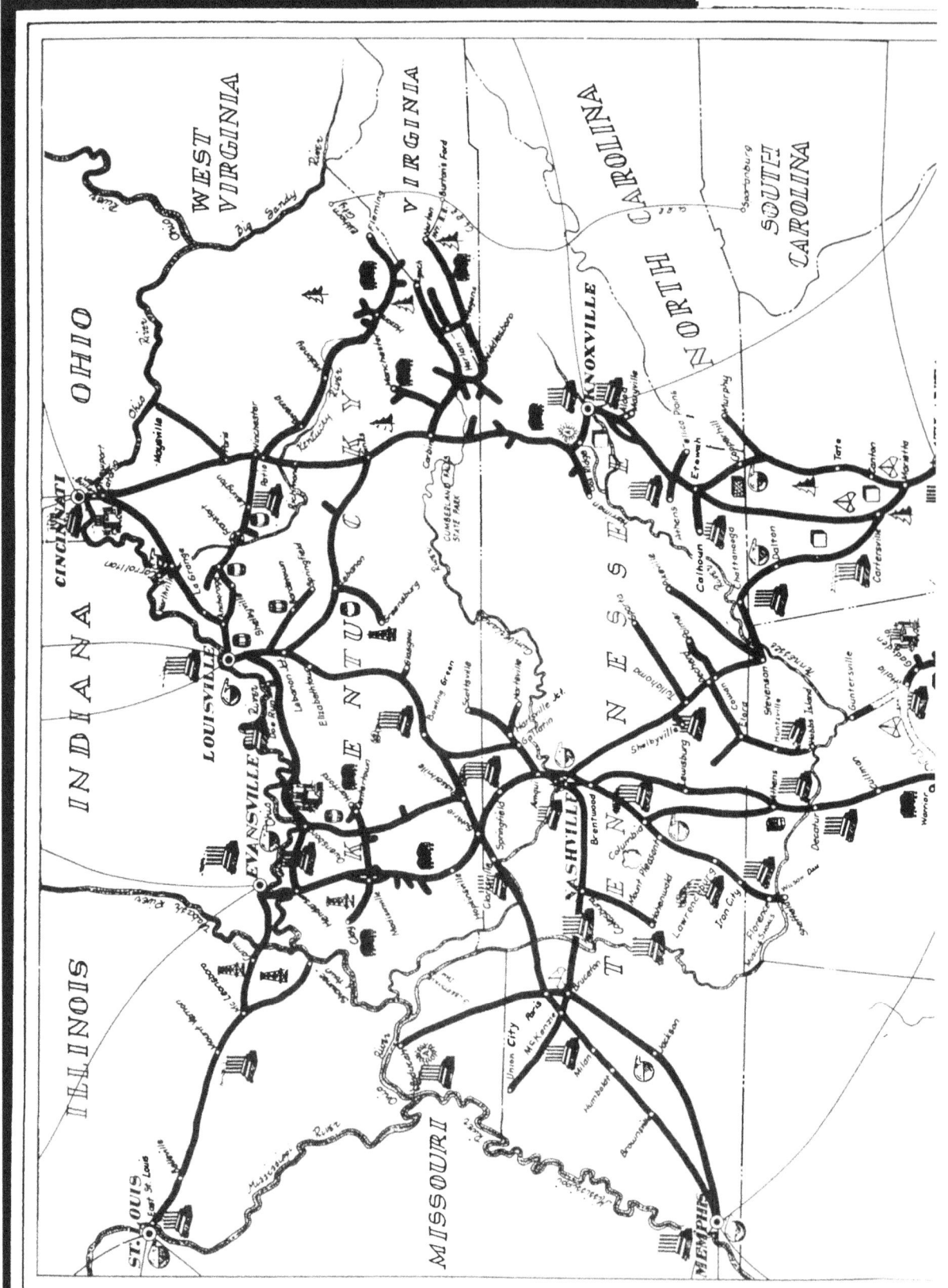

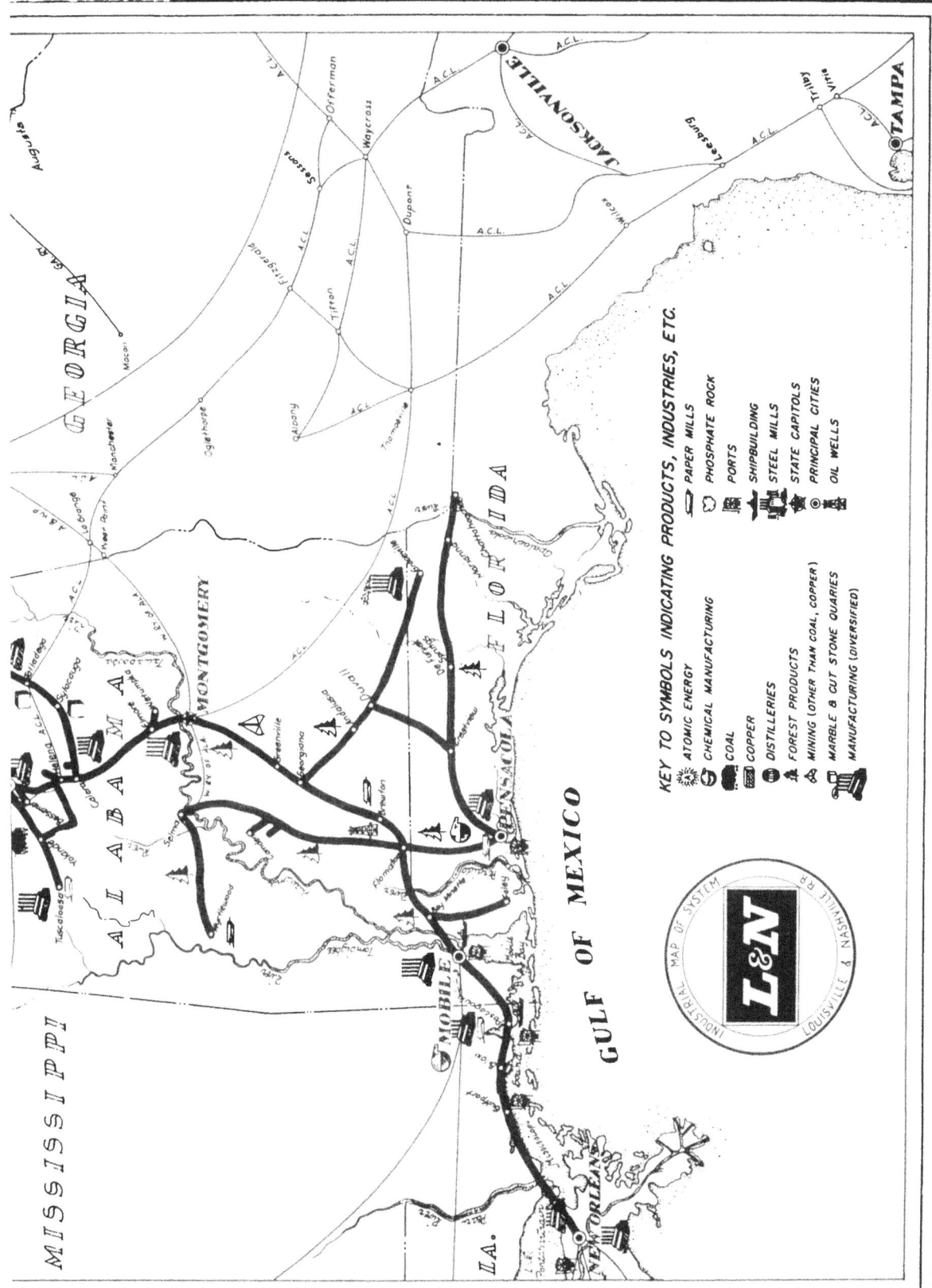

Author's Note

This history of the L. & N. had its inception in the pages of the L. & N. Magazine where it ran serially for 43 issues, beginning with January 1939.

The first edition was thereafter published in April 1943, with three other editions subsequently printed at various times to cover developments up to 1959, with new material added as necessary.

This fifth edition, which is being published on the 114th anniversary of the Railroad, in response to a continuing demand, represents a thorough revision and contains a new chapter, "Into the Space Age," which brings the record up to date by dealing specifically with the period 1959 through 1963.

At this time the author wishes to gratefully acknowledge his debt and to express his appreciation to the many employes of the L. & N. Railroad whose kind cooperation either made valued contributions to the text or was helpful in the compilation and publishing of the book. A by no means complete list of these appears on page 389, following the appendices.

The author's research also was aided by material previously published, especially those items listed on page 389.

The writer's chief function, in fact, as stated in the first edition, has been to research, read, digest and then dove-tail the factual material obtained from various sources.

No startling disclosures are made and the volume does not pose as either an **unbiased** or a **complete** history of the L. & N. We do feel, however, that it is worthy to reemphasize in this note that the Railroad has never changed its corporate name and has never been in receivership. It has always met its obligations to the public, paid every dollar to its workers, its creditors and its stockholders, and with very few exceptions, has regularly declared dividends to those stockholders since 1864.

With such a record a little partiality on the writer's part is perhaps excusable . . . and we have tried to be as complete as possible within the bounds of readability.

—K. A. H.
March 5, 1964

CHAPTER I

An Acorn is Planted

AT THIS distance, the ante-bellum days of the Civil War have an undeniable quaintness – as do all yesteryears. However, to those who lived in that era, they were **modern** times. In fact, judging from the newspapers of that day, one would be pardoned for assuming that the millenium was being ushered in at a somewhat undignified rate of speed.

Just as the 1960s have been called the beginning of the Space Age, the 1850s could be described as blossoming of the Railroad Age. Every community east of the Mississippi was afflicted with Iron Horse fever and this had had its inception as early as the 1830s, following the building of the Baltimore and Ohio, the Lexington and Ohio, and other pioneer railroads.

Thus, in 1850, following a decade or more of typical discussion, argument and widely divergent viewpoints, the agitation for a railroad between the cities of Louisville, Ky., and Nashville, Tenn., reached its climax. Its final flowering occurred on March 5, 1850 when the Louisville and Nashville Railroad Company was granted a charter by the Commonwealth of Kentucky for the purpose of building and operating a railroad from Louisville to the Tennessee state line in the direction of Nashville. The new company's name coincided perfectly with its aims which, however, were not at all modest ones for that time. On the contrary they were quite ambitious and in some quarters were even considered to be on the visionary side.

The granting of the charter on March 5, 1850, meant that victory had perched upon the banners of certain forces; for others the day brought no rejoicing. These latter had opposed the project for a variety of reasons; some sincerely, some according to the dictates of self-interest. Subsequent events proved how ill-directed such opposition was. At this distance, it can safely be said that March 5, 1850, was a momentous day in the history, not only of Louisville and Nashville and intermediate points, but of the entire Southland as well.

The new venture's first president was to be Levin L. Shreve, a prominent Louisville businessman, who had been a foremost advocate of such a railroad from the very first. His election did not take place, however, until September 27, 1851, following the prior election by the stockholders of seven directors. He was to be succeeded on October 2, 1854, by John L. Helm, a former governor of Kentucky, who had also long been active on behalf of the railroad and whose election to high office was in recognition of his inspired effort.

Agitation for a railroad leading southward from Louisville had been started by the earnest citizens of Bardstown, Ky., as early as 1832, given impetus by the chartering of the Lexington and Ohio in 1830 and its subsequent construction. It is typical of those days that nothing ever came of this. The citizens of Louisville, who had most to gain from the venture, still regarded with a complacent eye the location of their city upon the banks of the Ohio, and the proposed route of the L. & O., before referred to, including as it did the Kentucky metropolis, solidified this feeling of satisfaction with the **status quo.**

The times were changing, however, and it was not long before it began to be realized that not only was the Ohio not a dependable servant, but that the wagon trails over which a large part of the state and nation's commerce moved, were too slow for a century that had already given birth to the steamboat and the telegraph. Insofar as the Ohio was concerned it was like the little girl in the poem: "When she was good, she was very, very good, but when she was bad she was horrid!" And the Ohio had a wide variety of unpleasant moods, ranging from snow-and-ice-clogged channels through flood to drought. During any of these, navigation was drastically curtailed and frequently cancelled entirely. This, of course, had an unfortunate effect upon the well-being of millions of citizens.

On March 5, 1850 the Louisville and Nashville Railroad Company was granted a charter by Kentucky for building and operating a railroad from Louisville to the Tennessee state line.

Moreover, the Lexington & Ohio, which was to supplement the river route and the wagon roads, had not reached Louisville by 1847 and, in fact, it was 1851 before the line between Louisville and Frankfort was completed. In the meantime, however, an aroused citizenry had realized that Louisville was slipping. Their city was ideally situated between the North and the South, but as stated, the rapid growth and settlement of the country made it imperative that a quicker way be evolved for exchanging iron, coal, etc., for the finished products of the factories of the North. There was a grave danger that the streams of trade and commerce might change their course and pass Louisville by.

Thus, consciously or unconsciously, the citizens of Louisville and vicinity were subscribing to Francis Bacon's statement made nearly three centuries earlier:

"There are three things which make a nation great and prosperous – a fertile soil, busy workshops, and easy conveyance of men and animals from place to place." (Of course, Lord Bacon's statement was made at the beginning of the Industrial Revolution – otherwise he might have supplemented it by adding ". . . and a ready exchange of raw materials and finished products.")

In the comparatively short span of two years, therefore, opposition was quelled, claims and counter-claims were reconciled and, as a result of enthusiastic meetings at Glasgow, Bowling Green and Louisville, a concrete program was evolved. The proponents of the proposed road at every opportunity repulsed opponents with such statistical shrapnel as the fact that the road would be tributary to 10,046,107 acres of land, having a tax value of $192,834,520 and with a population of 588,956. In this area were 174,369 horses, 42,999 mules, 390,896 head of cattle, 590,680 sheep and 1,839,831 swine. It had produced 1,143,201 bushels of wheat, 32,368,052 bushels of corn, 1,832,038 bushels of oats and 37,824,820 pounds of tobacco annually. Embraced within the area were rich timber belts and ore beds, etc.

Nor was the value of the proposed railroad's rail and water connections – the pathways to wider spheres of activity and influence – overlooked. The agitation in Kentucky for a railroad between Louisville and Nashville, as mentioned, was typical of the railroad fever then sweeping the country. Roads having terminals at Louisville and Nashville, or in their near vicinity, had just been completed or were being rapidly pushed to completion. At Louisville, for instance, in addition to the ever-present Ohio River there was the previously mentioned Louisville and Frankfort Railroad, which was rapidly putting the finishing touches to the track between the two cities of its corporate name. Across the Ohio River from Louisville, Jeffersonville and New Albany were the terminals of railroads nearing completion, or just recently completed, which were later to be absorbed by such systems as the Pennsylvania, the Big Four, the Baltimore & Ohio, the Monon and the Southern. These lines were then known by the less familiar names of the Louisville and Sandusky Railroad, the Louisville and Cleveland Straight Line Railroad, the Jeffersonville and Columbus Railroad, the Fort Wayne and Southern Railroad and the New Albany and Salem Railroad. (Although Louisville was the avowed destination of most of these roads, they were actually not able to reach that city until the early part of 1870, when the 14th Street bridge between Louisville and Jeffersonville was opened for traffic.)

At Nashville, in addition to the Cumberland River, the proposed road would connect with the Nashville and Chattanooga Railroad and the Tennessee and Alabama Railroad, the first of which (in 1850) was nearing completion, with the second still in the blueprint stage.

It was estimated also that some 7,000 persons traveled annually between Louisville and Nashville, most of these making the trip by stagecoach, this costing the patron anywhere from $12 to $18. The revenue to be expected from the transportation of "mails and expresses" was estimated at $40,000 per year and the through freight revenue which the road might expect annually from its hauling of cotton, material for bale rope and bagging, bacon, salt pork and bulk meats, flour, whiskey, tobacco, mules and merchandise of various sorts, was placed in the neighborhood of $275,000. This was exclusive of the revenue from the local traffic, which was expected to be not inconsiderable.

At a mass meeting in Louisville held during the early part of 1850, it was voted that Louisville invest $1,000,000 in the proposed venture. It was originally proposed to obtain a charter for a road between Louisville and Bowling Green, by way of Elizabethtown, but this was subsequently amended, the name of specific towns were stricken out and the less specific charter was obtained. The new company was also given the privilege by this charter of constructing several lateral lines to the main line.

The capital stock of the Company was placed at $3,000,000, with the proviso that this might be increased to $4,000,000 in case of necessity. The charter, as granted, of course, provided only for the construction and operation of the railroad in Kentucky.

This original charter granted the Louisville & Nashville Railroad was carefully drawn up and consisted of about 5,000 words. It specified that shares in the new venture should sell for $100 each and that each of the counties through which the proposed road would operate had the privilege of subscribing for as much stock as seemed expedient, this money to be raised via the tax route, after the sentiment of the community with regard to the propriety of the step had been sounded out by a vote.

In case of disputes arising over the value to be placed on land, timber, earth, stone and other materials needed and acquired by the railroad, the sheriff of the county was empowered to select a panel of 20 men, 12 of whom, after the railroad and the other party had eliminated four each, would "justly and impartially fix the damages which the owner or owners shall sustain by the use and occupation of the said property."

The president and board of directors were given the privilege of selecting and determining the right-of-way, with the proviso that it could not be wider than 66 feet. As many sets of tracks might be constructed as were deemed necessary.

The charter gave the railroad the privilege of charging three and one-half mills per mile for every 100 pounds of goods, merchandise or property handled, provided the distance carried was over 20 miles and under 50 miles. For all persons, livestock and "every other description of freight and property," it was specified that "they shall charge no greater rate than is authorized to be charged on the railway from Lexington to Frankfort."

The State also promised not to grant charters for 30 years to any railroads which might compete with the L. & N. but very cannily inserted that inclusive phrase, "that nothing in this act shall be so construed" with regard to its right to authorize the "Kentucky and Mississippi Railroad Company" to extend their said road from Hopkinsville to Louisville.

It was necessary to obtain an additional charter for that portion of the line in Tennessee. This involved certain difficulties; difficulties which were magnified and exaggerated to a large extent by sectional rivalries and understandable jealousies. Nashville, while welcoming the proposed railroad, feared that Louisville directors would gain complete control of the company, and that the capital of Tennessee would not obtain any real benefits.

The charter first granted by the State of Tennessee, therefore, was not an especially liberal one, compared to that granted by the Kentucky, or even compared to charters which had been granted other roads by the State of Tennessee. It is specified that the proposed railroad must pass through the town of Gallatin, that it should approach no closer to Nashville than the northern bank of the Cumberland River and that the Company could only convey its freight across the river and into Nashville proper by means of **horse-drawn vehicles.** A further clause inserted in the Tennessee charter required the Louisville & Nashville Railroad to start construction at both ends of the road at the same time. Oddly enough, the original Tennessee charter was granted on February 9, 1850, almost a month before the one was obtained from Kentucky. The Tennessee charter was subsequently amended and liberalized and the Company was given the privilege of entering the city proper and of erecting a depot convenient to that of the Nashville & Chattanooga Railroad. In return for this concession, the Tennessee legislature requested that a charter be granted by Kentucky for a railroad from Nashville to Lexington. This never materialized.

Its charter difficulties finally overcome, the Louisville and Nashville's troubles were far from over, of course. Two of its most immediate problems were (1) the obtaining of the necessary money for the construction of a project of such magnitude and (2) the determining of the most practicable route, taking all factors into consideration.

Chapter II

Behind the Blueprints

THE Louisville Courier of July 1, 1851, carries a significant item, an item, however, which at the time was treated rather insignificantly, not to say negligently, and whose three or four lines were sandwiched in between the patent medicine ads and the account of a ruckus on Water Street. This item merely stated with undue reticence, that L. L. Robinson, who was employed as engineer with the Maysville and Lexington Railroad, would arrive in the city the next day to start the survey of the proposed route of the Louisville & Nashville Railroad. It informed its readers that the party would work southward by way of Elizabethtown and Bowling Green, returning via Glasgow and Bardstown.

One thereafter looks in vain for any mention of the progress of the surveying party. This is rather odd for all three of Louisville's dailies, the Courier, the Journal and the Democrat, were enthusiastic supporters of the road. It would seem that they would have aroused the public to the necessity of celebrating such an event with appropriate fanfare and would have given their readers a blow-by-blow account of what was happening. But perhaps the papers mentioned were slightly satiated with discussion of the railroad, for it was a favorite topic of the day and letters signed "Locomotive," "Railroad," and the like dotted their columns.

From other sources, it is learned that the party consisted of L. L. Robinson, Colonel William Riddle, Joshua Bullitt and S. B. Thomas. They encountered formidable natural obstacles lying in the path of each proposed route. It also was early apparent that the task of the company's directors was not going to be made any easier by the various intervening communities and counties, many of whom seemed to have a somewhat exaggerated idea of the benefits that might reasonably be expected as a result of the coming of the Iron Horse. Sectional jealousies, more or less dormant, were fanned into flames and more heated debates took place.

The survey, which was undertaken by Mr. Robinson and associates, was in the nature of a preliminary reconnaissance and the railroad got down to real brass tacks in August of the same year, placing two surveying parties in the field. One of these under James P. Robinson, not to be confused with L. L. Robinson, who later became chief engineer of the L. & N., started out from Seventh and Broadway. The second party, under John V. Gould, ran a line west of the one being run by Mr. Robinson. Later on a third party of engineers took the field, working northward from the north bank of the Cumberland River, opposite Nashville.

It is interesting to note that James Geddes, the Company's first diamond button (50-year) man, was a member of Mr. Gould's party. Mr. Geddes later headed a surveying party himself, when the line of the road was being definitely located.

The task of surveying parties in those days was no easy one. The country was sparsely settled, good roads were few and far between and accommodations for man or beast, with a few widely-separated exceptions, were indeed scarce. But if their task was a hard one, it was soon realized that that of the construction forces, which would necessarily follow them, would be monumental in comparison. There was a great deal of rugged country between Louisville and Nashville and obtaining an appropriate right-of-way was obviously going to be more than a matter of finding the shortest distance between any two given points and then leveling off the intervening space in the necessary width with pick and shovel.

Two of the parties moved south from Louisville. The one under James P. Robinson, working in accordance with a pre-conceived plan, had fairly easy sailing until it hit Pond Creek, 19 miles south of Louisville. Because of the adjacent terrain, it was realized that much heavy construction would be necessitated here. Then came Salt River and Muldraugh's Hill, each of which offered its own peculiar problem. Muldraugh's Hill was an especially difficult obstacle and of it, President Shreve, of the L. & N., said: ". . . once passed the battle is won!"

The party under John V. Gould ran a series of surveys from Louisville via Shepherdsville and Bardstown, all of which converged at a point on the Green River. Each of these surveys, as well as the ones run by Mr. Robinson, necessarily encountered Muldraugh's Hill. It was finally decided that the obstacle provided by this immense natural barrier could be overcome by only two routes that would meet requirements of grade and curvature. (As finally decided upon, the maximum grade was 70 feet to the mile; minimum radius of curvature was 955 feet.) These were by either the Mill Creek route or by the Clear Creek route and possessed an additional advantage in that either would converge naturally upon Elizabethtown. The latter route was the one eventually adopted.

Upon the completion of the surveys during the early part of 1852, the Company was faced with the difficult task of deciding just which route should be chosen. Any route, because of the nature of the intervening terrain, with its numerous rivers, Muldraugh's Hill, the knob country around Green River, Tennessee Ridge, etc., would present a difficult engineering problem. The board of directors had stated as early as October 18, 1851, that they had no preference for either route, the upper or lower, i.e., the so-called "Airline," route by way of Elizabethtown, Bowling Green and Franklin or the "Glasgow" route by way of Bardstown, New Haven, Glasgow, Scottsville and Gallatin, and that the location of the road would be determined largely by the stock subscriptions of the various sections.

It should be borne in mind, therefore, that the surveys mentioned did not definitely locate the road, but merely tentatively explored the ground, seeking the best possible route within the limits imposed by the inclusion of certain cities.

Thus, in September 1852, when the Board ordered the location of the railroad, it was an event that cast a long shadow, influencing the lives of many living persons and of generations yet unborn. Specifically, it meant that after about a year of intensive work, a year in which over 2,000 miles of territory had been surveyed at a total cost of $24,598.52, the railroad was ready to conform to a certain definite pattern. Once chosen, surveying parties could again take the field, contracts could be let for the construction of the road and ere long a railroad between Louisville and Nashville would be an actual reality instead of a very desirable possibility.

Ironically enough, although the inhabitants of Bardstown were leading spirits in early-day agitation for the railroad, that town was not on the route of the L. & N.'s main line, as finally located. The story is told that Isaac Stone and Ben Hardin, two of Nelson County's most famous sons, bitterly fought a proposed $300,000 bond issue, which the county was asked to float as its contribution to the projected railroad, and were eventually successful in having it defeated. James Guthrie, a native of Bardstown, and at that time one of the commissioners of the recently-chartered railroad, is said to have used his influence then to exclude Bardstown from the main line. The citizens of Nelson County soon saw their mistake, however, and later voted $300,000 in bonds to build a railroad from Bardstown to a connection with the L. & N. at Bardstown Junction. This 18-mile line was completed in March 1860, and soon afterwards became a part of the L. & N. system.

Following the selection of a route, surveying parties were put into the field to locate this definitely between the points included and by the spring of 1853, they had completed their task. In all, a total of $50,000 was spent for engineering expenses, but it was with a real measure of satisfaction that the engineer in chief reported on October 1, 1853, that "the line as located is upon the only practicable route, as regards cost and ability to construct the road, that can be found between Louisville and Nashville."

At about the time the main line was being definitely located, a tentative survey was also being made southwest of Bowling Green to the Tennessee state line with a view of making a connection with a proposed railroad from Memphis and surveys were also being run through Nelson, Washington and Marion counties with the thought of making Lebanon, Ky., the terminus of a branch line leading off from the main line in the neighborhood of Shepherdsville.

Simultaneously with the efforts that were being made to locate the line, a real battle was being waged to obtain the necessary money to insure eventual construction and completion of the road. As early as September 4, 1851, subscription books had been opened in the offices of Guthrie and Tyler, in Louisville, and when $100,000.00 had been subscribed, the books were closed and, in accordance with the provisions of the charter, a permanent organization was effected, with the subsequent election of seven directors, by the stockholders of the before mentioned stock. The election of the president, L. L. Shreve, and other officers, then followed. As previously stated, Louisville had agreed to furnish $1,000,000 of the estimated $3,000,000 felt necessary. Nashville and intervening counties were expected to furnish the remainder.

The voters of Hardin County had, as early as July 10, 1851, approved overwhelmingly a bond issue of $300,000, the proceeds from which would be used to purchase that amount of stock in the new venture, provided Elizabethtown should become a fixed point on the new road. Other

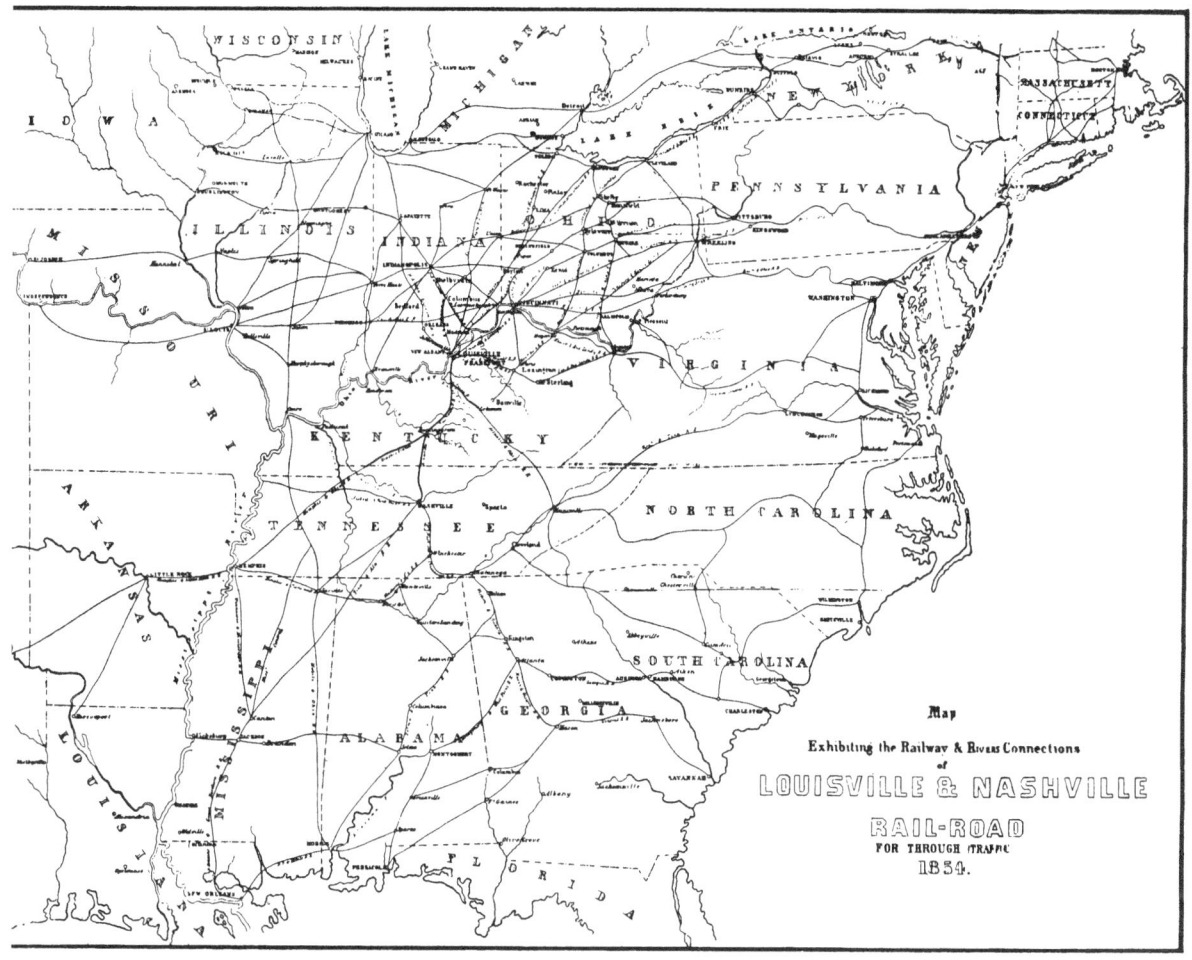

The accompanying map was included with the Annual Report for 1854. Many of the railroads shown thereon, like the L. & N. Railroad, were at that time still in the blueprint stage.

counties followed suit. Grayson County, Ky., subscribed $100,000; Warren County, Ky., $300,000; Davidson County, Tenn., $300,000; and Sumner County, Tenn., $300,000. Hart and Simpson Counties (Ky.) each subscribed $100,000 contingently. Private subscriptions in the amount of $928,700 and an additional subscription of $500,000 from the City of Louisville eventually swelled the original total to $3,828,700.

The manner in which Bowling Green insured its being included on the route of the Louisville & Nashville Railroad, which action antedated Warren County's stock subscription, is worthy of especial mention. Citizens of Bowling Green and the adjacent southern part of the state, anxious to have their section served by a railroad, had obtained a charter for the Bowling Green and Tennessee Railroad Company on March 5, 1850, the same date upon which the L. & N. had obtained its charter. The charter of the B. G. & T. Railroad thus had a certain "nuisance value," although its backers were undoubtedly sincere in their determination to build a railroad from Bowling Green to Nashville. A charter was obtained from the State of Tennessee on February 13, 1852, a party of engineers was placed in the field, surveying the proposed route of the road and stock subscription books were opened.

It was soon realized, of course, that the construction of two parallel lines south of Bowling Green and leading into Nashville would work to the advantage of neither. Fortunately, therefore, an understanding was reached before any serious duplication of effort was involved and the two roads were consolidated some time during June 1852, with the L. & N. receiving the charter of the B. G. & T. Railroad and all the rights thereof. Bowling Green had previously voted $1,000,000 for the purchase of stock of the B. G. & T. Railroad, so the L. & N. was assured of the enthusiastic support of the Warren County citizenry, especially when it became definitely known that Bowling Green would be a point on the Louisville & Nashville Railroad.

With the right-of-way finally definitely located and with some $3,000,000, or more, subscribed for its stock, the railroad was at last in a position to commence the work of construction. A subsequent amendment to the original charter also gave the Company the privilege of borrowing up to $800,000 on the capital stock, through the issuance of bonds, for the purpose of meeting a part of the costs of construction.

Thus in the early part of 1853, it seemed that the 185-mile railroad would soon become a reality and it was expected that trains would be running between Louisville and Nashville by January 1, 1855.

CHAPTER III

Wresting a Passageway

IN THE early part of 1853, the Louisville & Nashville Railroad Company, after a phase of existence replete with discussion, argument, counter-argument, glowing claims and sober conclusions became a full-fledged railroad. Before, it had been one with numerous ventures, many of which never approached any closer to reality than the imaginations of their backers or ornately-inscribed letterheads and stock certificates, complete with puffing engines, sheaves of wheat, Grecian goddesses and other contemporary symbols of prosperity and well-being.

In January 1853 Morton, Seymour & Company, prominent contractors of the day, submitted a proposal to the board of directors of the Louisville & Nashville Railroad to construct the entire road and this was subsequently accepted.

Under the terms of this contract, Morton, Seymour & Company were to turn over to the L. & N., after or within a period of two and one-half years' time, a complete railroad, ready and able to haul freight and passengers. They were to furnish labor, as well as materials, and were to be paid at the rate of $35,000 per mile. The work was to be done according to specifications and instructions furnished by the road's chief engineer. The time of commencement was set as the first Monday in May 1853, which was the 2nd.

May 2, therefore, was the day upon which it may be said that the L. & N., speaking physically, first came into being. Much preparation had preceded this occasion which like so many notable events took place rather quietly.

Lurking in the background of every venture, large or small, is usually the ubiquitous dollar-mark, or corresponding symbol. Obviously, since payments were to be made monthly to the contractors, a certain amount of cash in hand was not only desirable, but highly necessary. As stated, the L. & N. had been **promised** enough money for the construction, necessary equipment, buildings, etc., but payment for the stock purchased by the various communities was to be over a long period of time. The stock was generally paid for through the issuance of county or city bonds, which, in turn, were to be retired by a special tax upon property within the county or city, as the case might be. Obviously, such promises to pay had a very definite value but they didn't supply ready cash.

A bit of refinancing, therefore, became necessary. An amendment to the original charter gave the Company the privilege of paying for one-third of the construction cost in such bonds and of issuing bonds itself in an amount not to exceed $800,000.00, the same to be secured by a deed of trust upon the road and the proceeds to be applied to the construction of the road.

At that time the European bond market was the market and British and continental investors invested heavily in American ventures. Unfortunately, however, at the time the L. & N. attempted to dispose of its bonds (its own and the various city and county bonds tendered in payment of stock), the Russians and the Turks were having one of their wars, things were unsettled in general and the Company's agent was not able at first to dispose of the approximately $2,500,000 worth of first mortgage bonds which he had for sale. Eventually some $750,000 worth of L. & N. bonds were sold in Paris and another block disposed of at Frankfort-on-the-Main, but, even so, heavy financial sledding was encountered.

Construction proceeded rather fitfully because of financial difficulties, and in May 1854, was suspended entirely. Some $70,000 had been spent by then for rolling stock and about 156 tons of rail had been delivered. Delving further into the little road's status at that time, it is found that a total of $402,000 had been spent on the four divisions into which the railroad was divided, most of this being for grading. Iron purchased amounted to $225,000, money spent for lands and right-of-way totaled $64,000 and that bane of auditors, miscellaneous expense, came to $90,000. In all, $861,000 had been spent by June 1, 1854.

The undesirable state of activity lasted for almost another year, with a few half-hearted attempts being made to ready the line for about 30 miles out of Louisville. At the time work was suspended, quite a bit of grading, masonry, bridge and railway superstructure had been executed on all four divisions, but no part of the track was ready for operation for the very good and sufficient reason that no rail had as yet been laid. Some work had also been done at this time on the grading of the Lebanon Branch, extending from a point on the main line near what is now Lebanon Junction to the town of Lebanon, Ky., in Marion County, a distance of 37 miles and, as a whole, this enterprise was coming along more favorably than the work elsewhere.

In September 1854, despite the somewhat feeble state of its finances, work was re-commenced on the road with the end in view of at least placing in service that portion of the track which extended south to where the proposed connection with the Lebanon Branch was to be made. The advantages of this were two-fold; some revenue would be realized and the Company's credit would be vastly improved. By October 1, 1855, therefore, with Justin, Edsall and Hawley batting for Morton, Seymour & Company, with whom the original contract had been cancelled, the roadbed for that distance out of Louisville was placed in readiness for the track.

From all accounts, it seems that the first actual laying of the rail took place in July 1855. The crossties, cut to specifications furnished by the chief engineer (they had to be not less than eight and one-half and not more than nine feet in length; with a six-inch face and a thickness of six inches, and of white oak, cedar or black locust), were laid two feet apart, center to center, averaging about 2,700 to the mile. The gauge of the track was five feet. Here a difference of one foot meant a loss of several thousands of dollars to the Company for the gauge as originally decided upon was six feet and much of the rolling stock was purchased to fit that gauge. The change to five feet was made because this was the gauge employed by most of the other southern railroads and while it was possible to adapt some of the rolling stock to the new order of things, this was not invariably so, as intimated, and the misfits had to be discarded.

The track slowly penetrated the country south of Louisville. By August 22, 1855, it had reached a point eight miles from Broadway, in Louisville, where some 23 acres in the vicinity of 9th and 10th Streets had been purchased for the erection of a depot and other facilities. By September 17, 1855, the rails extended some 12 miles from the city.

On August 25, 1855, things were sufficiently progressed to permit a train to make the first formal trip over the rails of the L. & N. Railroad. This feat would now be in somewhat the same category as a bus trip to the suburbs, and many a harried commuter, bounding back and forth between domicile and desk, or work bench, achieves a much greater daily mileage. But, in 1855, it was an event calling for special recognition. An excursion train, filled with gentlemen of the press, distinguished citizens and hiliarious folk in general, made the trip to the end of the line in about 27 minutes. Warming up to his task, the engineer made the return trip in only 20 minutes.

The L. & N., in the early days of construction, was beset by many calamities. An epidemic of cholera killed many of the laborers engaged in the project and so hindered the work; a crop failure caused great suffering, and an unprecedented drought brought river traffic to a standstill and so delayed the delivery of necessary materials. War in Europe and the gathering clouds of fraternal strife in the United States also added to the general gloom.

With such adverse factors weighed in the scale against it, it is small wonder that construction proceeded at the proverbial snail's pace and that the goal was so long in being reached. Hand in hand with the financial and other assorted difficulties mentioned, marched another handicap that even under the most auspicious of occasions, would have been truly formidable. It has been previously mentioned. This was the nature of the terrain encountered between Louisville and Nashville; country that for a goodly part was rugged in the extreme. At the time construction of the Louisville & Nashville was commenced, railroads had been an item on the American scene long enough for certain practices in connection with their construction, operation and maintenance to have become standardized and accepted through being tested and proven worthy in the crucible of experience. To some extent, therefore, the L. & N. profited by the experience of even earlier pioneer roads, but it had its own peculiar problems.

A reading of the specifications of the chief engineer of the Louisville & Nashville, established for the contractor, impresses one with the great strides the railroad industry had made in less than a quarter of a century. The roadbed, after the necessary grading, was to be formed to a depth of one foot with clean gravel and sand. Rock excavations were to be 18 feet wide at the grade and the sides were to have a slope of one foot horizontal to five feet vertical. The most exacting specifications were laid down for tunnels, bridges, masonry, trestles, etc.

Two of the most formidable obstacles over which a passageway had to be gained were Muldraugh's Hill and Green River, near Munfordville, Ky. It is interesting to read that the proposed tunnel through the crest of Muldraugh's Hill was to be 1,986 feet long and was to pass through the Hill 135 feet below its summit. The cost of grading this section of the road from the base to the summit was estimated to be $520,000, or about $104,000 per mile. (Report of the Chief Engineer, 1854.)

The same report states that it was estimated that it would cost $140,000 to effect the crossing of Green River. Plans called for a deck bridge of five spans, each of 200 feet and two shorter spans of 100 feet each. The total length of bridge and approaches was placed at 1,800 feet However, the plans were changed somewhat before actual construction was begun and the completed structure, the largest iron bridge in America at that time, eventually cost some $165,000 instead of the estimated $140,000.

CHAPTER IV

The Course is Shaped

IT SHOULD, of course, be remembered that the builders of a railroad are to a certain extent trammeled by the limitations within which they have to work. Certain points have to be included on the line of road, certain obstacles have to be overcome, but a certain degree of curvature can never be exceeded nor can the track ascend or descend more than a certain number of feet per mile. In mountainous or rugged country, the result, before the days of mechanized, heavy-grading equipment, was apt to be a pretzel-like arrangement, making operation of trains difficult and perhaps unprofitable, even though the line represented quite an engineering feat. The L. & N. Railroad was fortunate in that its completed line was **sound**, considered from any angle.

Work on all five of the Railroad's divisions was done more or less simultaneously insofar as readying the right-of-way for the roadbed was concerned. After the cancellation of the contract with Morton, Seymour and Company, much of the work of grading was done under contract with local farmers living along the line, many of whom occasionally used their slaves in this work.

Had the financial skies been clear, the 187 miles between Louisville and Nashville doubtlessly could have been completed well within the two-and-one-half years specified within the original contract, even though such obstacles as Muldraugh's Hill, Tennessee Ridge and Green, Nolin, Salt and Cumberland rivers had to be overcome.

Some of the factors which complicated the situation and which retarded construction have already been memtioned. Mention might also be made of a record-breaking low stage reached by the Ohio River, which prevented the delivery of iron rail in the summer of 1854; the sale of the depot and grounds at Edgefield Junction to satisfy a disgruntled creditor; the refusal of certain counties to meet their obligations incurred by the purchase of L. & N. stock; the factional squabbles and disputes between the Louisville board of aldermen and the L. & N. board of directors, which eventually resulted in the resignation of President L.L. Shreve and the subsequent election of former Governor John L. Helm to this post; the difficulty of disposing of the Company's bonds with only a little, if any, trackage to secure them; and dissatisfaction on the part of all concerned, egged on by the press of the day, with the terms under which the contract for the building of the road had been let. It was argued that $35,000 per mile was too high, that it would be better to let the construction of the various portions of the road out on contract to local contractors and thus obtain some good will for the Company, through the use of local labor, etc., etc. As has been seen, the contract with the original contractors, Morton, Seymour & Company, was abrogated, but at some pecuniary loss and in the face of bitter opposition.

It is thus not surprising to discover that by 1856 only some 26 miles of road were in operation, although $1,212,137 had been expended for this work. However, most of the right-of-way had been graded and work on the various bridges, trestles, buildings, etc., was well under way.

Work on the Lebanon Branch was progressing satisfactorily and a survey was undertaken in the early part of 1856 to locate a line from Bowling Green, Ky., to a connection at the state line (Guthrie, Ky.) with the Memphis, Clarksville and Louisville Railroad.

The latter part of 1855 and the early part of 1856, however, saw a great change in the Company's fortunes. Although, as indicated, the amount of actual track laid was rather slight, much of the ground work necessary for the construction of the road had been done. The financial picture was brightening, more modern rolling stock had been purchased, and by June 9, 1856, a mixed freight and passenger train was making a round-trip each day between Louisville and Lebanon Junction, a distance of 30 miles. This was most encouraging for the money realized from the sale of stocks and bonds could now be supplemented with earned revenue derived from the operation of a train-on-track.

Meanwhile, the pioneer railroad was growing in yet other directions than trackage. At Louisville, a turntable some 45 feet in diameter had been constructed, along with a tank house and two tanks of 12,000 gallons capacity each. Shops for the construction and repair of locomotives, freight and passenger cars and other items, had also been build, but these were not as yet owned outright by the Company and this work at this time was being done under contract. Quite a bit of rolling stock had been purchased and work was progressing satisfactorily on various structures of one sort or another.

Another important event that took place in the Road's history during the year 1856 was the second subscription of the City of Louisville to the stock of the Louisville & Nashville Railroad. This was in the sizable amount of $1,000,000, such purchase being authorized during the latter part of 1855. It was specified, however, that payment should be made by three bond issues in the amounts of $500,000, $250,000 and $250,000 on the dates of April 1, 1856, October 1, 1856, and April 1, 1857, respectively. These bonds had a life span of 30 years and paid interest of six per cent per annum.

Along about this time two other railroad projects originated which have since been embraced within the L. & N. fold. These were the Barren County Railroad Company (later to become the Glasgow Railway Company) and the Louisville & Bardstown Railroad. These lines were to tap the main line of the Louisville & Nashville Railroad at some convenient point and were in the nature of consolation prizes for the communities of Bardstown and Glasgow, which, for one reason or another, it had been impossible to include on the L. & N.'s main line. Neither of these projects were initiated by the L. & N., although naturally it had a live interest in their development. Digressing for the moment, it might be pointed out that the Louisville & Bardstown Railroad was completed on March 19, 1860, and was thereafter operated by the L. & N. for four years, with a subsequent outright purchase occuring at the expiration of that time. It was subsequently known as the Bardstown Branch. The Glasgow Railroad continued to operate as an independent carrier, following its completion on September 1, 1870 and its leasing by the L. & N.

The year 1856 was also notable, in a left-handed sort of way, for the fact that the Company experienced its first casualties as a result of its operation. Two persons were killed by its trains but, surprisingly enough, no damages were paid, because "both accidents were unavoidable."

The commencement of the year 1857 saw the work of construction progressing favorably. The Lebanon Branch was doing especially well and by November 10, 1857, the line had been completed to the town which gave the branch its name. This was some 22 miles beyone New Haven, also on the branch, or 67 miles from Louisville and although through trains did not venture upon the newly-laid track until March 8, 1858, the more hardy locals were making connections with the regular trains at New Haven as early as November 1, 1857. It took almost four hours to make the trip between the latter point and Louisville.

On the main line, things also were happening, despite the fact that the contractors were having a rather difficult time in fulfilling their contracts, due to the high cost of living, which was soaring. In some cases, the contracts had been entered into when prices were lower and the fact that the contractors were strenuously engaged in making both ends meet meant also that the railroad was having some difficulty in making its "ends" meet. Some trackage had been constructed north of Nashville. However, Muldraugh's Hill, Green River and a few other assorted obstacles had yet to be conquered, although the frame-work for their eventual subduing was growing stronger day by day.

At this time the railroad had no ills that money couldn't have cured. It seemed, however, that the estimates frequently failed to coincide with the actual cost of construction and this led to states of emergency, hurried conferences, a certain amount of acrimonious debate and a bit of re-financing, now and then. Through all of this the financial condition of the railroad remained sound and the generous response of the various communities was instrumental in preventing a financial dictatorship of outside capital. The president and board of directors, in a report made in 1857, indicated that they were not unaware of the dangers that lay in catching the first life-line that might happen to be tossed in their direction, saying:

"It will be a proud achievement if Tennessee and Kentucky will, as they can, build this great connecting link in the chain of roads north and south, without subjecting it to liens and mortgages, held by capitalists who have no other motive than that of profit and ultimate ownership."

The agitation for a line of road branching off in the vicinity of Bowling Green to a connection with the contemplated line of the Memphis, Clarksville and Louisville Railroad, at Guthrie, Ky., was also coming to a boil nicely at this time (circa 1857). The chief engineer had some surveys made and submitted some estimates, which might have been taken with the proverbial grain of salt, in view of some of the Road's past experience, revealed that the outlay might be as follows:

Russellville Route - 48.5 miles $980,462
Central Route - 45.5 miles 960,361
Franklin Route - 34.5 miles 756,542

Nothing concrete took place for some little time, although arrangements were made with the Memphis & Ohio Railroad (Memphis to Paris, Tenn.) and the Memphis, Clarksville & Louisville Railroad (Paris, Tenn., to Guthrie, Ky.) for the operation of through trains, between Memphis and Louisville, if and when connections should be made.

Thus, the L. & N. had several irons in the fire at this time and seemed assured of a goodly portion of the trade and commerce of the Southwest, as well as of the Central South and the Southeast (via the Lebanon Branch). The Annual Report for the year ending October 1, 1858, contained this exuberant language: " . . . Who that is capable of reasoning can fail to perceive from these vast connections that the Louisville & Nashville road is destined soon to be numbered among the most important roads in the United States?"

The construction chart showed that while no trains were being run over the second division (extending south of Elizabethtown) some $226,-108 had been expended upon it and it was estimated that it would take about $279,198 more to get the division ready for operation. Trains were running on the first division of the main line as far south as a point seven miles north of Elizabethtown by the latter part of 1857. Pending the completion of the tunnel through Muldraugh's Hill, it had been decided to lay a temporary track over the crest of this barrier and it was estimated that the track should reach Munfordville (73 miles from Louisville) not later than September 1, 1858.

Perhaps two of the most important influences on the future history and growth of the Company were first encountered in 1857. These were the addition of two men of unusual calibre to the L. & N.'s "working" personnel. They were Albert Fink and James Guthrie. The two presented a strange contrast, but teamed together they formed an unbeatable combination. James Guthrie was a typical Kentuckian, a native of Bardstown, Ky., and had long been active in the agitation for railroads. A former Secretary of the U.S. Treasury, he had been one of the L. & N.'s incorporators and his elevation to the vice-presidency in 1857 meant that he was being groomed for the presidency, the ill health of the incumbent, John L. Helm, making such a step imperative.

Albert Fink, on the other hand, was not native to these shores. He was born in Germany and was one of those rare beings who seemingly excel in any field to which they may happen to apply their talents. A giant in stature, six feet, seven inches, he had great executive ability and a flair for mechanical ingenuity. He came to this country in 1849, and was not long in achieving considerable status as an engineer. The bridge over the Monongahela River at Fairmont, Va., and the Fink Bridge Truss gave him fame; the Green River Bridge and the L. & N. depot at

Louisville enhanced it. He entered the employ of the L. & N., as construction engineer, at the age of 30; soon advanced to general superintendent and vice-president.

This depot at Louisville, located at 9th and Broadway, was far in advance of similar structures of its kind of that day and cost some $34,000 to build, an immense sum in those times. The building and shed were 400 feet long and 153 feet wide and embraced within their commodious confines six tracks and three platforms. This depot was dedicated in 1858 and Inauguration Day, as it was known, was one of great rejoicing. Mayor John Barbee proclaimed a half-holiday and the citizenry turned out **en masse** to inspect the new station. There were speeches, of course; the future was painted in glowing colors and with a fine dramatic flourish, the president of the road, John L. Helm, rolled the first item of freight to be handled at the depot, a barrel, contents unknown, into a freight car which had a maximum capacity of 20,000 pounds. A cheer went up from those assembled and the little wood-burning locomotive, which was so effectively to supplant the stage-coach and the river steamer, soon moved off with its precious cargo. The crowd then inspected the premises. The holdings at that time in the vicinity of 9th and 10th and Broadway consisted of about 23 acres of land. It is said that engine cord wood, for the hungry Iron Horses, occupied a goodly portion of the acreage. This was considered in the suburbs at that time and the streets leading thereto were not paved or in very good condition. "The Gateway to the South" only had a population of about 45,000 then and it had only been a short time before that Charles Dickens, the well-known English novelist, following a visit to Louisville, had made some rather humorous remarks about the pigs which had their habitat in the streets of the Kentucky metropolis.

Chapter V

First Through Train

THE Louisville & Nashville Railroad, although a small railroad by present-day standards, was big for its age, and moreover when completed would have the distinction of being the first railroad west of the Alleghenies to effectively link the North and South. True, at that time there were other routes of communication in existence between the two sections, between which the Ohio River was approximately the dividing line, but these were highly unreliable and were of such a nature that a trip over them assumed the proportions of a major project. On land, stage-coaches and freighters jolted along over roads usually in a bad state of repair, even in the best of weather, impartially jostling passengers and freight, and by water the vagaries of the rivers were something to deplore.

The Louisville & Nashville's projected line was, therefore, an important one and realizing this importance, the press of the day, and its readers, voluntarily appointed themselves as members of the board of directors, **ex-officio,** and supplied oceans of gratis advice, laboriously transmitted via hand-set type.

Mention has been made before of the proposed branch from a point near Bowling Green, Ky., to a connection at the state line, with other lines extending north from Memphis, Tenn., in order to effect the operation of through trains between Louisville and Memphis. In 1858, the board of directors took steps to insure the completion of this branch and in so doing brought down upon their heads the wrath of the contemporary press and the readers thereof, aforesaid. Such opposition was, in part, the result of selfish interest as it was felt that the building of the proposed branch and the subsequent linking of the Ohio and Mississippi rivers by the rails of the Iron Horse, would not be to Louisville's advantage, nor indeed to that of several other towns. Such short-sightedness was allied, however, with more potent reasoning. Why, asked the Louisville Courier, with some disregard for fact, should a railroad which had already obtained $4,000,000 in aid from the City of Louisville and which had only constructed 35 miles (it was actually operating trains over at least 109 miles of track at that time – 1858), talk of branches?

Moreover, where was the money to come from? Notwithstanding much potent opposition and plaintive appeals to the taxpayers' pocketbooks, the citizens of Louisville, early in November 1858, overwhelmingly approved the ordinance which had previously been passed by the city council, subscribing $300,000 to the construction of the Memphis branch. Certain conditions were attached to this subscription and the Louisville Courier, more or less gracefully acknowledging defeat, fired this parting shot:"Let us see the locomotive thundering from here to Nashville and from Bowling Green to Memphis and we shall forgive all the chicanery by which this route has been selected, to the detriment of others more desirable." Previously, it had sounded off in this wise a few weeks before: "We do not wish or intend to attack the past or present management of the Louisville & Nashville Railroad, unless we are driven to it, though much, very much, might be truthfully said upon this subject which would startle the community."

It was estimated that it would cost around one million dollars to construct the branch and it was expected that the amount subscribed by the City of Louisville would be supplemented by similar amounts subscribed by the various counties through which the line would pass. As a matter

L. & N. passenger train on Green River Bridge, just south of Munfordville, Ky., in 1859.

of fact, at the time the Louisville ordinance was approved, the Company already had on hand bonds of Logan County in the amount of $300,000 and the other counties involved eventually came through with stock subscriptions. Grading of the line was begun in the early part of 1859 and continued through a part of 1860. The building of this branch to eventual completion and the operation of through trains between Memphis and Louisville will be discussed at greater length further on.

While the proposed line to Memphis would tap a rich agricultural region, its chief value to the L. & N., and the other two roads involved, was in the important connections which would be made not only at Memphis, but elsewhere along the line. First and foremost, of course, there was the mighty Mississippi River, a potent artery of trade and commerce. There were also crossings of the Cumberland and Tennessee rivers, and between

Bowling Green and Memphis the proposed line would connect with the Henderson and Nashville Railroad at Guthrie, Ky.; with the Nashville and Northwestern Railroad at McKenzie, Tenn.; with the Mobile and Ohio Railroad at Humboldt, Tenn.; and with the Memphis and Little Rock Railroad, the Memphis and Charleston Railroad and the Memphis and Grenada Railroad at Memphis, Tenn.

Getting back to the main line the year 1858 was chiefly notable for the speed with which the work was being pushed. The rails were being gradually placed into position all along the line and the gap between the road's northern and southern extremities was rapidly narrowing. A number of important steps were taken in 1858. A contract was entered into with the U. S. Government for the transportation of mails at the flat rate of $100 per mile per annum, weight or quantity apparently not entering into this agreement. Under this arrangement, the L. & N. Railroad and Messrs. Carter and Thomas, stage coach proprietors of the day, collaborated to carry the mail between Louisville and Nashville.

The completion and subsequent dedication of the Louisville station has already been mentioned. In addition, the Iron Horse now had places in which to hang up his hat in Edgefield, Elizabethtown and Gallatin and other similar structures were nearing completion elsewhere. The Kentucky Locomotive Works, Louisville, engaged in the manufacture of a high grade of rolling stock, was purchased outright by the L. & N. for the sum of $80,000. This was lifting an item from the bargain counter for the plant had originally cost $140,000 to build and it was still in very good condition.

In addition, along about this time, a $2,000,000 mortgage upon the physical assets and franchise of the Louisville and Nashville Railroad in the State of Kentucky was executed in order to obtain money with which to complete the line. A somewhat lesser sum would have been sufficient, but it was thought best to be on the safe side and avoid the possibility of having to execute a second mortgage at some later date.

June 15, 1858, saw the operation of the first train to Elizabethtown, Ky., which meant, among other things, that the barrier imposed by Muldraugh's Hill had finally been overcome. The Louisville Courier enthused thusly: "We, who remember the long and tedious stage ride of olden times, the sand roads and the crossing of Muldraugh's Hill, will hail this blessing of time and distances with appropriate exclamations of joy . . . And so, step by step, our Iron Horse enters the valley of Green River."

Much unconscious humor is displayed in reports on the operation of the road in those early times. Thus, the report of the superintendent for the year 1858 states that with respect to operation between New Haven and Lebanon: ". . . this train (a mixed one) ran through the winter with tolerable success, occasionally running off the track. It was never run at a speed to injure passengers or freight."

At this time it was considered the "thing" to make a journey by a judicious use of both railroad and stage coach and the L. & N. reaped a nice profit from business of this sort. This, along with local passenger revenue, the handling of freight and mail, etc., gave concrete evidence to the road's backers that the long, lean years were things of the past. A total of $163,288.44 was derived from such operation in 1858, the principal items handled, besides citizens of the Commonwealth, being those other distinguished adjuncts of the state, tobacco and whiskey, along with sizeable consignments of bacon, wheat, salt, sugar, flour, coffee and livestock.

Sixty-two miles of track, south of Louisville, on the main line, had been laid by the end of 1858, the Lebanon Branch had been completed to Lebanon and the Company placed each mile of track in service as soon as it was built. At this time a total of 10 locomotives, 7 passenger cars, 3 baggage cars, 32 box-cars and 102 rack, platform, boarding, hand, hand dump, stone and sawyer cars were owned.

The year 1859 was one of great rejoicing and celebration in the history of the Louisville & Nashville Railroad, marred only by demands from certain sectors that President John L. Helm tender his resignation. Some of this dissatisfaction seems to have been engendered by the selection of the route for the Memphis Branch; a larger part, however, was the result of inevitable differences of opinion. President Helm stuck by his guns though and refused to resign until the operation of through trains between Louisville and Nashville became a reality.

Many a hamlet and town along the right-of-way saw its first train in 1859 and informal, and, occasionally formal celebrations were the order of the day. Thus, when the road was opened from Nashville to Bowling Green on August 10, 1859, a great barbecue was held at Nashville with some 10,000 people downing the "vittles." A special train was run from Bowling Green to Nashville and it was greeted by an enthusiastic audience. The oratorical taps were turned on full blast and a carnival spirit prevailed throughout the city.

At that time, by use of stage coach and Iron Horse, travelers could make the trip between Louisville and Nashville in 16 hours and the newspapers of the day listed schedules of arrival and departure, calling attention to the fact that the trip could be made with "only 30 miles staging." This was a big improvement over the former time of 27 hours of only a few months before, when the railroad mileage and the stage coach mileage was not so disproportionate. In June 1859, for instance, travelers leaving Nashville journeyed by rail to Franklin, Ky., and "stage-coached" it from there to Munfordville, Ky., a distance of approximately 60 miles. At Munfordville they renewed acquaintance with their track-bound steed and so arrived in Louisville.

As the gap between the northern and southern ends lessened and as the railroad's part of the haul became greater and greater, the time necessary to make the trip decreased by whole hours at a time.

The completion of the Green River Bridge, near Munfordville on July 1, 1859, removed a very potent obstacle to the through operation of trains. It is a sad commentary upon human nature that this magnificent structure, erected only after the expenditure of huge sums of money and after much thought and effort, should, within less than three short years, be partially destroyed, not by the fury of the elements, nor obviously by the heavy hand of time, but by man engaged in his favorite outdoor sport of war.

This bridge, hithertofore mentioned more or less briefly in this account, was one of the engineering marvels of the day and Harper's Weekly for February 25, 1860, carried a complete description of it, along with the illustration reproduced with this article. Said they in part: "This structure, of which we present an engraving herewith, is one of those great works which, as triumphs of man's intelligence and energy over the obstacles interposed by nature to his free communication and commerce with his fellows, are looked upon in every country as fit subjects of national pride and eulogy. ... Before the regular use of the bridge it was thoroughly and severely tested with the heaviest loads that could possibly be placed upon it, as also with loads moving with the greatest attainable velocity. The deflections caused by the different loads agreed in all cases with those previously calculated from the known extension and contraction of the materials, thus affording mathematical proof of the excellence of the design, the faithfulness of its execution and the correctness of the builders' estimates of its proportions and consequent strength."

As the road neared completion in the waning days of the year 1859, elaborate plans were evolved for the operation of the first through train. Such plans called for considerable thought and ingenuity. It was a momen-

This is the first through time table of the L. & N. Railroad.

tous occasion, looming large among the current events of the day and the management did not wish to slight or offend anyone who had lent his moral, physical, spiritual or financial support to the building of the railroad. Obviously such a trip would be a glistening tid-bit to be handed down to one's posterity, even unto the fourth generation, and just as obviously this loyal legion of friends, whose numbers became mysteriously augmented over-night, could not all be accommodated upon the first through train. At last, the list was finally pruned down to about 200 and these lucky ones made the first trip by rail between Louisville and Nashville. Included in this valiant company were the board of directors; the Mayor of Louisville, councilmen, newspapermen and other citizens of Louisville.

This special train, consisting of an engine, tender and several coaches and with the American flag prominently displayed fore and aft, left Louisville, Ky., in the early morning of October 27, 1859, and because of the numerous stops, took about 10 hours to make the trip. The citizenry all along the road turned out almost en masse to witness the passing of the special and cheered it lustily. Some of the stops made were at the larger towns; others were at some of the principal engineering feats to permit the passengers to get a closer glimpse of just what had been accomplished. The tunnel through Muldraugh's Hill had not yet been completed and so the ascent was made via the temporary track. This temporary track was to be used until the first of January 1860 when the tunnel was completed and placed in service.

Food was present in abundance upon the special and the guests of the railroad dined royally. When the train reached a point about 20 miles from Nashville it was met by a sister train from that city, also loaded to the creaking point with notables. Included in the latter's "consist" were President Helm, of the L. & N., and V. K. Stevenson, president of the Nashville and Chattanooga Railroad Company. The reporter of the Louisville Courier, which had so often opposed the road on matters of policy, implied that such jaunts were an old story to him, saying: "The cars ran with smoothness and ease and for a new road it is decidedly the best we have ever traveled upon."

At Nashville, the excursionists were wined and dined to repletion, being formally welcomed by the mayor of the city and its council and later being entertained at the State Capitol. They witnessed among other things the first crossing of the Cumberland River Bridge by locomotives. (Evidently they had detrained at Edgefield, across the river from Nashville, the night before.) On this occasion three locomotives were placed upon the bridge at one time and it stood the test nobly. This bridge, as well as the line from Edgefield Junction to Edgefield, 10½ miles, was constructed jointly by the L. & N., and the Edgefield and Kentucky Railroad Company.

The excursion party returned home to Louisville on Saturday, October 29, 1859. They were in a merry mood and celebrated the crossing of the state line on so many numerous occasions and upon such slight provocation – in the time-honored fashion – that one passenger finally decided that it must run parallel to the right-of-way and that the train crossed it frequently in flagrant disregard of the laws of probability. Before arriving in Louisville the travelers drew up a joint resolution of appreciation for the splendid hospitality which had been shown them by the management of the Louisville & Nashville Railroad upon the trip and for the many courtesies which had been showered upon them.

As shown by the old time-table reproduced with this account, regularly scheduled trains did not operate on the Louisville & Nashville Railroad until on and after Monday, October 31, 1859. An examination of this time-table will reveal that in those days it took over nine hours for a passenger train to make the trip between the two cities, while a freight train's schedule called for approximately 18 hours' running time. It was not long, however, before the increasing demands of traffic and a subsequent improvement in the right-of-way not only caused and permitted these schedules to be accelerated, but resulted in other regularly scheduled trains, both freight and passenger, being placed into service. The impending War Between the States paradoxically enough was eventually to redound greatly to the advantage of the little railroad. But when the road was opened for through traffic, the war clouds had been an item of the landscape for so long that they were taken for granted.

Just beginning to take its first faltering steps in the world of transportation at the start of the Civil War, the L. & N. was so located as to have great strategic value to both the North and the South. Like most bones of contention, it emerged from the experience badly scarred and battered.

Mention has already been made of the fact that the Louisville & Nashville incurred some displeasure by reason of its choice of a route for its proposed Memphis Branch extending from Bowling Green to Guthrie, Ky., 46 miles. John L. Helm, as president, bore the brunt of this criticism, being subjected to it both from within and without. The dispute between the president and some of his directors came to a head on February 4, 1860, with the publication of a letter signed by Directors William Garvin and B. J. Adams, demanding the resignation of Governor Helm. These gentlemen claimed that they had only voted for his reelection with the understanding that he would relinquish the reins of leadership when the operation of through trains between Louisville and Nashville was an accomplished fact.

Mr. Helm countered with the assertion that he had always thought of the Memphis Branch, then under construction, as an integral part of the railroad and that he felt it his duty to the citizens of Logan County, from whom he had obtained stock subscriptions, to stand by until the Branch was completed.

After a great deal of acrimonious debate, in which the rift between President Helm and his board of directors steadily widened, the former eventually tendered his resignation on February 21, 1860, and Vice President James Guthrie assumed the duties of the presidency.

Despite the disputes raging in the "front office," work on the Memphis Branch was steadily pushed forward during the year 1860. This paralleled similar activity on the Memphis & Ohio Railroad, and the Memphis, Clarksville & Louisville Railroad Company, the two other links in the chain which was to connect Memphis and Louisville. The former company had been originally chartered as the Nashville & Memphis Railroad on

This early-day painting of the double tunnel near Fountain Head, Tenn., gives a good idea of the difficulties that confronted the builders of the line from Louisville to Nashville.

February 4, 1852, changing its name and its purpose somewhat on December 16, 1853. It was then empowered to build a railroad between Memphis and Paris, Tenn., a distance of 130.6 miles, to a connection at the latter point with the Memphis, Clarksville & Louisville Railroad Company, which had obtained its charter on January 28, 1852.

This latter road was to connect with the L. & N.'s Memphis Branch at Guthrie, Ky., on the Tennessee-Kentucky state line, a distance of 82.50 miles. The history of both of these little roads, long since embraced within the L. & N. fold, closely parallels the saga of the L. & N. itself.

In the case of the Memphis & Ohio Railroad, actual work was begun in August 1854, and thereafter progressed rather slowly. However, trains were in operation for a distance of 30 miles out of Memphis by November 1, 1855. The road was completed in the early part of 1861, but so bitter were some of the enmities which had been aroused that trains were frequently derailed by obstructions which had been placed across the tracks by irate and long smouldering citizens.

Work on the Memphis, Clarksville & Louisville Railroad was started in the fall of 1854 and completed in the latter part of 1860. In this connection it is interesting to note that the bridge of the M. C. & L. R. R., over the Cumberland River at Clarksville was originally built too low and steamboats frequently collided with it, resulting in numerous damage suits. An allowance had been made in the construction of the bridge to permit the passing of river craft, but the swiftness of the current and the comparative narrowness of this passageway made travel beneath the bridge exceedingly dangerous.

In the meantime, work had been progressing smoothly upon the L. & N.'s Memphis Branch between Memphis Junction, four miles south of Bowling Green, and Guthrie, Ky. The grading was completed on August 15, 1860, with the laying of track occurring almost immediately thereafter at many points. This 46-mile stretch of line was completed on September 18, 1860, and the occasion was appropriately celebrated by the operation of a special train between Louisville and Clarksville on the date mentioned. At the state line, General William A. Quarles, president of the Memphis, Clarksville & Louisville Railroad, and James Guthrie, of the L. & N., symbolically shook hands and there was no dearth of speechmaking by the many distinguished visitors. At Clarksville, another oratorical deluge took place and that night a banquet was served for some 700 persons.

The regular operation of trains was commenced on September 24, 1860, between Bowling Green and Clarksville and these made the 64-mile jaunt in about three and one-half hours. At this time, Russellville boasted a handsome passenger station built of brick, as well as a freight shed, while combination freight and passenger stations had been erected at Auburn, South Union, Whippoorwill and Olmstead. In addition, numerous water tanks had been constructed and six engine stalls had been added to the facilities at Bowling Green. Fifty-four-pound rail was laid in the track and despite the fact that trains were operating over the branch regularly on and after September 24, 1860, by October 1 of the same year only 14 miles had been fully ballasted, a condition frequently encountered in those days.

At this time (September 24, 1860) little yet remained to be done on the entire stretch of track between Memphis Junction and Memphis, a distance of approximately 262 miles. Chief obstacle to the through operation of trains was the uncompleted bridge over the Tennessee River at Danville, Tenn., north of Paris. When this was completed the operation of through trains between Memphis and Louisville became a reality in the early part of 1861 and the L. & N., in anticipation of a large passenger traffic between the two cities, re-routed its regular main line passenger trains to the branch, with the subsequent establishment of connections to and from Nashville at Bowling Green. Thus, for a short time, the main line became the branch. The arrangement mentioned, with abundant optimism, was commenced on April 14, 1861, just two days after the battle at Fort Sumter finally lit the fuse.

The actual commencement of hostilities found the Louisville & Nashville Railroad operating some 269 miles of track in Kentucky and Tennessee and with a small and somewhat inadequate array of rolling stock consisting of 30 locomotives, 28 passenger and baggage cars, six cabooses and 297 freight cars. From its operations for the fiscal year ending with June 30, 1861, it had derived a gross revenue of $807,934.67, $461,970.42 of which was **net**. This was a gain of about $100,000 for net and gross each over the preceding year and was largely the result of the current war scare which caused the Southern states to "import" huge quantities of provisions and supplies. It must be remembered that although actual combat did not take place until April 14, 1861, as early as February 1 of the same year, seven Southern states (Mississippi, Florida, Alabama, Georgia, Louisiana, Texas, and South Carolina) had already seceded from the Union.

Chapter VI

Mars in the Ascendant

AT THE outbreak of the War Between the States, the Louisville & Nashville Railroad, like its parent state of Kentucky, decided to remain neutral. This, a difficult feat at best, was easier said than done and a state of equilibrium which existed through the delicate balancing of two opposing forces could not long endure. In the end, one or the other was bound to prove the stronger.

In the beginning it seemed as if any influence which the L. & N. might have on the future outcome of the conflict, would certainly tend to tip the scales in favor of the Confederacy. Oddly enough a lively trade continued between the North and the South even after the formal declaration of war, with the bulk of this traffic moving toward the Southland. The L. & N., being one of the few intersectional routes of travel, received a large part of this business. As a matter of fact it received more business than it could handle and on April 29, 1861, a temporary embargo on freight of all sort was placed into effect. By May 8, however, the congestion was relieved and the L. & N. once again started supplying the South with the sinews of war.

The good citizens of Louisville became greatly alarmed over this vast exodus of provisions and materials into Dixie and a near panic resulted from the rumor that the city was on the verge of actual starvation. (This fear was, of course, groundless. It was developed that enough foodstuff was on hand for 10 years – normal consumption.) When the panic was at its height though the railroad's tracks were torn up south of Louisville and it was necessary to send armed guards ahead to

Green River Bridge on the L. & N. as it appeared after partial destruction by Confederate troops.

protect trains from violence.

The laxity of the Federal Government in permitting this commercial intercourse between the states may be attributed to several things. Kentucky was one of the important border states and President Lincoln was extremely anxious that she remain within the Union, even though Governor Magoffin, of Kentucky, had declared that the state would remain neutral. Such a course of action, from the Federal viewpoint, was at least preferable to outright secession and it has been argued that President Lincoln did not wish to do anything to deliberately antagonize Kentucky, the citizens of which were profiting by this commerce.

On the other hand such trade was extremely hard to control because of the indefinite status of the border states. It was admittedly difficult to prevent goods consigned to such border states from later finding their way into the hands of the Confederacy, either through direct reconsignment or through smuggling operations. High legal authority of the Federal Government had declared that the border states were to be considered as loyal regions, even though some of their citizens might be disloyal.

As has been intimated a large part of this traffic was open and above board, comparatively speaking, although on May 2, 1861, the Treasury Department had issued an order forbidding the carrying of

A troop train passing through the big cut on the L. & N. Railroad during the Civil War.

provisions and munitions into the Confederacy. This was at first entirely disregarded, but later events, culminating in a decision handed down by Judge Muir, of the Jefferson Circuit Court on July 11, 1861, made it politic for the L. & N. to comply with this order, at least formally. Nevertheless, large quantities of provisions and supplies continued to pour into the Confederacy, chiefly via the L. & N. and various rivers, a frequent subterfuge being to haul the goods by wagon from Louisville (where close supervision was exercised) to some small station on the line nearby and then transfer them to the railroad.

—Contemporary drawing

A Civil War Hospital Train.

Although the L. & N.'s compliance with Judge Muir's decision at first was merely nominal, it soon placed the carrier in hot water with the rebels. Previously, on May 21, 1861, the Congress of the Confederacy had prohibited the exportation of cotton internally, viz., to points in the Union, and somewhat later sugar, rice, molasses, tobacco, syrup and naval stores were also prohibited. This Confederate blockade was more rigid than that of the North, where a very flexible permit system supplemented an outright closing of one eye at the provisions of the embargo, and, ironically enough, tended to reduce sympathy for the South in Kentucky.

Such sympathy was also further alienated by the seizure on July 4, 1861, of all of the L. & N.'s rolling stock in the state of Tennessee, i.e., five locomotives, three passenger and baggage cars and about 70 freight cars, by General Anderson, of the Tennessee Military, acting under orders of Governor Isham G. Harris.

Following the seizure there ensued much correspondence between President Guthrie and Governor Harris, with proposal and counter-proposal following in rapid succession. The net result was that Tennessee kept the appropriated rolling stock and the L. & N. refused to recognize a fact accomplished. For fear of additional seizures, the railroad ceased the operation of trains past the state line and made formal demand that the equipment be restored and that the Company be compensated for any losses sustained.

The loss in Tennessee, however, while it deprived the L. & N. of some 45 miles of track and some rolling stock was a small calibre catastrophe compared to one of the first magnitude which was to follow. On September 18, 1861, the Memphis Branch and the Main Stem from the Tennessee State Line to Lebanon Junction were seized by order of General Simon Boliver Buckner, of the Confederate States, the Company thereby losing about one-half of its remaining rolling stock and motive power. A portion of this trackage remained in the hands of the Confederates but

Railroad hospital car used in Civil War.

a short time and Home Guards, which sallied forth from Louisville under the command of General W. T. Sherman, had, as early as September 20, 1861, cleared the track as far south as Elizabethtown. The Confederates in their retreat destroyed the railroad bridges over Rolling Fork, Nolin River, and Bacon Creek, necessitating their replacement at considerable expense.

In rebuilding these bridges and repairing damage done to the line, the construction forces of the railroad frequently were in advance of the Federal troops and because of this the bridge over Bacon Creek had to be rebuilt a second time, the Confederates again destroying it before it could be given the proper protection.

The Confederates eventually fell back to the southern bank of Green River, but during the remainder of the year 1861, the L. & N. only operated trains as far south as Elizabethtown, rejecting a proposal made by General Buckner that it operate the portion of the road under his control, subject to his supervision and in a manner not inimical to the interest of the counties through which the line passed.

Following his seizure of the road and his subsequent falling back beyond Green River, General Buckner, a native of Hart County, incidentally, strongly entrenched himself at Bowling Green and the operation of trains between Louisville and Elizabethtown, before mentioned, was made under the constant protection of Union troops.

In falling back the Confederates had also partially destroyed the bridge over Green River, which had taken so much time, effort and money to build, and this gap was once again an obstacle to rail travel southward, just as it had been in the days of construction. It was not possible to immediately rebuild it, because of fear of attack and the lack of sufficient protection, the Federals not advancing beyond this point until February 12, 1862.

The lines of the L. & N., south of Elizabethtown, Ky., remained in the hands of the Confederates until shortly after the beginning of the year 1862. At that time, General Don Carlos Buell, utilizing the lines of the Louisville & Nashville to the fullest, began an advance into Dixie with a huge force, which had Nashville, Tenn., as its ultimate objective. On February 15, 1862, the "boys in blue," entered Bowling Green, Ky., and less than two weeks later they were in the capital city of Tennessee.

The Confederates, in their retreat, destroyed bridges, trestles and track with reckless abandon and before leaving Bowling Green almost completely destroyed the railroad's facilities at that point. Depots and other structures elsewhere had not escaped their blighting attention and damage to the railroad, either intentional, or otherwise, was enormous. The L. & N. immediately set about putting its house in order. By the middle of March 1862, service of a sort had been re-established between Louisville and Nashville. The sadly depleted ranks of the rolling stock, the make-shift bridges and trestles, and the constant threat of cavalry raids from the hard-riding Confederates all combined to make successful operation difficult and elusive.

Fortunately for the L. & N., the raiding cavalry men especially had little inclination or patience for truly effective railroading in reverse. Generally, they contented themselves with mere removal of the rails – or with the burning of bridges and trestles, in which latter task the licking flames did most of the work. It was perhaps this understandable desire to achieve a maximum of result with a minimum of effort that led to the exercise of considerable ingenuity on the part of the Confederates in wrecking the railroad. Illustrative of this trait is the manner in which the tunnel at South Tunnel, Tenn., was rendered "hors de combat." Several freight cars were set on fire and then rolled well into the tunnel. The supporting timbers soon ignited and the immense heat thereby generated caused great quantities of material to fall into the tunnel, filling it up to an average height of 12 feet, for a distance of 800 feet.

Despite the handicaps mentioned, however, a through train between Louisville and Nashville was operated again as early as April 8, 1862, and was soon followed by others.

Chief fly-in-the-ointment, to the successful operation of trains, was General John Hunt Morgan. Although nominally the territory between Louisville and Nashville was in Union hands, at least for the time being, General Morgan was not long in letting the rival forces know that he was in the vicinity. The first of his many railroad raids on a large scale took place at Gallatin, Tenn., on March 15, 1862, where he sabotaged the railroad's facilities very effectively. His next public appearance was at Cave City, Ky., on May 11, when he destroyed a train, consisting of three passenger cars and 37 freight cars, "27 of which belonged to the Company," according to the Annual Report for that year.

Munfordville, Ky., in 1861, on the L. & N. main line.

At the time much of the rolling stock on the lines of the Louisville & Nashville belonged to

The wharf at Louisville, Ky., with the inhabitants leaving the city at the approach of Bragg's Army, September, 1862. Sketched by H. Mosler for "Harper's Weekly" of October 11, 1862.

other railroads. This was because the Federal Government had become cognizant of the "out-at-the-elbows" condition of the L. & N.'s equipment and had transferred a number of locomotives (for which the L. & N. paid a rental of 15 cents per mile each) and freight cars from Northern lines to its rails. This was not the simple feat that it would be later on because of the differences in gauge. (At that time the gauge of the L. & N. was five feet; that of the Northern roads four feet, nine inches, or four feet, eight and one-half inches.)

To facilitate the delivery of this rolling stock to the L. & N. at Louisville, a temporary track was laid from the canal, near 12th Street and the Ohio River, to the L. & N. depot at 10th and Broadway and this remained in place for several months or until it was necessary to utilize it in repairing track farther south.

The period consisting of the 12 months from July 1, 1862, to June 30, 1863, was an especially trying one and according to the pertinent Annual Report, the road was only operated for its full length for seven months and 12 days.

With Morgan carrying the ball, the Confederates did considerable damage to the facilities of the Louisville & Nashville in the summer of 1862, the railroad sustaining losses totaling $108,690 during the period July 1, 1862, to October 1, 1862, this resulting chiefly from destroyed bridges. General Morgan struck first at Lebanon, Ky., about the middle of July, with subsequent re-appearances along the line of road at Gallatin and Tunnel Hill, Tenn., about the middle of August, in each case throwing a very potent monkey-wrench in the operation of the railroad. At this later time the telegraph wires were cut and the northern and southern ends of the road were isolated, each from the other.

More trouble was shortly to follow. The theatre of war changed its location rather suddenly, in the late summer of 1862, necessitating a postponement of the vital work of reconstruction. Chief actors in the drama which now drew the attention of the nation were Generals Kirby Smith and Braxton Bragg, of the Confederacy, and General Buell, of the Northern forces. General Smith entered Kentucky, from his base at Knoxville, about the first of September, defeating a large Northern force at Richmond, Ky. Thus encouraged, the L. & N. Railroad next drew his attention and bands of cavalry attached to his command destroyed numerous bridges on the main line and the Lebanon Branch. In typical fashion, the Company commenced re-building just as soon as the bands had withdrawn. In view of Bragg's almost simultaneous invasion of Kentucky, with a force of 35,000 men, from his headquarters at Chattanooga, this may have seemed a bit hasty, but the re-built bridges were a God-send in that they permitted trains to be moved northward to Louisville to escape confiscation by the Southern general's forces.

Well-timed and executed, General Bragg's surprise attack at first seemed destined to succeed and the capture of Louisville seemed imminent. By the 12th of September, 1862, he was in Cave City, with the goal only 85 miles away and on September 15, he was thundering at the gates of Munfordville. Balked on that date and the day after in some of the bloodiest fighting of the Civil War, he was finally successful on September 17, compelling the garrison to surrender and burning the L. & N.'s Green River Bridge, as was the custom in those days.

In the meantime, General Buell had set out in pursuit of General Bragg from his headquarters at Nashville, with the intention of reaching Louisville before the Confederate leader. It was evident that the force that reached there first would have a big advantage, because of the strong fortifications that encircled the city.

General Bragg, however, with victory in his grasp, chose to procrastinate a short distance from Louisville and thereby lost a rich prize for the Confederacy. These were obviously parlous times for the L. & N. and the operation of trains in and out of Louisville was entirely discontinued. Upon the authority of President Guthrie, employes were released from their duties, which, to be sure, in most cases were non-existent at this time, and were formed into military companies to repel the invader. Defenses were strengthened and ladies with Southern sympathies surreptitiously tore up petticoats to make Confederate flags. But neither the expected battle or the flag-be-decked welcome ever materialized. On the misty morning of September 25, the blue-clad hosts of General Buell's army began to clatter into the streets of Louisville and the danger of capture was past. General Bragg, in the meantime, had elected to halt at Bardstown.

At this time there was in possession of the L. & N. only about 20 miles of track north and south of Bowling Green. The Annual Report, with some pardonable exasperation, remarks that following the occupation of Louisville, it was expected that "the presence in Louisville of the whole of Buell's army might be sufficient to protect at least 18 miles of the line of our road." It goes on to report, however, that such expectations were unduly optimistic and that on the 28th of September, 1862, the sad news

—*From Frank Leslie's Illustrated Newspaper, 1862.*

Bridge over Bacon Creek (near Bonnieville, Ky.), after destruction by the Confederates. Note the stockade at the right, built for the defense of the bridge against Confederate raiders.

Lebanon Junction, Ky., in 1861, when it was headquarters for General Sherman.

came that the Confederates had occupied Shepherdsville and were engaged in demolishing Salt River Bridge. This latter project took them about three days and from their point of view was one of the most successful ever undertaken, the bridge being a mass of ruins when they finally decided to call it a day.

The pendulum commenced its swing the other way on September 30, Buell's army moving southward out of Louisville on that date and driving the Confederates before them. Shepherdsville was re-captured on October 2, the Company's bridge forces moved in and by the 11th, a new bridge was in position. In the meantime, the battle of Perryville, near Danville, Ky., had been fought between the forces of General Bragg and Buell and while it was indecisive in that neither side could claim the victory, it did result in the ultimate withdrawal of Bragg from Kentucky.

The construction forces followed close on the heels of the army and except for some slight interruption caused by the ubiquitous General Morgan, the work of reconstruction proceeded smoothly and trains were running over a re-built Green River Bridge as early as November 1, 1862.

With the assistance of the engineering forces of the U. S. Army, bridges and trestles south of Munfordville on the main line, and on the Lebanon Branch, which had been destroyed, were restored, the railroad reimbursing the Government for this work. With such cooperation the entire line was again ready for the through operation of trains on November 25. Although open for traffic its entire length, the L. & N. at this juncture resembled a railroad in the same degree that a scare-crow may be said to resemble the well-dressed man. Bridges and trestles were necessarily of a temporary character and the track, many miles of which were as yet without ballast, was rough and uneven. It was hard to obtain sufficient fuel for the locomotives, because of the scarcity of wood and woodchoppers alike, and it was at this time that the Company first experimented with coal as a fuel. The Annual Report for the year ending with June 30, 1863, shows that during that period some 13,000-odd bushels were so used. However, this, too, was hard to obtain and eventually, with the assistance of the military, a plan was evolved whereby some 500 slaves, in each of the 13 counties through which the railroad operated, were conscripted to supply its locomotives with fuel, i.e., wood. This seems to have worked fairly well and a major worry was thereby eliminated.

The winter of 1862-1863 was a very hard one and a heavy snowfall at Louisville, Ky., supplemented the destructive work of the Confederates, caving in the roof of the blacksmith shop. This necessitated an outlay of $3,153.25, a high price to pay for a "white Christmas." At this time, the Company's shops at Louisville were especially vital, manufacturing 132 box-cars, 10 passenger cars and four baggage cars, besides many other items, during the year ending June 30, 1863, to replace those lost, strayed or stolen.

These shops also manufactured the superstructures for the bridges and trestles which had been destroyed and as fast as they were completed they were shipped south to replace the ones of a makeshift nature which had been hurriedly erected on the ground.

Christmas Day, 1862, was an especially memorable one in the annals of the railroad. On that date, General Morgan suddenly appeared at Glasgow, Ky., with a force of about 4,000 men. Cannily avoiding the fortifications at Munfordville, which had been primarily erected for the protection of Green River Bridge, he struck the railroad at Bacon Creek, a few miles nearer Louisville. From Bacon Creek (Bonnieville) to Lebanon Junction, Ky., is a distance of about 35 miles and the general and his forces celebrated the Christmas holidays by destroying every bridge, culvert, depot, water station, trestle and fuel concentration point within this 35-mile stretch. It is ironical that Colonel Basil Duke, one of Morgan's most daring lieutenants, later became a leading member of the L. & N.'s law department.

The trek of General Morgan, and company, was finally halted at Lebanon Junction on December 30, 1862. The management set about to repair the damage at once and when its labors appeared to be crowned with success, the through operation of trains was again prevented by unseasonable freshets, which destroyed the Company's bridges over a number of streams.

By the spring of 1863, insofar as the L. & N. was concerned, the worst of the war was over. Through service was re-established between Louisville and Nashville on February 1, 1863, and between Louisville and Clarksville, Tenn., on July 1. Bands of guerrillas still attacked and plundered the trains and stations of the railroad and General Morgan, shortly before his capture in Ohio, sacked the Company's facilities at Lebanon, Ky., on July 4, 1863, he seemingly having a predilection for remembering his favorite railroad on holidays.

Such attacks by guerrilla bands were common occurence throughout 1863, 1864 and 1865, despite the fact that by now the Federal Government was somewhat tardily providing heavily armed guards for all trains and had erected forts at various strategic points along the line. The theatre of war had also moved far southward and a goodly part of the L. & N.'s rolling stock was appropriated by the Northern armies for use in their various campaigns. Some of this equipment unfortunately, never reached its parent rails again, becoming permanently lodged in the Deep South.

Disputes with the military over the proper way to run a railroad also enlivened the waning years of the conflict for the L. & N. and despite the constant patching and repairing it was forced to do, it, on the whole, turned in a first class job of meeting the demands of the Government and of private interests alike, and, of course, both were considerable. The War Between the States was probably the first major conflict in which railroads had played such an important role and the L. & N. may be said to have been a part of the original testing ground for many practices later commonly accepted as standard in the movement of troops, the supplying of armies and the efficient utilization of rail facilities in large scale advances – and retreats.

Recapitulating it may be said that the L. & N. emerged from this conflict in somewhat the same condition as a battered prize fighter who has just fought a losing battle in a bout that has attracted a million dollar "gate." He has been badly beaten, but his share of the purse will more than pay for the damage. So with the L. & N. When the last gun had been fired and the uniforms of blue and gray alike had been traded for civilian garb, it was found that the total amount of the damage sustained by the railroad as a result of the war amounted to $688,372.56. This was according to the Annual Report for the year ending June 30, 1865. To offset this figure, however, the L. & N. could show net profits in each of the five years involved (1861-1865, inclusive) as follows:

    1861 - $ 461,970.42 (10 months ending June 30)
    1862 - 508,591.00 (12 months ending June 30)
    1863 - 1,062,165.09 (12 months ending June 30)
    1864 - 1,803,953.16 (12 months ending June 30)
    1865 - 2,172,515.42 (12 months ending June 30)
    Total - $6,009,195.09

With such a "back-log" the Company was in an excellent position to aid in the work of reconstruction as well as in the subsequent development and industrialization of the Southland, and it lost little time in so doing.

CHAPTER VII

Recovery From War

IT IS noteworthy that the L. & N. even in the midst of the uproar caused by having a civil war in its own back yard, still had time and initiative enough to place other irons in the fire. Chief among these was the further extension of its Lebanon Branch; another step towards tapping the rich coal fields of Eastern Kentucky and Tennessee and ultimate valuable connection north of Knoxville with other rail lines.

An amendment to the charter for such extension was granted on February 26, 1863, by Kentucky, the construction being financed by borrowing $600,000 from the City of Louisville and by the issuance of $600,000 worth of the Company's own mortgage bonds.

The work of locating the line was immediately begun thereafter and by the summer of 1864 this was established to Stanford, in Lincoln County, 36½ miles from Lebanon and 104 miles from Louisville. The grading of the line followed in short order and by May 17, 1866, the Iron Horse had reached Stanford, triumphal entries having previously been made into Parksville on February 19, 1866, and into Junction City (known variously and previously as Shelby Church, S. Danville Station and "Briartown") on April 9, 1866. Crab Orchard, ten miles from Stanford, was reached on July 1, of the same year. Management was highly enthusiastic over the possibilities of the extension, such enthusiasm having been engendered, in part, by the latent possibilities of the coal fields before mentioned, as revenue producers, and by the fact that the desired connections at or north of Knoxville would enable the Company to better compete with other Southern rail carriers for through traffic moving between the Middle West, Georgia and the Atlantic Seaboard and intermediate points like Atlanta.

When the extension east of Lebanon was first projected, the resulting contracts were based upon a written agreement between the railroad and General Ambrose E. Burnside, of Fredericksburg fame, who at that time was in command of the Federal forces in Kentucky, for a supply of negro labor, stores and tools, to be furnished by the Government at stipulated prices. This happy state of affairs did not last long and after three months' time, or on January 1, 1864, the arrangement was discontinued. New contracts were subsequently drawn and the work proceeded thereafter without governmental assistance.

During the latter part of 1865 and the early part of 1866, the right of way had been established or located from Crab Orchard to the state line by way of Mt. Vernon, Livingston, London, Lynn Camp (Corbin) and Williamsburg, a distance of 87 miles. Because of the rugged nature of the terrain, construction work proceeded rather slowly. Many tunnels and cuts had to be blasted out of solid rock in preparing the Iron Horse's bridle path between Crab Orchard and London (43 miles) and it was September 8, 1870, before the iron trail reached Livingston, Ky., 25 miles from Crab Orchard, Ky. At that time all work on the Branch was suspended, the management having decided it would be wisest to postpone further construction until the lines with which it was to connect gave some evidence of their intention to complete the necessary trackage northward from Knoxville to the state line.

The Civil War, of course, had wrought a great many changes. Not the least of these was the transformation which it had effected in the character of the L. & N. Railroad. Prior to the war, the L. & N. was merely a local road, with a very great portion of the traffic which it handled originating upon its own lines. The War between the States by bettering the financial position of the road, not only enabled it to extend a helping hand to other lines less fortunate, but also permitted it to prosecute the construction of extensions and branches, which in time were to give it valuable outlets and connections. The Lebanon Branch was, of course, one of these.

It is a tribute to the L. & N.'s leadership that it did not follow a policy of "let well enough alone," but rather early realized the advantages of close cooperation between the various rail carriers in handling the available traffic. Even so, executive opinion was far from unanimous as to the course the Railroad should pursue, it being the opinion of some that the road should place all its eggs in one basket and then watch that basket very closely. Illustrative of this is the fact that balloting on the further extension of the Lebanon Branch (from Crab Orchard to the state line) at the annual meeting of the stockholders on October 1, 1866, resulted in 24,867 votes being cast for the Extension, while 18,419 were cast against it.

Possibly the deciding factor which assured the future of the Lebanon Branch as a vital link rather than as a "dead-end" spur line, was the fact that at that time conditions were decidedly unsatisfactory at Nashville, insofar as the handling of interline freight was concerned. The N. & C. was assessing the L. & N. the rather startling sum of $10.00 to move each car of freight over a stretch of track some 2,500 feet long, which was equal to the cost of transportation over about 43 miles of the L. & N. Moreover, for some unknown reason, shipments originating on the L. & N. and destined for points beyond Nashville had to be reloaded at Nashville. It was hoped that the eventual extension of the Lebanon Branch to a connection at or near Knoxville with other lines would permit a rerouting of through traffic destined for Southern points and a subsequent avoidance of the pitfalls at Nashville.

Another example of the growing trend towards cooperation on the part of all railroads was the establishment of through fast freight lines in the years immediately following the Civil War. At first, such lines were operated by the concerned railroads themselves and the profits and expenses were shared equitably. One of these was known as the "Green Line" and operated between Louisville and such Southeastern and South Central points as Charleston, S. C., Montgomery, Ala., and Macon, Ga.

Another, the "Louisville and Gulf Line" operated between Louisville and Mobile and New Orleans. The chief advantages were that the roads synchronized their schedules, permitted the freight to be interchanged without breaking bulk and, in general, expedited the handling all along the route. Immediately after the establishment of the "Louisville and Gulf Line" (in 1867), the management pointed with some pride to the fact that freight could now be handled between Louisville and New Orleans in three and one-half days' time.

Things are proverbially not always what they seem and the shippers of that distant day could not understand why the freight rates on a short haul should be any greater than those on a long haul. Management very logically presented its case, stating that through business had been obtained that would have otherwise been lost, had it not been for the attractive rates granted. It must be remembered that in those pre-I. C. C. days each road established rates as it saw fit, being guided only by its conscience, the somewhat generous provisions of its charter, and the competition. The L. & N. argued plausibly enough that the greater the amount of business handled, the lower the average freight rate would be. Hence, it would be to the ultimate advantage of the local shipper for the road to secure as much through business as possible, regardless of whether or not the rate for this traffic was in strict conformity with the local rate. They cited the example of the Baltimore and Ohio Railroad, which handled a greater volume of business than the L. & N., over approximately the same mileage, and whose average charge for moving one ton of freight one mile was somewhat less than that of the L. & N., which was a fraction over two cents per ton per mile.

The board of directors of the L. & N., had on October 5, 1863, voted favorably upon a resolution, offered by President Guthrie, to invest a sum of money not exceeding $300,000 in the stock of the Louisville Bridge Company, which proposed to build a railroad bridge across the Ohio at the Falls. It was felt that this direct rail connection with the railroads of the North would be of distinct advan-

Advertisement which appeared in Edwards' Louisville Directory for 1866-67.

tage to the L. & N. and would be money well spent. The Civil War had proven that. The Company played a prominent part in the construction of this bridge, which was opened for traffic in the early part of 1870 and Albert Fink, by that time the L. & N.'s general superintendent, drew up the plans and superintended the erection.

With money in its pocket, the L. & N. was as receptive to new proposals as a recently-paid youth at a carnival; consequently, the plea of the citizens of Lincoln, Garrard and Madison counties, in Kentucky, for a railroad extending from Stanford, on the Lebanon Branch, to Richmond, through Lancaster, did not fall upon deaf ears. Building of this line, some 33 miles long, was commenced in July 1867, and was completed on November 8, 1868, at a total cost of about $750,000. The construction was financed by the sale of $750,000 worth of L. & N. stock to the citizens of the three counties involved, the right-of-way and depot grounds being donated to the Company.

An eyewitness to the running of the first through train between Louisville and Richmond, which occurred on or about November 8, 1868, has left an interesting, if somewhat scandalous, account of this inaugural jaunt. This train was so crowded that by the time it arrived in Lebanon passengers were literally being parked upon the cow-catcher. Souvenirs in the form of bottles of whiskey and wine, along with generous samples of chewing tobacco and cigars, were passed out all along the route with the result that: " . . . When we reached Richmond, away late in the afternoon, the interior of the coaches were a wreck as the celebrants had practically all gotten drunk and then got mad and threw fried chicken and baked ham and butter and macaroni, pickles, etc., all over the cars, messing up everybody and everything aboard. Windows were smashed, seats broken, heads cracked and noses bloodied. There being then no restrictions about employes imbibing, the riot extended from the rear end to the cow-catcher, engineer, fireman, and brakeman all participating and not a few high officials of the Company."

One of the "problem children" of L. & N. management in the years immediately following the Civil War was the operation of through trains between Louisville and Memphis. This service, after being entirely disrupted by the war, was again resumed on August 13, 1866, but all concerned held their breath much in the manner of an audience which has just witnessed a gentleman balance three billiard balls atop each other. The Louisville & Nashville participated in the through operation of trains between the points mentioned with two other carriers, whose condition was admittedly shaky. The L. & N., realizing the importance of the Memphis connection, had made a most generous offer to the managements of the Memphis & Ohio and the Memphis, Clarksville & Louisville, the other lines involved, to operate their properties for them, but so attractive was this offer that they were confused by its resemblance to the well-known gold brick and refused it.

The inevitable was not long in happening and both roads were soon on the verge of bankruptcy. In September 1867, the L. & N., to prevent the Memphis & Ohio from falling into the hands of a receiver, leased the line for 10 years, under an agreement whereby all monies, after the L. & N.

Courtesy—"This Fascinating Railroad Business" by R. S. Henry. Published by the Bobbs-Merrill Company.

The 14th Street Bridge across the Ohio River at Louisville, Ky., which was first opened for traffic on March 1, 1870, as it appeared when completed. A deck- and through-truss type structure, it was designed by Albert Fink and the contemporary press referred to it as "the first and only connecting link between the great railway systems of the North and South."

had been reimbursed for its necessary expenditures, were to be paid to the M. & O. Some five years later, in October 1872, the L. & N. acquired the Memphis & Ohio outright via the purchase route.

In the meantime, the Memphis, Clarksville and Louisville Railroad, which encountered rough sledding, both financial and otherwise, almost from its very inception, had run the gauntlet of bad luck provided by an extremely open-handed unkind fate. Finally, on February 6, 1868, the operation of trains thereon was discontinued entirely, due to an understandable unwillingness on the part of its employes to work without being paid. This dolorous state of inactivity continued until February 17 of the same year when the L. & N. took over the operation of the road (under much the same agreement previously entered into with the M. & O.), with outright purchase of the line occurring on September 30, 1871. During the fortnight when the M., C. & L. R. R., was inoperative, trains between Memphis and Louisville were routed via Nashville and McKenzie, over the Nashville and Northwestern Railroad.

The Louisville & Nashville spent a great deal of money in rehabilitating these two railroads and, although in each case it was "in the red" for considerable sums when it finally purchased them outright, it was expected that the advantages of having a through line to Memphis would more than compensate for past liabilities incurred.

On October 11, 1866, the Louisville & Nashville Railroad was host road to an incident which was to be the forerunner of a throng of comparable ones. This incident, a commonplace during the troubled days of the war, was somewhat unexpected during the peaceful autumnal days of 1866 and involved the wrecking and subsequent robbing of the L. & N.

pay car at Bristow, Ky., about five miles north of Bowling Green. This seems to have been the L. & N.'s first peace-time experience with the gentry who were later to look upon railroads as fertile fields for plunder.

L'affaire Bristow was seemingly the work of three men, as subtle and as clever a trio as ever decided the world owed them a living and effected collection with a thunder-stick. The pay car, for obvious reasons did all of its traveling in the day-time. Every precaution was taken to see that the cash aboard reached its rightful owners and up until the fatal day of October 11, 1866, its trips to and fro over the line had never been marred by anything more momentous than some inconsequential disputes as to the correctness of the wage disbursed.

On this occasion, however, the train wreckers had unfastened a rail from the tracks, but had left it in position. They had then ingeniously affixed wires thereto, which hidden from the casual gaze, trailed off into the underbrush, affording a direct and unfortunate connection between the evil-doers and our roadbed. The engineer on the locomotive pulling the pay car always kept an eye peeled for potential disasters and proceeded at a wary pace, but rails which suddenly leapt from the track upon the approach of the train were a novel phenomenon to him and a frantic tugging at the reverse lever and a call for "brakes!" were not sufficient to avert catastrophe. The entire train overturned and all was confusion. The pertinent Annual Report relates that the paymaster, G. W. Craig, "through his judicious conduct," saved $6,222.65 of the funds aboard. Nevertheless, the wily daylight robbers, taking full advantage of the uproar, disappeared into the shrubbery with some $8,264.70. A posse was hastily formed and scoured the countryside, but the train robbers were not to be found. In this hold-up, the Company not only lost the cash, but also sustained a loss of several thousands of dollars due to damaged equipment. The conductor, a Mr. Church, was hurt through being hit on the head by a roving water cooler.

Less than a month later, while the Company was still hopefully advertising in the daily papers, offering a reward of $2,000.00 for the capture of the robbers, as well as one-fourth of all the money recovered (a clever attempt evidently to induce one of the trio to turn state's evidence) another outrage of similar character was perpetrated. This time the scene was near Franklin, Ky.; the date November 9, 1866 the victim, a passenger train loaded with a hundred or more passengers. The holdup occurred in the early morning hours, the train being thrown from the track by a barricade of crossties. This was in the days before electricity had been harnessed to use in headlights; consequently the engineer was almost on top of the obstruction before he saw it. With the train derailed and at their mercy, a band of 12 men, with their faces blackened, descended upon the chaos and plundered the passengers at their leisure. They were subsequently captured, however, and adequately punished.

Chapter VIII

Southward to Coal and Iron

IN 1870, the farthest outposts of the Louisville & Nashville in the Southland were Nashville and Memphis, Tenn. The events of the Civil War had, of course, determined the Company's future course of action and its status as a local road was gradually changing. Its various branches were all projected with the idea of bringing the carrier into closer contact with the country's network of rail lines and its expansion was chiefly to the south; either by purchase, lease or construction.

There were many reasons for this trend. The L. & N. was a Southern road and the Ohio River was a part of the Mason and Dixon Line which imposed a barrier more than symbolic. Moreover, the Northern roads had one gauge track and the Southern roads another and this at the time seemed a vexation that was likely to endure ad infinitum. Freight, at the various points of connection, where difference in gauge was involved, had to be either transferred item by item, or the bodies of the freight cars had to be lifted by steam hoist for an exchange of trucks.

Lastly, and most influential of all, the Southland offered a fertile field for expansion and many systems which had not been as fortunate as the L. & N. during the War between the States were placed upon the bargain counter. A golden transfusion of outside capital was needed and the L. & N. was one of the few roads in a position to extend this aid.

Far south of Nashville lay the Gulf ports of Mobile, New Orleans, and Pensacola, which even at that early day loomed as important goals to the eyes of the L. & N. directorate. Here ships from the seven seas and flying the flags of all the nations of the globe discharged their cargoes and reloaded with the products of the New World. Through service on both passengers and freight was available between Louisville and these shipping centers far to the south, but the route was circuitous and only a small portion of the trackage involved belonged to the L. & N.

The road's first chance to penetrate farther south came early in 1871 and the events leading up to the L. & N.'s acquisition of a line extending from Nashville right through the heart of Dixie to Montgomery, Ala., about 303 miles away, deserve extended mention.

This route was achieved by leasing and obtaining control, respectively, of the Nashville and Decatur Railroad Company (122 miles) and the South and North Alabama Railroad Company (183 miles) in April and May 1871. Both of these roads were approximately of the same vintage as the Louisville & Nashville Railroad. With the always laudable desire to avoid too much tiresome detail, perhaps it might suffice to say each had its inception in the days of frenzied railroad building in the 1850s. The parentage of the N. & D. Railroad was a somewhat piebald affair, consist-

The L. & N.'s depot at Birmingham in 1873.

ing as it did of the Tennessee & Alabama Central Railroad Company, the Tennessee & Alabama Railroad and the Central Southern Railroad Company.

All of these companies were chartered around 1853 and industriously commenced construction soon thereafter. The first named sounded off from Decatur, Ala., to the Tennessee line, the second built from Nashville to Mt. Pleasant, Tenn., by way of Columbia, Tenn., and the third bridged the gap from Columbia to a point of connection with the first at the state line. The three batches of trackage involved were completed by 1860, but endured the hardships of the Civil War as separate entities, it being November 21, 1866, before adversities necessitated a consolidation which was henceforth known as the Nashville & Decatur Railroad Company.

The history of the South & North Alabama Railroad Company was no less variegated. A decade or so prior to the Civil War and almost simultaneous with the chartering of the predecessor lines of the N. & D., the citizens of Alabama had dreamed of driving a line of railroad from the state capital, Montgomery, straight through the tangled mountain fastnesses of Shelby and Jefferson Counties, to Decatur, principal city of Northern Alabama. These mountain barriers, with their fabulous stores of coal and iron, perversely ran at right angles to any south and north railroad, and their penetration was not an easy matter.

It had been realized early in the 19th century that Alabama possessed an abundance of iron ore and coal. However, as late as the Civil War, these were not especially important factors in the life of the state, although Selma, somewhat to the south of what was later to become Birmingham, was one of the Confederacy's chief ordnance manufacturing centers and there were a number of foundries, furnaces, rolling mills, etc., throughout the state at that time. Pig iron had been produced commercially as early as 1818, but there were several reasons why this had not reached the status of a large scale industry.

First, there was the lack of adequate transportation facilities and a consequent increase in the cost of marketing the products. Second, the industrial age was still in its swaddling clothes and existing sources of supply were sufficient to meet the demands for either coal or iron. Lastly, what in later years was to prove a most happy juxtaposition, i.e., that of iron, coal and limestone, essential ingredients in the present day manufacturing of steel, was not especially relevant to the making of pig iron in antebellum days. Charcoal, because of its supposedly superior heating qualities, was used almost exclusively as fuel for the furnaces, making the process a somewhat expensive one and it was 1876 before the first coke pig iron was produced.

It was to remedy the first of the deficiencies mentioned that the Tennessee & Alabama Central Railroad Company was incorporated on December 19, 1853, being authorized to build a railroad from Calera, Ala., to the Alabama-Tennessee state line. As previously mentioned, the best it achieved was a line from Decatur to the state line and on December 13, 1860, it passed along its rights for construction south of Decatur to the Mountain Railroad Contracting Company, which later was absorbed by the South & North Alabama Railroad Company. The latter had been incorporated on February 17, 1854, and had in mind the building of a line from Montgomery to Guntersville, Ala., on the Tennessee River. Subsequent amendments finally fixed the proposed railroad between Montgomery and Decatur and on April 12, 1869, after a period of hibernation enforced by the Civil War, a contract was drawn up between the S.&N.A., and Sam Tate and Associates. The latter thereby agreed to finish the line north of Calera to Decatur, rebuild that portion of it from Calera to Montgomery, which wasn't much to start with and which the War had made even less, and to turn over to the S.&N.A. Railroad by December, 1871, a railroad ready for operation and fully equipped with rolling stock, shop facikities, depots, etc.

Thus, at this time (1869) between Calera and a point about 20 miles

The Relay House — Birmingham's first hotel, built 1871.

south of Decatur, there loomed a gap of about 100 miles through some very rugged country. Sam Tate and Associates fell to with a will, first rebuilding the trackage between Montgomery and Calera. This was completed in November 1870. Next came pioneer construction work with no predecessor guidance, but even so the rails were gleaming far north of Calera when the tangled financial affairs of the S. & N. A. became so ensnarled that a major operation became necessary.

The cost of construction of the S. & N. A. had been set at $5,014,220, not an especially generous provision, payable in bonds of the company. These bonds were endorsed by the State of Alabama to the extent of $2,200,000 and had been hypothecated, not sold, to a group of New York financiers, which included Russell Sage and V. K. Stevenson, a former president of the Nashville & Chattanooga Railroad. However, these pledges had the privilege of taking the bonds up, or of selling them, if the interest payments were not met. A potent ally of theirs in financial matters was John C. Stanton, a prominent citizen of Chattanooga, who was interested in the Alabama & Chattanooga Railroad (later to become the Alabama Great Southern) with which the S. & N. A. was to make connection near Elyton. Previously, in 1870, speculating upon the development of a town at the intersection of the two railroads mentioned, the Elyton Land Company was formed and purchased a tract of 4,000 acres in Jones Valley, the site of present day Birmingham. Among the names appearing on the application for a charter are such prominent ones in the history of Alabama as J. R. Powell, J. N. Gilmer, John T. Milner and Sam Tate.

It is interesting to speculate that the "Pittsburgh of the South," which incidentally was named after the great manufacturing center of the same name in England, might have been named Elyton, had not a last minute decision of the engineers placed the point of intersection of the two railroads somewhat to the east of Elyton. Elyton is today, of course, a part of Greater Birmingham, but at that time it was the county seat and the most important town in Jefferson County.

Little time was lost in laying out the new township and its mud streets and crude frame dwellings were to offer a strange contrast to the modern metropolis that was soon to spring up almost overnight. Meanwhile, as intimated, the South & North Alabama had been having its troubles. Because of the meagre appropriation for its building, the engineers in charge had been forced to be "penny wise and pound foolish," and were constructing a line upon which practical operation would be almost an impossibility. The money for the requisite tunneling or cutting through the rugged country north of Birmingham could not be spared and the engineers perforce had to wind around the mountain barriers with many a fantastic "scenic railway" curve and dip, in the best and cheapest way they could. In fact, the watchword of John T. Milner, the chief engineer in charge of construction, a capable man, was, by necessity: "More curves, more curves, more stiff grade."

At this time the State of Alabama was impoverished, the dual disaster of the Civil War and carpet-bag rule having proven to be too much progressive misfortune. Consequently, in April, 1871, when the management of the S. & N. A. failed to meet the interest payments on the hypothecated bonds, the State of Alabama could only figuratively wring its hands and say "Too bad, too bad!"

This gave John C. Stanton the chance he had long awaited. He had an old score to settle with John T. Milner, dating back to the founding of Birmingham (he had been forced to forfeit his options on the Birmingham acreage to the Elyton Land Company, because of a lack of funds) and at his bidding, the Russell Sage interests calmly offered to the thunderstruck S. & N. A. management this bristling alternative: immediate settlement on the bonds and the interest due thereon or the complete transfer of the S. & N. A. Railroad, lock, stock and barrel, to the Nashville & Chattanooga Railroad, in which both Stanton and Stevenson were deeply interested. They proposed, among other things, to stop the construction of the railroad at Birmingham, which meant in effect that the city's glowing future would be transferred to Chattanooga, that Birmingham would become a mere way station and that Chattanooga, not Birmingham, would be the capital of Alabama's rapidly growing empire of iron and coal. Stanton had large investments at Chattanooga and, of course, his actions were not dictated by mere pique alone.

No. 29, "The Southern Belle," built by the L. & N. in its own shops in 1871.

After a stormy session between the S. & N. A. management and the Russell Sage interests at the Exchange Hotel in Montgomery, which is said to have rocked the very doors of that eminent hostelry, the S. & N. A. rejected the proposition and the meeting broke up. The outlook was admittedly gloomy and ruin loomed starkly ahead. But by morning the marines in the shape of the L. & N., as represented by Albert Fink, had landed and after the usual period of adjustment soon had the situation well in hand.

The president of the Nashville & Decatur Railroad at that time was Colonel James W. Sloss, and he and his road, of course, had a vital interest in the welfare of the S. & N. A. Knowing of the plight of his neighboring road to the south, he proposed to the L. & N. that they lease his road for a period of 30 years, take up the bonds of the S. & N. A., meeting the interest payments thereupon, and complete the S. & N. A. between a point just south of Birmingham and the northern end, which dangled some 20 miles below Decatur, a gap of 66 miles. The advantages to the L. & N. were many and obvious.

After a special meeting of the L. & N. board of directors, this proposition was tentatively approved and Albert Fink bore it in triumph to Montgomery. Following this preliminary discussion, a committee from the S. & N. A. Railroad, consisting of Frank Gilmer, Bolling Hall, E. K. Mitchell, John Milner and Sam Tate entrained for Louisville where they met with the L. & N. directors in the Blue Parlor of the famous Galt House.

Here a snag was struck as three of the L. & N. directors favored the proposition and three did not. President H. D. Newcomb (he had succeeded Russell Houston, who had in turn succeeded James Guthrie, just prior to the latter's death on March 13, 1869) was on the fence. Before he had time to make up his mind one way or the other, Sam Tate, who up until now had remained wrapped in the silence which is so often portentous, shattered the air of harmonious accord and good fellowship with a demand for a bonus of $100,000.00 for surrendering his contract with the S. & N. A. Chaos erupted in that sedate room. We quote from Ethel Armes' excellent book, "The Story of Coal and Iron in Alabama":

"Colonel Newcomb leaped to his feet, his wrinkled hands trembling.

This is one of the annual passes issued by the L. & N. in 1876, when it was toying with the idea of changing its name to the Louisville & Great Southern Railroad, or the Louisville & Nashville & Great Southern Railroad, following its acquisition of a line to Montgomery, Ala., in 1872.

He was a very old man and a choleric one. 'D'ye think I'll stand for any highway robbery!' he cried, and declared the meeting adjourned sine die.

"Tate then sprang at Newcomb. The two men met in the middle of the room.

"Tate raised his stick as though to strike Newcomb, but he did not strike. He said he would not give such as Newcomb even the little end of his stick. Then he stated that he had already arranged a transfer with the Sage and Stevenson party, but was willing to make a trade with the Louisville & Nashville people. Newcomb went savage at this. Both men grappled. Big Fink sprang between them. Though both Colonel Tate and Colonel Newcomb were tall men, Albert Fink towered head and shoulders over both. He laid hands on their shoulders and succeeded in parting them, saying in his broken English: 'Colonel Tate, you stop this! Colonel Newcomb, you come along with me,' and he got Newcomb out. Milner remarks at this point, 'The fat was then all in the fire.' "

However, good Kentucky Bourbon eventually did its part in cementing the scattered wreckage and the next day the James W. Sloss proposition, as it was called, was accepted as it stood, Colonel Newcomb who was mollified by Albert Fink and a slight concession on the part of Sam Tate, who reduced his original bonus demand to $75,000.00, casting the deciding vote.

Contracts between Sam Tate and Associates and the L. & N., between the S. & N. A. and the L. & N., and between the N. & D. and the L. & N., were subsequently drawn up, these being dated respectively May 19, 1871, May 19, 1871 and April 20, 1871. These were very inclusive and covered just about everything except the length and color of the directors' moustachios and the political affiliations of the section hands.

The legal niceties attended to, the L. & N. immediately started construction of the unfinished portion of the S. & N. A., completing this task on September 24, 1872. The work was done under the direction of J. W. Robertson, and cost the L. & N. some $4.6 million.

The through operation of trains between Louisville and Montgomery was commenced on September 29, 1872, the Nashville & Decatur lease having previously become effective on July 1, 1872. Incidentally, prior to the leasing of the N. & D., the L. & N. had no physical connection with that road at Nashville and several thousands of dollars had to be spent in procuring the right-of-way, for grading, for iron rail, etc.

It is indeed unfortunate that with a portion of its dream to reach the Gulf thus translated into reality, hard times should have come a'knocking at the L. & N.'s door so soon. Hardly had the S. & N. A. been completed than the panic of 1873 became a full-fledged reality, with wide-spread repercussions on the commercial and industrial activities of the nation. The traffic on the S. & N. A., for which such high hopes had been held, after an encouraging start, dwindled away, as did to a lesser extent, traffic on the other divisions of the L. & N. The Railroad, by cutting expenses to the bone, nevertheless managed to show net operating incomes of $1,484,047.38 and $1,565,382.34 in the years ending with June 30, 1873 and June 30, 1874, respectively.

However, these figures do not tell the whole story. Huge expenditures had been made, not only to complete the S. & N. A., but also to rebuild the N. & D., and these incomes were offset by these advances. Insofar as mere figures go, both the S. & N. A. and the N. & D. could boast of the fact that their gross earnings exceeded their operating expenses in each of the years ending June 30, 1874, June 30, 1875 and June 30, 1876, but these net earnings were comparatively small and did not go very far towards reimbursing the L. & N. for its initial expenditures, interest payments, etc., upon their behalf.

It is recorded that in the darkest days of the panic in 1873, there was not enough business available on the S. & N. A. between Decatur and Calera to warrant the operation of more than one passenger coach a week and that freight business was almost as bad, one freight car a day being more than adequate on the 118-mile stretch.

The story is told that Albert Fink encountered John Milner, who helped build the S. & N. A., on the street in Montgomery one day during the panic of 1873, and turned on him with these words: "You have ruined me, you fool, me and the L. & N. Railroad! The railroad (the S. & N. A.) will not pay for the grease that is used on its car wheels. Where are those coal mines and those iron mines you talked so much about and wrote so much about? Where are they! I look, but I see nothing!" A few years later, when things were really booming on the S. & N. A., Mr. Fink handsomely apologized to Mr. Milner for his impetuous words.

The L. & N. realizing that some of its troubles might arise from the sparsely-settled country traversed by the S. & N. A., spent large sums of money in the '70s to attract not only industries, but settlers as well to Northern and Central Alabama. Cullman, Ala., for instance, owes its origin to the L. & N., the railroad having entered into a contract with John S. Cullman, a German, in 1872, to bring settlers to a point about 53 miles north of Birmingham in what is now Cullman County. Here, the enterprising Mr. Cullman eventually located about five hundred families.

These rapid-fire acquisitions and the road's expansion southward gave General James F. Boyd, then general passenger agent, the idea in the '70s that the L. & N. deserved a more fitting and sonorous title and he suggested to the management that its name be changed to the "Louisville and Nashville and Great Southern." This seemed like a good idea at the time and accordingly such letterheads were prepared for Milton H. Smith and Albert Fink bearing this designation. It should be emphasized, however, that the Company's official name under which it was chartered was never changed.

It was about this time also that the red-and-white trade-mark, used by the L. & N. for many years, came into existence. This was designed by the late George Schumpp, who was master painter at the South Louisville Shops at the time of his retirement on July 1, 1929. At the request of General Passenger Agent C. P. Atmore, Mr. Schumpp prepared and submitted several designs in 1880; was always proud of the fact that the one shown, in this chapter, was selected and used for many years.

Shortly after the adoption of this trade-mark, the L. & N. was also affectionately referred to for the first time as "The Old Reliable," a phrase which was synonymous with the Railroad for many years. According to one set of facts, R. M. Rawls, then editor of the Alabama Courier, of Athens, Ala., first used this in referring to the L. & N. in an editorial in his paper in 1884. Mr. Rawls, of course did not coin the phrase.

Chapter IX

Yellow Jack and Teredos

MANY troubles beset the L. & N. in the half-a-decade ending with 1875. Epidemics of cholera and yellow fever plagued the Southland in the summer and fall of 1873, leaving a wake of death and destruction and seriously interfering with the operation of trains. Everything went wrong. The cotton crop was short in 1874 and in the spring of that year floods and storms played havoc with the Company's property, especially on the Memphis Line.

To aggravate matters – for the L. & N. at least – the Ohio and Mississippi rivers during 1873 were navigable the whole year, a condition that was most unusual in those days. This had the effect of diverting from the railroad a certain amount of traffic that it otherwise would have had. The firm hand of President H. D. Newcomb was removed from the road's helm by death on August 18, 1874, and the depots and engines were draped in mourning for a period of 30 days. He was succeeded by Thomas J. Martin, who in turn, was succeeded by E. D. Standiford on October 6, 1875.

In the meantime, on July 1, 1875, Albert Fink resigned and the L. & N. obviously suffered a severe loss. It is said that Mr. Fink left the L. & N. because of the until then disappointing results from the acquisition of the N. & D. and the S. & N. A. Fortunately for the L. & N. it had in its employ at that time one who was to more than duplicate the monumental achievements of the Teutonic giant.

Milton H. Smith's first connection with the Louisville & Nashville was as local agent at Louisville in 1866. Less than three years later he was made general freight agent and as such was an eye-witness to the exciting events incident to the L. & N.'s entrance into Alabama. He was firmly sold on that state's possibilities and was to do much that was to lift it to the position of eminence which it came to enjoy.

In the previous chapter we concentrated on the Railroad's acquisition of the N. & D. and S. & N. A., and relevant events, because of the importance which they were later to assume, but it is a fact that momentous things were happening elsewhere on the System.

A constant process of change was going on and the railroad was pouring out a steady stream of money for new depots, passing tracks, shop facilities, roundhouses, freight platforms, stock pens and the like. It was also keeping an open mind about the latest innovations in railroading and at the beginning of the '70s had not only ordered 15 of the latest type locomotives from Baird & Company, of Philadelphia, but was building five in its own shops from the designs evolved by its superintendent of machinery, Thatcher Perkins. All of these were to be coal burners and a number of its old engines had been converted so that coal could be used as fuel. The

Railroad was firmly convinced as to the superiority of coal over wood and it was estimated that when the L. & N. could utilize coal exclusively, its fuel bill would be reduced 25 per cent, or about $45,000 per year.

Along about this time a gentleman by the name of George Westinghouse invented the air brake, admittedly crude, but the L. & N. was so impressed with its possibilities that in 1871 it purchased 24 sets of straight air brake equipment for its locomotives and 94 sets for other items of rolling stock.

At the beginning of the '70s, steel rail was just beginning to be incorporated in the trackage of American railroads, replacing the less durable iron. The Annual Report for the year ending June 30, 1873, shows that at that time the Company had some 55 miles of steel rail sandwiched in between the more plebian metal on the Main Stem and Memphis Line.

Management was eyeing Cumberland Gap hopefully as a point of connection with roads serving the Atlantic Seaboard and a survey was made of possible routes from that spot to Livingston, Ky., the Lebanon Branch's jumping-off place. A conservative estimate set the cost at $2,180,000 and it was thought that the expense would probably run much greater because of the rugged nature of the country.

In the early part of 1872, the L. & N. had purchased a steam-boat, "The Dick Johnson," which plied leisurely back and forth on the Tennessee River between Danville, Tenn., and Florence, Ala. Barges were also pur-

The Barrett Lighting Matinee Train from New Orleans to Mobile and return, February 3, 1874. Running time from New Orleans, 3 hours and 11 minutes.

chased and a wharf-boat was placed in position at Danville for the exchange of freight, it being thought that the "Dick Johnson" would serve as a feeder to the railroad. This supplementary service was operated with indifferent success and the L. & N.'s one-boat merchant marine was finally discontinued on July 1, 1874.

Construction of a new general office building at Second & Main streets in Louisville was commenced in 1875, but the work proceeded rather slowly, not to say unenthusiastically. The panic of 1873 and assorted misfortunes largely eliminated the once crying need for increased space of which there was now plenty, due to reduced forces.

Knocked groggy, so to speak, by its acquisitions of the N. & D., and the S. & N. A. in 1871, as well as by other misfortunes, the L. & N. moved very circumspectly for the next several years. It still felt, however, that its expansion southward was a timely one and that the years would prove the wisdom of its policy. Its contemporary directorate was liberal-minded and hence when the opportunity arose in January 1877 to purchase the Cecilian Branch of what was formerly the Louisville, Paducah and Southwestern Railroad, they did not hesitate. It was snapped up instanter and the road thereby obtained trackage from Louisville to Cecilian Junction (near Elizabethtown, Ky.) some 46 miles long, which largely paralleled its main stem out of Louisville and which obviated, for the time being, the necessity of constructing a double track south of Louisville.

The L. & N., through its operation of refugee trains, played a prominent role in the relief of victims of the South's yellow fever epidemic of 1878.

The Cecilian Branch did not remain in the family long, it having been later leased to the Chesapeake, Ohio and Southwestern Railway Company and eventually sold to the Chicago, St. Louis and New Orleans Railway (Illinois Central Railroad) on December 19, 1901. The pertinent Annual Report (1877) referred to the Cecilian Branch as a "constant disturber of rates," and implied that its purchase was a self-protective measure. This same Annual Report grew somewhat lyrical over the possibilities of this branch, speaking of the rapid growth of the city of Louisville into the region traversed by the Cecilian Branch "as it meanders along the Ohio."

Encouraged by a sizeable net profit in the fiscal year ending with June 30, 1877, the L. & N. paid a dividend, but the majority of the "edge" was applied to the reduction of the bonded and floating debt. Encouraged by favorable signs and portents, the Company at this time also felt emboldened to construct a line of road from Columbia, Tenn., to Lewisburg, Tenn. (later to become a part of the N. C. & St. L. Ry.), a distance of 20 miles, and to build the Wetumpka Branch, some seven miles long, extending from Elmore to Wetumpka, Ala. It also entered into negotiations which had as their ultimate aim the construction of the Southern Division – so-called – of the Cumberland & Ohio Railroad between Lebanon, Ky., and Greensburg, Ky. (31 miles), with a subsequent leasing and operation of the line.

Some $1,600,000 had already been sunk into this venture and its backers, who originally had the idea of linking Louisville and Cincinnati, on the north, with Nashville and Chattanooga, on the south, were bankrupt in the year 1878. It was estimated that it would cost but $180,000 to complete the line and accordingly the L. & N. commenced construction in October 1878. Such work was largely one of filling in the gaps and the road was completed to Campbellsville in August 1879 and to Greensburg in October of the same year. The total cost of constructing this branch – to the L. & N. – was around $255,000 and it was operated by the L. & N. under contract until October 2, 1903, when the property was purchased outright.

In the meantime the new general office building at 2nd and Main streets, in Louisville, had been completed (in 1877) and some of the space was rented to outsiders.

These slight skirmishings for advantageous position in the rail structure of the nation were taking place in an atmosphere surcharged with woe and on other fronts potent monkey-wrenches were being tossed into the whirring wheels. A severe train wreck in 1878 killed several employees and marred an impressive safety record. In the latter part of July 1877, serious labor disturbances rocked the country and the L. & N. was caught in a damaging cross-fire of conflicting views and opinions. There were especially violent upheavals at Louisville and the other larger cities, with some subsequent damage to property.

Emerging from this man-made storm, the L. & N. soon encountered a fiercer one engendered by nature working through the medium of the yellow fever mosquito (stegomyia fasciata) and the yellow fever virus. This disease made its appearance at New Orleans (where it took a toll of 4,056 lives) in the summer of 1878 and swept rapidly northward through Mississippi. It soon reached Memphis, in which place it was declared epidemic in August 1878. Other points upon our lines, which at that time extended only as

The monument erected by the L. & N. in Cave Hill Cemetery, Louisville, Ky., in honor of Mr. and Mrs. Ernest, who gave their lives in the service of the Company during the yellow fever epidemic.

far south as Montgomery, were somewhat hard hit, but it was at Memphis and elsewhere on the Memphis Line that the death toll was greatest.

A panic-laden flood of citizens poured forth from the stricken city for several days, severely taxing the facilities of the L. & N., whose forces were also greatly decimated by the disease. Trains left the station with skeleton crews, the coaches crowded to suffocation, the engines straining to pull loads that were almost beyond their capacities. No attempt was made to collect fares and as the refugee trains with their melancholy cargoes rolled north they passed on the sidings all along the route other trains loaded with medicine, supplies, food, doctors and nurses, hurrying to the aid of Memphis and nearby towns.

At that time it was not known that the disease was transmitted by the mosquito before mentioned and persons from infected areas were generally shunned. Most of the towns north of Memphis and other disease-plagued spots had established rigid quarantines against these fear-inspired migrations and Bowling Green was the first point on our lines at which passengers were allowed to alight. At other points, shot-guns or similar potent items in the hands of a determined citizenry discouraged the usual inalienable right of a citizen to disembark from a train at whatever point it might stop. Smoke – and lots of it – was considered an excellent prophylaxis against the disease and, as a consequence, huge bon-fires blazed on the principal downtown streets of Bowling Green and elsewhere.

Too much credit cannot be given to the L. & N. and its employes for their conduct during the dark days of the epidemic. Employes remained at their posts of duty, exposing themselves to infection, and of 145 employes stricken with the disease, 71 lost their lives. The Annual Report for the year ending 1879 pays especial tribute to a heroic couple, husband and wife, of Paris, Tenn., who had charge of the Company's hotel at that point. This couple, Mr. and Mrs. G. W. Ernest, remained at their posts, nursing impartially those infected with the disease whether they be of high or low estate, until they in turn were stricken, their deaths occurring within a few days of each other. In grateful recognition of the services of these employes, the Company erected above their graves, in Cave Hill Cemetery, Louisville, a handsome memorial, suitably inscribed.

Management estimated that the visitation of the plague had caused it to suffer a loss of $300,000, as a result of the interruption of traffic. It had carried free of charge 150,000 pounds of freight and had handled free or at reduced rates the transportation of sufferers to the amount of $50,000. Some 500 employes had been thrown out of work, due to the chaotic conditions imposed by the epidemic, and the railroad had run, according to the 1878 Annual Report, some **1550 miles of special trains** for physicians, nurses, supplies, refugees, etc.

The Annual Report for the year ending June 30, 1880, contains this sentence: "The year under review has probably been the most eventful and stirring in the history of your company."

Trackage was acquired right and left, either through purchase or lease, and a railroad extending from the Ohio River on the north to the Gulf of Mexico on the south, which only yesterday had seemed many tomorrows away, became, almost overnight, a full-fledged reality. The L. & N.'s iron horse finally entered the rich Gulf ports of Mobile, New Orleans and Pensacola.

The Railroad's further march through Dixie was achieved by two closely-linked steps: first, the purchase of the majority of the stock of the Mobile and Montgomery Railway, some 180 miles long, on January 15, 1880, and, second, through the leasing of the New Orleans, Mobile and Texas Railroad Company on May 8, 1880. (It was subsequently purchased outright by the L. & N. on October 5, 1881.) This latter road was some 141 miles long and extended, as its name would imply, from Mobile to New Orleans. The L. & N. also obtained at this time, the Pontchartrain Railroad, a Lilliputian carrier some five miles long, which serviced New Orleans and Milneburg, on the shores of Lake Pontchartrain. It was famous as the first railroad completed west of the Alleghenies, having been chartered on January 20, 1830, and opened for traffic on April 14, 1831. It was abandoned in 1935.

The Mobile and Montgomery Railway Company was the result of two ventures: the Alabama and Florida Railroad and the Mobile and Great Northern Railroad. The A. & F., which had been chartered on February 11, 1850, completed a line of road from Montgomery to the state line (Alabama-Florida) via Pollard, Ala., on May 3, 1861.

The Mobile and Great Northern Railroad, on the other hand, was not chartered until February 5, 1856, but it finished a line from Pollard to a point on the Tensas River, now known as Hurricane, Ala., a distance of about 45 miles, during the fall of 1861. At Hurricane passengers and freight were transferred to boats to make the 22-mile trip down the Tensas River to Mobile. It was, of course, the original intention to build straight on through to Mobile, but the Civil War, as well as the engineering difficulties that were encountered, made Hurricane the southern terminus for a decade or more. A huge pier was built out in the Tensas River there to consummate the juncture of rail and river and this remained in position long after the line to Mobile was finally built. This last-mentioned event, which involved the construction of some 15 miles of track over swamps, marshes and rivers, was completed, with the usual fanfare, on March 5, 1872, a previous consolidation of the A. & F. and the M. & G. N., having taken place on August 5, 1868. After the completion of the line to Mobile, a feat which rapidly became a Pyrrhic victory insofar as the treasury was concerned, the line was sold and purchased by the trustees, the subsequent

Typical scenes at the L. & N. station at Mobile, Ala., around the turn of the century

re-organization being known as the Mobile and Montgomery Railway Company.

Descriptions of the old M. & M., which have been left by eye-witnesses, are not very flattering. Shortly after completion, it locked horns with the Civil War and after much bedeviling emerged from this conflict as from a concrete mixer. The right-of-way and rolling stock were both greatly dilapidated, the former consisting, in part, of two parallel (and not always at that) streaks of rust, badly overgrown with bushes and grass. The operation of trains over this phantom of Southern Alabama was at a snail's pace, 20 miles per hour then being the maximum speed limit. Section crews "poled" their way to and from their work upon this decrepit line on crude contrivances, achieving their momentum in much the same manner as the gondoliers of Venice do theirs. The meeting of trains was a social event, with train crews and passengers fraternizing.

Life was leisurely on the M. & M., and, as a consequence of all this, therefore, the L. & N. had to spend huge sums of money to remove this quaintness and to place its newly acquired property in good condition.

The New Orleans, Mobile and Texas Railroad Company, as a contrast, was in good physical shape when it was taken over by the L. & N. It had originally been chartered on November 24, 1866, as the New Orleans, Mobile and Chattanooga Railroad Company, with an intention,

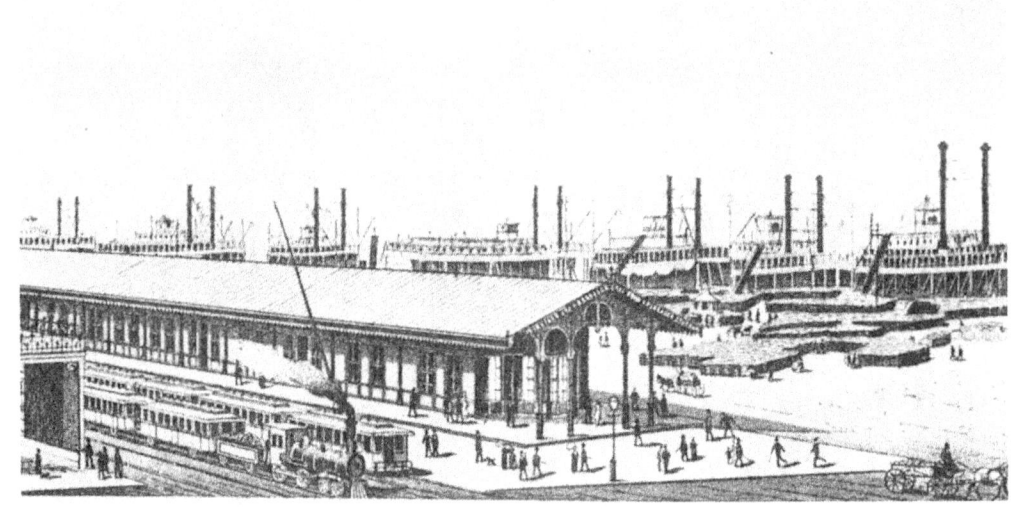

This is how the L. & N.'s Canal Street Station at New Orleans appeared in the 1880s.

among several others, of building a line of road from Mobile to New Orleans. Other aims included, as implied, a road to Chattanooga and a road to Houston, Texas. Following the granting of its charter, there ensued a period of construction and high finance, with the line between New Orleans and Mobile, which is our principal concern, being completed on October 29, 1870. It was this portion of the venture whose name on April 18, 1871, had been changed to the New Orleans, Mobile and Texas Railroad Company, which the L. & N. obtained through lease on May 8, 1880, with subsequent outright purchase a year or so later.

The building of the original line of the N. O. M. & T. R. R. Company had presented a peculiar problem from an engineering standpoint, due to the many inlets, bays, bayous and other bodies of water which had to be crossed. There are, in all, nine miles of bridges and trestles on this 140-mile stretch of track. Although the property was in good shape when acquired the status quo was difficult to retain, due to the insidious underwater activities of a pest known as the teredo navalis. The latter is a worm native to salt waters, whose principal item of diet is untreated timber.

The construction of the railroad from Mobile to New Orleans had been manna from heaven to this marine nuisance. It was known when the line was built that creosoted timbers would withstand the ravages of the teredo, and a plant was constructed at Gautier, Miss., in 1869 for such treatment, but the work, at first, was imperfectly done. As a consequence, a goodly part of the piling which supported the road-bed for long distances between Mobile and New Orleans, and which had been driven into position in 1869 and 1870, was destroyed in nine months' time by the teredo, whose potentialities for damage are all out of proportion to his size, which is about that of a lead pencil, or somewhat larger, when fully grown. He, or she, works in much the same manner as the termite, honeycombing the structure attacked and terminating its usefulness in short order.

The activities of the teredo were obviously of an expensive nature and further aggravated a situation which was badly frayed around the edges and wearing thin in the middle. In some places, in order to prepare a road-bed for the original line, a canal had been dredged through the marshes and watery waste-lands encountered and the displaced material, with some admixture of foreign soil, was piled on the south side of the canal, forming an embankment for the road-bed.

This latter had a tendency to slip back into the canal, so more expensive piling had to be driven as a protective check against such slides. The old N. O. M. & T. also had the distinction of being one of the few railroads, if not the only one, in the United States to have an anchored road-bed. Because of its proximity to the Gulf of Mexico, as well as because of the fact that in a good many places the road-bed was not very much above sea-level, high tides frequently washed over the tracks, sometimes returning to "home base" with booty in the shape of segments of the road-bed aforesaid. To prevent such disasters, posts were driven down at intervals between the rails and were then bolted to adjacent cross-ties, thus securely anchoring the track and discouraging any seagoing tendency.

After its first disastrous experience with the teredo, the management of the N. O. M. & T. went into the matter of creosoting timber a little more closely and eventually emerged with a process of forcing the creosote oil into the timber under pressure – an importation from England. This proved to be quite successful, so much so that the L. & N., soon after its acquisition of the line, extended such treatment to all timbers used along its lines in trestles, etc., in order to balk decay. (As a matter of interest, it was not until 1912 that it was decided to give cross-ties the creosote treatment as well.)

The operation of trains on the N. O. M. & T., like that of those on the old M. & N., was somewhat haphazard. Freight trains took about 12 hours to make the 141-mile trip between Mobile and New Orleans and storms blowing in from the Gulf Coast played hob with the schedule.

CHAPTER X

Coke Feeds the Furnace

OTHER acquisitions of the L. & N. in the Deep South included the purchase of the Pensacola Railroad (45 miles), extending from the Alabama-Florida state line at Flomaton, Ala., to Pensacola, Fla., on February 27, 1880, and the Pensacola & Selma Railroad (34 miles), which at that time had trackage only between Gulf Junction, on the Alabama River, opposite Selma, to Pine Apple, Ala. (Trackage arrangements with the Western Railroad of Alabama – then a leased line – consummated on July 1, 1881, gave the L. & N. access to Selma via the Alabama River Bridge.)

The Pensacola Railroad was an offshoot of the Alabama and Florida Railroad, previously mentioned, and the construction of this branch from Pensacola to a point of connection at Flomaton, with the main line, was commenced in 1861 and completed in May, 1869. It was necessary to rebuild the road completely after the Civil War and this branch of the Alabama and Florida Railroad became subsequently known as the Pensacola and Louisville Railroad Company, and still later as the Pensacola Railroad Company.

The Pensacola and Selma Railroad Company, originally incorporated as the Selma and Gulf Railroad Company, on January 30, 1858, was primarily projected as a link between the mineral wealth of Central Alabama and the bustling Gulf port of Pensacola. At the time it was acquired by the L. & N., however, the trackage extended only from Gulf Junction to Pine Apple, to which point the line had been completed in 1871. On February 28, 1880, the L. & N. entered into a contract with the Selma and Gulf Railroad whereby it agreed to complete the line from Pine Apple to Flomaton, a construction chore of 74 miles. The Pensacola and Selma Railroad was the result of these proceedings and by 1881 the line had been extended from Flomaton to Repton, some 30 miles away, leaving a gap of about 44 miles between the latter point and Pine Apple. This property was conveyed to the L. & N. by deed dated November 23, 1880, but it was January 1, 1900, before the line was completed between Pine Apple and Repton.

The L. & N. had also acquired at this time through lease the Selma Division of the Western Railroad of Alabama, extending from Montgomery to Selma. It later surrendered this lease and the line again became part of the Western Railroad of Alabama.

Farther north the corporate structure was also experiencing growing pains. In 1880 the L. & N. also acquired a majority of the capital stock of the N. C. & St. L. Railway, some 508 miles long. (This carrier continued to operate as a separate entity, however, until the merger in

First shaft opened at Pratt Coal & Coke Company mine, near Birmingham, as it appeared after its opening in 1879.

1957.) As a result of this control, the L. & N. subsequently leased the Illinois and Indiana divisions of the St. Louis and Southeastern Railway Company, Consolidated, on May 1, 1880. It may suffice to say that predecessor roads of these divisions, among which were the Mount Vernon Railroad Company and the Shawneetown and Eldorado Railroad Company, had been chartered as early as February 15, 1855, with the St. Louis and Southeastern Railway Company, as such, coming into existence on March 10, 1869.

Subsequent consolidation with the Evansville and Southern Illinois Railroad Company, and the Evansville, Carmi and Paducah Railroad Company, supplemented by some original construction work of its own, gave the St. Louis and Southeastern Railway (the "Company" had been dropped following still further reorganization on February 28, 1871) by January 1, 1872, a line of railroad extending from East St. Louis, Ill., to Evansville, Ind., via McLeansboro, Ill., and Carmi, Ill., with branches extending from McLeanboro to Shawneetown, Ill., and from Bellville, Ill., to O'Fallon, Ill., 208 miles in all. Access to St. Louis, Mo., across the Mississippi River from East St. Louis, Ill., was soon gained via the Eads Bridge, which had been constructed in 1874, and a tunnel, which "holed in" at the western terminal of the bridge and emerged at 8th and Poplar streets. The total distance from the relay depot in East St. Louis to the Union Station in St. Louis via this "underland" and "overwater" route was 3.84 miles.

When the track was completed between Equality and Shawneetown, Ill., on the Ohio River, a free train trip was arranged for the jubilant citizens and many Equality people went to Shawneetown for a day's outing and picnic. One very fat lady was unable to get through the narrow door of the coach but, nothing daunted, rode the cow-catcher all the way to Shawneetown, some 11 miles away, returning in the same manner.

Engine No. 18 did the honors on that occasion and was decorated with a pair of deer horns, which remained a part of its standard equipment for a number of years.

Later, on December 6, 1879, the L. & N. purchased what were known as the Kentucky and Tennessee divisions of the same St. Louis and Southeastern Railway Company, Consolidated, operation of these properties having been begun by the L. & N. on July 25, 1879. The trackage involved was some 146 miles in extent and lay between Henderson Ky., and Nashville, Tenn. The Tennessee Division extended from Nashville to Guthrie, Ky., the original predecessor line being known as the Edgefield and Kentucky Railroad Company, incorporated on February 13, 1852, and completed in the latter part of 1859.

The Kentucky Division extended from Henderson to Guthrie, at the state line, and had its original inception in the incorporation of the Henderson and Nashville Railroad, first chartered as early as February 8, 1837. The line, as above described, was completed in January 1871, by a company known as the Evansville, Henderson and Nashville Railroad Company, and this was subsequently taken over by the St. Louis and Southeastern Railway Company, Consolidated, on October 1, 1872.

The first L. & N. General Office Building, completed in 1877, at Second and Main Streets, Louisville. It was used until 1907 when the building at 9th and Broadway was constructed.

The L. & N. additionally acquired at this time (in March, 1880) a controlling interest in the stock of the Owensboro and Nashville Railroad Company, extending from Owensboro, Ky., to Central City, Ky., with additional prolongation to Adairville and Russellville, as well as to the Western Kentucky coal fields, ardently desired. It had been incorporated on February 27, 1867, and had completed its line from Owensboro to Central City during the summer of 1872.

The acquisition of the various divisions of its one-time flourishing rival, the St. Louis and Southeastern, theoretically, at least, gave the L. & N. a through line of railroad, some 321 miles long, from St. Louis to Nashville. However, the flaw in this tenuous life-line of steel, iron and wood was the fact that at this time there was no bridge across the Ohio River at Henderson, Ky., hence passengers and freight had to be ferried across by boat. This greatly hindered operation and shortly after acquiring the property, the L. & N. took steps to remedy the deficiency.

A charter for the construction of such a bridge between Evansville and Henderson had been issued to the Henderson Bridge Company on February 9, 1872, but nothing further was ever done until October 1881, when construction was commenced, the L. & N. having previously insured the success of the venture by becoming a principal stockholder. Of this vital link between North and South, more anon.

A little recapitulation may be in order at this point. At the end of the fiscal year ending with June 30, 1880, as a result of the acquisitions heretofore mentioned, the L. & N. owned and operated some 1,839.95 miles of track (independent of the 508 miles of the N. C. & St. L. Ry.) located in eight states of the Union. Notwithstanding its abnormal expense in connection with this expansion, it had declared a dividend of 8 per cent, the largest in years, and had purchased quite a batch of new equipment. With an eye to the future, all rolling stock procured had been manufactured so that the wheels could be moved over to conform with the proposed standardization of gauge of all American railroads, more and more being discussed as a very desirable possibility.

Meanwhile, back in Alabama, the S. & N. A., which had originally proven to be such a disappointment, was rapidly becoming a sparkling asset. The turn of the tide may be traced to one definite event: the decision of the Eureka Company, at Oxmoor, Ala., a few miles south of Birmingham, to experiment with the making of pig iron with coke. The Louisville & Nashville Railroad, realizing the portentousness of this experiment, had invested $125,000 in it, upon the recommendation of Milton H. Smith, then the Company's general freight agent. Mr. Smith's action was based upon the logical conclusion that if pig iron could be produced with Alabama coke, then the future of the Birmingham district was assured, for it possessed both coal (of which coke was a by-product) and iron in abundance and in close juxtaposition.

The experiment was a huge success and on February 28, 1876, the first coke pig iron was manufactured in Alabama. Mr. Smith left the service of the L. & N. Railroad in 1878, not to return until 1882, but before he departed he initiated policies which had much to do with the rapid growth of the Birmingham District. It was he, when the pig iron industry was a toddling infant, who introduced the sliding scale of rates in connection with the movement of that commodity. That is, when pig iron was a drug on the market, so to speak, the rates were low, when better times came around and the price for this commodity increased, the rates were stimulated accordingly. An apt illustration of Mr. Smith's firm belief in the importance of the Alabama iron and coal industry occurred a few years later, during one of the country's periodical panics. His message to the embattled iron and coal men was: " . . . Keep in blast! It doesn't make a bit of difference what the freight rate is – keep in blast! I'll carry the product to market, if I've got to haul it upon my back!"

Following the success of the Oxmoor experiment, additional furnaces and ovens were constructed at that point and at Helena, Ala., a few miles further south, one hundred coke ovens, costing thousands of dollars, were rapidly built. Blast furnaces and ovens sprang up like mushrooms all along the S. & N. A. As a result of this activity, business boomed and 97,000 tons of coal were hauled over this line in the year ending with June 30, 1876.

The L. & N.'s investment in the venture at Oxmoor was but one of a series of comparable ones, although these latter, for the most part, were admittedly upon a smaller scale. Realizing the ultimate value to the railroad itself, it was eager, whenever possible, to extend a helping hand to the then dislocated fragments of what was later to become a mighty empire of coal and iron.

In 1876 the L. & N. Railroad still owned approximately 500,000 acres of valuable lands in Central Alabama and disposed of a goodly part of this acreage at a nominal price in order to encourage colonization and industry. The day was to come when such lands as the Company had retained were to be worth fabulous sums. But, in 1880, the Company made a decision that was to have a far-reaching effect. It chose to dispose of such lands, even at a loss, rather than to mix the operation of trains on a track with the mining of coal or associated ventures.

The successful experiment at Oxmoor greatly increased the demand for Alabama coal. In 1876 the largest coal mining operation in the state was at Montevallo. Prior to the production of coke pig iron, the mining of Alabama coal had also been stimulated by its introduction into New Orleans, an innovation made possible, in part, by the L. & N., through its granting of a very attractive freight rate for the movement of this coal.

The combination of the various factors mentioned creating as they did an increasing demand, lead in 1878 to the formation of the Pratt Coal and Coke Company, which immediately began extensive operations somewhat to the west of Pratt City (later to become a part of Greater Birmingham) in the heart of the great Warrior coal field. It was the first of the state's industrial empires within an empire and it greatly expedited the growth of Birmingham.

It would take a volume or two to fully describe the history of iron, steel and coal in the Birmingham District and in this account, of course, since our concern is principally with the L. & N. Railroad, we can but touch the high spots. From time to time, as it becomes chronologically fit and proper, additional mention will be made of the progress of the Birmingham District and the very essential part played therein by the L. & N.

The various acquisitions mentioned, as well as other expenditures, constituted a severe, although not a dangerous drain upon the treasury, and it was decided in 1880 to fund the Company's entire indebtedness thereby created by a general mortgage of $20,000,000, secured by its properties in Kentucky and Tennessee. This sum would not only take care of the Company's newly incurred indebtedness, but would also enable it to retire its first and second mortgage bonds and fund the floating debt.

Shortly thereafter at a meeting of the stockholders on October 6, 1880, it was almost unanimously agreed to increase the capital stock of the L. & N. (20 votes being cast against the proposal) since the value of its property by far exceeded the total of stock capitalization. No definite figure was set at this time, this being left to the discretion of the board of directors, but it was decided that the additional stock so issued should be paid (by the Company) and distributed among the stockholders on a pro rata basis, according to the stock they then possessed. Subsequently, the capitalization was increased from $9,059,361.30 to $18,130,913.17, which meant that the fortunate stockholders were the recipients of a 100 per cent stock dividend; a bonanza which grew more impressive with time.

Chapter XI

Presidential Parade

IT IS not generally known that George Washington was a vice president and director of the Louisville and Nashville Railroad for several years. However, like so many startling statements with a "Believe-It-Or-Not" tinge, this one owes its effectiveness as an eye-brow lifter to a happy coincidence. The L. & N.'s George Washington was not the "father of our country" but was rather an esteemed employe of L. & N. nearly 100 years after his namesake had died. He served the L. & N. as director from 1876 through 1884 and as second vice-president from 1881 through 1884, and one may be sure that when Mr. Washington was finally gathered to his fathers he had heard every possible reference that could be made anent the identity of his name and that of the country's first president.

Mr. Washington's period of service coincided with an epoch in L. & N. history that was especially eventful. Entering the decade that was the forerunner of the Gay Nineties, the L. & N. was solidly entrenched in the nation's rail structure, owning and operating some 1,872 miles of track, not including the 521 miles embraced within the N. C. & St. L. system. It immediately proceeded to add to this trackage. In 1880, it secured a half interest (the other half being secured by the Central of Georgia Railroad) in a 99-year lease of the Georgia Railroad and dependencies, 641 miles in all, and including such valuable properties as the Atlanta and West Point Railroad, the Rome Railroad of Georgia, the Port Royal Railroad and the Western Railroad of Alabama. These lines had valuable and strategic connections and outlets, served fertile and prosperous territories and it was thought that the lease would prove of real benefit to the Company.

Work was also resumed on the Lebanon Branch after a lapse of about 10 years, during which dormant decade the branch's terminal had remained on "dead center" at Livingston, Ky., about 140 miles from Louisville. A contract was entered into with the East Tennessee, Virginia and Georgia Railroad (to become part of the Southern System) for a cow-catcher-touching ceremony at the state line (Jellico) by January 1, 1883. Once started the work progressed rapidly and the line was opened to London, Ky., 18 miles from Livingston, on July 1, 1882. The shores of the Cumberland River were reached in December of the same year and although the state line was not reached on schedule, still all concerned felt that the date of April 2, 1883, was a very acceptable substitute.

Then ensued a period in which viewpoints were reconciled and compromises were broached, with the operation of through trains between Louisville and Knoxville via the L. & N. and the E. T. V. & G., being ultimately achieved on June 4, 1883. Steel rail had been used exclusively in laying the 60½ miles of the Extension and a glance at the record shows

Opening of the Pewee Valley, Ky., station in 1867.

that at the end of the fiscal year ending with June 30, 1883, the score for the entire System stood: steel rail – 1,276 miles; iron rail – 789 miles.

Meanwhile quite a few other irons were glowing among the embers. The Company obtained control on May 9, 1881, of the Pensacola and Atlantic Railroad Company, through a purchase of the majority of the capital stock. This railroad had been incorporated on March 4, 1881, and had received a generous land grant from the State of Florida of nearly 4,000,000 acres. It proposed to build a line of road from Pensacola, some 170 miles long, eastward across the northwest corner of Florida to a connection just east of the Apalachicola River (Chattahoochee) with major systems serving the Atlantic Seaboard.

Shortly after the L. & N. obtained control, construction was started (in June 1881) and thereafter proceeded at a rapid pace. The country it traversed was thinly settled and there was not a great deal of heavy work to be done. Consequently, it reached the Apalachicola River in January 1883, and the completion of a bridge across this stream to Chattahoochee enabled the L. & N. in April 1883 to connect with railroads serving a vast territory.

This line was a "land grant" railroad, some 3,890,619 acres having been donated to it by the state of Florida, as grantor for the U. S. Government, but only 2,830,065 acres were ever actually delivered. Much of the territory which it traversed, especially in the west, was surprisingly fertile, cotton being the principal crop. The growers depended mainly upon the Chattahoochee River for the floating of their cotton to the big market at Columbus, Ga., and periodically lost money when the river was low.

The eastern end of the line crossed wilder country, and such fauna as panthers, deer and wild turkeys abounded. Train and engine crews frequently combined business with pleasure for a good many years after the line's completion, by obtaining fresh meant for their larder whenever the opportunity presented itself.

The construction of the road was delayed somewhat in its latter stages by an outbreak of swamp fever, but even so it was completed in an amazingly short time. The only two real towns in existence at that time were

Marianna and Milton and these were served by depots of the orthodox type. Elsewhere, set-off boxcars were utilized as stations for quite some time. Much of the credit for the subsequent development of this section of Florida is due to the L. & N.

Contrast this feat of construction – 170 miles in 22 months – with the building of the L. & N.'s original line from Louisville to Nashville – 185 miles in six years; a striking illustration of the potency of a well-filled purse. Definite schedules for the operation of through trains were established on November 18, 1883, and high hopes were held that the venture would pay out in short order. Following the building of the line a number of sawmills were built and turpentine began to be shipped in large quantities, all of which was highly encouraging.

On January 1, 1883, the L. & N. departed minutely from its policy of expansion through acquisition and construction, by leasing its Richmond Branch, extending from Stanford to Richmond, to the then up-and-coming Kentucky Central Railway.

One of the most important steps taken by the L. & N. in the "pre-mauve" decade was its acquisition of the Louisville, Cincinnati and Lexington Railway on July 1, 1881, through the purchase of its entire capital stock. The L. & N. began operation of this property on November 1, of the same year.

The addition of this road to the L. & N. network gave the railroad ingress to Cincinnati, O., Lexington, Ky., and the Northern Kentucky cities of Newport and Covington. The lines of the L. C. & L. stopped at the southern bank of the Ohio River, but entrance was gained into Cincinnati via the Newport and Cincinnati Bridge, which had opened for traffic on April 1, 1872. This bridge was subsequently purchased by the L. & N. from the Pennsylvania Railroad on April 2, 1904. Predecessor roads of the L. C. & L. were of an even more ancient vintage than the L. & N., the former having its inception in the incorporation of the Lexington and Ohio Railroad Company on January 27, 1830.

The Lexington and Ohio, one of the real pioneer roads of the country and sometimes referred to as "the first railroad west of the Alleghenies," encountered all of the buffets that pioneers are habitually exposed to. It was the original intention to construct a railroad from Lexington to some point on the Ohio River, but for many years the line got no closer to **La Belle Riviere** than Frankfort, the state capital, some 29 miles away.

The management of the Lexington and Ohio went overboard for quaintness with a splash. Iron strap rail were imbedded in limestone sills, which were laid in the direction of the track, instead of at right angles, as are crossties, and horses were used to draw the coaches and other equipment. These passenger coaches were double-deckers and when a steam engine finally made its appearance it was so impractical that it was hastily shunted into freight service where dependability was not such an important asset!

The original line between Lexington and Frankfort wended its way between those two points in a manner which gave rise to the suspicion that the engineering forces who located the road might have been slightly intoxicated at the time. The numerous curves have been more plausibly explained in various ways. Some said they were to avoid steep grades;

others stated the road respected property lines, thereby protecting the integrity of the barn-yard and the apple orchard, while a hopeless minority contended that curves were deliberately placed in the track so that the engineer could see the rear of his train ever and anon, thus assuring himself that all was well.

Be that as it may, the road reached Frankfort on January 30, 1834, with due recognition being accorded this achievement. It did not enter the city proper, but came to rest at the top of a large hill, which lies northeast of Frankfort. Here the cars of the L. & O. were handled by a stationary engine down an inclined plane, some 2,200 feet long and with an inclination of 40 degrees. There was no additional charge for a ride on this Kentucky counterpart of rail travel in the Alps and it seems to have been fairly safe. Occasionally, however, cars would get out of control and would careen wildly down the plane onto Broadway, greatly frightening the citizens and passengers alike, but doing no great damage.

Many passengers however, abandoned the railroad at the top of the hill and entered Frankfort by cab, even though such a transfer of allegiance cost them an additional 25 cents. The tunnel at Frankfort, which later enabled the railroad to enter directly into the city, seems to have been built in 1848 and was a truly herculean feat since it had to be dug some 500 feet through the hill, without the use of dynamite or any other high-power explosives.

Some spasmodic effort was made to continue the line from Frankfort to Louisville in 1835, but this met with no great success. At Louisville, a dislocated fragment of the Lexington and Ohio was built about this time, this being known locally as the Portland Railroad. It was only about three miles in length and was to serve as the western terminus of the Lexington and Ohio, if and when that road ever reached Louisville. The proposed right-of-way in the city traipsed down Jefferson Street through the heart of the town to Portland, then a separate municipality. The Portland Railroad, however, only extended from 6th and Main streets in Louisville to Portland and prolonged lamentation greeted its building, it being thought that city streets were no place for a railroad and especially the locomotives thereof. Most vocal were the drayage and transfer interests who reaped a rich harvest hauling freight between the two cities located on opposite sides of the Falls.

The Lexington and Ohio was sold to meet its debts in 1842, the State of Kentucky being the purchaser. After improving the road by an expenditure of $100,000, they in turn leased the road to the firm of McKee and Swigert in 1845. After several years of such operation the line was sold outright to the newly-organized Lexington and Frankfort Railroad Company in 1849, and much of the line between Lexington and Frankfort was rebuilt. In the meantime, in 1847, a company had been organized to build a road between Frankfort and Louisville. After buying out the interest of the old Lexington and Ohio in such a line, construction was started at both Louisville and Frankfort, with completion of the trackage occurring on September 8, 1851. Despite the fact that Louisville and Lexington were now connected by rail, through trains were not operated for a number of years. Passengers solemnly changed cars at Frankfort and when the Lexington and Frankfort and the Louisville and Frankfort were finally consolidated on September 7, 1869, and thereafter operated as one entity, the Louisville, Cincinnati and Lexington Railroad Company, the good citizens of Frankfort were highly indignant over their town being made a mere way station.

Prior to the formation of the Short Line, as the consolidation was also known, the Louisville and Frankfort had undertaken the ambitious

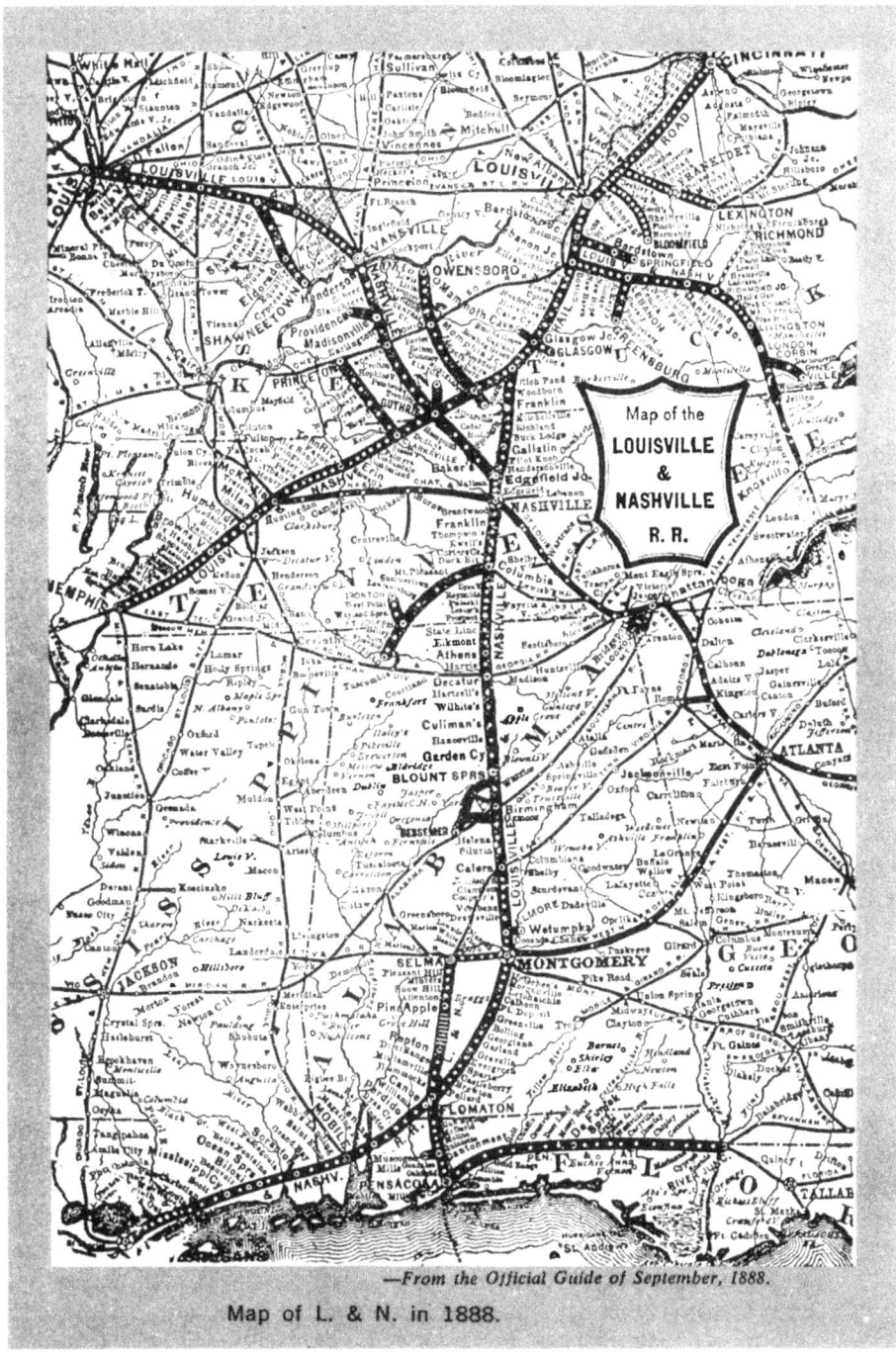

—From the *Official Guide* of September, 1888.

Map of L. & N. in 1888.

project of building a branch line from LaGrange to Covington. This was started in 1867 and completed in 1869. The L. C. & L. was placed in the hands of a receiver on September 21, 1874, such a disaster being largely the result of the drain imposed by the building of the Cincinnati line. In 1877, the Short Line emerged from beneath the stigma imposed by receivership, being now officially known as the Louisville, Cincinnati and Lexington **Railway** Company. Its chief contribution to the railroad scene was the construction of a four-mile line connecting Covington and Newport.

At the time it was taken over by the L. & N. the Short Line had a gauge of four feet, nine inches, and the two roads had been physically connected at Louisville some time before by the construction of what was known as the Railway Transfer, some four miles long and extending from East Louisville to South Louisville. This was built with three rails, because of the differences in gauge (that of the L. & N. being five feet at the time), thus facilitating the transfer of equipment between the two carriers. At the time it was taken over by the L. & N. the Short Line was also the proud possessor of 11 miles of narrow gauge (3 feet) line, this being known as the Louisville, Harrods Creek and Westport Railroad.

Still another item of trackage which came into the possession of the L. & N. at this time, through its purchase of the L. C. & L., consisted of a line from Anchorage to Bloomfield, Ky., by way of Shelbyville, some 45 miles in all. The line from Anchorage to Shelbyville had been completed by the Shelby Railroad Company in 1871 and was later leased to the L. C. & L. The road from Shelbyville to Bloomfield, on the other hand, was not completed until 1880. This work of construction was done by the L. C. & L. for the Northern Division of the Cumberland and Ohio Railroad and was subsequently operated by the former.

One day in 1882, the L. & N. General Office Building at 2nd and Main streets buzzed with excited comment. Nor was that all. Ties were straightened, unruly locks were combed and slicked back and each detail of attire received careful attention. Those were stirring times, but the matter under discussion and which was responsible for this sudden awareness of possible deficiencies of dress and deportment,dwarfed such then-accepted railroad phenomena as wrecks, strikes, the building of new lines, etc. And, indeed, in the light of what has happened since, this emphasis was justified, for on the day mentioned the first woman entered the employ of the L. & N.; the opening wedge into a profession that had theretofore been exclusively masculine. Oddly enough, the male employes did not resent this embargo upon profanity and other vices peculiar to the male, but cordially greeted the young lady in question as a welcome addition to their daily routine.

This plucky pioneer in skirts was Miss Sallie Curtis Murphy, the first woman to take shorthand dictation in Louisville. Miss Murphy later became Mrs. Charles E. McBride. Mrs. McBride's, or Miss Murphy's, first service with the L. & N. was as secretary to Andrew Broaddus, then assistant general freight agent.

As before mentioned, the Civil War had changed the status of the L. & N. from that of a local road, controlled by local capital, to that of an interstate carrier, with increasing importance in the rail and financial structure of the nation. As a consequence of this expansion, more and more outside capital was attracted and British and Dutch financiers invested heavily in L. & N. stocks and bonds during the 'eighties and late 'seventies. As a result the board of directors began to gradually change. Where once this body had been composed almost exclusively of citizens of Kentucky and Tennessee, with Louisville names predominating, here and there an outsider began to creep in. Prominent among these outsiders was Col. Edward H. Green, the husband of famed Hetty Green, lady wizard of Wall Street and contiguous territory. Colonel Green not only served as director of the L. & N. for several years, but was also president of the road briefly from December 1, 1880 to February 26, 1881, at which time he or his wife either owned or controlled a large block of L. & N. stock.

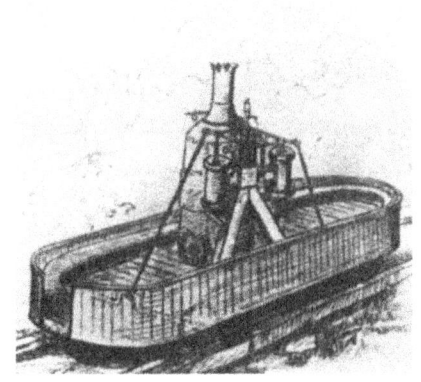

Replica of the first locomotive of the old Lexington & Ohio Railroad.

Then in 1884 came Jay Gould, Thomas Fortune Ryan, and Russell Sage, famous financiers all, who however, were directors for but a short time.

Milton H. Smith became president on June 11, 1884, succeeding J. S. Rogers, successor to C. C. Baldwin, who had, in turn, succeeded Colonel Green. This presidential parade had its origin in the panic of the spring of 1884, during which hectic period the market price of the Company's stock declined from 48 to 31 within four days' time. An unwise direction of the Company's financial affairs culminated in the resignation of C. C. Baldwin on May 19, 1884, and the election of J. S. Rogers in his stead. Mr. Rogers despaired of unraveling the financial snarl and resigned on June 11 of the same year, Milton H. Smith then becoming president. Shortly thereafter the names of Jay Gould, Thomas Fortune Ryan and Russell Sage disappeared from the L. & N.'s directorate. Subsequently, a representative of the British and Dutch majority stockholders appeared on the scene and under his guidance the L. & N.'s ship sailed into more tranquil financial waters. In a subsequent confidential report to the L. & N.'s directors dated September 14, 1885, Mr. Smith was severely critical of the L. & N.'s financial leadership during the period 1875-1884 and closed with the remark that a repetition would inevitably lead to disaster, even though the road was inherently sound.

Serving as vice president during the troubled days mentioned was Eckstein Norton, who was a native of Russellville, Ky., and who was in the cotton exchange business in New York with his partner, Thomas Slaughter. Mr. Norton was the financial representative of certain Dutch interests and it was largely due to their influence that Mr. Norton was made president of the L. & N. on October 6, 1886. Mr. Smith was appointed vice-president in charge of all details of active operation at the time and as such his work was deemed of equal importance to the Company as that of Mr. Norton, the salaries of the two being equal.

These various changes in the financial control of the Louisville and Nashville did not affect its money-making capacities in the slightest, nor indeed its basic policies. A glance at the record shows that its net earnings (before interest charges, taxes, etc., had been deducted) in the fiscal years ending with June 30, 1881, 1882, 1883, and 1884, were respectively $4,198,518.32, $4,558,374.20, $5,135,320.53 and $5,527,310.25.

Maintenance and the usual work of routine rehabilitation occupied a large share of the railroad's attention in the 'eighties, but at the same time it was also pushing its lines through wilderness and farmland to goals greatly desired. On January 1, 1884, for instance, the O. & N. Branch reached Adairville, 47 miles from Central City and 12 miles from Russellville. For the construction of this line the L. & N. had formed the Owensboro and Nashville Railway Company, and upon the completion of the extension, operated the road as an owner of the majority of the capital stock. Prior to its completion to Russellville on the Memphis Line, the O. & N. had no physical connection with the rest of the System and because of this fact had not paid its way.

Sixteen miles of railroad were also built westward from Madisonville, Ky., the Iron Horse reaching Providence in the heart of the Western Kentucky coal fields on November 1, 1882.

The first L. & O. Railroad passenger car. Note bench for passengers on top.

At the time the L. & N. was extending its lines into the Western Kentucky coal fields, that section (roughly Ohio, Union, Crittenden, Webster, Hopkins, Muhlenberg, McLean, Christian, Davies, Henderson and Caldwell counties) was the state's leading coal producer and embraced an area of approximately 4,000 square miles. Its output rapidly increased from a modest 200,000 tons in 1874, to 760,300 tons in 1882, to 1,299,797 tons in 1890 and to over 3,000,000 tons in 1901. Due to the efforts of the L. & N. in popularizing the Western Kentucky fuel, it soon largely replaced Pittsburgh coal in such nearby cities as Louisville, Evansville, Memphis and Nashville.

When the L. & N. experimented more extensively with coal as fuel for its motive power in 1871, Pittsburgh coal was used exclusively at first. It was soon displaced, however, by Western Kentucky coal, upon the recommendation of Albert Fink, who had witnessed the fine results obtained on the old Evansville, Henderson and Nashville Railroad, which ran through the very heart of the Western Kentucky fields. At that time the L. & N. paid a price of $1.62½ per ton for lump coal, f.o.b., at Western Kentucky mines. Prior to the coming of the railroad, the prevailing freight charge by wagon-haul for the 39-mile trip between Madisonville and Henderson, Ky., – from 50 cents to $1.00 per 100 pounds, depending upon the condition of the roads – precluded the commercial marketing of Western Kentucky's hidden wealth.

Another road in which the L. & N. also had a vital interest at this time (1883) was the Nashville and Florence Railroad Company, which had been incorporated on February 24, 1879, and whose purpose, after some pruning of legalistic verbage, was to construct a line from Columbia, Tenn., to Florence, Ala., a distance of 79 miles. The proposed line traversed finely timbered country and it was hoped that the iron ore deposits located in Lawrence County, through which 38 miles of the road passed, would prove to be important revenue producers.

The L. & N. soon thereafter acquired a majority of the capital stock in this company and advanced the cost of construction, which by July 1, 1883, had reached a point about 20 miles south of Columbia. The N. & F. rebuilt the line between Columbia and Mt. Pleasant (11 miles) formerly the property of the Nashville and Decatur, and by February, 1884, its line had reached St. Joseph, Tenn., 56 miles from home base. Here it rested for several years and on January 19, 1887, the Tennessee and Alabama Railroad Company (no relation to the predecessor line of the Nashville and Decatur) was chartered in Alabama for the purpose of building a railroad from Sheffield, Ala., across the Tennessee River from Florence, to a point of connection with the N. & F. at the state line (Tennessee-Alabama).

The T. & A. Railroad, however, never turned a spade or wheel and it was consolidated with the N. & F. on May 16, 1887, to form the Nashville, Florence and Sheffield Railway Company, which completed the line from St. Joseph to Florence, 24 miles, on July 1, 1888. Access to Sheffield, across the Tennessee River, was gained through the use of the bridge and other facilities of the Memphis and Charleston Railroad Company, which became part of the Southern Railway System. The West Point Branch (now abandoned) was completed the same year. As owner of the majority of the capital stock of the Nashville, Florence and Sheffield Railway, the L. & N. operated this road for its owners from July 1, 1887, to May 31, 1900, when it purchased the property outright.

The Sheffield & Tuscumbia Railway Company, 2½ miles long, which had originally been incorporated on November 23, 1886, as the Sheffield & Tuscumbia Street Railway Company, was completed and placed in operation on September 10, 1895, by the Nashville, Florence and Sheffield Railway Company.

The tri-city area of Sheffield, Florence and Tuscumbia in Northwestern Alabama was at this time enjoying a boom, which threatened Birmingham's supremacy as a center for the manufacture of iron; a boom which to a large extent owed much to the completion of the railroad. Another potent factor in its development was Colonel Enoch Ensley, who had trekked northward, following certain disappointments in the Birmingham district. Under his energetic guidance and that of his associates a number of blast furnaces were built at Sheffield.

The building of the blast furnaces attracted other industries and a number of factories manufacturing pipe, stoves, etc., sprang up. The formation of Lady Ensley Coal, Iron and Railroad Company in 1891, predecessor of what later became the Sheffield Iron and Steel Company, added impetus to the development of the Sheffield-Florence-Tuscumbia District.

CHAPTER XII

Changing the Rail Gauge

AN EVENT of some importance in the history of the L. & N. occurred on July 13, 1885. On that date, the Henderson Bridge which spanned the Ohio River at Henderson, Ky., was completed and opened for traffic. The orators who graced this dedication with their presence and the contemporary press which reported the event were equally enthusiastic. This enthusiasm, as a matter of fact, was founded on a good solid base of truth for the opening of the bridge forged another link to connect North and South and meant that thereafter the handling of freight and passengers through the Evansville gateway would be greatly expedited. Passengers, for instance, could now be carried between St. Louis and Nashville in 12 hours' time and between Chicago and Nashville in 16 hours, while freight moving between the same points could now run on 22-hour and 34-hour schedules respectively; an improvement in each case of several hours' time.

Previously, it had been necessary to transfer both freight and passengers by boat between Evansville and Henderson, a trip of some 12 miles, and winters being what they were in those days, ice frequently cancelled the service altogether.

Many difficulties were encountered in the construction of the bridge and a number of humorous or unusual incidents occurred. For instance, when one of the caissons was lowered into the muck of the Ohio River bed it landed astride a pair of railroad car wheels. Just how these wheels and their connecting axle arrived at their watery resting place is a matter for conjecture, but at any rate they provided a serious obstacle to the laying of the bridge's foundation and it was necessary to cut the axle in two with cold chisels. The inside half of the axle with its wheel was then sent up through the air lock to the outside world, while its companion piece on the outside of the caisson was unceremoniously shoved out of the way with crow-bars.

The water was kept out of these caissons, of course, by compressed air, and it frequently happened that when the caissons were lowered they would strike shale. This latter had to be removed by blasting until bed rock was reached. This blasting would force considerable air out of the caisson and the river water would rush in to take its place, often rising waist-high before the air pressure could be raised. The pressure crews, as the "sand hogs" of those days were called, had their little jokes to relieve the monotony (!) of the daily grind and a favorite one took the form of omitting to tell new laborers of the crew about the blasting and its attendant effects. These latter seeing the water beginning to flow into the caisson would invariably believe an accident had happened and that they were doomed.

The members of these pressure crews were mostly Negroes and their working conditions being what they were, they early formed the habit of working in the nude, resuming their garments in a shanty-boat anchored nearby. The story is told that a young lady of Henderson, insistent in her desire to witness such a bit of color as a pressure crew coming off duty, but unaware of the sartorial lack of the laborers, finally had her wish gratified. She was taken to a partially-constructed pier near a point where the men emerged, but unfortunately she saw much more "color" than she had bargained for. The Negroes, as was their wont, all trooped forth in their birthday clothes, and one of them, upon perceiving the young lady, was so panic-stricken that he dived back into the river whose bed he had just left.

Scene in 1884, during the erection of the piers for the original Henderson Bridge across the Ohio River, an important connecting link between the North and South.

The new structure was a thing of beauty and was entirely adequate for the demands of the traffic of the day. It was single-tracked and was designed to carry the weight of two 118,000-pound engines each followed by 60,000-pound tenders, with a maximum capacity of 2,500 pounds of uniform load per foot of bridge. Its total cost was around $2,000,000 and once actual construction had commenced, it was completed in less than one year.

The bridge proper was about two-thirds of a mile long, extending from the north line of Main Street, in Henderson, to the low water mark on the Indiana side, from which latter point some nine and one-half miles of track were laid, a goodly portion of it on trestle work and fills, to a connection at Evansville with what had formerly been the St. Louis and Southeastern Railway. The chief engineer in charge of construction was F. W. Vaughan, and the channel span of the bridge, 525 feet in length, was reported to be the largest trestle span in the world at that time.

An enthusiastic crowd of 8,000 persons, "from all parts of the country," according to the Louisville Courier-Journal of July 14, 1885, witnessed the passage of the first train across the bridge on July 13 and several of those present, either as spectators, or as active participants in the drama unfolded high over the muddy waters of the Ohio, were to be on hand when the new Henderson Bridge was dedicated some 47 years later on December 31, 1932.

From time to time mention has been made in these dispatches of a constant source of inconvenience and inefficiency inherent in railroading during most of the past century; namely, the differences in gauge that existed between the various railroads of the country. Most of the railroads north of the Ohio River had gauges of four feet, eight and one-half inches, the so-called standard gauge, or of four feet, nine inches, while lines south of the Ohio, for the most part, had gauges of five feet. Hence, points of connection between roads of different gauges had common denominators in the form of track with three rails, steam hoists and a great number of sets of trucks, some of one gauge, some of another. Each point of connection was a "frontier," in effect, between two "foreign countries" and much time was lost in effecting compensation through a hoisting of equipment and the subsequent interchange of trucks. On the L. & N. alone, for instance, there were steam hoists, etc., at Louisville, East Louisville, Rowland, Mobile, New Orleans, Milan, Nortonville, Henderson and Evansville.

The traffic demands of a constantly growing country had, by 1880, created a situation that was rapidly becoming intolerable, even though it took but about four minutes to change the trucks of each car. The population was increasing by leaps and bounds, and the era of mass production was just being ushered in. Rapid communication and a more expedited flow of raw materials and finished products between the various sections of the country became a vital necessity. At this distance it is perhaps hard to understand why such a vexatious problem remained unsolved for so long. There were two chief reasons for this. First, the magnitude of the task itself (involved in any standardization of gauge) and, second, the inability of the roads to agree as to what was the most desirable gauge to adopt, with each line being understandably prejudiced in favor of its status quo.

However, it was eventually decided in 1885 that roads south of the

A view made during the erection of the channel span of the original Henderson bridge.

The original Henderson bridge which carried L. & N. trains across the Ohio for 47 years.

Ohio River should change their various gauges, mostly five feet, to the standard gauge of four feet, eight and one-half inches, or to four feet, nine inches. It was possible for the Southern roads to have this choice, because a one-half inch difference in gauge, from an operating standpoint, was negligible. Rolling stock that could roll along over track with a gauge of four feet, nine inches, could do the same on track with a gauge of four feet, eight and one-half inches, or vice versa.

It is generally supposed that when the L. & N. changed its entire gauge on May 30, 1886, that the change was made from five feet to the present day standard of four feet, eight and one-half inches. This is slightly erroneous, or to the extent of one-half inch. At that time, the change was made to four feet, nine inches and it was not until some ten years later that a gradual change was made to four feet, eight and one-half inches.

It was early realized that the change of gauge would necessitate the expenditure of large sums of money and that this expense would be greatly increased unless the change took place with hair-line accuracy and precision. Such expense was roughly divided into two parts; first, the cost involved in the actual change (extra help, parts, tools, etc.) and, second, in the purchase of equipment to replace that which for one reason or another could not be adjusted to conform with the revised track. Illustrative of the extent of this latter expense is the fact that because of this narrowing of the track, it was necessary to add 40 additional locomotives to the road's roster of motive power, involving an outlay of about $340,000, not all of it, it must be admitted, properly chargeable to change of gauge.

The decision to change to four feet, nine inches, rather than to four feet, eight and one-half inches, was reached only after a careful weighing of all the pros and cons by a committee of six especially appointed for that purpose by the Executive Committee of the Southern Railway and Steamship Association. Reuben Wells, the L. & N.'s general manager at that time, was a member of this committee and was in charge of all of the details incident to the change of gauge upon the L. & N.

Insofar as the L. & N. itself was concerned, two of its divisions (the St. Louis and the Short Line) already had a gauge of four feet, nine inches, and a number of connecting lines, notably the Pennsylvania Railroad and the Missouri Pacific, also had this width. Moreover, certain of the L. & N.'s equipment could stand the stress and strain involved in having its underpinning "dislocated" three inches, but an additional half inch would prove difficult. The preference of the L. & N., one of the leading, if not the leading road in the South, naturally had great weight. There were, in all, some 13,000 miles of trackage in the Southland involved in the change and of this the L. & N. owned and operated well over 2,000 miles.

The intense and elaborate preparations that were carried on in the winter of 1885 and in the spring of 1886 culminated in the actual change of gauge on May 30, 1886, which fell on Sunday; the day of rest, for obvious reasons, being an ideal one for the consummation of a project of such magnitude. Some of the L. & N.'s less important branches, however, had had their gauge changed just previous to that date on Friday, May 28, and Saturday, May 29.

Two branches of the service were chiefly involved in the change; the mechanical and the maintenance of way departments. Although the decision to change the gauge did not occur until March 5, 1885, for several years before all new equipment purchased, or manufactured by the Company's own shops, had been built to specifications which would permit its use upon a track of narrower gauge.

Railroad equipment in those days was not as complex as it is today and it was, therefore, fairly simple to press in the freight car or coach wheels upon their axles and to prepare a number of sets of trucks in advance which conformed to the gauge of four feet, nine inches. The chief problem of the mechanical department was the driving wheels of the locomotives.

Out upon the track itself (about one week before) spikes had already been driven into position to receive the west rail when it should be moved in, the old spikes on the inside had been removed from alternate pairs of cross-ties and the shoulders that the west rail had worn in the ties had been adzed off to facilitate the rail's journey east.

Tie plates were not generally used in those days, and the change was thus comparatively simple. The changing of switches presented a more difficult problem, of course.

The early morning of May 30, 1886, saw the battle lines tightly drawn and train schedules temporarily suspended. On the one side were some 2,000 miles of track, the west rail of which had to be moved east three inches (in some tunnels and at other points along the right-of-way with close clearances, it was necessary to move each rail in one and one-half inches), and nearly 300 locomotives, as well as about 10,000 other pieces of freight and passenger equipment. On the other side was a small army of about 8,000 men, composed of the Company's mechanical and maintenance of way forces, their ranks having been swelled for this one day by additional recruits. They were adequately supplied with ammunition and weapons in the form of claw bars, spike mauls, track gauges, spikes, jacks, wheel presses and the like.

The men were out to make a record and keen rivalry existed between the various sections and shops. Many of the section foremen had promised their men a special treat in the form of a barbecue, or some other event centering around food and drink, if they made a good showing, and a generous cash prize was to be given to the section foreman of each division who changed his section to the new gauge in the shortest time.

Once commenced, the change of gauge took place in a manner that exceeded the management's fondest expectations and that can only be described a spectacular. With the exception of a certain amount of passing track and siding, the entire trackage was changed to four feet, nine inches, by nightfall and a goodly number of the section crews had finished their part of the chore by noon, with subsequent commemorative antics. Each section was given a quota of four men to each mile of track (five where there were numerous curves, bridges or trestles) and the force assigned to each section was divided into two parts and worked both ways from the middle, the plan being for these crews to move rail until they met forces from the neighboring section. This was not always done. It frequently happened that when the limits of the section were reached, there was a wild hurrah and a concerted rush for the nearest water-cooler, with some pointed remarks about those lazy and far from top-heavy gentlemen on the next section. The change of gauge proved to be one of the biggest outdoor attractions of the year and throngs of the curious flocked to track-side to witness the progress of the work and loyally give it their undivided attention. Fortunately, the occasion was blessed with fine weather, with the single exception of a heavy rain in the vicinity of Memphis.

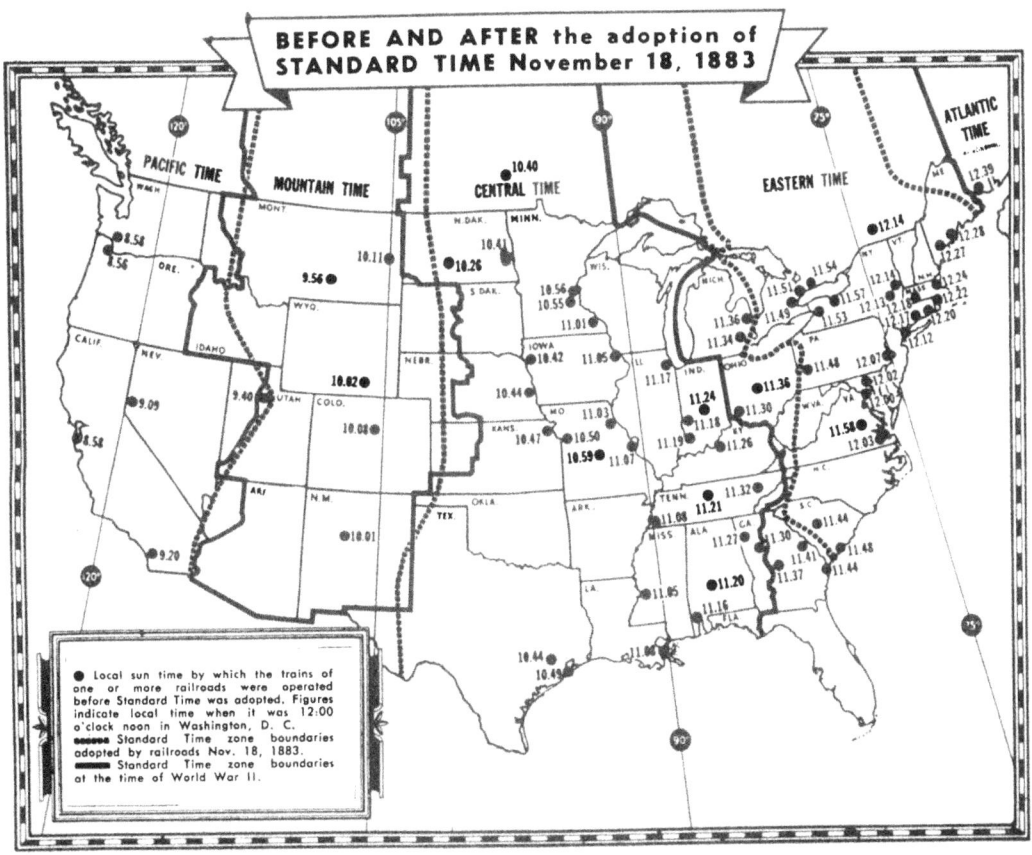

By far the greater part of the rolling stock was also ready for use on the new gauge track at the close of the day and by 6:00 p.m., after the track had been thoroughly tested, trains were running over the lines of the L. & N. about as usual.

Indicative of the speed with which the work took place is the record achieved by one section foreman and his gang; 11 miles of track changed to the new gauge in four and one-half hours. One shop changed 19 locomotives, 18 passenger coaches, 11 cabooses, 1,710 revenue freight cars and a number of pieces of non-revenue (work, etc.) equipment between sun-up and sun-down on May 30.

For the next week or two maintenance of way and mechanical forces were kept busy, disposing of various odds and ends, incident to the change of gauge, but this, for the most part, was spare time work and was not pressing. The change of gauge was an accomplished fact and in the short space of 12 hours, more or less, order had been brought forth from chaos of long standing; henceforth, with some slight negligible variation, America's railroads would speak the same language, for the events which had taken place upon the L. & N. on May 30, 1886, had been, or were shortly afterwards, duplicated elsewhere in the Southland. Some of the Southern roads changed their gauge a short while previous to May 30. Some waited until early June, and a few did not change upon that Sunday because of conscientious scruples in connection with the day of rest.

A silent but industrious witness to all these "high jinks" was the Company's auditing department and when the gauge had been completely changed, they dexterously produced their figures as to the actual cost of the incident, exclusive of that of new equipment, procured as a consequence thereof. These revealed that the L. & N.s bank-roll had been nicked to the tune of $195,055.69, the damage being allocated as follows: track – $91,977.51; locomotives – $53,480.98; cars – $49,577.20. This red ink entry was reduced somewhat by $29,605.22, which was realized from the sale of third rail, no longer needed at such points as Louisville, Henderson, Evansville, etc., and by an unspecified sum realized from the sale of steam hoists and other items which had now served their usefulness.

While the change or standardization of gauge in 1886 was a vital factor in the continuing successful evolution of American railroads, it had been antedated by 1883 by a standardization equally important, namely, the adoption of Standard Time by the nation's rail carriers on November 18 of that year. Prior to that date each community had its own time known as solar or sun time, which might be the same as that of the neighboring hamlet, only a few miles away, or which might vary therefrom by several minutes. It was based upon the passage of the sun across the meridian, that is, it was noon when the sun had reached the highest point of its heavenly arc. The sun time thus established was not exact for true sun time varied with the season of the year.

Obviously, a railroad such as the L. & N., with its 2,000-mile sprawl through the Southland, passed through dozens of localities having different local or sun times and this created a situation that was extremely vexatious. A railroad could not attempt to correlate these dissimilar times and was forced to operate its trains by one or more solar times which it had selected as standard. East-and-west railroads sometimes operated their trains by as many as a dozen different standard railroad times. The L. & N., from the first, operated all its trains on the solar time for Louisville, Ky., its headquarters, and Rule 27, of the rules and regulations of an L. & N. working time table issued on September 27, 1858, states: "Conductors and engineers must daily compare their watches with the clock in the Louisville depot, which is the Standard Time by which all watches of men on the Railroad must be regulated."

Matters thus remained unsatisfactory for a number of years with missed trains and connections being a frequent and irritating occurrence. Finally, the railroad heads took cognizance of the increasing chaos in the realm of Father Time and their efforts and investigation eventually resulted in the General Time Convention of October 11, 1883, which was held at Chicago. At this meeting America's railroads definitely adopted a Standard Time, which is substantially the same as it is today. The plan as there adopted provided for the establishment of five time zones in the United States and Canada, these being known as Intercolonial (now Atlantic) time for the eastern provinces of Canada, and Eastern, Central, Mountain and Pacific times for the remainder of the continent. The last four mentioned, which involved time observance in this country, were based upon mean sun time on the 75th, 90th, 105th and 120th meridians west of Greenwich. The time of each zone differed from that of its neighboring zone by exactly one hour.

Instructions were subsequently issued to all railroads directing them to have all their clocks and watches set to the new Standard Time at exactly 12 o'clock noon, November 18, 1883. The move involved the abandonment of some 70 or more official railroad times and hundred of local times. The L. & N.'s preparations for the change were placed in the hands of its general superintendent, D. W. C. Rowland. (The new Central Standard Time which was to be the prevailing time in most L. & N.-served territory, was 18 minutes slower than Louisville solar time.) Shortly prior to November 18, 1883, Superintendent Rowland issued a circular to all trainmen and other operating department employes and we quote herewith from it: "Should any train or engine be caught between telegraph stations at 10:00 a.m. on Sunday, November 18, they will stop at precisely 10:00 o'clock wherever they may be and stand still and securely protect their trains or engines in the rear and front until 10:18 a.m., and then turn their watches back to precisely 10:00 o'clock, new standard time, and then proceed on card rights or on any special orders they may have in their possession for the movement of their trains to the first telegraph station where they will stop and compare watches with the clock and be sure they have the correct new standard time before leaving. . ."

The switch in time was made without a hitch on the L. & N. and almost without exception all of the communities along its lines adopted the new time. This new Standard Time did not have the official sanction of the Federal Government for many years, even though it, in common with everybody else, adopted it. The adoption of Standard Time led subsequently to such kindred innovations as standardized inspection and maintenance of time-pieces and the L. & N. adopted this service in 1893.

CHAPTER XIII

Growth in Mining Areas

AN IMPORTANT nucleus for the L. & N's further growth had been created in July 1884, following the completion of the Birmingham Mineral Railroad. The latter (owned and operated by the L. & N.) had a modest beginning and, as its name would imply, was projected to serve the iron and coal industries of the Birmingham District. It was originally only 11 miles long and consisted of two branches, the North and South. However, the Company had ambitious plans for this seedling and it was the intention to encircle Red Mountain, thereby tapping the rich mineral deposits and serving the many industries which had sprung up mushroom-like in the vicinity. The original trackage extended from a junction with the S. & N. A. at Magella, Ala., (about three miles south of Birmingham) for a distance of about seven and one-half miles along the northern base of Red Mountain to what later became the town of Bessemer, so named with prophetic insight by H. F. DeBardeleben, its founder. The South Branch led off from the S. & N. A. about four miles south of Birmingham at Graces, Ala., and skirted the southern base of Red Mountain for a distance of about three and one-half miles to Redding, Ala. As mentioned, these two small lines (later to be linked together by additional construction) served as bases for the L. & N.'s many and extended beneficial forays into the Birmingham District.

By the year 1886, the city of Birmingham, a lusty adolescent of 15 years, was experiencing phenomenal growth. Nearby towns, too, like Bessemer (1887) sprang up overnight and for a brief space seemed to threaten the very supremacy of Birmingham itself, but in the end they but contributed to the greater glory of the Magic City. Speculation was rife and one would have to go to the Florida boom of the 1920s for adequate comparison. But whereas the Florida boom was largely the result of real estate speculation alone, Birmingham's 1886-1887 crashing crescendo was a hectic mixture of the selling of real estate, the mining of coal and the making of iron, with other less important items flavoring the heady brew of growth and expansion.

The Magic City's glittering future, as well as the demands of the traffic, seemed to justify the L. & N. in its construction of a new depot there and this was completed in 1887, at a total cost of $134,163.95, this sum representing expenditures not only for the station itself, but for passenger tracks, a trainshed, etc.

The Railroad's faith in the future of Birmingham and the Birmingham District was thus based not alone on wishful thinking. Its Birmingham Mineral Railroad, which received its initial impetus from Milton H. Smith, was rapidly bringing it in touch with many flourishing iron and coal operations and the Annual Report for the fiscal year ending with June 30, 1887, states that at that time there were in existence upon the lines of the L. & N. and those of its sister road, the N. C. & St. L., a total of 32 furnaces producing huge quantities of pig iron, 11 of these furnaces, utilizing charcoal and 21 of them using coke. In the Birmingham District alone there were 33 coal and iron companies. There were also under construction at the time 28 additional furnaces, only six of which were of the charcoal variety. It was estimated that the coke furnaces then operating could each produce 115 tons of pig iron a day, while the charcoal ones had a rated daily capacity of 50 tons each. As a matter of possible interest, the recipe for one ton of pig iron at that time was two tons of iron ore, one and one-half tons of coke, and one-half ton of limestone.

Prominent among the industries at that time (1887) in the stronghold of iron and coal were the Tennessee Coal Iron and Railroad Company, which was just completing four large furnaces at Ensley known as the "Big Four," the Pratt Coal and Iron Company (soon to be absorbed by T. C. I. & R. R. Co.), the Sloss Furnace Company, the DeBardeleben Coal and Iron Company (capitalized at $13,000,000), the Cahaba Coal Mining Company, the Pioneer Mining and Manufacturing Company (later to become a part of Republic Iron and Steel), the Woodward Iron Company and the Eureka Furnace Company, each representing an investment of many hundreds of thousands or, in some cases, millions of dollars.

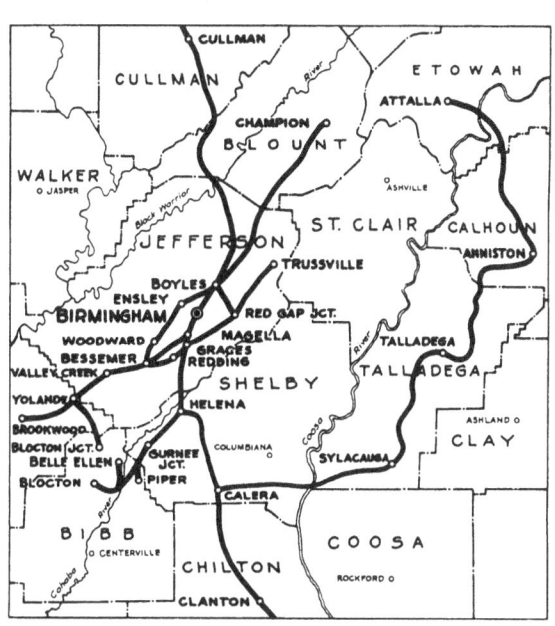

The L. & N. lines in the land of coal and iron in 1890.

These properties were owned or operated by men who have since become almost legendary figures in the world of coal and iron: Daniel Pratt, Truman H. Aldrich, Henry F. DeBardeleben, Enoch Ensley, James H. Sloss, William T. Underwood (the brother of that Senator, Oscar W. Underwood, for whom years later Alabama Democrats were so persistently to cast their 24 votes for Presidential nominee), John T. Milner, T. T. Hillman and many others.

While it is true that the manufacture of pig iron and the mining of coal monopolized the picture, there were a number of other flourishing industries in the Birmingham District and their number was constantly being increased. For the most part these industries manufactured products such as pipe, car wheels, axles, stoves, nails and hardware of all sorts and descriptions for whose making large quantities of pig iron were required. Numerous rolling mills were also established to serve as middlemen between the furnaces and the factories.

In this connection it is interesting to note that steel was first produced in Alabama as early as 1888. On March 8, of that year, the Henderson Steel and Manufacturing Company produced a ton of that metal, utilizing ordinary Alabama iron ores. This steel was subsequently successfully used in the manufacture of razors, carving knives, etc., but the fruits of this achievement were highly deciduous. In all, the Henderson Company produced about 1,800 tons of fine steel, but the cost of operation was entirely out of proportion to the price that could be obtained for the product in the open market and in 1890 the company's furnace was turned over to a committee from the Birmingham Chamber of Commerce as a possible proving ground for the introduction of steel-making into the Birmingham District. One of this committee was Pulaski Leeds, the L. & N.'s superintendent of machinery. This committee reported favorably upon the furnace and its process, but outside capital strangely enough was somewhat coy and the plant was subsequently abandoned. It was years later, in 1897, to be exact, before steel was manufactured again in the Birmingham District. But, of that, more later.

Other railroads, too, were being attracted to Birmingham, each anxious to serve as Mercury to Vulcan. Lines which later became parts of the Southern, the Central of Georgia and the Frisco were all completed to Birmingham during the 'eighties. Thus, the position of the South and North Alabama Railroad, long the dominant one of the district, was being challenged by these new arrivals.

A less alert leadership might have allowed this early-gained and hard-won advantage to be forfeited through sheer inertia or a too-fond recollection of past glories. But that was not the policy of the L. & N. Its rapid-fire construction of innumerable branch lines and industrial spurs more than kept it in the running. Nourished by L. & N. capital, the Birmingham Mineral Railroad, that rapidly-growing satellite of the S. & N. A., shot out tendrils of steel and wood in every direction, allowing the Iron Horse access to remote mountain fastnesses where large coal mining operations were being prosecuted or where huge quantities of red and brown hematite ore were being removed from the bosom of Mother Earth.

This account, endeavoring as it does to preserve a judicious balance of power between bare statistics and the more colorful aspects of our Road's building, will not attempt to list in iron-clad detail the gradual evolution of the Birmingham Mineral Railroad. This has already been done by very competent authorities. Then, too, some of these branches, spurs, etc., once projected to serve then vital needs, have long since been abandoned and nowadays no trace of them remains. Others have been sold to other railroads. In a broad way, however, we shall endeavor to sketch the growth of the Birmingham Mineral Railroad as it occurred year by year in that territory which largely lies to the southwest of Birmingham.

Mention has been made heretofore of that "basic" trackage which skirted the south and north bases of Red Mountain, just south of Birmingham. These two branches were soon connected, forming a loop of some $18\frac{1}{2}$ miles around Red Mountain. (A portion of this trackage, from Redding to

An L. & N. flat car proudly carried this 11-ton lump of Alabama coal to the World's Industrial and Cotton Centennial Exposition at New Orleans in 1884. It was shipped by the Pratt Coal and Iron Co., near Birmingham. Reading from the left, the men are: Col. Enoch Ensley, L. W. Johns, Joshua Collins and William Gude.

Bessemer, was later abandoned.) On January 1, 1888, the North Branch which extended to Bessemer was further extended to Blocton Junction, some 27 miles distant, by way of Valley Creek and Yolande, this being known as the Blue Creek Extension. In addition to the trackage previously mentioned, construction was completed of a line from Bessemer to Boyles, (Huntsville Branch No. 1) nearly 16 miles long and extending through the thriving communities of Woodward and Ensley. A line (east of the S. & N. A.) from Boyles to Red Gap, a distance of about 6½ miles, was also built.

Then, in 1889, or thereabouts, some 60 additional miles were added to the Birmingham Mineral's trackage, making in all a total of 132.60 miles. Included in such construction was a line from Boyles to Champion, a distance of 36 miles, and the further extension of the road from Red Gap to Trussville, some 11 miles away. During the fiscal year ending with June 30, 1890, some 24 additional miles were constructed, resulting in the Birmingham Mineral then having a total trackage of 156.22 miles to its credit.

Various spur lines were constructed in conjunction with these branches and the Birmingham Mineral and the South and North Alabama between them rendered a real service to the industries of the District. Then in 1890, they were joined by a potent ally, the Alabama Mineral Railroad Company, which was incorporated on July 28, 1890, with the L. & N. owning a majority of the capital stock. This venture was the result of the consolidation of the Anniston and Atlantic Railroad (incorporated on May 24, 1883) which boasted of some 53 miles of narrow gauge track, extending from Anniston to Sylacauga and the Anniston and Cincinnati Railroad (incorporated on January 31, 1887) which ran between Anniston and Attalla, a distance of 35 miles. Both of these roads were built by A. L. Tyler and Samuel Noble, the founders of Anniston, that city (Annie's Town) being so named in honor of Mr. Tyler's wife.

Each of these roads was acquired by the L. & N. shortly after completion, or on July 19, 1889, and it immediately set about to correlate their activities with the rest of the System. The formation of the Alabama Mineral Railroad was the first step towards this end. The Anniston and Atlantic's narrow gauge line was changed to four feet, nine inches, the 30-pound rail was replaced with 58-pound rail and the line was changed at a number of points to reduce grades, eliminate curves, etc. New construction work was also commenced in March 1890, the line eventually being extended from Sylacauga to a connection with the South and North Alabama at Calera, 34 miles south of Birmingham. This linking was completed on January 1, 1891, with the result that the Alabama Mineral Railroad now consisted of 119 miles of main line track and 13.23 miles of spurs and branches, extending from Calera through Sylacauga, Talladega and Anniston to Attalla. These lines formed, when viewed on the map, a rough-hewn masculine profile which, with some pardonable imaginative license, suggests the features of the "Father of our Country."

This left a gap of some 26 miles between Attalla and Champion, which at that time was the northern outpost of the Birmingham Mineral's Huntsville Branch No. 2. The L. & N., for obvious reasons, was extremely anxious to complete its "great circle," embracing St. Clair county in totality and large portions of Shelby, Talladega, Jefferson and Calhoun counties. The Alabama Mineral Railroad served a territory which was rich in marble, limestone, brown hematite ore and other mineral deposits and to move these commodities to Birmingham or to the South and North Alabama from Attalla, Gadsden, Anniston and other points on the "forehead" of the profile was a roundabout procedure. There were other railroads providing short cuts to Birmingham from various points on the Alabama Mineral; nevertheless it was May 28, 1905 before the missing link of the Alabama Mineral was completed between Attalla and Champion, providing a more direct route to Birmingham via the L. & N.'s Alabama Mineral.

Much iron ore and coal also moved over the Alabama Mineral Railroad from Birmingham and points nearby to the numerous iron furnaces in operation at Attalla, Gadsden, Anniston, Talladega and Shelby. It was also planned that the cars moving onto the Alabama Mineral after being unloaded, could be re-loaded with the brown hematite ores heretofore mentioned for shipping to the Birmingham District for subsequent admixture with the red hematite ores, it having been found that

Left: Barren River Bridge, Bowling Green, Ky. Right: Bowling Green Shops. Taken in 1879.

a better grade of iron, as well as a larger yield, was thereby produced.

The L. & N.'s Annual Report for the year ending June 30, 1889, carries a very interesting comparison of the tonnage provided by the cotton crop for **the country as a whole** and the tonnage that iron and coal provided **the L. & N. Railroad alone,** in the supplying of the numerous furnaces along its lines, chiefly in the Birmingham District, with the necessary raw materials, i. e., coal, coke, iron ore and limestone. Using the last 15 years as a standard, it was estimated that the average annual weight of the total cotton crop during this period, was 1,434,126 tons. On the other hand, the raw materials before mentioned and handled over the lines of the L. & N. alone totaled 1,438,292 tons for the year 1888.

The increasing traffic handled by the Louisville & Nashville Railroad necessitated the purchase, or the manufacture in its own shops, of large quantities of rolling stock of every description. The Annual Report just mentioned reveals that at that time (June 30, 1889) the Company owned and operated 439 locomotives, 338 passenger coaches and 14,274 freight cars, a sizable increase in each case over the ownership of the year previous. For some time past the L. & N. had been replacing its light engines with heavier ones of the Consolidation type, these weighing from 115,000 to 135,000 pounds and being used exclusively in heavy freight service.

The capacity of its freight cars had also been increased from 15 tons to 20 and 30 tons; the rail in the track was gradually being replaced with heavy (for that day) 68-pound steel rail, and bridges and trestles were being strengthened in order that they might safely support the weight of the heavier rolling stock. Illustrative of the growing demands made upon the equipment is the fact that during the fiscal year ending with June 30, 1889, the L. & N. carried 4,334,175 passengers and hauled 14,443,983 tons of freight, this last being an increase of 2,271,973 tons over the year previous. The average tonnage of each freight train was 159.72 and the average number of tons carried in each car was 12.09.

This increasing traffic not only necessitated the purchase of new equipment, it also played hob with existing rolling stock and there was a pressing demand for more adequate shop facilities. To expedite this work of construction, replacement and repair, the L. & N. started building new shops at Decatur, Ala., in the year 1887. Fifty-five acres of land were purchased as a site and once started the work progressed rapidly. This paralleled similar activity at Howell, Ind., near Evansville, where shops were being built to serve the Henderson and St. Louis divisions.

Both of these shops were placed in active operation in the early part of 1890, there having been expended upon the new shops at Decatur, including the cost of machinery, a total of $346,178.80, as of June 30, 1890. The sum of $212,931.54 had similarly been spent at Howell. A goodly portion of the sums mentioned had been spent for new machinery.

The completion of the shops at Decatur and Howell gave the L. & N. four major shops, the other two being located at Mobile and Louisville. There were somewhat less adequate facilities at Bowling Green, Rowland and a number of other points. The L. & N.'s shops at Louisville at that time were located at 10th and Kentucky streets, but a clue as to future developments in the Kentucky metropolis might have been gained from the Company's purchase of 44 additional acres of land at South Louisville, Ky., in the year 1890. At that time it was the intention merely to construct yards there to relieve the congestion at East Louisville and at 10th and Market Streets, although it was candidly admitted that the shop facilities at 10th and Kentucky were far from adequate for the fast-growing railroad.

CHAPTER XIV

Entering the Cumberlands

THE Company had long eyed Cumberland Gap, Tenn., Big Stone Gap, Va., and Norton, Va., as possible points of connection with other railroads and accordingly on April 29, 1886, a start was made toward those goals from Corbin, Ky., the necessary authority having been granted upon that date by the board of directors. The Cumberland Valley Branch, as it was to be known, was located (not built) as far east as Pineville, Ky., 31 miles away at that time. The directors had visions of the creation of another "Birmingham District" and with good cause for the Annual Report for the fiscal year ending June 30, 1887 states: " . . . On good authority we learn that good coking coals exist in very large quantities in Bell and Harlan counties, and that they extend to the Cumberland range of mountains which divide the states of Kentucky and Virginia. It is also stated that large deposits of iron ore are in Poor and Powell's Valleys in Virginia, immediately south of the Kentucky state line and also that an abundance of limestone and good water is found in that region and it is believed that large iron and other manufacturing interests will be developed as soon as transportation facilities are supplied."

The line was completed to Pineville on April 1, 1888, and a contract was let on July 3, of the same year, for the completion of the 15½ miles south from Pineville to Cumberland Gap. It was eventually decided to reach Big Stone Gap and Norton via that passageway and by laying the steel along the south base of Cumberland Moutain, in Poor and Powell's valleys. In this connection it is interesting to note that a report made upon the mineral resources of Southeastern Kentucky and Southwestern Virginia by Andrew S. McCreath and E. V. D'Invilliers, mineralogists of Philadelphia, Penn., as a result of investigations undertaken in 1887 at the instigation of President Milton H. Smith, was rather pronouncedly of the opinion that the better route of the two proposed to Big Stone Gap was to be found in a general north eastwardly direction from Pineville. This route followed the Cumberland River and its Clover Fork and then dipped southward through Black Mountain to the point mentioned.

Messrs. McCreath and D'Invilliers were not particularly concerned with the comparative merits of the two routes from an engineering standpoint, but based their conclusions largely upon the superiority of the mineral deposits in the Cumberland River district. The following is quoted from their report: " . . . The Cumberland River district necessarily presents by far the largest area of coal measures and numerous opportunities for development through the many branch streams watering the region. The Cumberland River itself, in its low grades, presents an exceptionally favorable route for the location of a railroad line designed to meet the

Blast furnaces for the making of pig iron erected by the Watts Steel and Iron Syndicate, of Middlesborough, England, at Middlesborough, Ky., in 1890. They were capable of producing about 400 tons of pig iron per day.

requirements of cheap and readily moved freight and this feature it possesses in common with its principal tributaries of Clover Fork, Martin's Fork and Poor Fork."

The report concluded on this note: "From a review of all the facts collected by us in the several districts, we are of the opinion that the Cumberland River route presents the most advantages for the location of a railroad line designed to best develop the resources of the district between Pineville and Big Stone Gap."

However, the establishment of Middlesborough as an **entre-pot** for a newly developed mineral kingdom and the subsequent rapid growth of that city and surrounding territory, made it imperative that the railroad pass through that section. As a matter of fact, the extension of the road from Pineville to Cumberland Gap was almost completed before it was finally decided to locate the road south of Cumberland Moutain. This existing trackage undoubtedly greatly influenced such a choice for very little of it could have been utilized had the Cumberland River route been chosen.

Perhaps the chief factor, however, in the decision to so build was a report made by R. E. O'Brien, a civil engineer who was an expert on such matters and who had been especially hired to investigate the two routes and weigh their merits pro and con. Mr. O'Brien strongly recommended the Poor Valley route, as it was called, stressing as points in its favor its lower cost, its closer proximity to the iron ore deposits of the region, as well as the fact that it was closer by some 32 miles to such large cities as Knoxville and Atlanta than the Cumberland River route and hence could expect greater through traffic. Mr. O'Brien's recommendations were subsequently adopted by the board of directors at a meeting on March 20, 1889, following a favorable report upon the same by a committee of three, which had been previously appointed to weigh the facts in the case.

Mr. O'Brien pointed out that the money saved by adopting the Poor Valley route (about $1,000,000, he estimated) could be later utilized in building a branch line up the Cumberland River. However, the cost of building the line between Cumberland Gap and Norton was much greater than estimated and it was a number of years before the L. & N. began that intensive penetration of Harlan County, which made Harlan coal a household word, and which so completely fulfilled the predictions of the mineralogists before mentioned.

At this distance, when almost every landscape is at least within whistle-shot of a railroad, it is hard to realize that the Iron Horse was not always welcomed with open arms and the strewing of rose petals. Mountain folks are proverbially clannish and they sometimes resented its invasion of their privacy. The L. & N. in locating, building and afterwards maintaining and operating its lines in Southeastern Kentucky, Northeastern Tennessee and Southwestern Virginia was hampered to a certain extent by this understandable hostility: understandable, that is, when environment and other factors are taken into consideration. Outsiders were generally suspect, especially so to a certain small percentage of the population which practiced the illegal distilling of "mountain dew." Quite a bit of the law was concentrated in the barrel of a rifle or a revolver and fingers were quick on the trigger in the days before the turn of the century. Such a hazardous overhead had a tendency, of course, to keep the Company's forces from doing their best work.

Illustrative of the remarks contained in the foregoing paragraph, we quote from the reminiscences of A. J. Lamb, former assistant superintendent, Birmingham Division, now deceased. Mr. Lamb and J. D. Haydon, later superintendent of the Eastern Kentucky Division, helped to locate the L. & N.'s lines between Corbin, Ky., and Norton, Va.

Said Mr. Lamb: "All the mountaineers seemed to be good shots with a rifle and one night a 'blarsted Englishman' rushed into the depot (at Middlesborough) and anxiously inquired when the next train would leave town as it was not a safe place to stay just because some fellow had shot out the light in his hand lantern.

"On another occasion a brakeman was throwing a switch when three shots rang out, one taking out the red glasses in the switch lamp, another the white glasses and the third the brakeman's hand lantern and all he got was one bullet through his arm."

The further completion of the road to Middlesborough, Ky., on or about September 1, 1889, lent impetus to a boom which the town was experiencing and it began to grow and expand rapidly.

At that time Middlesborough (this is still the official name of the town, but popular usage has shortened it to "Middlesboro") was but one year old, being the outgrowth of the efforts of the American Association, Limited, capitalized at $2,000,000. This Association was largely composed of English capitalists and industrialists, among whom were numbered Baring Brothers, of London, England, and the directors of the Watts Iron and Steel Company, of Middlesborough, England, after which city the Kentucky mountain town was named. The

Cumberland Ave., Middlesborough, 1891.

names of the latter's streets, such as Aylesbury, Ashbury, Bloomsbury, Salisbury, etc., also indicate its English origin.

Chief instrumentality in the decision of the English financiers to invest so heavily in the New World wilderness was Alexander A. Arthur, a young Scotch-Canadian then residing in Tennessee, who is known as the founder of Middlesborough. In 1886, Mr. Arthur explored and reported favorably upon the vast mineral wealth centering around Middlesborough and somewhat later he and a group of friends, known as the "Gap Associates," bought and secured options on thousands of acres of land in the valley of Yellow Creek. Out of their endeavors grew the American Association, Limited, aforesaid, the parent of what later became the American Association, Inc.

The Association supplemented the purchases of the "Associates" and eventually was the possessor of some 60,000 acres of land rich in coal and iron ore and located in Claiborne County, Tenn., Lee County, Va., and Bell County, Ky. Soon afterwards the Middlesborough Town Company was formed for the purpose of owning and selling lots in the proposed township in the valley of Yellow Creek. By May 1889, the city had begun to assume definite tangible shape and the Watts Steel and Iron Syndicate, the Middlesboro Water Works and many another venture were well along with their construction work. The **piece de resistance** of the Syndicate, before mentioned, in addition to many other irons which it had in the fire, was a 400-ton daily capacity blast furnace (iron) and a 700-ton daily capacity open hearth steel plant.

Men flocked by the hundreds to the new metropolis, for man-power was greatly needed, not only to build the forges of Vulcan, and associated ventures, but to operate them as well. Accommodations could not be provided fast enough for the newcomers, many of whom were Englishmen, sent out from home to gain a little experience in a raw new land, and, incidentally, to keep an eye on Papa'a investments. A tented city sprang up on the outskirts of the town to care for the overflow, but the ceaseless sound of saw and hammer made ringing declaration that its presence need only be regarded as a temporary evil.

The coming of the L. & N. in the fall of 1889, added impetus to a boom which until then had blazed fitfully but determinedly under the handicap of somewhat inadequate transportation facilities. The town's population increased from 50 in May 1889, to 6,200 in August 1890, and then eventually to well over 15,000 when the peak was finally reached. Numerous coal mines were opened up in the vicinity, factories sprang up intra-nocturnally in vacant lots, two blast furnaces were operating at full capacity and producing hundreds of tons of pig iron each round of the clock and these and many other operations added their tributary wealth to the golden stream which flowed through Middlesborough in the early 1890s. Oddly enough, however, the steel plant before mentioned, although completed, was never operated to any great extent.

Even a disastrous fire shortly after the incorporation of the city in 1890 checked its growth but slightly. Phoenix-like, it arose from its ashes and at this and immediately subsequent periods in its history, it presented an aspect closely akin to that of a Western frontier town. Hardy moun-

This locomotive and these men helped to build the Cumberland Valley Division. They are (left to right): Frank Kearns, William Duncan, Logan Davidson, Engineer Dave Burgess, George McCarthy, James Middleton and Conductor Joe Doody.

taineers with rifles at the ready rubbed incongruous elbows in the streets with civil engineers, metallurgists, geologists and with many an Englishman with an Oxford accent. Coal miners, farmers, gamblers and the usual boom-town "camp followers" added color to the scene.

Smaller towns came into being and were immediately attracted into the Middlesborough orbit. Soon, suburban trains plied back and forth between Middlesborough and such satelite towns as Cumberland Gap and Harrogate, Tenn. From time to time railroad surveyors and construction gangs adroitly wound additional trackage around the town and through the adjacent valleys, the better to serve this overflow and the coal mining operations. In all, it was a happy time and everyone had high hopes both for himself and the community.

The existing rooming houses proved to be inadequate to the demands made upon them and the story is told that the Middlesborough Hotel, one of the first in town, was filled to overflowing before it was completely finished; indeed while the walls were still without plaster and the windows without sashes and, of course, such inconsequential trifles as glass, curtains or shades.

Another hostelry which was built near Middlesborough at this time was the "Four Seasons Hotel," located at Harrogate, Tenn. A 700-room building, it was erected at a cost of $750,000 and nearly $2,000,000 was expended upon the project of which it was an integral part. This hotel had a gala house-warming in 1891 with a ball which was led by the late Ward McAllister, of '400" fame, and it is said that its silverware alone cost $35,000. Erected with the hotel were an elaborate casino and sanitarium and the latter structure was later used as the nucleus for Lincoln Memorial University. A number of prominent Eastern socialites attended the opening and the resort was for a few brief years, before rapidly falling into disuse, a mecca for the wealthy, who were entranced by the scenery

The "Four Seasons Hotel" at Harrogate, Tenn., built in 1891.

and the invigorating mountain air. The wealthy, as is their wont, provided elaborate playgrounds for themselves for the spending of their leisure time and Middlesborough had one of the first golf courses laid out in the United States.

To publicize the wonders of Middlesborough and adjacent vicinity, Mr. Arthur borrowed a large L. & N. coach and loaded it down with specimens of rock, coal, iron ores and the various timbers of the region. This coach, which he termed a "Traveling Exposition," made flying trips in the spring of 1890 to New York, Boston, Philadelphia and other large Eastern cities and did much to bring the new development in the Cumberlands to the attention of the outside world.

From this modest beginning evolved a super-publicity scheme in the fall of the same year, with the operation of a 22-car special train, including the Exposition Car, to most of the large cities of the East and Midwest. Lecturers and guides accompanied the Special and illustrated publicity was handed out with a lavish hand.

While it lasted it was a glorious party, but like so many parties, it had its sad aftermath; largely, however, through no fault of its own. The banking firm of Baring Brothers, of London, failed in 1892 and completely paralyzed English investments in Middlesborough. Then came the panic of 1893 and Middlesborough experienced a number of lean years. The pendulum swung the other way with a vengeance. The citizenry left in droves. Factories closed, residences and stores by the hundreds were left without tenants and only a few of the more hardy stayed on and tried to eke out a living from chaos. In those troubled times, the railroad loomed up as a lighthouse in the storm, its very presence bringing the hope of better days.

Those dark times eventually became but an unpleasant memory and Middlesborough leveled off as a city of 15,000 prior to World War I, not another Birmingham, as was hoped, it is true, but still in all, one of Kentucky's most thriving and progressive cities.

Chief obstacle to a more expedited prolongation of the line to Norton, Va., had been the tunneling at Cumberland Gap. This tunnel was built by the Powell's Valley Railroad and its successor, the Knoxville, Cumberland Gap and Louisville Railroad, and the L. & N. entered into contracts in 1888 with these for its joint use when completed. The question might well be asked why the railroad did not build through the "Gap," instead of beneath it and the answer comes pat enough that the ascent to the "saddle" was too steep for the railroad to negotiate. It is somewhat ironical that the railroad by necessity had to pass beneath this breach in nature's barricade, for since time immemorial the Gap had been used as a passageway; first by the Indian tribes and later by Boone and the other hardy pioneers who were the vanguard of the mighty migrations of the 18th and 19th centuries.

Because it is one of the few adequate gateways through the Cumberland Mountains, the Gap has always had great strategic importance. During the Civil War, it was first in the hands of the North and then of the South. It was eventually re-taken by the Union forces, and these, learning a lesson or two from the previous conflicts over its possession, fortified it in such a manner that its re-possession by the Confederates would have been an extremely formidable undertaking.

The tunnel which passed beneath this historic gateway and which was completed in the summer of 1889 was a real engineering feat, albeit a somewhat faulty one, and was possessed of several distinctive peculiarities. It burrowed beneath the states of Kentucky and Virginia, was some 3,741 feet long and two separate and distinct grades were encountered within this man-made cavern. The east portal of the tunnel was only a few hundred feet from the town of Cumberland Gap, Tenn., and trains entering it from that end encountered a grade which had a rise of .76 feet per 100 feet. The summit of this rise was

Middlesborough's "Big Fire" of 1890.

reached about 1,000 feet within the tunnel, at which point a new grade of 1.18 feet per 100 feet was met, descending toward Middlesborough. At the time there was undoubtedly some reason for such construction. At any rate, regardless of the direction in which a train was traveling, it had an uphill climb part of the way and the "peak" created by the different grades had a tendency to hinder ventilation, with the result that smoke from passing trains did not disappear as rapidly as would be desirable. The tunnel caved in on July 4, 1894, and again on July 4, 1896 and for a time after the ravages of the last debacle had been repaired engines did not use the tunnel as it was feared they might cause another cave-in. One engine would push freight cars in one portal of the tunnel and another would draw them out of the other portal, a slow process at best. Passengers were transported through the Gap by hack, wagon or horseback between the two rail-heads until the tunnel was deemed fit for re-use.

As stated, the Powell's Valley Railroad was later known as the Knoxville, Cumberland Gap and Louisville Railroad, one of the predecessor roads of the Southern Railway System. In 1889, the K. C. G. & L. decided to build a line of its own between Middlesborough and Cumberland Gap, Tenn., although it could have utilized the existing trackage of the L. & N. between those two points, this having been completed a short time before. However, at this time the two railroads were engaged in a bit of a squabble as to just who possessed the title to several hundred feet of track located at both the west and east portals of the tunnel and this may have been one of the reasons why the K. C. G. & L. decided to build its own line.

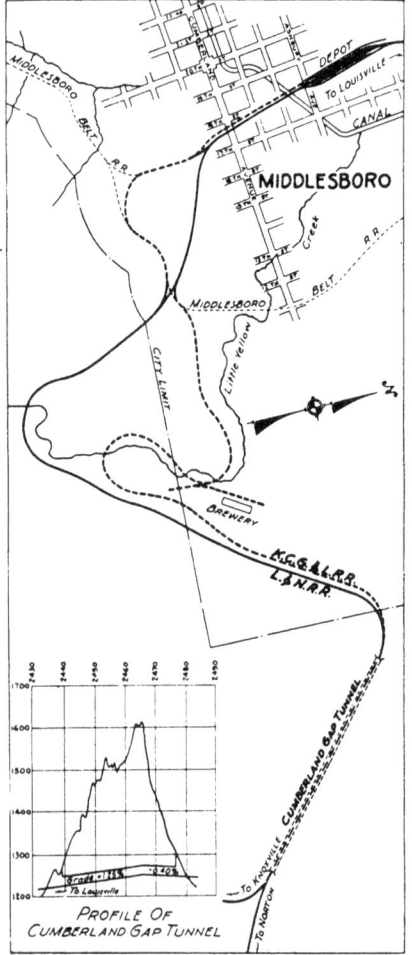

Other influential factors may have been the generosity of the American Association, Limited, in donating rights-of-way through Bell County, Ky., to both railroads, which lowered construction costs considerably, and the desirability of building on through to Louisville, as was originally intended and as the name of the road would imply. The dispute aforesaid was eventually settled amicably by an agreement dated June 30, 1890.

This trackage of the K. C. G. & L. Railway (re-organization in 1895 having changed the "Railroad" to "Railway") was rather circuitous and was subsequently abandoned for the most part when the L. & N. came into the possession of it and the tunnel in 1896, as a result of negotiations presently to be described.

On November 4, 1896, the L. & N. acquired the Middlesborough Railroad, which owned and operated about 21 miles of track encircling the city and serving most of its industries. (Twelve miles of

Map showing lines of the L. & N. Railroad and the Knoxville, Cumberland Gap and Louisville Railway, between Middlesborough and Cumberland Gap, at the time of the agreements dated November 4, 1896. Inset shows profile of Cumberland Gap Tunnel at the time it was built.

"Niggerhead" Rock, a scenic oddity encountered on one of the L. & N.'s lines branching off from the C. V. main at Pennington, Va.

this was later abandoned in 1897.) This railroad was the outgrowth of the Middlesborough Belt Railroad, incorporated in Kentucky on March 1, 1890, the transformation having taken place on August 22, 1895.

Principally, this trackage seemed to have been the vehicle by which the L. & N. could lease certain properties to the K. C. G. & L. These were its Middlesborough-Cumberland Gap trackage and the tunnel, the latter having – that same day – November 4, 1886 – come into the possession of the Middlesborough Railroad. Thus, at that time the L. & N. leased to the Knoxville, Cumberland Gap and Louisville Railway for a period of 50 years, with privilege of renewal for like periods forever, the joint use of its line from its connection with the K. C. G. & L. in Tennessee just east of the east portal of the tunnel to the station at Middlesborough, a distance of 4.342 miles, which, of course, included the ubiquitous tunnel. Similar provisions of the contract provided for the joint use of certain designated station buildings, yards and terminal facilities, and, as stated, most of the K. C. G. & L's line between Middlesborough and Cumberland Gap was abandoned.

Soon after its acquisition of the properties of the Middlesborough Railroad, the L. & N. lined the bi-state tunnel and made other improvements in connection therewith at a cost of approximately $125,000.

We have gotten a bit ahead of the chronological procession in telling the history of the trackage between Middlesborough and Cumberland Gap and have left the Railroad's Cumberland Valley Division dangling at the latter point. The steel was subsequently pushed on further to Big Stone Gap, Va., where it met the South Atlantic and Ohio Railroad, on April 15, 1891, following the completion of the tunnel on September 1, 1889. Exactly one month later, or on May 15, 1891, the railroad reached Norton, Va., its goal, where it connected with the Norfolk and Western Railway. The total cost of extending the line from Corbin to that point, a distance of 118 miles, had been $4,397,328.97. Incidentally Norton, Va., originally known as Prince's Flats, was named in honor of Eckstein Norton, who was president of the L. & N. from October 6, 1886, until March 9, 1891.

Exclusive of the net earnings of the Cumberland Valley Division derived from traffic handled upon its lines alone (which were largely offset by interest and taxes) it had a far greater value as a "feeder" to the rest of the System. The records show that the revenue derived from traffic interchanged with that division totaled approximately $2.5 million in the six-year period following the completion of construction.

CHAPTER XV

Expanding Services

FROM the evidence already spread upon the record, it can readily be seen that the events leading up to the creation of a landscape complete with railroad tracks, have followed thus far a certain definite pattern. First there was the virgin territory, the early settlers and their pioneer civilization. These settlers through their efforts wrestled order of a sort from chaos and life became more urbane. A reciprocal demand was thereby created for the goods and services of the outside world and of the community itself, which, in turn, led to the subsequent demand for a railroad. Frequently, as has been illustrated, this demand was expedited by the discovery of iron ore, of coal, of gold, or of some other inertia-disturbing element. When the need is great enough there will always be those to supply it and following this need, therefore, there came in rapid and more or less consecutive order, the incorporators of the railroad, the lawyers, the stockholders, the engineering crews and the track forces. And, finally, as a symbolic reward for all their varied but associated activities, the first train itself.

The history of the L. & N. and that of its predecessor lines, prior to 1900, is studded with repetitions of this familiar pattern, and while occasional re-enactments of this theme were to take place after the date mentioned, they were to become more and more infrequent. The great day of railroad building, at least insofar as the country east of the Mississippi River was concerned, was on the wane; henceforth, with some exception, additional mileage added to the L. & N.'s system would be via mileage acquired, rather than through trackage constructed. In brief, the trend was towards consolidation, rather than expansion of existing rail facilities.

In detailing the railroad's major activities in the decade ending with 1890, some loose, although not unimportant, ends have been overlooked until now. One of these involved the extension of the Bardstown Branch from the home of "My Old Kentucky Home" to Springfield, Ky., 20 miles away. Such prolongation was authorized in December, 1885, and the work was completed on February 1, 1888.

Also, on August 30, 1884, the L. & N. had entered into a contract with the Elkton and Guthrie Railroad Company (incorporated on February 10, 1871, as the Elkton Railroad Company) whereby it was to complete the road from Guthrie to Elkton, Ky., and was to lease the resultant 11-mile stretch of track for a period of 25 years. The work of construction was completed on February 1, 1885, and the road was subsequently operated under lease by the L. & N.

An amendment to the original charter of the Elkton and Guthrie gave it the privilege of charging as much as five cents per mile for transporting a passenger, while the maximum freight rate was set at 15 cents per pound for the whole line. A still later amendment gave it the privilege of charging six cents per mile to those through passengers who neglected to purchase their tickets from the ticket offices of the company at Guthrie and Elkton.

Another acquisition of the Louisville & Nashville along about this time was a narrow-gauge railroad, known as the Tennessee, Alabama and Texas Railroad Company, Consolidated, extending, incongruously enough, from Clarksville, Tenn., on the Memphis Line, to a point near Gracey, Ky., some 32 miles away. At the time the L. & N. formally took over the T. A. & T. R. R., on April 9, 1887 (it had previously acquired its stocks and bonds on August 14, 1886), the line was in very poor physical condition. Although the road with the tri-state name had long since compromised on Princeton, Ky., as a northern terminus, after relinquishing

The "August Belmont" (top) and the "E. O. Saltmarsh" docked at Pensacola during the days when they were operated by an L. & N.-owned company.

the dreams of greater glory implied in its name plate, it was at that time still stymied 20 miles from the goal. After its acquisition by the L. & N. a number of changes were made. The gauge was changed from three feet to the then standard of four feet, nine inches, and about six miles of the line was re-located. This latter step moved the southern terminus from Clarksville to Princeton Junction, two miles north, where contact was made with the tracks of the L. & N., the two roads having had no previous physical connection. The work of extending the line to Princeton was started immediately thereafter and the railroad reached that town on December 1, 1887. The completed railroad, 52.74 miles of it, did not long rejoice in a purely L. & N. status. On July 26, 1892, that portion of the road lying between Gracey and Princeton was leased for 99 years to the Ohio Valley Railway, later to become a part of the Illinois Central System. Freight and passenger anemia forced the abandonment of the remaining trackage by the L. & N. on May 13, 1933.

Another chore completed about this time (1888) was the changing of the gauge of the Louisville, Harrod's Creek and Westport Railroad from three feet to four feet, nine inches. Because such a step, in the case of the L. H. C. & W., was such a radical one, this had not been done when the general change of gauge was made. While they were changing the gauge of this picturesque 11-mile line (Louisville to Prospect, Ky.) the Company's forces substituted a heavier steel rail for the lighter one of iron that had seen service for so many years. The widening of the track made it necessary to junk, or sell, most of the road's equipment and the total net cost of the change of gauge, etc., amounted to $15,128.09.

It is rather surprising, but none the less true, that at the end of the fiscal year ending with June 30, 1888, 965.22 miles of the 2,546.33 miles owned and operated by the L. & N. were still unballasted. Such trackage, of course, was found on lines where traffic was light or on lines which had been in the possession of the L. & N. for but a short time. The "content" of the 2,546.33 miles before mentioned was as follows: unballasted, 965.22 miles; sand ballasted, 300.67; partly ballasted, 600.97; fully ballasted, 679.47.

In 1889, the capital stock was increased from $35,000,000 to $48,000,000. The stockholders had the first chance to purchase this additional $13,000,000 worth of stock, and the proceeds, in part, were used to retire $10,000,000 worth of six per cent trust bonds. A hopeless minority, representing 55 shares of stock, voted against the proposal to increase the capitalization when it was presented to the other stockholders at their annual meeting on October 2, 1889. A total of 232,560 shares were voted in favor of the resolution, which increased the capitalization by about one-third, the resulting figure being still considerably less than the total cost of the road and branches. (The Company's charter, of course, gave it the privilege of increasing its capitalization to a point where it was equal to such total cost, this being $73,730,905.42, as of June 30, 1889.)

It was at this time (June 2, 1890), also, that the L. & N. undertook to further place its financial house in order by the issuance of a $75,000,000 Unified Mortgage, consisting of 50-year four per cent gold bonds. Part of the proceeds from this mortgage was used to retire prior bond

The L. & N.'s Muscogee Wharf at Pensacola around the turn of the century. The center track led to the coal tipple which may be seen in the background and it was here that the "August Belmont" and the "E. O. Saltmarsh" received their cargoes of coal.

issues which constituted liens on portions of the road, or branches thereof, and the remaining sum ($33,082,340) was used for the purchase or construction of additional trackage, and for the purchase of new equipment, bridges, terminal facilities, etc. These bonds were issued and sold from time to time as the need for additional funds arose.

The advantages of the Unified Mortgage were manifold; it reduced the interest charges on existing bonded indebtedness by $963,833.20 annually and it additionally eliminated the time and trouble involved in floating a bond issue every time the Company acquired or constructed a branch line or purchased a sizeable amount of new equipment.

Shortly previous to the issuance of the Unified Mortgage, or on July 1, 1887, the stockholders had voted that for a three-year period, effective as of that date, all dividends paid should be stock dividends, rather than cash dividends, in order that the Company might have a workable margin for improvements, etc. This was adhered to until July 2, 1890, when, heartened by a net operating income of $7,426,911.45 and a net income (after taxes, interest, rentals, etc., had been deducted) of $2,866,641.91, a three per cent stock-and-cash dividend was declared; 1.90 per cent being in stock and 1.10 per cent being in cash.

In addition to those previously mentioned, several other small batches of trackage were readied for traffic in the 1880s. Some of these lines are now no longer in existence and would not be singled out for especial mention at this time were it not for the fact that their heydays were particularly colorful. Excellently representative of those carriers whose rails were the background for much of moment, but which have now been gathered up unto the Iron Horse Valhalla (via track removal gangs) was the Mammoth Cave Railroad, a rare nonesuch of the transportation world if there ever was one. This pike's tenure of service to the shipping and traveling public (mostly the latter) extended from 1886 to 1931.

The Mammoth Cave Railroad was not built by the L. & N. Railroad, but prior to its construction a contract was entered into between the two companies whereby the L. & N. leased the Mammoth Cave Railroad for a period of 25 years from date of completion. Under the terms of this agreement the L. & N. furnished the requisite rolling stock without rental charges, stop-over privileges at Glasgow Junction were given the L. & N.'s patrons, and the net earnings of the line were to be paid quarterly to the Mammoth Cave Railroad. This arrangement was continued until August 12, 1895, when a receiver was appointed for the Cave carrier. The road was subsequently sold under foreclosure on March 17, 1898, and later taken over by a re-organized company, representing the original stockholders, shortly after the turn of the century.

While the Mammoth Cave Railroad operated under its own power after 1903, it was a virtual "protectorate" of the L. & N., and that road and the Glasgow Railway were its only rail outlets to the outside world. The Mammoth Cave Railroad extended from Glasgow Junction, Ky., to Mammoth Cave, a distance of 8.7 miles and, of course, was built to accommodate the visitors to the subterranean wonderland. Elbert Hubbard, writer and philosopher, used its facilities on a pilgrimage to the Cave shortly before his death on the **Lusitania** and has immortalized the lilliputian road in a blistering little sketch. This, while full of sardonic wit, is, on the whole, unfair to a carrier which, for 45 years, faithfully served its public, generally made money for its owners and never had a wreck, a passenger killed in a train accident, or a law suit brought against it.

Said **Fra Elbertus**, in part: " . . . To reach the Mammoth Cave you take the Louisville & Nashville Railroad to Glasgow Junction. There you change cars and take the Mammoth Cave Railroad, an institution that has an equipment of one passenger coach and a dummy engine. I was interested in seeing a Kaffir cutting the grass between the two streaks of rust, and was told this had to be done three times a year, and is the thing that keeps down the dividends."

The coming of the automobile forecast the eventual discontinuance of

The L. & N.'s Tarragona St. Wharf at Pensacola, Fla., about 1900. This wharf was used for the loading and unloading of inbound and outbound merchandise shipments.

the railroad on September 1, 1931. For several years prior to that date business had been very bad and a number of experiments were tried in a vain endeavor to lure back the fickle traffic. It is ironical that the passing of the railroad was but a short time prior to the establishment of Mammoth Cave National Park on May 22, 1936.

Other and more strictly L. & N. developments were also achieving fruition at this time. Notable among these was the extension of a line of road into the Cahaba coal fields leading off from the S. & N. A. at Helena, Ala. This branch of the Birmingham Mineral was completed to Gurnee Junction, 10 miles away, about the first of July, 1889, and the subsequent obtaining of trackage rights from the Brierfield, Blocton and Birmingham Railway Company (later a part of the Southern Railway System) gave the L. & N. eventual access to Blocton, Ala., and somewhat later to Belle Ellen and Piper, in the heart of the Cahaba coal fields aforesaid. The completion of the line to Blocton shortened the coal haul to Gulf points by about 40 miles and greatly increased the demand for Bibb County's valuable "black diamonds." The Red Gap Branch from Graces to Red Gap Junction, Ala., a distance of 10 miles, and the Dudley Branch from Yolande to Brookwood, 3.39 miles, were also constructed at about this time.

The "Hercules," famous old engine of the Mammoth Cave Railroad, at Mammoth Cave, Ky., around the turn of the century.

The completion of the Helena & Blocton Branch subsequently led to the formation of the Export Coal Company, under the laws of the State of Florida, and under the aegis of T. H. Aldrich, president of the Cahaba Coal Mining Company. It was thought that such an agency could not only stimulate the demand for Alabama coal in foreign lands, and facilitate its handling thereto, but that it might also do the same for other products as well. The L. & N. was greatly interested in the success of the venture, of course, and subscribed $75,000.00 for the stock of the company.

At that time the facilities for the handling of exports and imports at Pensacola were far from adequate and such interchange was constantly increasing. Accordingly, in 1889 and 1890, the L. & N. spent large sums of money at that port to help consummate the union of rail and water. Some $30,000 was spent for dredging Pensacola Bay and an additional $26,700 was expended in providing coaling and fertilizer facilities, tracks and improvements to Muscogee Wharf, etc.

At that time the Export Coal Company had a fleet of two ocean-going steam tugs and four barges for the transportation of coal and other freight to Cuba, the West Indies and Central and South American ports and for the handling of return loads. It was the delight of the ranking officers of the company to invite a few selected guests and review this flotilla as it lay anchored on occasion in Pensacola Bay.

The following news item which is from an Evansville, Ind., newspaper of January 13, 1893, gives some idea of the optimistic glow which surrounded the operations of the Export Coal Company at that time:

"The steamship Barocoa, recently placed in the Gulf trade between Pensacola and Havana, in the interest of the freight traffic of the Louisville and Nashville Railroad, left Pensacola yesterday afternoon on her third trip to Cuba, loaded to her fullest capacity. This steamer started on her first trip on the 16th of last month and L. & N. General Traffic Manager Van den Berg has been officially informed that the Company's venture to the West Indies has proven to be a grand success. The steamer's cargo into Pensacola last Sunday consisted of sea island sugar, rice and fine woods in large square logs, all of which were closely piled on the decks, thus utilizing every inch of the space for storing freight. The cargo out yesterday was made up mostly of Southern products, brick and manufactured goods from all parts of the country. So well satisfied are the officials of the L. & N., that the next grand stride they expect to make is to ascertain an approximate amount of manufactured wares from the North and West that could be sent to Cuba, Mexico and the Central and South American republics, after which, at least three, and probably five, new steamships will be built especially for the Company's service. The new vessels will be colossal freight carriers, with clipper speed, so arranged for passenger accommodations as to be rated first class in every particular."

There were large deposits of Bessemer iron ores (necessary for the making of steel) in Cuba and it was thought that the establishment of steel plants at Mobile and Pensacola might be a practical move, inasmuch as those cities were nearer to the ores than the large steel producing plants of eastern Pennsylvania which, at that time, depended principally upon Cuban ores for the manufacture of their product.

The establishment of such steel plants would have been, of course, a great boon to the L. & N. and the Export Coal Company, for it would have given the latter guaranteed tonnage for its ships on their return trips from Cuba and near-by ports. At that time it was apparently not realized that the day was not far distant when the Birmingham District would begin to manufacture steel itself, utilizing basic pig iron evolved from its own ores.

The formation of the Export Coal Company and the chain of events which this set in motion may be said to have led to the eventual establishment in November 1889, of the L. & N.'s foreign freight department, which was directly concerned with export and import freight traffic.

The L. & N. itself later made a bid for the Pan-American trade with its Gulf Transit Company, which succeeded the Export Coal Company, which had not lived up to expectations, although the Railroad derived a revenue of $377,970.45 from coal alone as a result of its operations during the five-year period 1889-1894. The Gulf Transit Company was organized on January 21, 1895, and the L. & N. owned all its capital stock, it, in turn, owning all the capital stock of the Pensacola Trading

Company, organized and existing under the laws of Great Britain. This latter corporation owned two steel screw steamers, the August Belmont and the E. O. Saltmarsh (gross tonnages of 4,640 and 3,630 respectively), which plied the waters of the Gulf and the Caribbean, delivering coal to foreign ports and returning to home base at Pensacola with tonnage of a highly diversified nature. The August Belmont was named in honor of the L. & N.'s then chairman of the board, while the E. O. Saltmarsh honored the L. & N.'s then superintendent of the Pensacola and Pensacola and Atlantic divisions. Some years after the formation of the Gulf Transit Company, the intineraries of the vessels were broadened and they made regular trips across the Atlantic, touching at Liverpool and other ports in the vicinity.

Both the August Belmont and the E. O. Saltmarsh flew the British Union Jack and were the only physical assets of the Pensacola Trading Company aforesaid. At one time the Gulf Transit Company had also owned another vessel named the Pensacola but this was sold to A. H. Bull and Company on February 17, 1906. The August Belmont and the E. O. Saltmarsh were themselves subsequently sold in the early part of 1915 to the C. C. Mengel & Brother Company, of Louisville, Ky., in a transaction whereby the latter secured complete ownership of the Pensacola Trading Company (July 1, 1915). The combined purchase price of the two vessels came to $385,000.00 and they were afterwards used by the Mengel Company in hauling mahogany from South American ports. One of these vessels was later sunk by a German submarine during World War I.

As a result of the formation of the Gulf Transit Company, the L. & N. spent additional large sums to improve its port facilities at Pensacola. This involved the construction of new wharves and warehouses and roughly paralleled similar activity at Mobile and New Orleans.

The opening of the L. & N. Passenger Station (first known as the Union Station) at Birmingham was a momentous event back in 1887. Suitably decorated and attended, Engine No. 95 had the honor of hauling the first passenger train into the new station, with Engineer W. K. Rosser at the throttle. The original photograph belonged to his grandson, Charles H. Rosser, Jr.

Chapter XVI

Builders and Wreckers

THE increasing traffic which the L. & N. was being called upon to handle made it imperative that a certain amount of double-track be constructed if the freight were to be moved swiftly and satisfactorily. The nation's railroads (1888) were now carrying approximately 700,000,000 tons of freight annually, as contrasted with 5,500,000 tons in 1851, and the L. & N's tonnage had also increased proportionately. Accordingly, in 1888, authorization was given for the construction of an additional track between East Louisville and Anchorage (10 miles); between South Louisville and Shepherdsville (15 miles); between Edgefield Junction and East Nashville (8½ miles); between Birmingham and Boyles (3 miles); and between Birmingham and Oxmoor (6 miles). In 1889, additional authority was given for construction of second tract between East Louisville and South Louisville (3 miles) and between Shepherdsville and Lebanon Junction, Ky. (12 miles). All of this trackage, with the exception of that last named, was completed in 1890.

As of July 1, 1891, a total of $726,636.57 had been spent upon this work and the subsequent ironing out of various wrinkles was to cost many thousands more.

One of the show places of Louisville in the Gay 'Nineties and one that was invariably shown to country cousins, visiting firemen and other temporary infiltrations into the civic scene, was the L. & N.'s new Union Passenger Station, which was formally opened for traffic on September 7, 1891. This dedication thus transmuted into reality a dream of long standing for it had been realized for some time that such a structure was needed. As a matter of fact, land for this purpose had been purchased as early as 1880 in the vicinity of 10th and Broadway and some work upon the foundations had been done. Following the purchase of the Short Line in 1881, however, the job was suspended and not resumed until the early part of 1889. Prior to the completion of the station in 1891, Short Line trains used the Water Street Station at 1st and Water, while Main Line trains used the old depot at 10th and Maple streets, somewhat to the south of Broadway. In order, therefore, to permit Short Line trains to utilize the facilities of the new station without too much lost motion, the "A" Street (Gaulbert Ave.) Cut-off was built, this connecting the main line with the Railway Transfer, which, in turn, connected East Louisville and South Louisville. Short Line trains could thus run in and out of the new station without the necessity of making a roundabout trip all the way out to South Louisville. The trains of the Monon and the Pennsylvania also used the new station from the very first. Somewhat later the Louisville, St. Louis & Texas Railway (later to become a part of the L. & N.) also began to hang up the hats of its trains therein.

It had been estimated that the construction of the new station would cost approximately $336,415, a fairly accurate conclusion for the final figures revealed that such cost was $310,656.47. Besides the station proper this money had been expended upon such diverse items as a trainshed, a coach shed, granite paving, sidetracks, a water supply and fencing.

F. W. Mobray, chief architect for the L. & N., designed the plans for the new station and resigned from the employ of the Company a few days after its opening, evidently having been hired especially for the prosecution of this work. Newspaper accounts of the dedication were unanimous in their praise of the structure and it was said to be the largest and most complete in the West – anything to the left of Pittsburgh in those days – with the

The L. & N.'s first passenger station in Louisville, Ky., which was opened in 1858. At that time the structure was used both as a freight station and as a passenger depot. It was located at 9th and Broadway and shortly after the War Between the States its use as a passenger depot was discontinued, a station being erected in the vicinity of 10th and Maple streets for the accommodation of passengers. A considerable portion of this old building continued to be used by the L. & N. as a freight shed, a section of the front having been removed in 1905 to make room for the construction of the present day general office building.

single exception of Chicago's train hostelry. Huge crowds of the curious thronged in and out of its doors on opening day and marveled at its many excellencies. A unique feature and one that might be said to be the forerunner of present-day air conditioning, was its heating plant, which could "blow" hot or cold, as the occasion demanded. While this feature does not seem to have been used in the summer-time, the heating plant was so arranged that if its pipes overdid their job of warming the station, cold air could be pumped through them in order that the temperature might be quickly regulated.

Another momentous event which took place during the 1880s and which affected not only the L. & N., but all other railroads as well, was the passage by Congress on February 4, 1887, of the Interstate Commerce

Law. The five-man commission thereby created was given certain powers in connection with the rate-making activities of the railroads, chief among these being the power to prohibit and declare illegal all fares and freight rates which were not just and reasonable. (At that time several of the states had railroad commissions which determined rates and fares, insofar as purely intra-state shipping and travel were concerned.) These powers granted the I. C. C. were more implied than actual, however, and subsequent rulings of the Supreme Court greatly nullified what authority the Commission had. One of these decisions was momentous in that the Court ruled that under the Act of 1887, the I. C. C. had no power to actually fix railroad rates.

It was not until after the turn of the century and the passage of the Elkins Act in 1903, which sharpened the original Act's teeth, and the Hepburn Act in 1906, that the authority of the Interstate Commerce Commission was greatly widened and strengthened. The Hepburn Act specifically gave the I. C. C. the power to determine and prescribe just and reasonable maximum rates. This was subsequently upheld by the Supreme Court in 1910 and may be regarded as the keystone of present day I. C. C. policy and practice.

Closely paralleling these legislative developments was the evolution occurring within the railroad itself. Heavier steel rail was placed in the track, bridges and other structures were strengthened, and more powerful 10-wheeled locomotives made their appearance. These latter stressed utility and not adornment and the proud-stepping, brass-bound little locomotives, with their flaring smoke-stacks and their exaggerated cow-catchers, began to gradually disappear from the L. & N. scene. They lingered on for some while, even after the turn of the century, however, and a considerable portion of the time of the fireman who did his shoveling aboard one of these proud beauties was spent in polishing the brass on his engine until it shone like the sun at noon-day. At that time an engineer was generally assigned to one particular locomotive and hence he took an especial pride in seeing that it was kept spic and span. If the occasion demanded it the engineer was not above doing a little brass-polishing himself, but it was essentially the task of the fireman and woe betide the hapless tallowpot who was inclined to regard this as the lesser part of his duties and hence most apt to be neglected.

Although neither Jesse James nor the Dalton Boys ever honored the Louisville & Nashville with the pleasure of their fleeting presence, their nefarious activities were duplicated upon our road by a host of other gentlemen, during a period which covered a number of years and which lasted, in fact, until World War I. Reference is had, of course, to train robbers and wreckers.

Just prior to the turn of the last century, the troubled times, as much as anything else, engendered not only a swarm of lesser criminal fry, but other and more daring criminals as well. Not for these latter the brief profitable glory to be found in petty larcenies of one sort or another. Theirs were deeds which made the front pages for the proverbial seven days and since theirs were the greater risks, theirs were also the correspondingly greater awards. With shot-gun and pistol, with rifle and black-jack, they perpetrated misdeeds which caused large sums of cash to change

This is the Union Station at Louisville, which was dedicated in 1891, and which superseded the strictly L. & N. station near 10th and Maple. With some superficial exception, the exterior of the station looked the same in 1963 as in 1891.

hands in the twinkling of an eye and which more often than not involved violence and bloodshed.

Crime rode the rails in the Gay 'Nineties and on the L. & N. it was personified by such choice of characters as Morris Slater, alias "Railroad Bill," Gus Hyatt, Harry Lester and many others.

In this connection special tribute is due the L. & N.'s former chief of police, J. B. Harlan, who first became connected with the Company's police department in 1893 as special agent. Three years later he was appointed chief special agent and, as such, for over 40 years, or until his death on December 12, 1936, he directed the fight against the forces of lawlessness and disorder whenever they invaded L. & N. territory. His son, Marion B. Harlan succeeded him; still later M. B. Harlan, Sr., was succeeded by M. B. Harlan, Jr.

In the days when the 20th Century was just around the corner and even for some time thereafter, the territory served by the L. & N. Railroad was, for a large part, thinly settled. Much rugged country was traversed by its lines and the hills, pine woods, and swamps which bordered its right-of-way for many miles afforded excellent cover for criminals and outlaws, both before and after their crimes. This, of course, rendered their apprehension all the more difficult.

The case of Morris Slater, alias "Railroad Bill," supplies an excellent example of the difficulty of finding a rather vicious needle in a haystack. "Railroad's" usual habitat was the pine woods and swamps of Southern Alabama and Northwestern Florida and in them he led a charmed existence for a number of years, eking out a living by "working" on the railroad at periodic intervals. "Railroad Bill" was a Negro and it was commonly believed by members of his race that it would take a silver bullet to kill him. After a long and varied career as a bandit and a plunderer of our depots and freight cars, he was finally killed, however, by an ordinary bullet at Atmore, Ala., on March 7, 1897.

Another slightly tarnished blade of the 'Nineties whose story does not whittle so pointed a moral was Gus Hyatt, a lone wolf of the steel trail.

Mr. Hyatt is chiefly remembered upon the L. & N. for two feats;

each involving the armed robbery of one of its passenger trains. The first of these occurred near Calera, Ala., in March 1897, No. 4 being the train dispossessed. On that particular March night, No. 4 was carrying a large sum of money and Augustus Homer Hyatt and a confederate by the name of Lowe, introduced themselves to the engineer and fireman via the six-shooter route, while the train was stopped at a water-tank just north of Calera. On this occasion they decamped with about $20,000, which they obtained from a safe in the express car. Later, L. & N. passenger train No. 102 was held up and robbed on June 22, 1897, at St. Bethlehem, Tenn., about six miles north of Clarksville, by Mr. Hyatt.

On this occasion Gus, accompanied by two Colt 45's and an empty (but not for long) bran sack, did a change of pace that would have done credit to Dr. Jekyll and Mr. Hyde, changing in a trice from peaceful passenger to marauding malefactor. Following this transformation, he leisurely robbed the safe in the express car of its contents, consisting of money and other valuables, and then left the train at St. Bethlehem.

Some months later at Kansas City, Mo., Gus's foot slipped and he was brought back to Tennessee for trial. Subsequent conviction on the charge of robbing No. 102 landed him in the penitentiary at Nashville. He eventually escaped for keeps, however.

The Alabama train-wreckers who infested the lines of the L. & N. during the 'nineties, were of a somewhat different caliber than Gus and "Railroad Bill"; their handiwork being distinguished by its apparent aimlessness. The first of these wrecks occurred to an L. & N. freight train near Catoma Creek, a few miles south of Montgomery, Ala., in 1896, and was caused by a crosstie which had been placed on the track. Then, on November 12, 1896, No. 3, heavily loaded with passengers, mail, express and baggage, and running at a high rate of speed, was derailed at McGehees, Ala. None of the passengers was seriously injured, although naturally quite a few of them were severely shaken up and jarred and the train's equipment was very badly damaged.

While the L. & N. was still checking up on the wreck at McGehees, No. 3 was wrecked again; this time in the early morning of April 22, 1897, upon Trestle No. 76, near Wilcox, Ala., which was at a point about 64 miles south of its first mishap. The engine and tender, along with the

No. 3 near Wilcox, Ala., the morning of April 22, 1897—the work of train wreckers. As may be seen the engine was badly damaged and both engineer and fireman were killed.

Trials and tribulations of a railroad — the Company's shops at Bowling Green, Ky., following a disastrous storm in 1893.

postal, express and baggage cars, and one coach, plunged from the trestle (a "ditch switch" having been made by the malefactors) and in so doing thoroughly demolished it. The locomotive turned completely over, killing the engineer and fireman most painfully with clouds of scalding steam. As in the former wrecks, the train wreckers, however were conspicuous by their absence.

One Nels Williams, a Negro, was subsequently convicted of this crime and given the surprisingly light sentence of six years in the penitentiary. He disclaimed any knowledge of the first wrecking of No. 3 and the perpetrators were never apprehended. In addition to the three actual wreckings mentioned, there were a number of attempts to de-rail other L. & N. trains in Alabama, all of these occurring, however, prior to the first wreck at Catoma Creek.

Previously back home in Kentucky, the L. & N. had also been having its misfortunes. Outstanding among these were an unsuccessful attempt to wreck the paycar in the fall of 1893 on the high fill south of Mt. Vernon, Ky., and a partially successful similar attempt upon Train No. 26, near Hazel Patch, Ky., in the latter part of 1894. In the latter instance, no one was hurt, although the engine and tender were de-railed. In each of these instances, the train wreckers were captured and convicted.

CHAPTER XVII

More Bluegrass Pastures

A MAJOR acquisition of the Louisville & Nashville Railroad in the 'nineties was the Kentucky Central Railway, which served a large portion of the Bluegrass region of Kentucky. In December 1890, the L. & N. contracted to purchase not less than two-thirds of the outstanding capital stock of this road and the system was actually acquired on September 22, 1891. At that time the Kentucky Central was owned by the Collis P. Huntington interests, who contemporaneously were engaged in a factional squabble with the leadership of the Chesapeake and Ohio. The disputes over right-of-way precedence which raged between the K. C. and the C. & O., frequently culminated in blows and cracked heads. The sale of the K. C. to the L. & N. tended to formalize the relationship between the two carriers and a friendly association eventually emerged.

At the time it was taken over by the L. & N., the K. C. Railway consisted of 248.43 miles of track, some 217 miles of this being owned outright; the remainder being leased from the L. & N. The line from Covington to Sinks accounted for 149.88 miles; that from Paris to Maysville for 49.32 miles and that from Paris to Lexington for 17.86 miles. The leased trackage extended from Fort Estill Junction, near Richmond, to Rowland (later abandoned in part) and, as stated, this was the property of the L. & N. Connection with the outside world was made at Milldale (Latonia), at Lexington, at Rowland, at Livingston and at one or two other points. Ingress into Cincinnati was gained via the bridge of the Covington and Cincinnati Elevated Railroad and Transfer and Bridge Company, generally known as the C. & O. bridge. This structure was completed on Christmas Day, 1888. Engineer Edward P. Maurer had the honor of piloting the first locomotive across the bridge.

Some 500 persons were crowded on a special train, consisting of six flat-cars, as it made the trip from Covington to Cincinnati. Aboard as passengers doing it the hard way were many C. & O. and K. C. notables, a large proportion of the workmen who had built the bridge and at least one alertly observant reporter from one of the Queen City dailies who has left the following interesting account of the occasion:

"As the ascent to the bridge was reached with a rush, Maurer let go his whistle, long and loud, and the shrill answer came from everything with steam up on the river, or on either shore. The engine went up the grade swiftly, giving scarcely an opportunity to admire the splendid completed wagonway, but when it reached the level the orders were to go slow, on account of insufficient brakes for so heavy a train.

"The engine and tender weighed about 90,000 pounds, the cars 120,000 and the people 80,000, on a rough estimate – but that was considered a bagatelle so far as weight for the structure was concerned. The suspension bridge to the right seemed so near, in a sense, that one could almost reach down and touch it with his right hand. The ice floe in the river, up and down, lent variety to the landscape. Everybody that was met took off his hat and shouted. The workmen on the cars cheered. They cheered when the bridge was reached. They cheered in the long span. They cheered as the descent to the Ohio shore was made. Answering plaudits came thundering from the hundreds below."

It is said that this bridge cost $5,000,000 to construct and at the time it was the finest truss bridge of its kind in the world. One of its interesting features was its switchback approach, a necessity because of the nature of the terrain. The designer of the bridge, Epes Randolph, was at that time superintendent of the Kentucky Central. It was superceded by a more modern structure in April 1929. Only those trains of the L. & N. which operated over the old Kentucky Division (Cincinnati Division) used this bridge, or its successor, to gain access to Cincinnati for a great number of years. Then, in April 1933, the opening of Cincinnati's $41,000,000 passenger terminal made necessary the re-routing of Short Line trains and all L. & N. trains began to use the new C. & O. bridge.

The history of the Kentucky Central is rather an involved one. In the beginning, there was the Maysville and Lexington Railroad, which was exactly one day older than the L. & N. By December 19, 1854, the 18-mile stretch between Lexington and Paris had been completed and this was subsequently leased to the Covington and Lexington Railroad, incorporated 1849. The Maysville and Lexington, after many financial vicissitudes (the trackage from Lexington to Paris having come back into the fold in the meantime), eventually split up into two parts, known as the Maysville and Lexington Railroad, Southern Division (Paris-Lexington), and the Maysville and Lexington Railroad, Northern Division, which was charged with the responsibility of completing the line between Paris and Maysville. This corporate maneuver occurred on January 21, 1868. The Northern Division aforesaid completed the line to Maysville about 1873 and the two roads were subsequently (1876) operated as one entity until February of 1881. At that time, the Kentucky Central Railroad, which had

Corbin, Ky., yard in 1900.

come into existence as the result of steps presently to be described, leased the lines and subsequently purchased the majority of their capital stock.

We now touch upon the Licking and Lexington Railroad Company, which was incorporated on March 1, 1847, to build a railroad from Covington or Newport through Falmouth, Cynthiana and Paris to Lexington. In 1849, the name of this pioneer road was changed to the Covington and Lexington Railroad, before mentioned, and in July 1851, it commenced the construction of the 78-mile iron-clad trail from Covington to Paris. This was completed and placed in operation on March 9, 1856. That nemesis of early-day railroading, the defaulting of interest upon bonds, hauled the flourishing Covington and Lexington into the courts on August 13, 1859, and it eventually (in 1863) emerged as the Kentucky Central Railroad Association, which was formed for the express purpose of operating and acquiring the properties formerly owned by the Covington and Lexington, and, in general, tidying things up a bit.

The Kentucky Central Railroad Company, as such, was incorporated on February 22, 1871, and seems to have been dormant, at least technically so, until July 7, 1875, when it took over the properties of the Kentucky Central Railroad Association under the terms of the charter.

In 1881, or thereabouts, the Kentucky Central passed into the hands of the Collis P. Huntington interests and it was decided to extend its line from Paris to a connection with the L. & N.'s Knoxville Division (Lebanon Branch) at Sinks of Roundstone, Ky., just north of Livingston. This was done in two stages; Paris to Richmond, 39 miles, and Fort Estill Junction, near Richmond, to Sinks, 30 miles, the work being completed in 1883. Contemporaneously, as before stated, the K. C. also operated the L. & N.-owned line from Fort Estill Junction to Rowland (33 miles) and owned trackage between Lexington and Maysville by way of Paris, and between Covington and Paris. Trackage rights obtained from the L. & N. permitted

No. 7, a locomotive of the old Kentucky Central Railway.

Many farmers along the L. & N. in bygone years supplemented incomes by hewing crossties.

its trains to run to Jellico, Tenn., where connection was made with the East Tennessee, Virginia and Georgia Railroad, later to become a part of the Southern Railway System.

However, it was the Kentucky Central **Railway,** rather than the Kentucky Central **Railroad,** which was taken over by the L. & N. in 1891. the change from "road" to "way" having occurred on June 7, 1887, after a session with the receiver which had been initiated on January 28, 1886.

At the commencement of the War Between the States, there was in existence about 100 miles of track of the predecessor roads of the Kentucky Central. The line from Paris to Covington (there was, of course, no bridge across the Ohio to Cincinnati, at the time) was of especial strategic importance and it received much the same sort of blighting attention from raiding Confederate cavalrymen as did its confrere and neighbor, the L. & N. Many of the "Johnny Rebs" were natives of the section and hence had first-hand knowledge of the vital points at which to strike along the right-of-way.

When the capture of Cincinnati by General Kirby Smith, U. S. C., seemed imminent, a pontoon bridge was hurriedly thrown across the Ohio River and troops were rushed into Northern Kentucky via the railroad to man the forts and other fortifications which had been erected in the hills of Kenton County.

These stirring but troublous times were followed by the dark days of the Reconstruction Era, and, as outlined previously, the predecessor lines of the Kentucky Central Railroad did not come through this period unscathed.

By extending its line from Paris to Sinks of Roundstone in 1881, 1882 and 1883, the Kentucky Central left its Bluegrass pastures and encountered somewhat rougher going. At that time the citizenry of that part of Southeastern Kentucky, like their native hills, were somewhat rugged and unsophisticated. The entrance of the Iron Horse upon the scene helped to break the monotony of their routine but, on the other hand, it took them some little while to become accustomed to the novelty; a feat of acclimatization which was entirely mutual. Some of these frictions were accidental; others were deliberate. In the first category might be placed the hitching of horses to trains which had paused but temporarily and the subsequent chain of events set in motion by the departure of the train. In the second category could be placed the practice of using the wheels of trains as moving targets to improve one's marksmanship – an innocent enough pastime considering the unerring aim of its practitioners – but one never greatly appreciated by the passengers. These phases, however, soon passed and it was not long before the railroad was accepted as a part of the native flora and fauna.

It might be stated at this point that in those days the railroad station

Cumberland Furnace in 1929 about the time its operations were discontinued. At one time it was one of Tennessee's biggest producers of iron, with shipments handled over the Clarksville Mineral.

in most small communities, regardless of its geographical location, was the center of the town's civic activities; a club and a clearing-house at one and the same time. To that outpost of the outside world, at train time, were inexorably drawn that portion of the masculine population (and not a few ladies, too) who were not bedfast or otherwise prevented from attending by the struggle for a livelihood in a callous world.

Sometimes the train stopped and sometimes it did not, but it made no difference to the citizenry there congregated. There was compensation in either case. If it did not stop there was the thrill of seeing the "Cannonball Express," or some other "name" train, roar through their metropolis at 40 miles an hour in a swirl of dust and cinders. The resounding thumps created by a bundle of big-town papers and the mail pouch landing on the station platform (or thereabouts) were tangible evidence at least that the fast flyer was not entirely unaware of the town's existence.

And, of course, when the train did stop, as even the "Cannonball" did more or less frequently, depending upon the size of the town, there was a great hustle and bustle, involving the transfer of mail, express and passengers, accompanied by a brisk rattle of milk cans, the greetings and farewells of friends and the nonchalant conversations of the train crew. It was at such a time that the small boy's ambition to become a railroader became more firmly solidified. Then a stentorian cry of, "All aboard!" broke the spell, the big wheels began to revolve slowly and with bell clanging the train moved off, its departure leaving all concerned with a feeling of anti-climax, comparable to that experienced on the day after Christmas. But this gentle melancholy was softened considerably by the knowledge that there would be other trains and corresponding drama in the very near future.

Another addition to the L. & N. family in the 'nineties was the Clarksville Mineral, now abandoned, which was constructed in 1891-93, to reach the iron ore deposits in Montgomery and Dickson counties, Tenn. The road extended from Hematite, nine miles south of Clarksville, to Pond, on the N. C. & St. L. Railway, by way of Marion and Van Leer, a total distance of 31 miles, with a six-mile spur leading off from Van Leer to Cumberland Furnace. The line was completed on January 1, 1893, and was more or less successfully operated until 1929, when the furnace at Cumberland Furnace, in its day quite a revenue producer, ceased to cast its rosy glow upon the skies and closed down for good. This was the last straw, although the Mineral tottered along until November 1, 1936, before it was formally abandoned.

The Napier Branch, also now relegated to limbo, was another "ghost" line built about this time, its 10.92 miles being completed on September 23, 1891. It extended from Summertown on the N. F. & S. to Napier, Tenn., and was projected primarily to serve the various iron works at Napier.

As of June 30, 1893, there were 2,954.66 miles of track embraced within the L. & N. System proper, this figure including such leased lines as the Nashville and Decatur and the South and North Alabama, then, as now, considered integral parts of the railroad. Outside of this figure, but also operated under lease, were the 88.29 miles of such semi-independent lines as the Glasgow Railroad, the Elkton & Guthrie Railroad, etc. The N. F. & S. Railway and the Henderson Bridge and connecting track accounted additionally for 104.83 miles and 10.06 miles, respectively, making in all a System total of 3,157.79 miles of track. The trackage of the N. C. & St. L. Railway (at that time 810 miles) and that of the Georgia Railroad and dependencies (721 miles) were never included in any figure involving strictly L. & N. mileage, even though the L. & N. either owned a majority of the capital stock, as in the case of the N. C. & St. L., or was a joint lessee (the Georgia Railroad).

At this time (1893) the company still owned approximately 51,319 acres of agricultural and mineral land, largely located in Alabama and Florida; nevertheless, while it was disposing of this land as rapidly as was possible, it occasionally found it necessary to purchase additional land located at various points along its right-of-way so as to construct new facilities to accommodate its expanding needs and requirements. Thus, in the early part of 1891, the L. & N. purchased a sizeable parcel of land in Whitley County, near Corbin, Ky., formerly known as Lynn Camp, and shortly thereafter commenced the construction of a roundhouse and certain other facilities at this point.

Prior to 1893, when the roundhouse was completed, the mechanical facilities of the Cumberland Valley Division, such as they were, had been located at Shawanee, Tenn., where there were a frame engine shed and a few rudimentary items of shop machinery. And, of course, in case of emergency, the shop facilities at Rowland, Ky., could always be pressed into service, although, obviously, this meant the loss of a certain amount of time.

At that time the C. V.'s total mileage was embraced in the single line of track from Corbin to Norton, Va., a distance of 118 miles; consequently, the roundhouse aforesaid at Corbin and a blacksmith shop, along with the usual complement of tracks, etc., were sufficient for a number of years to take care of the division's mechanical needs, despite the increasing tonnage it was being called upon to handle.

In 1893, or thereabouts, however, despite the fact that the L. & N.'s facilities at Corbin were rather meager, the town commenced to grow in a startling manner and a number of buildings were erected. It is said that no less than 12 saloons lined the town's main street and the Shotwells and the Whites, then in midst of their feud, frequently enlivened the civic scene with a little plain and fancy shooting.

Chapter XVIII

Alabama Steel

THE 'nineties, of course, are noted as a decade in which many momentous events took place. Many of these, naturally, touched upon the L. N., but lightly, although in our closely-knit and integrated civilization it can hardly be said that any event deserving the adjective "momentous" is without its influence in even the remotest quarters, and the L. & N. certainly could not be relegated to that sector of the compass.

One event whose dimensions grew increasingly impressive with the years had its inception in 1891 at the Little Belle Furnace (at Bessemer) with the manufacture of the first basic iron ever produced in Alabama. Basic iron is iron with a low silicon content (about one-half of one per cent) and Alabama pig iron at that time had a high silicon content (an average of around two and one-half per cent). This basic iron was superior to the iron with a high silicon content in that it was much better adapted to the making of steel.

This production at the Little Belle Furnace was admittedly experimental and was undertaken primarily to prove that Alabama could produce basic iron from its ores and existing blast furnaces without the utilization of any special patented process. The venture produced definite tangible results a few years later when a determined effort was made by the Tennessee Coal, Iron and Railroad Company to commercially produce basic iron. After several discouraging failures, including the manufacture of several hundred tons of iron which had just a mite too much silicon to permit its classification as basic, a large cast was finally successfully achieved at the Alice Furnace, near Birmingham, on July 22, 1895.

(The chief bar to the successful manufacture of the basic iron had been the difficulty of simultaneously reducing the silicon and sulphur content. When the presence of the silicon had been sufficiently reduced, the presence of sulphur increased almost proportionately, due to the steps which had been taken to eliminate the silicon. It was the story of the ubiquitous dent in the slightly flawed rubber ball all over again and on a much larger scale. However, patience and the lessons learned from experience eventually carried the day.)

The Andrew Carnegie interests tentatively purchased 4,000 tons of the metal and this proved so satisfactory that 21,000 additional tons were subsequently ordered. The barriers were finally breached and in almost no time at all the Tennessee Company was selling its new product to a number of steel mills, located at Pittsburgh and elsewhere.

It is now generally agreed that this pioneer work of the Tennessee Company was the one single thing chiefly responsible for the subsequent birth of the steel industry in Alabama. It is not at all improbable that had not that company vanquished the legend that Alabama ores were not suitable for the making of basic iron that Alabama's gigantic empire of coal and iron might have crumpled into an obsolescent ruin. This was because steel was rapidly replacing iron in more and more fields and it was only a question of time until the production of pig iron which could only be utilized in the making of iron products would be economically unsound.

As indicated, the production of basic iron by Alabama furnaces was not an end in itself, and can only be regarded as a necessary stepping stone to the ultimate production of steel. It is obvious that the manufacture of steel in Alabama would be the logical result of the new departure for the latter brought into being for a brief time a set-up that also had its element of the weird. Basic iron produced in Alabama was transported to the Pittsburgh District (largely) some 1,000 miles away and there converted into steel. This was unsound for two reasons; first, the cost of transportation and, second, the increase in the cost of conversion, it being easier and cheaper to convert the basic iron into steel while it was still in the molten stage, or as part of one continuous process.

The railroads propped up this state of affairs by the granting of attractive rates, thereby making it possible for the Alabama furnaces, with their cheaper labor costs, to successfully compete with the Northern furnaces. At this time the Interstate Commerce Act lacked teeth and the chief function of its Commission was "viewing with alarm," which it did through the medium of voluminous reports issued periodically. Meanwhile, in a fiercely competitive world, the railroads trimmed their rates more or less to

An ore train at Ensley, Ala., in 1900. Left to right: B. M. Huey, flagman; J. A. Obenchain, chief clerk; E. F. Boone, cashier; H. S. Chiles, abstract clerk; Chas. Rosser, conductor; Engineer Whitfield.

suit themselves, i.e., to obtain the best possible revenue from any existing source of traffic, consistent, of course, with its welfare and the securing of future business, and the checks imposed by competition and the laws of the various states.

The unwieldiness of the set-up is effectively proven by the shortness of its duration. Two years later almost to the day – on July 24, 1897, to be exact – the Birmingham Rolling Mill Company (to become a part of Republic Iron and Steel) produced their – and Alabama's first cast of steel, utilizing two small open-hearth furnaces, which had been constructed but a short time before. The experiment was pronounced a success and it was suggested that the Tennessee Coal, Iron and Railroad Company provide the money for enlarging the plant to a daily capacity of 500 tons, in order that the commercial production of such steel might be done in a practical manner. Shortly thereafter the Tennessee Company did subscribe $100,000 for such purpose (payable in pig iron) as did the Louisville & Nashville Railroad, an unusual feature of the former's subscription being that it was made with the express stipulation that that company itself would not engage in the manufacture of steel. However, the Birmingham Rolling Mill was to purchase all of its basic iron from the Tennessee Company.

Here the matter languished for more than a year with nothing being done and the Tennessee Coal, Iron and Railroad Company finally decided to build its own plant for the manufacture of open-hearth steel. The subscriptions previously mentioned were rescinded and the building of the T. C. I. & R. R.'s steel plant was assured by the action of the L. & N. and Southern Railroads, each of whom agreed to purchase T. C. I. & R. R. bonds in the amount of $250,000 to help finance the construction.

After the raising of the capital, the Alabama Steel and Ship Building Company, a subsidiary of the T. C. I. & R. R., was organized and on July 14, 1898, a site for the proposed plant was selected at Ensley, Ala. Once started, construction work pushed forward rapidly with the result that the mills were ready for operation by the latter part of 1899 and produced their first cast of steel on Thanksgiving Day (November 30) of that year. Originally, the plant consisted of ten open-hearth furnaces and a blooming mill, each of the furnaces having a daily capacity of 100 tons.

The rest of the story belongs properly to the saga of coal, iron and steel in Alabama, from which this episode has been lifted. Various beginnings and highlights have been touched upon in this account because of the importance to this railroad, as well as because of the part the L. & N. played in such development. Suffice to say, therefore, that after 1899 Alabama's mighty empire of metals never took a backward step and in the decades to come progressed to the very front rank of the world of iron and steel; an advance which was hindered to a certain extent by the lack of an adequate industrial water supply.

Of the many events which occurred during the 'nineties, which directly concerned the L. & N., other than the acquisition of existing lines, or the construction of new ones, and which have not been previously mentioned, there were three which had especial significance. These were, not in the order of their importance, but as they occurred chronologically: the passage of the Safety Appliance Act on March 2, 1893, the gradual change of the

Top: Ensley blast furnaces of the Tennessee Coal, Iron and Railroad Company, in 1900. Bottom: Ensley Steel Works of the Tennessee Coal, Iron and Railroad Company, in 1900; Alabama's first large-scale producer of steel.

L. & N.'s gauge from four feet, nine inches, to four feet, eight and one-half inches, during the years 1896-1900, inclusive, and the yellow fever epidemic of 1897, which lasted from August 23 of that year until about the middle of December.

The enactment of the Safety Appliance Act on March 2, 1893, meant that henceforth all American railroads had to utilize as standard equipment such devices as the air brake and the automatic coupler. Insofar as the L. & N. was concerned, a goodly portion of its rolling stock was already so equipped and the Act merely had the effect of somewhat hastening a process that had been going on as rapidly as conditions of finance and operation would permit. The railroads were given until January 1, 1898, for complete compliance but extensions were subsequently granted. At the end of this history of the L. & N. will be found a somewhat briefer but more statistical history of the L. & N.'s motive power and rolling stock, which will supplement whatever pertinent reference has been heretofore made and which attempts to describe their evolution and development down through the years, insofar as the facts are available. Such an outline, of course, is an integral part of any history of the L. & N., for the day coach, the freight car and the locomotive of yesteryear had little resemblance to their successors.

The further lessening of the L. & N.'s gauge from four feet, nine inches, to four feet, eight and one-half inches, did not take place with the dramatic suddenness of the previous change which had occurred on May 30, 1886. As a matter of fact, it happened so gradually that for a number of years after it had become an accomplished fact (in 1900) a great number of people who should have known better would have flunked on a question directed

This car hoist was in use at Louisville, Ky., for a number of years prior to the change of gauge on May 30, 1886, being utilized to hoist rolling stock in order that the trucks might be changed to conform to the different gauges. The above picture was taken some time in the 'Eighties. The engine is No. 45, rebuilt in 1880 from a 4-4-0 type into a 0-4-0. Note the four-rail track.

to ascertain the gauge of the L. & N. Railroad. Thus, on March 3, 1902, we find the National Railway Publication Company, publishers of the Official Guide, writing in to ask if the gauge of the L. & N. was four feet, nine inches, or four feet, eight and one-half inches.

There was, of course, some reason for this confusion in the public mind, and elsewhere, for the change had taken place over a period of about five years and was done whenever rails, etc., were renewed or whenever any other favorable opportunity to kill two birds with one stone presented itself. The history of this one-half inch retreat from status quo may be traced briefly as follows.

In October 1896, the Committee on Standard Wheel and Track Gauges of the American Railway Association canvassed the membership of that body for their reaction to its recommendation that four feet, eight and one-half inches be adopted as the standard track gauge for all American railroads. The L. & N. voted in favor of this recommendation, principally because it would increase the safety of travel by rail, and instructions were issued on November 25, 1896, to carry out the change in the manner previously described, the majority of the roads (195 out of 242) having also favored this standardization. No change in the road's equipment was necessitated by this slight narrowing of the track.

No exact date can be established as the one upon which the entire system first rejoiced in a standard gauge of four feet, eight and one-half inches, but it would seem to have occurred some time during the year 1900.

The yellow fever epidemic of 1897 differed chiefly from its predecessor of 1878 (there had also been an epidemic in 1888), at least insofar as the

L. & N. was concerned, in the extent of the territory affected. At the time of the epidemic in the summer of 1878, for instance, the L. & N. reached only as far south as Memphis and Montgomery and its Memphis Line had been hardest hit. By 1897, of course, its lines had been extended all the way to New Orleans, Mobile and Pensacola and the plague striking as it did with varying degrees of intensity at most of the states south of Kentucky and east of the Mississippi River, affected a much greater part of our mileage. Fortunately, this visitation of the fever was distinguished by the mildness of its character and the low mortality rate. Insofar as the L. & N. itself was concerned, only a few of its employes died from the disease (about a dozen in all) and only 250 or so were stricken.

In 1897, the idea still prevailed that the disease was contagious through the usual contacts of every day life, and some of the restrictions which were put into force seem ludicrous in the light of modern medical knowledge. The operation of the L. & N. was seriously inconvenienced by the various restrictions and quarantines which were in effect for varying lengths of time and it was forced to discontinue the operation of a number of trains. At the time it so happened that traffic was unusually heavy – another contrast to previous epidemics – on all divisions and this added to the road's difficulties.

Some of these quarantines were so rigid that trains from infected areas were forbidden to stop within the corporate limits of a town, sometimes a whole county, even for water, and all their doors and windows were required to be kept tightly closed as they passed through. The minimum speed limit was generally 20 miles an hour. At some points, employes of the Company, because of their presupposed contact with employes at other and infected points on the system, were kept to the right of way by shotgun quarantine.

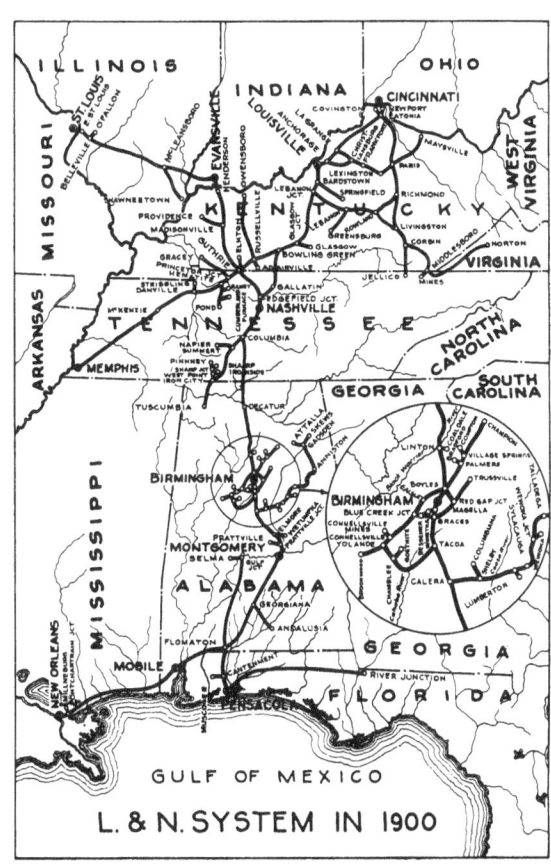

L. & N. SYSTEM IN 1900

The operation of local and refugee trains obviously offered the greatest problem. Most communities refused to accept refugees from the stricken areas and many of the fleeing unfortunates were forced to spend many days upon trains, traveling back and forth like so many shuttlecocks, until they somehow finally found sanctuary. Former Superintendent J. I. McKinney, of the old M. & M. Division, tells of one refugee train which was about ready to leave Montgomery (then infected) and which was loaded down with uprooted citizenry, who had, for the most part, arranged to be taken care of at various points along the line. At the last moment, word came that the governor had refused to grant permission for the train to stop at any point in the State of Alabama. Mr. McKinney disposes of the incident in these words: "When the train departed the quarantine officer was by some accident left behind and I have not since heard any complaint from passengers who failed to get off at local stations as they desired."

In order to carry on its business and at the same time comply with the various rulings, etc., of the different boards of health, the L. & N. was forced to establish relay stations located at some distance from towns which had established quarantines against other communities in order that crews from infected districts might not come in contact with the citizenry. There were, for example, 12 such relay stations between New Orleans and Birmingham and at each of these it was necessary to provide sleeping accommodations, food and shelter for the employes.

The requisite fumigating and disinfecting which for a time was extended impartially to passengers, freight, mail and baggage alike at certain selected points, also required additional time, effort and money.

Oddly enough, considering the chaotic conditions of the time, the L. & N.'s losses were surprisingly slight, it being estimated that the yellow fever epidemic caused a loss of revenue totaling only about $253,328.51. By the middle of December, the epidemic belonged to history and things rapidly began to revert to normal.

The Company was especially pleased with the attitude and loyalty of its employes during the crisis. Most of them stuck to their posts of duty, even though this frequently meant long periods of separation from their wives and families and the enduring of unaccustomed hardships. However, the trains kept moving, even though normal operation was greatly curtailed, and that was the main thing. Normal efficiency of operation was out of the question, but somehow food, supplies, and medicines were brought in; somehow the refugees were evacuated. It is indeed no exaggeration to say that the L. & N. Railroad, as ably represented by its officers and employes, by keeping its head during those troubled days, undoubtedly prevented the effects of the 1897 epidemic from being much worse than they were.

CHAPTER XIX

Consolidation Maneuvers

A RAILROAD map of the United States for 1890 presents a rather interesting spectacle. Much of the trackage that is being operated today was in existence at that time, at least insofar as the territory east of the Mississippi River is concerned, but the main difference lies in the fact that in 1890 this trackage was divided between many more railroads than it is now. In the 'nineties, the financial and physical condition of many of these lines was exceedingly poor and they barely managed to survive. New transportation giants were beginning to stir in the earth, however, and in the 1890s the trend toward consolidation of existing rail facilities became more intensified than it ever had before. This trend, once established, by not such far-fetched analogy, changed the railroad map into a gigantic chessboard, upon which moved majestically the kings and queens of the transportation world, with the short lines taking the part of pawns and other lesser light of the black-and-white arena. The Southern Railway itself was the result of the consolidation during the early 1880s of a number of comparatively small lines. Once it came into being, however, it forged ahead rapidly and since its lines served approximately the same territory as those of the L. & N., it soon established itself as the latter's principal rival. In order to protect its own interest, therefore, the L. & N. kept a wary and watchful eye on the remaining short line trackage for it was entirely possible (considering the success of the Southern) that portions of this might be welded together by a little additional construction thereby creating another major rival. Its officers and directors were then of the opinion that existing rail facilities were sufficient to care not only for contemporary traffic, but for any sizeable increase in the same that might reasonably be expected in the territory served by the L. & N. Their position, and it was a logical one, was that indiscriminate competition could only result in chaos and confusion, to the ultimate disadvantage not only of the railroad, but of the shipper and traveler as well. It should here be emphasized, however, that the L. & N. was always willing to aid in the construction of branch lines in its territory, or even to construct such lines itself, but it felt that this should only be done where there was a need for such construction.

Indicative of this willingness to build and let build let us quote from the testimony of William T. Underwood, a large coal operator of the day and a prominent figure in the history of coal and iron in Alabama, who has been previously mentioned in this account:

" . . . In the spring of 1900, I had secured control of a body of coal lands in Western Etowah and Blount counties (Alabama) and wanted to open mines. I wanted it badly, but my lands were many miles from a railroad, and I was not able to command one-third of the money needed. I preferred opening mines on that side of my property nearest to the Alabama Great Southern Railroad and took the matter up with the Southern officials, but got no encouragement. I then went to Mr. Milton H. Smith and found no difficulty in arousing his interest in it. I remember his saying to me: 'If you have the quality and quantity of coal you think you have, I will build you a road.' I then explained that I could not raise more than one-third of the money needed for opening and operating the mines and I asked him if he could aid me with that. He said that he did not know but would see. He did not keep me waiting, but acted immediately. He made me haul 30 wagonloads of coal 12 miles for test purposes. He sent experts and proved the correctness of my statement as to quantity. He then arranged with a Louisville bank to loan my company many thousands of dollars, which we were allowed to pay off from our earnings. He began building 12 miles of road for us in May, 1900, and the following October we were shipping coal over it. I started this business with but a few thousand dollars of my own and within four years' time had paid about $80,000 for the land, paid off the banks, and sold the property for a very large sum, most of which money came from outside of the State and remains invested in Alabama. The country through which he built the road and its extension on to Attalla, had been almost a wilderness. The population there has now increased ten times or more (this was written in 1910) and that city is prosperous.

"Other railroads had been asked to do this, but they did not. Had it not been for Mr. Smith's desire to extend the sphere of usefulness of his road, his comprehensive understanding of business men and their needs, as well as of railroads, and his personal inclination to help men with good propositions, that section of Blount and Etowah counties would still be asleep. Today and for fifty years to come, its mines can give a living to many thousands of people . . . The prosperity of the people of the Alabama mineral district is very largely due to the liberal policy of M. H. Smith."

At the proper chronological point a more detailed mention will be made of the L. & N.'s penetration of Etowah and Blount counties, via Altoona and Attalla. It is mentioned at this time as an excellent example of the L. & N.'s willingness to help where help was needed. But, in a frame of mind similar to that of a newsboy who defends his "corner," it didn't see the need, figuratively speaking, of a rival perched on each of the four corners and out in the middle of the street as well.

In latter years, the Interstate Commerce Commission, then largely dormant, has realized the dangers inherent in a laissez faire attitude towards indiscriminate construction and consolidation and has refused to sanction these where they result in a duplication of existing facilities. But at the time under discussion, the L. & N. under the leadership of Milton H. Smith, was forced to be the sole watch-dog of its own interests.

In this connection the files contain an interesting and – at this distance – enlightening account of a conference which was held between Milton H. Smith and Samuel Spencer, president of the Southern Railway Company, at Kennesaw, Ga., Sunday, October 28, 1894. Prior to that meet-

In January 1901, the L. & N. completed its line from Champion to Altoona, Ala., and its station at the latter point (shown here in the background) was the town's most imposing structure for some time. The above picture was taken in May 1902, and shows some of the town's beaux and belles in those "horse-and-buggy" days on their way to a big footwashing ceremony which was scheduled to take place at Flagpond on nearby Sand Mountain. From left to right those in the picture are as follows: David H. Crump, Underwood Coal Company; Miss Nan Lee; a Mr. McIntire, also with the Underwood Coal Company; Miss Jennie Crump; John Cole; Miss Annie Cole; Henry Meacham, the L. & N.'s agent at Altoona at the time, and a Miss Cornelius.

ing, the L. & N. had attempted to purchase the interests of C. P. Huntington in the Chesapeake, Ohio and Southwestern Railroad Company (to become a part of the Illinois Central) and in certain other properties. The Commonwealth of Kentucky brought suit against the L. & N. to prevent such purchase and this was eventually decided in the Commonwealth's favor, since the lines involved parallel trackage already owned by the L. & N., this being forbidden by State law. Negotiations for the purchase of the South Carolina Railway had also fallen through, but the L. & N. was shortly to acquire (on September 9, 1896) for its sister road (the N. C. & St. L. Railway) the Paducah, Tennessee and Alabama Railroad, extending from Paducah, Ky., to Lexington, Tenn., a distance of 118.6 miles, and the Tennessee Midland Railway, extending from Memphis to Perryville, Tenn., a distance of 135.6 miles.

These corporate maneuvers are mentioned at this time merely to supply a bit of background for the meeting about to be described. Both Mr. Smith and Mr. Spencer believed such a conference to the mutual advantage of their respective roads, but both of these gentlemen, in poker parlance, "played them close to their chests," and it is doubtful if either emerged from the meeting a great deal wiser than he was before. The primary purpose of this meeting was to ascertain the intentions of the L. & N. and the Southern with regard to the acquisition of certain small railroads, located for the most part in the territory south of the Ohio and east of the Mississippi rivers.

Both the L. & N. and the Southern were anxious to consolidate and strengthen their positions by acquiring lines which might be of value to them, either directly because of their traffic, or indirectly because such acquisition would keep them from falling into the wrong hands. A conference of the sort mentioned, therefore, by clarifying aims and intentions, might, among other things, prevent ruinous competitive bidding for such properties.

A stenographic transcript was made of this meeting and in the light of what later happened, portions of it are rather amusing. Both Mr. Smith and Mr. Spencer seemed determined to outdo each other in disclaiming any interest in certain lines.

"Miserable abortions," said Mr. Smith of several of these railroads.

"Decline to have anything to do with them," stated Mr. Spencer.

Of another railroad, Mr. Smith inquired: "What is going to become of it? Let it eke out a miserable existence?"

Mr. Spencer stated of yet another line: "We do not want it, unless you want to give it away with an endowment fund added, sufficient to take care of it for life."

The corporate ears of "Railroad X" must have indeed burned on the date of the meeting for it was the subject of some of the uncomplimentary remarks before mentioned. However, less than one year later this changeling was embraced within the Southern fold and remains there to this day.

As a result of what happened immediately after this conference, Mr. Smith recommended to August Belmont, then chairman of the board of directors, immediate and vigorous action with regard to certain short line trackage in Tennessee, Alabama and Georgia. These recommendations were never fully acted upon except in the cases of the Paducah, Tennessee and Alabama Railroad and the Tennessee Midland Railway, before noted, other factors entering upon the scene and rendering such acquisitions impractical.

In the 1890s, too, the railroads were unwillingly being established as dragons with which hordes of political St. Georges could gleefully joust; particularly around election time. This is not to say that there were not abuses of the public confidence by the railroads, but the tragedy was that the many suffered for the sins of the few. It is also true that a lack of adequate competition from other forms of transportation tended to make certain roads arrogant and caused them to assume, either consciously or unconsciously, a "take-it-or-leave-it" attitude. Perhaps the chief accusation that could be leveled at most railroads was that their struggle for survival was not always marked by that strict adherence to etiquette which is possible at a polite social gathering, but hardly so in a combat in which your opponent is doing his best to gouge out your eyes.

Death removed from the contemporary scene in the 1890s, within less than two years of each other, two men who deserve a large share of the credit for the L. & N.'s rapid growth and development. The first of its targets was Judge Russell Houston, chief attorney, who died in October, 1895, after a continuous association with the L. & N. which dated from October 6, 1862. Previous mention has been made of Judge Houston and his service with the Company, which included a brief term as president, and perhaps his best epitaph may be found in the words of the Annual Report which notes his passing and which states that

A happy family gathering at Bakers Hill, Tenn., on the Evansville Division, some time in 1903. The gentlemen are members of a bridges and building gang and the ladies are the nieces and sister of the foreman.

" . . . a record of his service would almost be a history of the corporation in itself."

Judge Houston was a great storyteller and one of his favorites was the one entitled, "No sooner down than skinned." As he told it, parable fashion, on occasion to prove a point, it went about as follows:

"A horse was killed by a freight train on our tracks one day, and its owner, being a thrifty farmer and thinking about all he could get out of him was his hide, had him skinned and left his carcass lying in the road. The night following it was dark and stormy as a man on horseback, almost feeling his way through the storm and guided by the flashes of lightning, arrived at this very spot, just as there came a flash of lightning, followed by a terrific clap of thunder. His horse, in terror, jumped from under him and he fell, straddling the carcass that had been left lying in the road. Feeling in the darkness for his mount, as he rubbed his hands over the carcass, he exclaimed: 'Jerusalem! That sure was quick work. He was no sooner down than skinned.' "

Judge Houston's death was followed by that of Albert Fink on April 3, 1897. That mighty titan of a man had resumed his connection with the L. & N. as a director in 1893, after a lapse of some 18 years. Mr. Fink was not connected with the L. & N. at the time of his death, however, but he always took an extremely keen interest in its fortunes and numbered his friends upon that road by the hundreds.

These two men, along with James Guthrie, Milton H. Smith and several others, were or had been the personification of the railroad and their passing saddened many. Luckily for the L. & N. both of these men, and others, had made almost a fetish of training younger men for responsible positions and there were a host of younger executives in the employ of the L. & N. in the 'nineties who were destined also to make their marks. There was Walker D. Hines, then one of the Company's young attorneys (made assistant chief attorney in 1898), who was later to become first vice-president on October 2, 1901. After leaving the L. & N. in 1904, he practiced law for a short while and in 1906 returned to the railroad field, eventually becoming chairman of the board of the Atchison, Topeka & Santa Fe Railroad. He was made assistant director general and then director general of all American railroads during the World War period of federal control. (He died on January 14, 1934, at Merano, Italy, after further brilliant successes.) There were many others like George E. Evans, who was executive vice-president at the time of his death on January 7, 1931, who had started in at the bottom of the ladder and who were just then reaching their peaks as first-rate railroaders.

Trio of Engineers

The engineers who piloted the Dixie Hummer on its record run. At the top is J. W. Rowe, L. & N.; center, F. N. Baker, E. & T. H.; and bottom, E. L. Wood, C. & E. I.

In addition to those then with the L. & N. there were others like J. T. Harahan, who had been general manager for a number of years, but who had left the service in the latter part of the 'eighties, and who later became president of the Illinois Central Railroad.

There were other men, in addition to those specifically mentioned, who were achieving brilliant successes in their chosen fields of law, finance, operation, engineering, traffic, etc., within the railroad fold, and from time to time, as the spotlight focuses upon the fruits of their endeavors, mention will be made of them. An account of this sort is more concerned with results naturally than with personalities, although it is readily conceded that "an institution is the lengthened shadow of a man."

Mention has previously been made of the opening of the Henderson Bridge in 1885 and of the great boon which this was to travel and commerce. Such construction reduced the time for passenger trains between Chicago and Nashville, for instance, to 16 hours, which was all very wonderful. It is approximately 444 miles from one city to the other and a 16-hour schedule for those times was not at all bad, representing as it did an average of nearly 25 miles an hour. By 1898, this time had been further reduced to about 13½ hours. Still greater miracles were yet to occur, however. On April 28, 1898, a train made the 444-mile jaunt in the startling time of 524 minutes; four hours and 51 minutes less than schedule time. Truth to tell, however, this was a tour de force and had required a great deal of careful planning. Since the L. & N. and its employes figured prominently in this bout with Father Time, a few details might not be amiss.

In 1898, therefore, the State of Tennessee was celebrating its 100 years of Statehood with the Tennessee Centennial Exposition at Nashville, Tenn. The year 1896 really marked the 100th anniversary of Tennessee's entrance into these United States, but like so many honeymoons with the past, this one, aided and abetted by the cash customers, had been repeated in 1897 and 1898. The old Chicago Times-Herald, ever alert to enhance its prestige, conceived the idea of printing a special Tennessee Centennial edition of its paper and of having it transported to Nashville in the fastest manner possible. The vehicle chosen for this scheme was a train to be operated over the lines of the Chicago & Eastern Illinois, the Evansville & Terre Haute (now a part of the C. & E. I.) and the Louisville & Nashville. This train was promptly dubbed "The Dixie Hummer" by the newspaper's staff and it subsequently certainly lived up to its name. The railroads cooperated by eliminating all stops save those absolutely necessary for taking water, changing engines, etc., and by giving the engineers carte blanche to do their darndest.

The results, as previously indicated, were rather surprising. Laden down with its commemorative 24-page edition of 200,000 copies (small bundles of which were tossed off at the various stations along the route) and with only a few selected railroad officials and members of the newspaper's organization, including a number of leather-lunged Chicago newsboys, aboard the three-car train (two baggage coaches and a private car) rolled out of the Dearborn Street Station in Chicago at 4:00 a.m., on April 28, 1898. The run to Terre Haute, Ind., 178 miles away, as the Iron Horse gallops, was made in 183 minutes. From that town to Evansville, 110 miles away, the going was somewhat slower due to recent washouts which had weakened the roadbed; still only 138 minutes had elapsed when the "Hummer" snorted into Evansville. At that point the L. & N. took over and we relinquish the descriptive reins to the anonymous scribe of a pamphlet which commemorates the train's feat. Said he:

"Evansville was reached at 9:23 and at 9:26 Colonel E. H. Mann, superintendent of the division, signaled 'Billy' Rowe, the Adonis of the Louisville & Nashville, to give engine No. 33 her head. In the full glory of a southern spring morning the train rolled over the long trestle, over the muddy Ohio and into old Kentucky.

RAIL RECORDS BROKEN.

Times-Herald Train Makes Unequaled Time to Nashville.

ALMOST A MILE A MINUTE

Fastest Long Distance Run in the History of Railways.

PAPER ON SALE AT 1 O'CLOCK.

Special Exposition Edition Distributed in Tennessee Nine Hours After Being Printed.

Facsimile of the heading of the story of the Dixie Hummer's record run carried in the Chicago Times-Herald of April 29, 1898.

"Colonel Mann is a large portly man with gray mustache and a little gray tuft on his lower lip. He is quiet of manner, scant of speech, and very reluctant to commit himself. One of the party asked him what time the special would get to Nashville. The Colonel allowed he would be in about 1:30 p.m., the scheduled time.

"The train came over Baker's Hill – thirty-four miles from Nashville – fifteen minutes ahead of time. The grade on Baker's Hill is 273 feet to the mile. The curves are awful. Billy Rowe then turned No. 33 loose and the 'Dixie Hummer' landed in Nashville at 12:44 – forty-six minutes ahead of its schedule and three hours ahead of the fastest run ever before made from Chicago to Nashville." (Incidentally, the train's record run caught Nashville napping and when the "Hummer" steamed in the committee of welcome and the citizens in general were still at their dinner tables.)

In addition to those previously mentioned, other acquisitions by the L. & N. before the turn of the century included the Montgomery & Prattville Railroad, 10.36 miles in length, which extended from Prattville Junction to Prattville, near Montgomery (completed October 28, 1895; acquired by the L. & N. June 13, 1896, and now abandoned) and the Shelby Cut-Off, approximately eight and one-half miles in length, which extended from Shelbyville to Christiansburg, Ky. This latter trackage had loomed as a desirable possibility for a number of years, creating as it did, in effect, double trackage between Anchorage and Christiansburg, but nothing was ever done until July 17, 1895, when the L. & N. started construction, it having acquired the lease of the Shelby Railroad, owner of the right-of-way, etc., when it purchased the old L. C. & L. in 1881. This was completed April 1, 1896, and shortened the distance between Lexington and Louisville by about 10 miles. Just prior to that date, the L. & N. and the Chesapeake & Ohio Railway and its associate road, the Elizabethtown, Lexington & Big Sandy Railroad (jocularly known as the "Eat Little and Be Satisfied") had entered into a contract which gave the latter roads the right to operate over L. & N. tracks between Lexington and Louisville, via Shelbyville, when the cutoff should have been completed. This contract which became effective April 1, 1896, runs for 100 years.

Most American railroads, at one time or another, have found themselves burdened with facetious nomenclature which generally corresponded to the initials of their corporate name. Thus, as previously mentioned, the E. L. & B. S. Railroad became the "Eat Little and Be Satisfied" ('tis said because of the parsimonious habits of one of its construction engineers in boarding his men) and the L. & N. itself, in addition to its dignified and appropriate soubriquet of "The Old Reliable" has been variously dubbed the "Late & Never Running Regular" and the "Long and Nasty."

A number of other important steps were taken during the decade under discussion. Some of these were rather metaphysical in nature and in this category might be placed the L. & N.'s lease of the Nashville & Decatur Railroad for 999 years, effective as of July 1, 1900 an act which comes as close to outright ownership as is legally permissible in the case of the N.&D.

The L. & N. also at this time (February 28, 1898) became sole lessee of the Georgia Railroad, and dependencies, after being a joint lessee with the Central of Georgia Railway for a number of years.

Chapter XX

Nashville's New Union Station

THE situation at both the Nashville and St. Louis terminals had been unsatisfactory for some time and steps were taken in the late 'nineties to remedy these matters. It was decided, in the case of St. Louis, to provide the needed facilities on the east side of the Mississippi River, at East St. Louis, Ill., and accordingly during the period 1896-1898, well over $200,000 was spent at that point for real estate, coal yard tracks, switching facilities, a freight depot, etc. In connection with this expansion at East St. Louis, the Baltimore & Ohio Southwestern Railway granted the L. & N. permission to use certain of its tracks at that point.

To further the prosecution of the work at Nashville, which it had been decided should be undertaken jointly with the N. C. & St. L. Railway, the L. & N. and that road formed the Louisville and Nashville Terminal Company, which was incorporated on March 22, 1893. The latter leased to the L. & N. and the N. C. & St. L. for a certain rental to be paid by the two roads in an appropriate proportionate manner, its properties in Nashville, including real estate, tracks, passenger and freight depots, etc., a portion of which had formerly, or before the formation of the Terminal Company, belonged to one or the other of the railroads. (It was the Terminal Company, however, which proceeded with the completion of the construction of the many items involved in the Terminal project.) This agreement, or lease, became effective July 1, 1896, and was originally binding for 999 years. Supplementary contracts of August 15, 1900, re-fixed the rental, the manner in which it should be allocated between the two roads and stated that the leased property should be known as the "Nashville Terminals." Many items, as implied, were involved in the providing of improved facilities at Nashville, Tenn., but perhaps the one of chief interest in an account of this nature, was the construction of a handsome union station there which was completed on September 3, 1900.

It had been realized for some time that Nashville needed a new union passenger station, but prior to June 1898, the city of Nashville and the L. & N. and the N. C. & St. L., could never get together on this important matter. The railroads were forced to seek concessions from the city in the carrying out of the many details involved in their Nashville Terminal project, such as the closing of certain streets, and the obtaining of rights-of-way, and they felt that some of the city's terms were rather onerous.

In addition, there were panics, strikes, epidemics, floods and other misfortunes which emptied the treasury and rendered it impossible for the roads to embark upon an undertaking of such magnitude. It was estimated that the building of additional freight depots, the Kayne Avenue freight train yards, a new union passenger station, viaducts, additional trackage and round-

L. & N. Engine No. 35 was typical of those engines used in work train service on the Alabama & Florida Railroad shortly after that road was completed by the L. & N. on July 16, 1902.

houses, as well as the re-arrangement of other facilities would cost in the neighborhood of $1,700,000.

The inadequateness of the passenger station facilities at Nashville at that time had been the result of a peculiar set of circumstances. The station which was then being used by both the L. & N. and the N. C. & St. L. had been originally built by the old Nashville and Chattanooga Railroad (the predecessor of the N. C. & St. L.) in the 1850s for its sole use. It was, of course, arranged for a very limited traffic. The L. & N. built a slightly larger station in the city soon afterwards and at one time there were no less than six passenger depots in Nashville and its environs. Shortly after its acquisition of a through line to Montgomery in 1872, the L. & N. made arrangements to stop its trains not only at its own station at College and Market streets, but at the N. & C. depot, as well. This latter arrangement continued until 1886, when the L. & N. station was destroyed by fire. This station was not re-built, a more suitable location being sought, and it was decided to make temporary use of the old N. & C. station, which by now was sole survivor still in use of the six stations previously mentioned.

In the meantime, of course, Nashville had grown and the old N. & C. station was woefully inadequate for the passenger business handled by the N. C. & St. L. alone. Nevertheless, it manfully managed to make room for its fellow public servant, thus establishing an irksome condition which even the most pessimistic did not think would last for over a few months, but which did last in fact until September 3, 1900, when the new Union Station was dedicated.

A portion of the press of the day did not think much of the new arrangement from the start and Nashville's station was one of their most popular topics of vitriolic comment. The matter of providing Nashville with an appropriate union station was a hardy perennial and the withering blasts of failure did not succeed in killing the hope that springs eternal. Mass meetings were held, letters were written to the papers and many a heated conference took place, but Nashville's historic train hostelry weathered all storms. It was a mighty stubborn grain of sand in the civic consciousness of the city and it took a long time to turn it into the cherished pearl of a handsome union station.

Thus, on one occasion in 1893, when it appeared as if the matter might be approaching fruition, Milton H. Smith returned a copy of the proposed revised version of the bill or ordinance, covering the many phases of the Terminal project, with this notation: ". . . The Bill which the Committee (of the city of Nashville) proposes to recommend for passage differs so radically from the one submitted by you (the L. & N.'s representative) that were I to comply with Mr. Kuhn's request to suggest amendments, I should propose to amend by substituting the original bill."

Again, in June 1896, it appeared as if the dream were about to blossom forth in all the gorgeous hues of reality. The city council of Nashville passed the Terminal Bill on the 25th of that month by a vote of 11 to 9, leaving in one or two slightly contentious clauses, apparently with the thought that they would be swept by the railroads on the broad flood-tide of popular approval. But such aggressive optimism was destined to encounter disappointment. The Bill, as passed, was not acceptable to the railroads (the maintenance of the viaducts over Broad and Church streets being bones of contention) and, moreover, the mayor of the city vetoed it. There the matter languished until the early part of 1898. At that time, the matter was re-opened and a Terminal Bill that was acceptable to both the city and the railroads was finally passed by the city council in June of the same year.

Much of the credit for the success of these negotiations belonged to Major E. C. Lewis, a prominent citizen of Nashville. Major Lewis for many years was manager of the Sycamore Powder Mills, of that city, and was also director general of the Tennessee Centennial Exposition (1896-1898). He had long taken an active interest in obtaining a new union station for Nashville and upon the resignation of Milton H. Smith from the presidency

Trials and tribulations of a railroad. In June 1903, East St. Louis, Ill., had one of the worst floods in its history and the above picture shows our freight house as it appeared on June 12, of that year, as a pertinacious driver decided to deliver some freight, flood or no flood. The river reached a stage of thirty-nine feet, six inches.

Left: Laying the foundations for the Nashville Union Station some time in the early part of 1889. Right: In August 1899, this is how the new station and viaduct looked from a point on old Broad Street, looking east.

of the Louisville & Nashville Terminal Company in the early part of 1898, he had succeeded him. It was under his leadership that an acceptable bill was finally passed and that the Nashville Terminals were built.

As a leading citizen of Nashville and as president of the Terminal Company and one of its defenders prior to his ascension to the presidency, Major Lewis was frequently between the gentleman with the pitchfork and the deep blue sea. The following from the Nashville Daily Sun of January 7, 1896, is typical:

". . . The union depot will require '200 men two years to complete it,' according to Mr. Lewis (Major E. C. Lewis). That is too dazzling for our untrained imagination. The suggestion that it will take 200 years to get two men started to work on the union depot would strike us as more probable . . . Wait until after the Centennial, says Mr. Lewis. Until after which Centennial, that of 1896, or that of 1996?" etc.

As stated before, Nashville's new union station was thrown open to the public, on September 3, 1900. This was a gala occasion and the celebration was appropriate. Thousands were on hand.

The Nashville American in its issue of September 3, 1900, under large headlines which read: "New Terminal Station is a Gem of Beauty. Its Exterior Has Been The Pride of the City and the Interior Decorations Will Be a Revelation," made this comment and gave its readers a last minute preview: ". . . The entire building is Romanesque in architecture, this idea being carried out even to the most minute detail. The main building is 150 feet square and constructed of Bowling Green stone and high grade Tennessee marble. The height of the structure is 219 feet, including the towers, while the bronze statue of Mercury, the souvenir relic from the Commerce Building of the Tennessee Centennial Exposition, adds an additional twenty feet. . . The main waiting room is finished in light-oak and Tennessee marble, while the decorations are elaborate. These decorations, it can be truly said, are second to none in the country and have been greatly admired by those who have had occasion to visit the building. The hall is a spacious floor, covering an area of about 67x125 feet, three stories in height, with a skylight of prismatic glass with trimmings of light and yellow green tint, covering the entire room. At each end of the room is a massive fancy fire-place of marble and stone. . .The first floor is of a deep olive green and rich with gold leaf. On each of the east and west sides are five arches in fresco work, over each of which stands in bas-relief two heroic-sized women. These recline over the arches holding the natural products of the Volunteer State, including tobacco, corn, wheat, cotton, mineral and other resources. The figures are done in life tints and are very beautiful, being of the Romanesque type. (Evidently, an example of carrying out the Romanesque 'to the minutest detail,' as previously mentioned.)

"Just over the clock in the south end can be seen in bas-relief figures of two young ladies, representing the Nashville and Louisville girls. These figures face one another, with outstretched hand, denoting welcome and ties of friendship. Over the north clock are a couple of figures, also in bas-relief, representing Time and Progress. These are very striking and highly tinted."

Then, when the dedication was an accomplished fact, the American enthused thusly in its issue of September 4, 1900: ". . .The handsome new union passenger station was used for arrival and departure of trains for the first time yesterday afternoon. All day yesterday a steady stream of people could be seen on Broad Street, wending their way to and from the station, and nothing save words of praise was heard. The handsome depot won the admiration of everyone who entered it.

"During the afternoon a representative of the American was standing at the elaborately decorated general waiting-room when a trio of commer-

Left: This is how Nashville's Union Station (left) and the old and new Broad Street viaducts looked in August 1899. The new viaduct is the one on the left. Right: Looking south from the west side of the Nashville Union Station on Broad Street. The station is on the left and to the right is the location where the middle yard and south yard and old Kayne Avenue roundhouse facilities were later constructed.

The Nashville Union Station as it appeared in 1900 after completion.

cial travelers (i. e. traveling salesmen) came along. 'Well,' said one of them, 'this is the prettiest depot I have ever seen. There is nothing finer in the United States and I have been very nearly all over Uncle Sam's country. You will go to larger cities and you will find depots on a larger scale, but you will not see one that is prettier, or, in my opinion, as conveniently arranged in appointments.' This seemed to be the verdict of the public.

"The last train out of the old passenger station was the regular L. & N. train No. 6, which left shortly after noon yesterday for Louisville. . . . At 3:35 p.m. yesterday (September 3) the first regular passenger train reached the new station rolling in under the big shed. It was the accommodation train (L. & N.) from Gallatin. Long before the arrival of this train, the Chattanooga train No. 5, (N. C. & St. L.) which leaves Nashville at 3:30 p.m., had backed into the shed and taken its place on one of the ten tracks. This train, the first to leave, pulled out on time and without ceremony.

"The rails in the new station are all set below the platform and this innovation will prove one of the greatest advantages of the new service. Heretofore, as in nearly every passenger station in the country, the tracks have been on a level with the platform of the depot, and the result has been that a passenger has had to mount a high step to reach the platform of the coach. Now, the first step is almost on a level with the depot platforms."

On December 11, 1899, the L. & N. purchased the Southern Alabama Railroad Company, which it had previously formed for the purpose of completing the 46.36-mile gap between Pineapple and Repton, Ala., which had been languishing around under the heading of unfinished business for a number of years. This gap was closed on January 1, 1900, giving the L. & N. a 109.29-mile stretch of track between Selma and Flomaton.

Another ambitious construction project undertaken by the L. & N. in the waning days of the past century was the building of a line from Georgiana, Ala., on the main line, southeastward to Graceville, Fla., approximately 100 miles away. This chore had originally been undertaken by the Alabama & Florida Railroad but on January 20, 1899, that road leased its completed line (Georgiana to River Falls; 28 miles) to the L. & N., and a subsequent deed dated December 17, 1900, conveyed to the latter its entire line of road, either actual or proposed, between Georgiana and Graceville. The L. & N. advanced the steel through the pine woods slowly but surely, the railroad reaching Andalusia on December 1, 1899; Geneva on March 1, 1901, and Graceville on July 16, 1902. From Duvall, Ala., on the A. & F., it was decided to drop a line to Florala, near the Alabama-Florida state line, some 22 miles away, where connection could be made with the Yellow River Railroad, which extended from Crestview, Fla., on the L. & N.'s Pensacola & Atlantic Railroad to that point, a distance of 26½ miles. The Yellow River Railroad had started out in life as strictly a logging pike, but shortly after its completion in 1894, it had commenced to handle passengers and freight in the regular manner. Following the completion of the L. & N.'s line to a connection with the Yellow River Railroad, near Florala, on July 1, 1903, the L. & N. subsequently incorporated the Yellow River Railroad into its system on July 1, 1906, it having previously acquired all issues of stocks and bonds in November 1902.

In July 1899, the L. & N. and the Southern Railway became joint purchasers of the Birmingham Southern Railway, which was a subsidiary

The Church Street depot of the N. C. & St. L. which was used both by the L. & N. and that road prior to the completion of the new station.

The bas-relief figures over the clock at the north end of the Nashville Union Station which represent Time and Progress.

of rapidly-growing Tennessee Coal, Iron and Railroad Company. This property consisted of some 28 miles of track in and around Birmingham and in 1907 reverted to the T. C. I. & R. R. with the exception of the 8-mile stretch between Woodstock and Blocton.

Mention has previously been made of the more outstanding developments within the Birmingham District and at the end of the decade terminating with 1895, the L. & N. could look with satisfaction upon the fact that in that time it had spent approximately $15 million for the construction and equipment of branch roads which had been primarily projected to serve iron and coal in the Birmingham district.

As of June 30, 1894, there were 54 iron furnaces in operation upon the lines of the L. & N., 25 of which were in the Birmingham District. It was estimated that these latter had a total annual capacity, or output, of nearly 1,000,000 tons. The total estimated capacity of the various coal mines considered within the orbit of the Birmingham Mineral Division was 2,625,000 tons per year.

Because of the panic of 1893, the yellow fever epidemic and other misfortunes, of 1897, the L. & N. was unable to comply with the provisions of the Safety Appliance Act within the time limit prescribed, which had set the date of January 1, 1898, for complete compliance. It was thus forced to apply on two occasions for the deadline upon which all of its rolling stock had to be equipped with with automatic couplers and power brakes.

It was, in fact, some time during the fiscal year ending with June 30, 1914, before **all** of the L. & N.'s rolling stock was equipped with both air brakes and automatic couplers. However, as early as 1902, automatic couplers had been applied to all of its equipment and only a few freight cars of obsolete make, and not used in interstate service, lingered on for several years, minus air brakes, to prevent complete unanimity within the ranks of the rolling stock.

It cost the L. & N. more than a million dollars to thus improve the safety of travel by rail and since such a development was also being paralleled on a hundred other roads its final consummation signalized the passing of a colorful figure, the old-time brakeman. Color, however, is frequently achieved at the expense of life and limb and this picturesque character, as often as not, was minus a finger or two and many a stump-legged crossing watchman, or other "grounded" employe, had seen more active days as a brakeman. It was the brakeman, who, when the signal came for "brakes!" clambored to the top of a swaying boxcar and scampered over the train, setting brakes, no matter how icy or uncertain the footing, or how rapid the momentum. It was the brakeman and his less itinerant fellow-workman, the switchman, who coupled trains together in the old days by link-and-pin, a device that was simplicity itself, but one that was singularly treacherous. Some of the more conservative elements of railroad management had objected to the application of the automatic couplers, it being thought that they were not trustworthy and it is a fact that several wrecks could be attributed to their failure to function properly. But this was just after they had first made their bow and all the kinks had not as yet been ironed out. Time was to prove that the air brake and the automatic coupler were two of the most important advances ever made by the railroads, for they not only made travel by rail more safe, but additionally rendered it more efficient, making it possible for heavier loads to be handled in less time.

    The invention and application of the automatic coupler and the air brake thus expedited a trend towards more efficient railroad operation which had established itself when the first steel had been placed in the L. & N.'s track in 1871 and when the first coal-burning locomotive had made its bow at about the same time. A detailed description of this evolution is found in the appendices.

Chapter XXI

Southward – to Georgia

PERHAPS one of the most important steps which the L. & N. took at this time was its creation of its present-day Cincinnati-Atlanta line.

It may be said that one of the main north-and-south "highways" of Middle-America is the route which starts at Chicago and passes through Cincinnati, Lexington, Knoxville and Atlanta, to branch off at the last named to ultimately reach such South Atlantic and Gulf Coast ports as Charleston, Savannah, Jacksonville, St. Petersburg, Tampa, etc. At the beginning of the 20th Century, the L. & N. was an integral part of such a route, operating between Cincinnati, O., and Jellico, Tenn., where connection was made with the Southern Railway. This arrangement was not entirely satisfactory, however, and on March 10, 1902, the L. & N. took the first of several steps which was ultimately to result in its obtaining a line of its own between Cincinnati, O., and Atlanta, Ga., a distance of 489 miles. At that time it purchased a majority of the capital stock of the old Atlanta, Knoxville & Northern Railway.

This obtaining of the control of the A. K. & N. was closely linked with the formation of the Knoxville, LaFollette and Jellico Railroad Company, under L. & N. auspices, on April 3, 1902, for the purpose of building a railroad from a point at or near Knoxville, Tenn., to a point at or near Jellico, Tenn., a distance of about 75 miles.

The Atlanta, Knoxville and Northern Railway which, as such, came into existence on June 3, 1896, was an amalgamation of a number of predecessor lines.

In the beginning there was the Ellijay Railroad, which was incorporated on February 9, 1854. Its name was subsequently changed to the Marietta, Canton and Ellijay Railroad Company and still later to the Marietta and North Georgia Railroad. By 1887, the latter had finally gotten around to constructing 96 miles of track between Marietta, Ga., and the Georgia-North Carolina state line. No construction at all was commenced until the year 1874 and the building of the long-deferred line seems to have received its initial impetus from the immense deposits of marble which were located all along the " old line" between Blue Ridge and Marietta, Ga. These marble deposits were among the largest and finest in the world.

At the time it was constructed the Marietta and North Georgia was a narrow-gauge pike (a third rail was added in 1886, making it standard gauge) and much of it was constructed by convict labor. Because of the mountainous country encountered, its building involved considerable expense, despite the convict labor and the fact that as had been the case with the old S. & N. A., its builders avoided the necessity of expensive cuts and tunneling by giving the line many a voluptuous curve and many a steep grade. It is said that on one occasion the blasting powder ran out, but the foreman in charge, nothing daunted, had huge fires built around the large rock ledges which barred further progress. Then, when these stony outcroppings of nature had been suitably heated, he cracked them by chilling them with quantities of cold water.

The Marietta and North Georgia's "jumping off" place was subsequently moved northward from the Georgia-North Carolina state line to Murphy, N.C., some 13 miles away, shortly thereafter. Then, in 1889, the Marietta and North Georgia Railway (re-organization having changed the "Railroad" to "Railway") was given permission to extend its line southward to Atlanta and northward to Knoxville. The Marietta and North Georgia Railway never got around to either of these chores and the Knoxville Southern Railroad, which in the meantime had been incorporated on June 23, 1887, finally filled in the gap by building a line of road from Knoxville to a connection with the Marietta and North Georgia at the Georgia-Tennessee state line, 107 miles away. This line was more or less completed by July 1890, the Marietta and North Georgia contributing some 13 miles of track between Blue Ridge, Ga., and Copperhill, Tenn., to make possible the connection. Shortly thereafter, or on November 25, 1890, the two roads were consolidated, the new set-up being known as the Marietta and North Georgia Railway.

Copperhill was then known as McCays and the copper ore deposits in the surrounding Great Copper Basin of Tennessee were at this time greatly in need of a better outlet to the outside world. Prior to the building of the Knoxville Southern, the copper was placed in primitive conveyances, powered by oxen, and hauled many miles over rough mountain trails, to the nearest railroad. Incidentally, this Great Copper Basin of

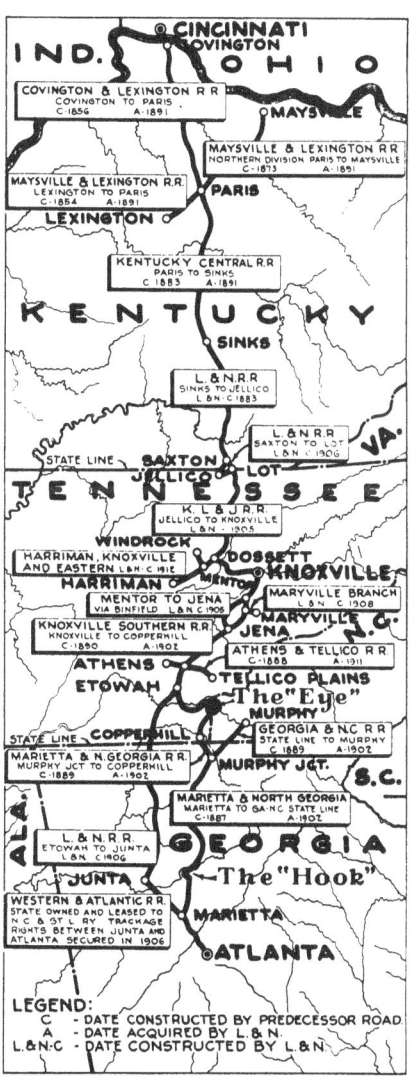

Map showing how the L. & N.'s Cincinnati-Atlanta line came into being. The construction dates shown refer to the year in which the trackage was completed; the acquisition dates refer to the year in which the L. & N. first secured control. The bridge across the Ohio River was built by the Covington and Cincinnati Elevated Railroad and Transfer and Bridge Company.

Tennessee was assuredly one of the world's most unique localities. At the time of the building of the Knoxville Southern, the Tennessee Copper Company had not as yet entered upon the scene and the mining and smelting of the copper ore was carried on in a highly inefficient and wasteful manner. In that year of our Lord (1890) and for some time previous – as early as the 1850s – it was and had been the practice to pile the mined copper ore in huge heaps upon the ground and smelt or "roast" it by burning huge quantities of cord wood beneath it. This released the volatile elements of which sulphur was the preponderant one and the Basin was generally blanketed beneath a cloud of evil-smelling smoke which very quickly destroyed all vegetation and very efficiently discouraged its return when elsewhere the flowers were blooming in the spring. This chemical-laden fog and the cutting down of the trees nearby to furnish the fuel used in the "roasting" process quickly combined to denude the adjacent landscape of the customary adornments of nature and to create a resemblance to some lost, fantastic world.

The entrance of the Tennessee Copper Company upon the scene in 1898 saw a gradual improvement in mining and smelting operations and this smoke, or furnace gas, was trapped and valuable sulphuric acid derived from it. And, too, whereas once upon a time copper was the sole product of the Basin, later a host of by-products such as copper sulphate, iron sinter, slag and zinc concentrates, were derived from the scientific treatment of the copper ore and other elements with which it was found combined.

The road between Knoxville and a point near Copperhill was constructed by George R. Eager, an Englishman, who agreed to build this 107-mile stretch at the rate of $20,000 per mile. The city of Knoxville, which owed its inception and subsequent growth to its strategic location on the Tennessee River at the confluence of the Holston and French Broad

Left: Here is how the L. & N.'s Hiwassee Loop, north of Farner, Tenn., crosses under itself, after encircling the mountain. Right: So near and yet so far! Mile post 263, just out of picture at the extreme right, is only a stone's throw from mile post 262 which is on the lower track that may be glimpsed through the trees.

Steam shovels frequently had their work to do all over again in building the Knoxville, LaFollette and Jellico Railroad, due to the extensive slides which occurred. The steam shovel here shown is busily engaged in re-establishing the status quo disrupted by a slide near Dossett, Tenn., in the early part of 1905. Due to these slides, much of the line was laid several feet above grade and was not completely lowered to true profile grade until after the line was opened to revenue traffic.

rivers, had begun to realize that river transportation alone was not sufficient and it was an enthusiastic supporter of the new line, subscribing $275,000 to the venture. It is said that Mr. Eager's contract with the Knoxville Southern at the rate before mentioned was predicated upon his completing the railroad into Knoxville by July 1, 1890. By many a feat of engineering "derring-do," Mr. Eager was enabled to join the north and south rails at Apalachia on the last day of June 1890, and the next day the Iron Horse made a triumphal entry into an enthusiastic Knoxville.

However, it was not until August 18, 1890, that the first through trains were operated between Knoxville and Atlanta and for some time thereafter only one train a day each way was scheduled between the two cities. It took a little over 12 hours to make the trip.

Mr. Eager, and his forces, in their race with Father Time, left the conquest of Bald Mountain, which lies about 16 miles north of Copperhill, Tenn., to the very last, being uncertain as to just how to tackle such a formidable obstacle. East of Apalachia the right-of-way had been surveyed to follow the gorge of the Hiwassee River for several miles and to reach the banks of this river it was necessary for the line from the south to drop several hundred feet within a comparatively few miles because of the presence of Bald Mountain which prevented a more leisurely descent. It was a problem that the Knoxville Southern could not solve by the adoption of its usual steep grade tactics and its engineering forces eventually emerged with the plans for a switchback, an engineering feat constructed on the zig and zag principle, which achieved the desired result and which subsequently resulted in Bald Mountain being adorned with a gigantic "W." This, although crudely effective, was highly unsatisfactory and only three or four cars could be handled over the switchback at one time.

The Atlanta, Knoxville and Northern, as such, came into existence on June 3, 1896, and shortly thereafter, under the impetus provided by the new blood in its management, its traffic began to increase. Six engines were purchased from an Eastern railroad to help handle this increased business and legend has it that Arbuckle coffee coupons were tendered in

The evolution of a town in the pine woods of Southern Alabama, following the coming of the L. & N. and the fine work done by its general immigration and industrial department, is graphically portrayed by the accompanying series of pictures. At the top is Main Street, Samson, Ala., as it appeared in March 1903, when the surveyors were at work. The middle picture shows Main Street in 1905, just two years later. The bottom picture shows the same street in 1907.

payment. At any rate, the engines were henceforth known as "Arbuckles." The switchback at Bald Mountain, however, was a constant thorn in the side of efficient railroad operation. Finally, in desperation, Henry K. McHarg, who was the new owner of the line, borrowed T. A. Aber from the L. & N., and told him to get rid of the stumbling-block at Bald Mountain. Mr. Aber was equal to the task and the result was the monument to his ability which is known as the Hiwassee Loop, which lies between the towns of Farner and Apalachia, Tenn., and which is said to be the third longest railroad loop in the world.

The Loop was constructed in 1898 and is some 8,000 feet in length. It was from it and the 15-degree double reverse curve at Tate Mountain between Whitestone and Talking Rock, Ga. (four miles via this curve, but only two and one-half miles as the crow flies), that the old A. K. & N., derived its name of "Hook and Eye." The "eye," of course, was the Loop and the "hook" was the curve at Tate Mountain. This road was also known by several other nicknames. The name "Narrow Escape" was derived from the mountainous country traversed and the "Black Satchel" sobriquet, which was often applied to the old A. K. & N., was said to have originated in the practice of natives of the section carrying black cardboard satchels with them whenever they took a train trip.

Several of the stations located on either the "old" or "new" lines of the K. & A. Division, received their nomenclature in rather unusual fashion. Toonigh, Ga., for instance, is said to be so named because when the citizens of that locality first petitioned the old Marietta and North Georgia to make their community a bona fide station, they were told that it was "too nigh" Holly Springs and Woodstock, Ga.

Chatsworth, Ga., on the other hand, is so named, or so legend has it, because some citizens discovered a board with that word written upon it, reposing in a field, and liking the effiuent sound of its syllables, they forthwith adopted it to designate their locality.

Talking Rock, Ga., is so-called, according to one version, from the custom of certain train crews in those unregenerate days to leave a dollar bill on a large boulder in the vicinity on their trips north or south. On the return trip they always found a quart of "mountain dew" in place of the dollar; a fair exchange which was by no means considered a robbery.

Getting back to the Loop, it may be said of it that it was much the same in 1963 as it was when it was first built. To accomplish a drop of 426 feet in the six miles from Farner to Apalachia, the line from the south, to reach the gorge of the Hiwassee River, goes completely around Bald Mountain, crossing under itself at the approximate point it first touches the mountain. The line then starts on another trip around the base of the mountain, but before the second loop is completed, it reaches the banks of the Hiwassee River and thereafter parallels that stream for about 15 miles, crossing it at Reliance, Tenn. In traveling over the loop, a train faces all points of the compass and it is a fact that two trains on the Loop may be going in the same direction and be only 60 feet apart. The book of rules is not being flouted, however, and there is no danger of collision for,

A momentous occasion; the laying of the last rail on the Knoxville, LaFollette and Jellico Railroad. This occurred some time during the early part of 1905 at the south portal of Black Oak Tunnel, near the station now known as Dossett, Tenn. Resident Engineer Charles E. Bright, now deceased, is among those present.

The St. Louis Union Station which was formally opened to the public on September 1, 1894. Said to be the largest railway station in the world at the time — it was served by 30 tracks — it was completed in the remarkably short time of two years and five months. It was built by the Terminal Railroad Association of St. Louis, composed and controlled by six railroads, including the Louisville & Nashville.

measured by track mileage, they would be several thousand feet apart. Three states – Tennessee, North Carolina and Georgia – may be seen from the top of the Loop and the beauty of the scenery spread far below is a treat to the eyes.

The "old" line also traverses a section that is rich in historical lore and during the War Between the States, especially in the year 1864, blue- and gray-clad armies battled furiously back and forth over the terrain in the vicinity of Marietta and Atlanta. The doom of the latter was forecast by General Joseph E. Johnston's defeat by General William T. ("War is Hell") Sherman at Kennesaw Mountain, a few miles northwest of Atlanta, in one of the bloodiest engagements of the Civil War; an engagement which lasted 34 days and which culminated when the Confederates fell back before the superior Federal forces to prepared fortifications to defend Atlanta.

Atlanta eventually fell on November 15, 1864, and Sherman's famous march to the sea followed immediately thereafter. All these bullet-tattered pages of history were written, of course, before much of the L. & N.'s present-day trackage between Knoxville and Atlanta came into existence, but grim reminders in the form of military cemeteries and battle memorials are not lacking.

Chapter XXII

Other Fields of Usefulness

PRIOR to 1903, the L. & N.'s activities for the colonization of the territories it served were carried on by a general immigration and industrial department. Among other things, to encourage immigrants and others to settle in the South, the L. & N. sponsored the publication of a magazine, North & South; its name was later changed to The Southland.

In 1903, the department was reorganized and a more intensive effort made to acquaint "outsiders" with the advantages of a location in L. & N.-served Dixie. Much literature was printed and samples of soil and raw materials were collected and indexed. Agricultural products and minerals were displayed at fairs and expositions; new settlers were helped with their problems.

As one result, colonies of French-Canadians, Greeks, Italians, Bohemians, Scandinavians and Germans were established in Southern Alabama and Northwest Florida along the L. & N.'s lines in the early part of the 20th Century. Thousands of acres of land that were once scarred and dotted with unsightly pine tree stumps were transformed into fertile fields, bearing in season bumper crops. Thriving communities came into being and industries moved in.

This colonization and agricultural activity was the direct predecessor of the L. & N.'s industrial development department which was subsequently to play such an important role in industry's move southward to Dixie.

As has been previously related, the L. & N. obtained control of the old A. K. & N., on March 10, 1902, the trackage of the latter at that time extending from Knoxville to Marietta, Ga. Subsequent to that date, companies were formed by the L. & N. for the building of a road from a point near what is now Etowah, Tenn., to Tennga, at the Tennessee-Georgia state line and between Mentor and Jena, by way of Armona and Binfield, Tenn. Both of these lines, prior to their completion, were formally conveyed to the A. K. & N. during the latter part of 1904, the L. & N. at that time, of course, owning the majority of the former's capital stock.

Prior to the completion of its own line between Cincinnati and Atlanta, the L. & N. operated its trains between Jellico, Tenn., and Knoxville over the tracks of the Southern Railway. The Knoxville, LaFollette and Jellico Railroad was thus formed by the L. & N. for the purpose of building a line of its own between Jellico and Knoxville. This work was started on May 12, 1902 and completed on April 3, 1905, at which time the first through trains were operated over the lines of the L. & N. between Cincinnati and Atlanta. The subsequent building of trackage between Saxton and Lot, Ky., at the state line, eliminated the necessity of through trains passing through Jellico, which was somewhat to the west of the Cincinnati-Atlanta "bee

This was the master mechanic's office force at Etowah, Tenn., in February 1907, shortly after headquarters were transferred from Blue Ridge, Ga.

line." Consequently, shortly after the completion of the K. L. & J., through service between Cincinnati and Knoxville was established via Lot, instead of Jellico. The original trackage of that portion of the old Knoxville Branch, extending from Saxton, Ky., to Jellico, Tenn., was abandoned.

At one time a mixed train was operated between Jellico and Saxton, where connection was made with the main line trains. This accommodation carried hundreds of passengers daily, not all of whom were experienced travelers, by any manner of means. The story is told that once upon a time a patron boarded the train at Jellico, en route to Williamsburg, Ky., and refused to surrender his ticket. For thus throwing a monkey-wrench in the smooth operation of a railroad, he was, after more peaceful forms of suasion had failed, put off the train about a mile south of Saxton. He still had the cherished ticket, however. As the train, which was studded with inquiring heads poked out of its windows, receded into the distance, he waggled it high into the air and shouted with gloomy satisfaction at Conductor Jim Gilmore, now deceased these many years, "You can put me off yer ole train, but this ticket is mine and you're not goin' to git it!"

Prior to the formal opening of the new line between Knoxville and Jellico on April 3, 1905, trains were operated more or less regularly over portions of the road already constructed and it is recorded that the first of these made the trip on August 8, 1904, between Jellico and Jacksboro, Tenn., a distance of about 31 miles.

A number of coal mines were opened up at Whitley County, Ky., between Corbin, Ky., and Jellico at this time, and in the fall of 1904 a mine run was added between these two points by the L. & N. This was manned, in part, by Conductor Green Harp and Engineer John Callahan and was known to the natives of the section as the "Turn-Around." It vied for popularity with the "Short Dog," a mixed run operating between the same two points. It is 32 miles from Corbin to Jellico and it was the unenviable lot of the flagman on the "Turn-Around" to walk much of this distance on foot since the train made 19 regularly scheduled stops between the two points, not to mention a number of extemporaneous ones, these varying in duration from ten minutes to three hours.

Subsequent amendments to the K. L. & J.'s original charter gave it the privilege of constructing a number of branch lines and such were eventually projected into the coal regions along such streams as Laurel Fork,

Hickory Creek, Clinch River and Cow Creek. Much of this trackage was built over the strenuous protests of a railroad which was already upon the scene and these protests did not confine themselves to a purely verbal or legal form. At Oliver Springs, Tenn., upon Cow Creek Branch, for example, it was necessary to pass above the tracks of this other railroad and the latter discouraged the passage with an "aerial attack" which consisted of dumping quantities of hot sand and hot water upon the heads of the hapless construction forces of the L. & N. as they labored to erect the necessary trestle work. The competing line also hindered the progress of the work by blocking the sidings, etc., with empty cars until finally, in exasperation, the L. & N.'s chief engineer of construction, J. E. Willoughby, instructed his forces to drive the pilings right through the empty cars. These physical encounters were always followed by legal "hang-overs" the next day, or shortly thereafter, in the form of law suits and the Company's lawyers were kept busy for a number of years in that vicinity.

The construction camp on the Clear Fork Branch of the Knoxville, LaFollette and Jellico Railroad near Pruden, Tenn., which was headquarters for Chief of Police J. B. Harlan, and his men, as well as the construction forces, as it appeared in May 1903. The L. & N. later abandoned the idea of building this line and it was completed by the Southern Railway. The former secured trackage rights from the latter, soon after completion, from a point near Holton, Tenn., to Fonde, Ky.

In the building of a number of its branch lines through the mountains of Eastern Tennessee, which were tributary to the Knoxville, LaFollette and Jellico Railroad, the L. & N. encountered a certain amount of opposition from other railroads and from feudists of the section and it was necessary for it to have special agents accompany its construction forces. The above picture shows J. B. Harlan (on horseback), former chief of police, now deceased, and his men on the Clear Fork Branch in May 1903.

At that time it was engaged in constructing a line north of Knoxville, through the medium of the K. L. & J. R. R., the L. & N. had a number of other irons in the fire in connection with the operation of trains between Cincinnati and Atlanta. It was contemporaneously engaged in rebuilding most of the trackage of the old A. K. & N. between Knoxville and what is now known as Etowah, and of its Knoxville Branch between Corbin, Ky., and Saxton, Ky., relocating portions of these lines, reducing grades, etc. It was also rapidly prosecuting the construction of a new "low grade" line, some 80 miles long, from Etowah to a connection with the Western & Atlantic Railroad at Junta, Ga., near Cartersville. This latter work was completed on April 1, 1906, and the prior obtaining of trackage rights from the N. C. & St. L.-leased Western and Atlantic on December 12, 1904 (the state of Georgia had passed a law in 1903, prohibiting any new and parallel road from being built within 20 miles of the state-owned Western and Atlantic) gave the L. & N. access to Atlanta at this time over its new line from Etowah via Chatsworth, Ramhurst, Fairmont and Junta. The A. K. & N. had been operating trains over the Western and Atlantic from Marietta, Ga., into Atlanta since July 1, 1904, and thus the L. & N. was now well-equipped to handle the traffic moving between Cincinnati and Atlanta. Large sums of money had also been spent in the construction of adequate terminals at both Knoxville and Atlanta, and the shops at Corbin, Ky., which had hitherto confined their activities to the making of light running repairs, began to emerge as one of the L. & N.'s major shops; a development which was to take place over a period of several years and upon which the L. & N. was eventually to spend millions of dollars.

Etowah, Tenn., at the junction of the "old" and "new" lines of the K. & A. Division, was a "railroad" town which owed its inception and much of its growth to the building of the line from that point to Junta, Ga. A few scattered dwellings and stores sprang up at this junction and the eventual decision of the L. & N. to establish shops and division headquarters there boomed the town amazingly. (Upon the completion of the shops at Etowah in November 1906, the master mechanic moved his office there from Blue Ridge, Ga., on

This is Etowah, Tenn., in the beginning, in the year 1905. Compared with modern-day Etowah, it seems a far cry. Top: The site of Third and Pennsylvania Ave. Center: Fourth and Pennsylvania Ave. Bottom: Etowah's first post office.

An aerial view of a portion of South Louisville Shops as the plant appeared in the late 1930s.

January 15, 1907, and division headquarters were subsequently transferred from Marietta, Ga., to Etowah on April 22, 1908.) Etowah thus gradually came to assume an increasing importance, a trend which was in evidence until the consolidation of the Knoxville and Atlanta divisions in 1931 and the subsequent removal of the divisional headquarters to Knoxville.

Those portions of Knoxville & Atlanta Division and already mentioned were the mighty trunks from which sprang forth a score of tributary roots, some of which have now been abandoned. Among the more important (and getting ahead of our story by some few years) were the Maryville Branch, four miles long, extending from Armona to Maryville, Tenn., which was placed in operation in June, 1908; the Pine Mountain Railroad, West (entire capital stock owned by the L. & N.), 21 miles in length, extending from Favoy, Ky., to Gatliff and Packard, Ky., which was opened for traffic on November 9, 1908; the Athens and Tellico Branch (the outgrowth of the Athens and Tellico Railway Company, which in its less than a quarter of a century of existence had greeted its patrons under no less than five names) which was purchased by the L. & N. on June 30, 1911, and which extended between Athens and Tellico Plains, Tenn.; and the Harriman, Knoxville and Eastern Railroad (entire capital stock owned by the L. & N.), 17½ miles in length, whose trackage extending between Allingham, Tenn., and Harriman, Tenn., was placed in operation on March 15, 1912.

Outstanding among the batches of supplementary trackage which came into existence shortly after the turn of the century was the further extension of that prong of the Birmingham Mineral known as Huntsville Branch No. 2. For many years (since 1889) its jumping off place had been established at Champion, Ala., some 36 miles to the northeast of Boyles. Then, in the spring of 1900, as previously related, William T. Underwood, a large coal operator of the day and a prominent figure in the history of Alabama, acquired a vast acreage of coal lands in Etowah and Blount counties, Ala., and interested Milton H. Smith in providing rail facilities for the mines which he proposed to open. A thorough investigation convinced Mr. Smith of the feasibility of the project and construction of the extension was started in May, 1900. The line reached Altoona, some 10 miles from Champion, on January 1, 1901. Here a stop was called upon construction for some time and it was March, 1903, before the filling-in of the 13.83-mile gap between Altoona on the west and Moragne on the east was commenced. This line which linked the L. & N.'s Birmingham Mineral and Alabama Mineral division, with the aid of trackage rights obtained over the N. C. & St. L. between Moragne and Attalla (1.63 miles), was completed on May 28, 1905, and greatly facilitated the moving of iron ore, coal, etc., over the divisions involved.

The L. & N. was extremely active in Alabama at this time, such activity, in part, being a reflection of the optimism which pervaded that whole district coincidental with the successful manufacture of steel in 1897 and the subsequent erecting of steel miles at Ensley in 1899.

To this new departure then may be attributed, in part, the L. & N.'s purchase of the majority of the capital stock of the Birmingham, Selma and New Orleans Railway on September 10, 1900, and the completion of the 16-mile Camden Branch (Camden Junction to Camden; an offshoot of the Selma-Flomaton line) at a cost of $160,490.66, on February 15, 1901.

The Birmingham, Selma and New Orleans Railway, above mentioned,

Above: This is how a locomotive underwent heavy repairs at the South Louisville Shops just after they were completed. A locomotive might be in the shops for two or three years. Below: An old wooden passenger coach in the embryo stage of construction at the South Louisville Shops. Such construction was an essential part of the work at these shops for some time after their completion.

The old planing mill, part of the early shop plant constructed near 10th and Kentucky, Louisville, in 1868. This still stood in 1963.

at the time of its purchase by the L. & N., extended only from Selma to Martin, Ala., a distance of 20 miles, all of this trackage being within Dallas County. In April 1901, the L. & N. commenced the construction of an extension from Martin to Myrtlewood, Ala., 40.25 miles away, and this was completed to Linden, 30.11 miles from Martin, by May 1902. Myrtlewood was eventually reached on August 10, 1902, and the subsequent building of the Meridian and Bigbee River Railway permitted connection to be made with a number of other carriers in that vicinity.

At this time also the new Sardis-Selma line of the Southern Alabama Division was completed and placed in operation on June 14, 1903. Prior to that date the L. & N. had used the line of the Western Railway of Alabama from Gulf Junction into Selma, a distance of about eight miles. The completion of the new line eliminated the necessity of using the Sardis-Gulf Junction-Selma "dog leg," and the old line from Sardis (or Selma Junction) to Gulf Junction was abandoned simultaneously with the opening of the new eight-mile line from Sardis into Selma. The opening of this new "approach" to Selma had involved the building of a new bridge across the Alabama River.

Nurtured by the prosperity which had descended upon the Birmingham District as a result of the successful making of steel, the various lines of the L. & N. in that vicinity shot out in every direction. Most of these were only two or three miles long and were projected to serve iron ore or coal workings. The Cain Creek Branch, however, which came into existence at about this time, deserves extended mention. Construction was started from Black Creek Junction, Ala., on the main line of the South and North Alabama, on August 20, 1903, and by April 28, of the following year, the construction forces had reached Vulcan, Ala., 15 miles away. Subsequently, the line was further extended to Praco, 13 miles from Vulcan and 28 miles from Black Creek Junction, this being completed on July 17, 1907.

The building of the Cain Creek Branch expedited the development of the Warrior coal field and Miss Ethel Armes in her interesting book, "The Story of Coal and Iron in Alabama," previously mentioned in the account, has the following to say about the L. & N.'s construction

Upper left: The old general office building at 2nd and Main. Upper right: The L. & N. general offices were located in this building prior to 1877. Lower left: The general office building as it appeared in 1963. Lower right: The general office building before the annex was added.

of this line:

"... By the end of 1903, it (the Pratt Coal Company in the Warrior coal field in Northwestern Jefferson County, Ala.), was operating 18 mines, and owned a total of 800 tenement houses, 14 churches and schoolhouses, eight stores and warehouses.

"... Through the action of Milton H. Smith, the Louisville and Nashville Railroad Company started the construction of a branch line – the Cane (sic) Creek Branch, 25 miles long, into the undeveloped section of the Warrior coal field. Fifteen miles of the railroad ran direct through the Pratt Company's properties. Additional mines were opened on the Pratt, Nickleplate and Big seams and small slopes on the Jefferson and Black Creek seams. Thus the five seams of coal were worked simultaneously in 1903 by the Pratt Coal Company, an achievement up to that year never before attained by any single mining property in the Birmingham District. No company in Alabama had ever worked more than two seams at the same time. The L. & N. track was completed to seven of the company's mines by May 1, 1903; the loading of coal began on a great scale, and this part of the country, the famous Warrior field, woke up from its century's sleep. The heart of the coal country of Alabama now beat with new life and energy. Just as the Birmingham Mineral, under M. H. Smith's lead, unlocked the riches of Red Mountain back in the 'eighties, so now, nearly a generation later, the L. & N. disclosed the treasures of the remote and long-settled, yet wealthiest, region of the great coal field.

"By the late summer of 1903 (we believe the date should be 1904 – K.A.H.) the railroad had reached Banner, the one shaft mine of the Pratt Company about twenty-five miles from Birmingham, and coal was first hoisted from this point on August 1 of that year. Out of Banner, the Company's 'prize mine,' which had once been a meager drift opened in the Big Seam in October, 1902, there has been made a coal mine strictly up to the highest standard. It is located in Jefferson County, near the Walker County line and, including both shaft and slope output, has a daily capacity estimated at two thousand tons." (This was written in 1910 – K.A.H.)

Elsewhere, of course, the L. & N. had not been idle.

Mention has been previously made of its efforts to secure a line of its own south of Jellico and of how this desire was eventually realized. This may be said to be the piece de resistance of the L. & N.'s efforts at the beginning of the century, as its other irons warmed nicely in the fire. Confining ourselves for the nonce to track construction exclusively these other irons (or this other "iron"), also included the completion of a line from Providence, Ky., to Morganfield, Ky., a distance of about 26 miles, on April 1, 1907, and the building of the Bay Minette and Fort Morgan Railroad, an L. & N.-sponsored venture, with completion to Foley occurring on May 11, 1905.

These last two lines were built for quite dissimilar purposes, the line to Morganfield coming into being to serve the coal fields in Western Kentucky and the Foley Branch (as the Bay Minette and Fort Morgan Railroad came to be known) being constructed principally to serve logging operations then being conducted among Baldwin County's many hundreds of thousands of acres of pine forests. Later on the resultant tree stumps were uprooted, the ground cleared and crops planted. This agricultural acreage increased year by year and Baldwin County began to gradually emerge as one of the country's biggest food producers.

The L. & N.'s general immigration and industrial department, as previously related, assisted this development by systematically and intensively advertising Baldwin County's advantages to the outside world.

Subsequently, L. & N. development men, cooperating with land owners, real estate men and others helped to attract an increasing number of newcomers from all parts of the United States through the medium of advertising and personal contacts. Settlers poured in and more and more acreage was cleared annually. When it is considered that Baldwin County is nearly as large as the state of Delaware, it can be realized that it is with truth called "The Last Frontier."

As its name would imply the Bay Minette and Fort Morgan Railroad had originally intended to reach the latter point on the shores of the Gulf of Mexico, but construction was stopped at Foley, 36½ miles from Bay Minette, after an expenditure of $225,728.57.

CHAPTER XXIII

L'Affaire Gates-Hawley

THE L. & N.'s acquisition of its line between Jellico and Atlanta was followed by certain unforeseen consequences. These latter eventually resulted in the Atlantic Coast Line Railroad securing control of the L. & N. in October 1902 and were a direct result of the re-financing which was made necessary by the acquisition and construction of the various portions of the Jellico-Atlanta line. This change in ownership came about in this wise:

On April 7, 1902, the board of directors voted to increase the road's capitalization from $55,000,000 to $60,000,000, this increase having been authorized by the stockholders some few years before. This involved the sale of 50,000 shares of stock. Shortly prior to that time Edwin Hawley, president of the Minneapolis and St. Paul and the Iowa Central Railroads, and John W. Gates, of "Bet-A-Million" fame, became independently interested in obtaining large quantities of L. & N. stock. They soon became aware of this mutual interest and eventually joined forces, entering into an agreement whereby the two "pools" would act as one in the disposal of any L. & N. stock accumulated. These two men also acted as agents for several other interests.

The directors of the L. & N., who held a comparatively small amount of stock themselves, were seemingly unaware that the road's "paper" was being concentrated in the hands of a few individuals and proceeded to sell the 50,000 additional shares which had been authorized, before they had been actually issued. It was their thought that such a disposition was to the best interests of the Company and would keep its stock from being a drug on the market. Unfortunately, their action occurred at a time when the Hawley-Gates pools were unusually active and the latter as chief buyers of the new stock began to put the pressure on for an immediate delivery of their purchases. This the L. & N. could not do because of a Stock Exchange ruling that new shares could not be listed and made good for delivery until 30 days after the application to list. Thus, the L. & N. was technically "short" on its own stock and the directors began frantically to try to borrow or obtain enough existing stock to make good the sales made in good faith. But, unfortunately, available stock was mostly in the hands of the Hawley-Gates combine, who had thus succeeded in cornering the market. Meanwhile, following the inevitable dictates of the old law of supply and demand, the price of the stock mounted sharply, which may or may not have been an unforeseen consequence. A panic, such as had been witnessed the year before when a "squeeze play" had been engineered on Northern Pacific (at one time it sold for as high as $7,000 a share), loomed as a dangerous possibility, but Gates and Hawley generously agreed not to press for immediate delivery. To be sure, this was to their advantage, for at the time they owned or controlled 306,000 shares of the 600,000 shares outstanding and anything that might have proved harmful to the L. & N. Railroad, would certainly have redounded to their disadvantage.

As indicated, this artificial popularity of L. & N. stock zoomed its listing upward and on April 9, 1902, for instance, 169,000 shares of L. & N. figured in the day's trading on the New York Stock Exchange; approximately one-fourth of the total volume of business. This activity in L. & N. stock created a great deal of interest, not only in Wall Street, but in the contemporary press, as well, and each "expert" had his own conjecture as to just what was actually happening behind the scenes. It was generally agreed that the ownership had changed hands and that August Belmont and Company, who owned a large amount of L. & N. stock, and who represented the foreign interests such as the Rothschilds, had been ousted from control. The Atlanta Journal in its issue of April 12, 1902, for instance, made this cryptic and cynical comment anent the "Gates-L. & N. incident." "We may not know which shell the L. & N. is under, but we know who's working the shells and that's enough for us!"

Thus the rumors were rife as to what would become of the L. & N. and the down-town streets of Louisville, its home city, had a somewhat fevered aspect, as if an invasion by some alien foe were impending. It was a popular topic of conversation in barber shop, pool-room, saloon and exclusive club, frequently ousting such tried-and true favorites as the weather, politics, horse racing, whiskey and the ladies.

One rumor was to the effect that the Southern was out to acquire the L. & N. in retaliation for the steps which the latter had recently taken to gain access to Knoxville and Atlanta. For a short and somewhat sub-rosa period in 1896, the L. & N. had been owner of the entire line of the Knoxville, Cumberland Gap and Louisville Railway, but had later relinquished this to the Southern, it being subsequently stated by those who claimed to be "in the know" that the L. & N. had agreed to keep out of Knoxville, if the Southern would keep out of Nashville.

About the middle of April 1902, J. P. Morgan and Company finally pricked all the bubbles of fact and fancy that were floating about by announcing that they had acquired 100,000 of the shares owned and controlled by the Gates-Hawley pool at the rate of $120.00 per share, this representing a cool, but neat, profit of several millions of dollars for Messrs. Gates, Hawley and associates. J. P. Morgan and Company also took an option to purchase the remaining 206,000 shares at this price before October 15, 1902, subsequently doing just that. The combine had claimed consistently that they had no interest in obtaining control of the L. & N. but had purchased its stock solely because they thought it was a good investment. And so it was – as things turned out!

In October of the same year, J. P. Morgan and Company sold their holdings in the L. & N. to the Atlantic Coast Line (the two roads had physical connection at Montgomery, Ala., and Chattahoochee, Fla.), thus giving that line the ownership of 51 per cent of the L. & N. capital stock. The L. & N.'s board of directors at a meeting on October 30, 1902, appended a matter-of-fact footnote to past history by including in the minutes of that meeting this statement: "Resolved: That the Louisville and Nashville Railroad Company hereby assents to the purchase and the holding of a majority of its capital stock by the Atlantic Coast Line Railroad Company." A little over 23 years before the stock of the L. & N. had been first listed on the New York Stock Exchange and the control of thr road had begun to pass from the cities and counties which had helped to build it.

Although nominally these financial maneuvers changed the status of the L. & N. from that of an independent line to that of a satellite of another system, in reality, the change was rather superficial. The L. & N. still retained its same official personnel and under the able leadership of Milton H. Smith it continued to carry out those policies which had played such an important part in the development of the South.

The purchases of Hawley, Gates, et al, was not the first time in the L. & N.'s history that its stock had proved to be an irresistible temptation to Wall Street manipulators, most of whom had never seen the road or been within several hundred miles of its track. An outstanding incident was the one involving famed Hetty Green, the "witch of Wall Street," and one-time wife of one-time L. & N. president, Colonel Edward H. Green (December 1, 1880, to February 26, 1881), and Addison Cammack, a noted "plunger" of the day. Both Mr. Cammack and Mrs. Green, however, were more familiar than most with the Louisville and Nashville.

Mr. Cammack was a native of Kentucky and during the 'eighties learned by somewhat devious means that the L. & N. was planning to reduce its annual dividend that particular year, or per chance let it go by the board entirely. Anticipating a decline in the stock's listing by reason of that fact, Mr. Cammack immediately began to sell it short. Everything went off as anticipated; in fact, too well. The dividend was passed and the L. & N.'s listing moved downward several points. Shortly, Mr. Cammack found himself in the unenviable position of having to borrow or buy – somehow – somewhere – several thousand shares of L. & N. stock to make good his commitments. Unfortunately for the plunger, no stock seemed available. In his own words: "I was in a slaughter-house and everywhere I looked I spouted blood." Hearing that Mrs. Green was the holder of several thousand shares of "Louisville" he paid that lady a visit.

Mr. Cammack eventually emerged from this conference with the 40,000 shares of L. & N. stock held by Mrs. Green, having purchased the same at cost – plus $10.00 per share. The incident is frequently held up as an example of Mrs. Green's sometimes latent generosity for she could have clipped Mr. Cammack for a much larger sum had she been so minded.

In some quarters there was ill-concealed jubilation over the fact that such a veteran of Wall Street as August Belmont had been whip-sawed out of the driver's seat by comparative upstarts. However, Mr. Belmont remained on as chairman of the board until July 9, 1903, at which time he resigned, giving as his reason the heavy press of other duties. He was, of course, at the time head of the banking house of August Belmont and Company and was also taking an active part in the affairs of the New York Rapid Transit Transportation Company, then engaged in building Manhattan's first subway. Mr. Belmont was succeeded by Henry Walters, a native of Baltimore, Md., who held this office until his death on November 30, 1931. At the time of his election as chairman of the L. & N.'s board, Mr. Walters was also chairman of the Atlantic Coast Line's board and had served that system in a number of capacities. He was 55 years of age at the time.

Although, as stated, the change in the L. & N.'s ownership did not greatly affect its status, or its basic policies, there were certain results directly traceable to the new set-up. Perhaps the most important of these was the joint acquisition by the Southern and the L. & N. of the Chicago, Indianapolis and Louisville Railway, otherwise known as the "Monon," on May 20, 1902. That road owned and operated 556 miles of track extending between the points listed in its corporate name and its acquisition involved the purchase of 38,734 shares of preferred stock and 97,469 shares of common stock. This purchase was covered by the joint issuance on the part of the L. & N. and the Southern of $11,877,642 worth of L. & N.-Southern-Monon Collateral Joint Four Per Cent Gold Bonds.

At this time (May 20, 1902) J. P. Morgan and Company controlled both the L. & N. and the Southern and although the L. & N.'s directorate, as a whole, and M. H. Smith especially, were not in favor of the step, there was not much they could do but assent to the purchase, the rapid-fire developments of the past few weeks having shorn them of much of their power. Nevertheless, three of them retained the courage of their convictions and cast a "no" when the matter was finally put to a vote.

Milton H. Smith, incidentally, had very little patience with, or liking for the financial titans in New York who were using L. & N. stock as a football. Gates he called a "bull in the china shop." And of the elder J. P. Morgan he had this to say: " . . . Mr. Morgan's idiosyncrasy is the creation of enormous combinations. He is in the position of a strong man in the circus, on his back, feet up, keeping an enormous cask revolving in the air, which sooner or later must come down."

This crossing of the Ohio River was a rather radical step for the L. & N., for with some negligible exception, it had previously confined its operations to the South. Milton H. Smith had never favored such an invasion of the territory north of the Mason-Dixie Line, but the new acquisition did give the L. & N. an entrance of its own into the Windy City and since it was shared jointly with the Southern, it had the further effect of eliminating a certain proportion of the competititve strife for traffic moving between Chicago and Southern points which had been waged for a number of years between the two roads. However, despite the fact that circumstances had dictated a joint ownership of the "Monon," elsewhere the two lines continued to badger each other whenever and wherever possible.

The press of the day was inclined, for the most part, to view these various developments with a jaundiced eye, since at the time both the L. & N. and the Southern were Morgan-dominated. It was thought, or feared, that an attempt might be made to establish a rate monopoly to the disadvantage of the public and the legal forces of the various states girded themselves for the fray, striking embattled attitudes. However, their anxiety proved to be a needless one and even if such an intention had been incipient among the financial titans, the passage of the Hepburn Act in 1906, which greatly strengthened the Interstate Commerce Law, would have blighted the scheme in its infancy.

Chapter XXIV

Shop Talk

AT A meeting of the board of directors on August 14, 1902, President Milton H. Smith was authorized to proceed with the construction of a new general office building at 9th and Broadway, in Louisville. Both the office building and the shops were badly needed, due to the L. & N.'s constantly-increasing business. The general office building then in use at 2nd and Main Streets had been completed in 1877, when the railroad's personnel was exclusively and aggressively masculine. At that time, the L. & N. owned and operated slightly less than 1,000 miles of track and hauled around 2,000,000 tons of freight annually. By 1902, when the authorization was granted, the trackage actually owned or operated was 3,444.13 miles in extent, over which were carried annually 38,158,009 tons of freight and 6,600,599 passengers (as of the fiscal year ending June 30, 1903.)

This increased business necessitated, of course, an expansion of the L. & N.'s clerical forces at Louisville and, as early as 1890, it had been realized that more commodious accommodations were imperative. Spurred into action by the sight of clerks practically sitting in each other's laps within the crowded confines of the once-impressive structure at 2nd and Main, a seven-story building was authorized in that year, but this came to naught and it was 1902 before the work of erecting a modern 11-story structure at 9th and Broadway was commenced. The "front yard" of the freight station at that point had been selected as the site for this edifice and before the work could proceed it was necessary to raze a portion of this historic building, which at one time had functioned as both a freight and passenger station. Through its doors had streamed the sick, the lame and the halt of the Civil War's holocaust and in more peaceful times its walls had witnessed tearful farewells, fond goodbyes, joyful reunions and the indiscriminate throwing of rice.

Although work on the general office building was commenced in 1902, it was January 1907 before this structure may be said to have been completely finished, the task being delayed by a strike of the structural steel workers in the fall of 1905. Approximately $650,000.00 were spent for its construction.

The L. & N.'s general offices at Louisville had been housed in a number of structures since the birth of the road in 1850. At one time they are said to have been located at 6th and Liberty streets in the pre-Bohemian days of that neighborhood and it is certain that a portion of them were in a building at Bullitt and Main Streets prior to the erection of the old general office building at 2nd and Main in 1877. The Bullitt and Main structure seems to have been rather inadequate and some of the

Locomotive repair section of the machine shop, South Louisville, Ky., as it appeared at the time of World War II, or during the hey-day of steam power.

general officers had their headquarters in a large frame building that stood where the Victoria Hotel was later to be built. Others, including Milton H. Smith (he was then general freight agent), were located in a building at 9th and Broadway, a part of the freight shed that was subsequently to make way for the present-day general office building.

The construction of the new general office building at 9th and Broadway roughly paralleled the erection of shops at South Louisville, Ky. Authority for such construction was granted in July 1902, and shortly thereafter contracts were allocated to several different companies. These included the Louisville Bridge and Iron Company, of Louisville, Ky.; the American Bridge Company; Grainger and Company, of Louisville; the Snead Architectural Iron Works, of Louisville; Charles Hegewald Company, of New Albany, Ind.; and the Southern Foundry Company, of Owensboro, Ky.

The old shops at 10th and Kentucky had been purchased in 1858 from the Kentucky Locomotive Works for the sum of $80,000. Subsequently in 1868-1872 the L. & N. erected several shop buildings at that location to supplement the original ones.

Once commenced the work proceeded rapidly and by the middle of August 1905, the entire shop plant and personnel at 10th and Kentucky streets had been moved to South Louisville, this migration of men and materials being done piece-meal, a certain "bottle-neck" having been formed by the inability to obtain certain materials and items of machinery when needed. While it is, of course, true that much of the equipment at the old shops was transplanted to the new, the older and more obsolete items were not.

The old buildings at 10th and Kentucky subsequently received blighting and destructive attention from wrecking crews with the exception of the old planing mill building at 11th and Garland and the old shop office building at 10th and Kentucky, the latter afterwards being used by the dining car department, the motor car repair shop, the signal department, and others. These two withstood the assault of the years, with some occasional assistance from the bridges and buildings forces, and the old planing mill was long used as a storage house for old records, tariffs, files, etc., being known colloquially as the "dead house."

Some idea of the size of the task undertaken by the L. & N. in the construction of its shops at South Louisville may be gained when it is stated that these shops, as originally built, covered over 50 acres of ground and that some 35 or more buildings, housing every type of facility used in the maintenance and construction of railroad equipment, were erected at that time. As of June 30, 1907, when all of the odds and ends, incident to getting settled in the new location, had been disposed of, a total of $2,396,644.52 had been expended upon the South Louisville Shops.

In 1914, the L. & N. completed the construction of a modern steel car shop for the building and repair of steel passenger and freight cars. Parenthetically, it should be explained that for a great many years prior to that time the L. & N. had been building its own locomotives and freight and passenger cars. Prior to 1910, however, the latter two items of equipment were largely of wooden construction. After their appearance steel freight and passenger cars were not long in proving their worth and the L. & N., along with most other American railroads, began to purchase more and more of this type of equipment, necessitating a somewhat radical revision of shop facilities. At first it was only intended that maintenance work should be done at this shop, but it was eventually decided that for a slight additional sum the L. & N. could also construct this type of equipment.

As to just what the L. & N. got for the many millions of dollars it expended at South Louisville, perhaps the following figures for the decade ending with December 31, 1915, (the first of the shops' existence) will be illuminating. In that time, its forces at South Louisville constructed 282 locomotives, 184 items of passenger train equipment (day coaches, mail, baggage and express cars, diners, etc.), 400 box cars, 9,430 gondolas, 1,600 coal hoppers, 250 ore cars, 1,200 flat cars, 200 refrigerator cars, 300 stock cars, 300 coke cars, 78 acid cars and 451 cabooses. (The "end-to-end" school, which conscientiously strives to make dry statistics more palatable, would inform us that this mighty armada of rolling stock would reach from South Louisville to Bowling Green, or thereabouts, a distance of 112 miles, and if this hypothetical train were moving south, its 282 locomotives would be well on their way to Nashville before its 451 cabooses had even received an inkling of departure.)

It should, of course, be also borne in mind that this construction work (which incidentally had an original inventory value of well over $16,-

000,000) was in addition to the millions of man-hours which were spent in the repairing and maintenance of equipment.

The years subsequent to World War II saw a gradual decline and finally a virtual cessation in the construction of cars and locomotives at South Louisville Shops, and locomotives, frieght cars, etc., acquired new in recent years have been purchased from concerns that specialize in such construction. However, in the early part of 1940 an extensive program of rebuilding freight cars of obsolescent types to make them into modern types, was entered upon at South Louisville and to this extent construction work has been resumed.

(The postwar years witnessed a gradual evolution of the L. & N.'s repair facilities and this became intensified after the introduction of the diesel locomotive and specialized equipment. Following complete dieselization the assembly-line method for repairing diesels was adopted at South Louisville in 1960. This was also applied there to hopper cars in the same year. Other major shop centers such as DeCoursey, Radnor and Boyles were likewise modernized.

For a more detailed look at the L. & N.'s shop evolution during 1959-1963, specifically, the reader is referred to Chapter 41.)

These construction activities at South Louisville roughly paralleled similar activities on a smaller scale at Paris, Tenn., Etowah, Tenn., and Boyles, Ala., the main distinction being that the South Louisville Shops were equipped for construction and maintenance, while the others mentioned were maintenance centers only.

The construction of the shops at Boyles, Ala., was slightly antedated by the work done in the Kentucky metropolis. The shops at Boyles were completed in 1911, although the seed was sown as early as 1904. Ever since the L. & N. had acquired and completed the South and North Alabama in 1872 there had been shops at Birmingham, although the importance of these had greatly declined following the completion of the L. & N.'s shops at New Decatur in 1890. The nucleus of the L. & N.'s present-day shops at Boyles seems to have been a roundhouse which was erected at that point in 1904. This innovation proved highly successful and led in the early part of 1906 to the eventual decision to establish Boyles as a major shop center. The actual work of construction, however, was not started until some few years later and it was 1911 before the facilities at Boyles were in sufficient shape to permit heavy repairs to be extended to equipment.

As has been previously stated, the shops at Etowah were placed in service in Novermber 1906. They consisted of a power station, machine shops, boiler and smith shop, planing mill, carpenter shop and a roundhouse. Simultaneously there had also been constructed a passenger depot and office building and a railroad Y.M.C.A., and the completion of all of this work was contemporary with the running of freight trains through from Corbin to Etowah and from Etowah to Atlanta, with the elimination of the previous stop for change of engines at Knoxville. This move became effective November 1, 1906.

The Railroad's new shop center at Etowah gave the Company's freelance spellers a great deal of trouble and it was some time before the correct spelling became firmly established in the personnel's consciousness. Some of the variations most frequently encountered in the files are "Etawa," "Etowa," and "Etawah."

Prior to the establishment of the shops at Etowah, this maintenance work for the Knoxville and Atlanta divisions had been done in varying degrees at Corbin, Knoxville, Atlanta, and Blue Ridge, Ga., the shops of the old A. K. & N. having been located at the last named. Some of the machinery, tools, etc., at Blue Ridge were transferred to the new shops at Etowah and in addition approximately $78,000 were spent for new equipment.

Meanwhile, to talk "shop" just a bit more, the L. & N. had not neglected the needs of its Iron Horse on its Memphis Line, one of the oldest parts of the System. Such work was originally done at Bowling Green, Memphis and Paris. The increasing traffic gradually rendered such facilities inadequate and in 1899 it was decided that more extensive shops should be provided at Paris, Tenn., that city being chosen because of its strategic location. At that time authority for the construction of four principal buildings (a planing mill, a machine shop, a boiler shop and blacksmith shop) was given and these along with a sprinkling of less important buildings, were completed in 1900.

The new shops at Paris cost approximately $60,000 and upon their completion approximately 100 additional men were employed to man their intricate facilities. These included trained workers of all sorts and a study of their then-prevailing compensation, which was typical of the rest of the system, is very interesting. Blacksmiths, boilermakers and machinists were paid $2.56 a day; helpers were paid $1.00 to $1.60 a day and woodworkers, $1.85. The basic working day had 10 hours.

The shops just recently mentioned, along with similar ones at Howell, Corbin, New Decatur, Mobile and Covington (this one having been inherited from the old Kentucky Central) constituted the back-bone of the L. & N.'s antidote for rolling-stock wear and tear at this time. They were supplemented by a number of smaller shops and roundhouses in certain strategically-located cities. Generally speaking, at these latter points only running repairs were extended to equipment, they not having the facilities for work of a heavier nature.

Fire Department, L. & N. Shops, Tenth and Kentucky Streets, Louisville, in 1898.

CHAPTER XXV

Y's and Otherwise

ONE of the phenomena that is essentially peculiar to railroading is the railroad Y.M.C.A. Frequently, these came into existence because of a lack of adequate housing facilities for employes at a point which had been selected by the Company for operating reasons as a shop center, or which had been automatically established as a terminal by the junction of two divisions. Or, as was the case at Louisville, because it was a convenience, both for the men and the Company, to have the employes reside close to their work. In either event, the railroad Y. M. C. A. served a multiple purpose. It offered the employe away from home base reasonable lodging and board (the latter was optional); it gave him a semi-directed social life and it placed his residence and his employment within easy walking distance of each other; a boon, as related, to both men and management.

The L. & N.'s first railroad Y. M. C. A. was located at Louisville at 1023 W. Broadway and was established in 1892. At that time, of course, the shops were still at 10th and Kentucky and South Louisville was terra incognita to most of the rest of the city, being separated therefrom by quite a few acres of nature in the raw. From 1023 W. Broadway, the railroad Y. M. C. A. moved to more commodious quarters in the Dulaney mansion at the southeast corner of 8th and Broadway. (This later became the Welsworth Hotel.) At that time the rental for this handsome edifice only came to $100 per month, but it cost some $3,000 to equip the dwelling for the occupancy of transplanted railroaders. The L. & N. defrayed a portion of this expense.

The removal of the L. & N.'s shops to South Louisville in August 1905, greatly nullified the utility of the railroad "Y" at 8th and Broadway, but the structure in South Louisville at 3rd and Central was not built as soon thereafter as one might imagine, it being May 6, 1912, before the cornerstone was laid and December 1, 1912, before the building, with appropriate fanfare, was actually dedicated. The root of all evil was at the root of this unavoidable procrastination, too, and it required a subscription of $20,000 from the L. & N. to finally do the trick.

The L. & N. in the early part of 1901 took action, admittedly upon a small scale at first, upon a problem which had confronted it for some time, i.e., that of the loyal employe, grown gray in the service, who could no longer efficiently perform his duties. This problem, of course, increased in knottiness with the passage of time and a more or less constant increase in the number employed. Human nature being what it was – and is – but very few employes made adequate provision for their declining years, when their earning power was lessened, or severed entirely. The L. & N. was naturally loath to remove from the payroll the name of any employe who could no longer capably perform his duties because of the infirmities of age, but in many cases no other course of action was possible, if the safe and efficient operation of trains were to continue.

Corporations at that time were perhaps not as aware of their employes as human beings as they are today and, in general, superannuation, or the pensioning of employes, was looked upon as an altruism inconsistent with the carrying on of the world's work. In fact, it may be said that it was 1910, or so, before the idea of pensioning employes was translated into reality by most corporations. In this field, our neighbor to the north was somewhat in advance of American practice, a pension system having been inaugurated by a Canadian railroad in 1873. (Although it was 1901 before an L. & N. pension system was adopted, several employes had been previously pensioned in the 'eighties and 'nineties, even though there was no regularly established plan.)

As stated, the L. & N.'s pension plan was started on a very modest scale and during 1901, 1902 and 1903, only one employe received the Company's gratuity. In each of the three years mentioned, this retired employe received the sum of $120.00. It is interesting to note how the L. & N.'s pension payments steadily increased from year to year, never taking a backward step. In 1904, the total annual payments to four employes amounted to $853. In 1908, the L. & N. paid out $7,244.72; in 1912, $14,091.72, and by 1916, the payments had reached such an impressive total ($31,011.50) that the management decided that it would be best to have the practice sanctioned by the board of directors. The matter was accordingly placed before that body at its meeting on April 4, 1917, and resulted in the adoption of the following resolution:

"Resolved: That this board hereby empowers the president or first vice-president to authorize the payment of pensions to employes who have rendered the Company long and faithful service when they have attained an age necessitating relief from duty, the basis of all pension allowances to be one per cent of average salary for the last ten years of service for each year of continuous service; report to be made monthly to this board for its approval of the employes pensioned in previous month, giving names, term of service, average salaries for the last ten years, and pension to be paid each employe.

"Resolved, Further: That this board approves the payment of pensions to living and deceased pensioners since the inauguration of the pension system in 1901, to November 1, 1916, aggregating $171,461.90.

"Resolved, Further: That the payment of pensions from November 1, 1916, as recited, to the following persons is hereby approved and authorized; said payments to be charged to operating expenses:

Number of living pensioners	131
Aggregate monthly allowance	$3,802.32
Equal to yearly allowance of	$45,627.84

"Resolved, Further: That the granting of pensions to employes, as above authorized is purely voluntary on the part of the Company, and may at any time be changed or abolished by action of this board.

"Resolved, Further: That the sum of $15.00 per month be fixed as a minimum pension to be paid in case the basis adopted should call for a

The Railroad Y. M. C. A. at 3rd and Central, Louisville, Ky., which was built in 1912, and torn down in 1963.

less amount."

In general, this confirmed the details of the practice which had been followed during preceding years. The pension payments continued to increase thereafter and the figures for the years 1918, 1922, 1926 and 1930 were $69,312, $115,098, $219,075 and $415,633 respectively. Up to 1926, or so, the increases in pension payments roughly paralleled the yearly increases in the number employed. Thus, in 1901, the L. & N. had 20,053 workers, their annual compensations being $11,124,609. In 1930 the L. & N. had 40,926 employes (and this was not the peak) whose compensation totaled $63,481,000 annually. (The "Pike's Peak" of L. & N. employment was reached in 1926, with 53,029 names on the payroll, representing an annual compensation of $78,177,106. However, a somewhat fewer number of employes had been paid $86,099,731 in 1920.)

In 1936, just prior to the year in which the obligations of the L. & N. were finally taken over for good by the Railroad Retirement Board, well over $500,000 was paid out to some 950 retired employes. A more specific mention will be made later on in this account of the provisions of the railroad retirement acts of 1935 and 1937, which largely replaced the individual pension plans of each road.

As related, a major portion of the L. & N.'s activities at the beginning of the 20th Century were devoted to construction and acquisition, but, of course, it was not neglecting its already-existing facilities. In fact, quite the contrary was true. Thus, in 1904, and 1905, it dipped deep into its corporate pockets and shelled out some $300,000 for improvements at Evansville; $104,035.36 for new facilities at East St. Louis, Ill.; $500,000 for terminal facilities at Atlanta and $117,673.37 for a freight station, etc., at

Front and Butler streets, Cincinnati, O. The improvements at Evansville and East St. Louis were especially pertinent for St. Louis was then beginning to emerge as one of the largest rail centers in the nation; a condition that was corollary to its rapid growth and expansion. (As early as July 26, 1889, the growing transportation needs of the city had resulted in the formation of the Terminal Railroad Association of St. Louis, this resulting from the combination of the Union Railway and Transit Company and the Terminal Railroad of St. Louis. Six railroads, including the L. & N., were charter members of this Association and subsequently, on February 26, 1903, they were joined by the ten other railroads entering St. Louis at that time.)

The reduction of grades on the Birmingham and Henderson divisions (in 1903), the completion of the long-deferred double track between Shepherdsville and Lebanon Junction (in 1900) and the re-building of the Rigolets and Chef Menteur bridges (both within the boundaries of Orleans Parish, La.), also occupied the L. & N.'s attention at this time. The latter task involved the erection of new superstructures and the driving of additional timber piling to strengthen the bridges against the terrific hurricanes originating in the eastern end of the Caribbean Sea. These "gentle breezes" often seriously interfered with the operation of trains, damage to the structures being a frequent occurrence. (Such troubles have long ago been overcome by construction of bridges built to withstand winds of the highest known velocity.)

The L. & N. also purchased the Newport and Cincinnati Bridge on June 16, 1904, this structure having been opened for traffic some 32 years before, or on April 1, 1872. After its completion the Pennsylvania Railroad Company subsequently obtained control and it was from this company that the purchase was made. (The Short Line trains of the L. & N. used this bridge to gain ingress into Cincinnati until April 1933 when they began using the C. & O. bridge.)

Entire shop force at Cloverport Shops, L. H. & St. L. Ry., about 1904.

On September 2, 1901, the Company's first 50-year man, Major James Geddes, completed a half-century of continuous service. At that time Major Geddes was superintendent of the Nashville and Decatur Division of the L. & N., but on the date mentioned he was promoted to the position of assistant to the general manager, with headquarters at Nashville. At this time also a very elaborate banquet was given in his honor in the Union Station at Nashville, the speakers including President Milton H. Smith, Major E. C. Lewis, president of the Nashville Terminals, and Judge H. W. Bruce, the L. & N.'s chief attorney.

A Scot by birth, Major Geddes had entered the service of the L. & N. on September 2, 1851, as a leveler in its engineering department and as such and as foreman of a construction force had helped to locate and build the line between Louisville and Nashville. Major Geddes died on November 13, 1914, after over 63 years of continuous service with the L. & N.

A glance at any railroad map of Kentucky will reveal that the L. & N. Railroad is well represented in every section of the state with the exception of the extreme western and eastern portions. Much of this trackage may be said to roughly parallel the Ohio River, the state's northern boundary, and it has been previously related how the L. & N. came into posession of a good part of this through the acquisition of its line from Cincinnati to Louisville. In 1905, it took the first of several steps which were eventually to give it undisputed possession of another line paralleling the Ohio: the purchase of a majority of the capital stock of the Louisville, Henderson and St. Louis Railway. This road extended from Strawberry, Ky., six miles south of Louisville, to Henderson, Ky., a distance of 137 miles, with a principal branch extending from Irvington to Fordsville, Ky., some 38 miles distant. (Although the L. & N. secured control on the date mentioned, the L. H. & St. L. continued to operate as a quasi-entity until April 2, 1929, when the Interstate Commerce Commission granted the L. & N. permission to lease the line for 99 years, with the privilege of renewal from time to time until the year 2396, which at this writing is still some distance in the future. At that time in 1929 the L. & N. owned 95.45 per cent of the common stock and 85.25 per cent of the preferred stock of the L. H. & St. L., and the road had been operated in close cooperation with the L. & N. for a great many years; in fact, since 1905.)

The old L. H. & St. L., which was often referred to as "The Texas" by old-timers, was so-called because its predecessor line was chartered as the Louisville, St. Louis and Texas Railway. This was on January 13, 1882, and its corporate name was not completely descriptive, W. V. McCracken, one of the builders of the road, summing up the matter succinctly when he said: "The Louisville, St. Louis and Texas didn't start from Louisville, never reached St. Louis and had no intention of going to Texas."

Actual construction of the line between Henderson and a point of connection with what is now the Illinois Central at West Point, Ky., was started on November 10, 1886. Prominent among the road's backers were R. R. Pierce, of Cloverport, Ky., the road's first president, Colonel J. D. Powers, of Owensboro, Ky., and Colonel J. C. Fawcett, of Louisville, Ky., who was also president for a short while. These gentlemen obtained financial backing

Sleeping quarters at Oak Hill Camp, Hopkins County, Ky., which was one of those established for the special L. & N. police force in 1901 in the strike of the Western Kentucky coal miners.

for the road and the project was largely underwritten, as well as built, by W. V. McCracken and Company, of New York. The head of this company, Major W. V. McCracken, was president of the "Texas" from September 3, 1888, until the financial panic of 1893, which forced the little line into receivership. The "Texas" was a real "family" road and at one time was officered by five McCrackens: W. V. was president, A. M. was superintendent, J. K. was general freight and passenger agent, H. M. was roadmaster and C. W. was chief engineer of the Louisville, Hardinsburg and Western, one of its branches.

At the time they commenced the building of the "Texas" the McCrackens had just finished the building of the Toledo, Saginaw and Michigan Railroad and brought many of these workers to Kentucky with them. A number of these remained with the road after it was completed.

The trackage between Henderson and the point of connection with the Illinois Central was completed on April 1, 1889, but it was April 1, 1905, before the line was subsequently extended from Howard, Ky., near West Point, to a connection with the L. & N. at Strawberry, a distance of 18 miles. Prior to that date entrance into Louisville had been gained via trackage arrangements with the old Newport News and Mississippi Valley Railroad (later to become a part of the Illinois Central), the road having been operated as a through line between Evansville and Louisville since 1897.

Rock Haven had the honor of being the point at which the first grading of the roadbed was done and the rail laying, once the line had been graded, was pushed forward simultaneously from Owensboro, towards Henderson and West Point and from West Point itself. The first trains on the road seem to have been operated between Owensboro and Stephensport in October 1888, the rail laying being speeded up a bit in order that the line might be ready for operation in time for the opening of the Owensboro Fair. Shops were subsequently established at Cloverport, Ky., and these remained in operation until the acquisition of the L. H. & St. L. by the L. & N. in 1929.

Much cannel coal was mined in the Tar Springs neighborhood, a few miles out of Cloverport and this reached the L. H. & St. L. via the Cloverport and Victoria Railroad, a narrow gauge "pike." It is said that the top layer of each shipment of coal was whitewashed in order that pilfering might be readily detected.

Contemporary with the construction of the "Texas" was that of its satellite, the Louisville, Hardinsburg and Western, also named with a bit of poetic license, which on July 6, 1891, completed the construction of what became known as the Fordsville Branch. (Irvington to Fordsville; Hardinsburg Junction to Hardinsburg; Dempster to Falls of Rough). The Louisville, Hardinsburg and Western was taken over by the "Texas" on August 6, 1892 and the "Texas" itself emerged from the shadow of receivership, before mentioned, on June 1, 1896, as the Louisville, Henderson and St. Louis Railway.

Not the least of the L. H. & St. L.'s distinctions was its excellent safety record of never having had a passenger killed in a train accident in its almost exactly 40 years of existence as a more or less independent carrier.

Closely related to the L. & N.'s obtaining control of the L. H. & St. L., was its formation of the Madisonville, Hartford and Eastern Railroad shortly thereafter and its eventual completion of this road on January 4, 1910. The L. & N. owned all of the capital stock in this venture and the road extended from a connection with the Morganfield Branch, near Madisonville, through Hopkins, Muhlenberg and Ohio counties, crossing the Ownesboro and Nashville line at Moorman, to a connection with the Fordsville Branch of the L. H. & St. L. at Ellmitch, Ky., a total distance of 55.49 miles. This line was intended as the hypotenuse of a triangle and did, in fact, create a shorter route between Louisville, Ky., and the coal fields and agricultural regions of Western Kentucky. However, the L. & N. was never able to take full advantage of this "short cut" because the construction of the line between Irvington and Ellmitch was such that heavy power and heavy tonnage trains could not be operated thereupon.

It was at about this time also that the L. & N. completed the Morton-Atkinson Cut-off (now known as the Earlington Cut-off) between the first two points mentioned. This took place on June 4, 1911, being approximately

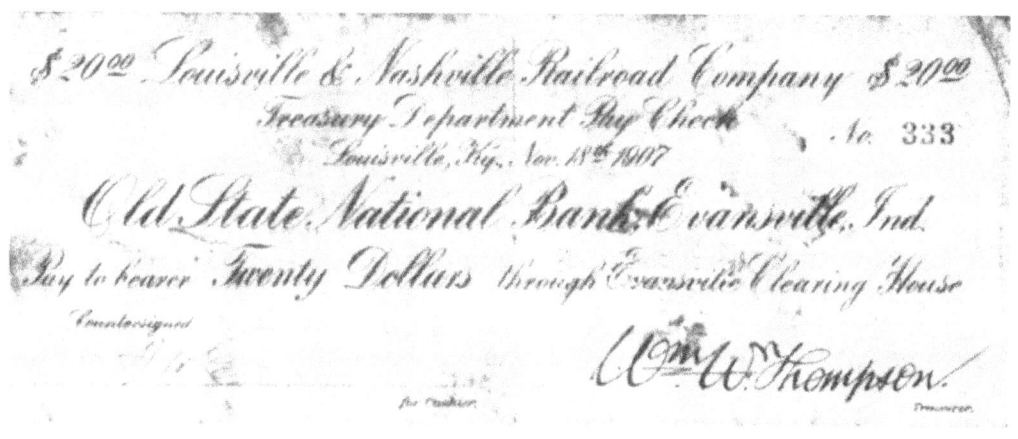

This is a reproduction of a piece of the scrip issued to employes by the Company during the money panic of 1907.

seven miles in length, as contrasted to the nine miles between the two points by way of Earlington and Madisonville.

At the end of the year ending with June 30, 1906, the L. & N. owned and operated a total of 4,205.55 miles of track and was interested, either as a joint owner or lessee, or as owner of a majority of the capital stock, in other roads whose combined mileage amounted to 2,366.83. About one-half of the strictly L. & N. trackage was laid with either 70- or 80-lb. rail, the remainder running to somewhat lighter weights although 12.52 miles boasted 85-lb. rail. This, of course, with the exception of 7.33 miles of track, which still had "heirloom" iron rail, was all steel rail.

The railroad's daily grind was enlivened by several untoward events during the period 1901-1907. Especial mention might be made of a disastrous fire which paritally destroyed the Louisville Union Station in 1905, necessitating its being re-built at considerable expense, the yellow fever epidemic of 1905, which was confined to New Orleans and vicinity; and the severe storms along the Gulf Coast in September 1906, which disrupted service for 8½ days, damaged the Company's property to the amount of $107,678, and decimated its potential traffic by leveling thousands of acres of pine trees adjacent to the just recently-completed Foley Branch. There was also the medium-sized "panic" of 1907, which, among other things, forced the Company to issue about $1,500,000 worth of scrip to pay off its employes, and the strike of the Western Kentucky coal miners which commenced in October 1901 and which lasted for over two years.

The last mentioned caused the L. & N. great inconvenience and expense, not only because it obviously curtailed a source of revenue, but additionally because an irresponsible element among the miners established a "stronghold" in the vicinity of Madisonville, Ky., and armed bands frequently sallied forth to interfere with the operation of trains, and to commit other acts of violence. Eventually, their depredations became so frequent and bloody that the L. & N. was forced to establish armed camps for its police forces at Oak Hill, Nortonville, Morton's Gap, Earlington and at other points along its lines in Western Kentucky for the protection of its property and in order to insure the operation of trains. As stated, this "state of war" continued for over two years and it was the latter part of 1903 before things gradually began to revert to normal and the L. & N. was able to dismantle its camps and withdraw its special forces.

The "panic" of 1907, before mentioned, was created by a condition of "money stringency," which means that there just wasn't enough money available to carry on the nation's business. It might seem that this condition is the cause of all "panics" or depressions, but that of 1907 differed from its predecessors in that "times" were not especially "hard" and there was only the normal amount of unemployment. The L. & N. Railroad, for example, in that year had a balance to the credit of its Profit and Loss Account (as of June 30, 1907) of $20,827,512.88, yet it was unable in November 1907, to obtain sufficient cash to meet its monthly payroll of approximately $2,000,000. The only solution seemed to be to issue scrip, and this was done in allocated amounts on each of the Company's depositories, the issuance being in denominations of $10, $20, and $50. In all, $1,100,000 worth of scrip was issued and distributed to employes and the

L. & N., realizing that employes would have a need for ready cash, purchased in the open market in New York City $625,000 in five-dollar gold pieces, paying for this "luxury" the tidy premium of $24,000; that is, it paid $649,000 for $625,000. Thus, employes in the months of November and December 1907, received 35 percent of their salaries in five-dollar gold pieces and the necessary odd change, and the remainder in scrip. Backed by the L. & N., the scrip was as "good as gold" and was everywhere accepted without question. The L. & N. was able to resume its usual cash payments in January 1908, and in about three months' time all of the scrip, with the exception of a few odds and ends, had come home to roost. Basically, scrip may be regarded as a promise to pay on the part of the one who issues it (all paper currency is, in effect, scrip) and it is a tribute to the L. & N. that its scrip was everywhere unhesitantly accepted as legal tender.

CHAPTER XXVI

A Look at Eastern Kentucky

ON JULY 1, 1906, the L. & N. assumed operation of two small roads in North Central Tennessee, one of which was yet another heir of the ill-fated Cumberland and Ohio Railroad, before mentioned in this account. Subsequent to their operation by the L. & N., the roads were combined into what was known as the Gallatin and Scottsville Railway and it conveyed all property, rights and franchises to the L. & N. on January 18, 1907.

The larger of these two roads – the Chesapeake and Nashville Railway Company – had originally been incorporated on February 23, 1882, as the Cincinnati, Green River and Nashville Railroad. The smaller of the two – the Middle and East Tennessee Central Railway – had been incorporated in Tennessee on February 19, 1883. To make a long story short, it might be said that both of these roads, the one extending from Gallatin, Tenn., to Scottsville, Ky., a distance of 35.44 miles (the C. & N. Railway), and the other extending from a point of connection with the Chesapeake and Nashville at Hartsville Junction to Hartsville, Tenn., 11.38 miles, were primarily projected, not as branch lines to their present termini, but as systems which would serve a large section of the Southland. Thus, it was the original intention of the Chesapeake and Nashville Railway to build north from Nashville to a connection with the Cincinnati Southern at Danville, Ky., via Glasgow, Ky., with a branch line from the latter point via Hodgenville to Elizabethtown. To further this aim the Chesapeake and Nashville secured on May 30, 1885, all of the interests of the Cumberland and Ohio aforesaid in its proposed road between Scottsville and Gallatin. This part of the contemplated line was completed and placed in operation in 1886 and was the only portion ever completely constructed, although some grading was done in the direction of Glasgow and the citizens of Nashville were so enthusiastic about the road that they had granted it a right-of-way and depot grounds and had even voted $100,000 towards building a bridge across the Cumberland River for it. However, the road passed into receivership on January 1, 1891, and after changing ownership several times finally was obtained by the L. & N. on July 1, 1906.

The Middle and East Tennessee Central Railway was incorporated to build from Gallatin eastward to Knoxville, but the best it could do was a line from Rogana (Hartsville Junction) to Hartsville. This was completed on January 1, 1892, and thereafter the little road changed hands rapidly like a lone lawnmower in a suburban neighborhood. It, too, was finally acquired by the L. & N. on July 1, 1906.

In both of these cases the L. & N. had acquired the properties, not because it especially needed them, but to keep them from falling into the

A street scene in Hazard, Ky., before the coming of the railroad in 1912.

wrong hands.

The need for another railroad paralleling the L. & N. between Elizabethtown, Ky., and Nashville, Tenn., was highly dubious, even at that time, and, on the whole, the Chesapeake and Nashville, as originally projected, may be taken as an excellent illustration of a well-meaning attempt to supply a non-existent need.

The abuses inherent in parallel trackage had early been recognized by the various states, but interpretations of "parallelism" differed widely and the law governing this matter was frequently contained only in the charters of the railroads which had arrived first on the scene. Large and commodious loopholes were thus provided for those sagacious enough to employ the best of legal talent. The Commonwealth of Kentucky, at least, however, had early decided that for one railroad to own parallel lines, or what the courts construed as parallel lines, was not in the best interests of the citizens of the Commonwealth and on several occasions the L. & N. was forced to surrender roads which it had acquired within that state. One of these "here-she-comes-there-she-goes" roads was the Frankfort and Cincinnati Railway, extending from Frankfort, Ky., to Paris, Ky., a distance of 40 miles, the legal title to which was conveyed to the L. & N. on October 28, 1909. (It had previously purchased all of the capital stock in 1901.) The Commonwealth of Kentucky brought suit against such acquisition, declaring it contrary to the state's constitution, and the case was eventually decided in its favor, the L. & N. ceasing to operate the Blue Grass carrier as of June 30, 1912.

At this time, the L. & N. was revising much of its older trackage in the interests of more efficient operation. Chief offender in the direction of tortuous track and "scenic railway" grade was the original line of the old South & North Alabama Railroad between Decatur and Montgomery which had been constructed as cheaply as possible because of a depleted

Engine No. 10 in 1891, at the Clay City, Ky., shops of the old Kentucky Union Railway, forerunner of the Lexington & Eastern Railway.

treasury. The L. & N. spent millions of dollars in rectifying this line to its liking and much of this work was done during the period 1911-1914. At that time the entire line between Decatur and Birmingham was revised, through the elimination of certain of the curves and grades aforesaid and the laying of a second track. This revision resulted in some re-routing, leading subsequently to the abandonment of much of its old line between Bangor and Newcastle, Ala., a distance of about 25 miles, the new line being located somewhat to the east of the original trackage. This new line was double-tracked and the revision necessitated the building of the Haydon Mountain Tunnel, 2,192.2 feet in length. All of this work was completed by November 15, 1914.

Roughly contemporary with this work on the S. & N. A. was that done between Saxton and Livingston, Ky., 59 miles, which was completed during 1908 and which involved the double-tracking of the line from the last-mentioned to Corbin; and the reduction of grades between Guthrie and Henderson, Ky., 97 miles, which was commenced in February, 1909, and completed in September, 1911. This latter involved the construction of some new line (including the Morton-Atkinson Cut-off before mentioned) and the completion of the work gave the L. & N. a line with a maximum grade of 0.6 per cent opposed to all trains. The revision of the line between Madison and Goodletts, Tenn., five miles, which construction was completed on August 28, 1910, also greatly facilitated the operation of trains between St. Louis and Chicago and Southern points and resulted in the building of a new line, 3.83 miles long, between Goodletts and Amqui, Tenn., and the abandonment of three miles of track between Goodletts and Edgefield Junction (Edenwold).

The constant effort made by the L. & N. to improve and refine its operations is illustrated in its Annual Report for the fiscal year ending with June 30, 1912, which contains no less than 66 closely-packed pages of type (8½" x 11½") devoted to Additions and Betterments to its properties during that year. The listings included such items as lumber sheds, ice houses, air pumps on locomotives, glass water gauges, wells, concrete mixers, telephone lines, bridges, cattle-guards, cross-overs, an interlocking plant, a rail unloader, section houses, stock pens, trestles, water cranes, water closets, wyes, etc.

The first decade or so of the 20th Century was a very profitable one for the L. & N. and its gross revenues increased from $35,449,377.84 (1902-1903) to $56,211,788.30 for the fiscal year ending June 30, 1912. During the same period net operating revenues increased from $11,478,565.40 to $16,585,460.86. However, the L. & N. was not really making as much money as these figures would seem to indicate. Operating Expenses had also increased greatly -- from $23,970,812.44 in 1902-1903 to $39,636,327.44 for the period 1911-1912.

There were other heavy drains upon the treasury as well. The acquisition and improvement of the L. & N.'s Cincinnati-Atlanta line had cost millions, as had its lines in Eastern Kentucky, whose story will be told very shortly. It was thought wisest to defray these extraordinary expenses by the issuance of bonds and by increasing the capitalization of the Company. Thus, the capital stock was increased by approximately 120,000 shares (about $12,000,000) in October, 1912, which increased the capitalization of the L. & N. from $60,000,000 to $72,000,000

In March 1903, an issue of $30,000,000 of Louisville & Nashville Railroad Company Five-Twenty Collateral Trust Four Per Cent Gold Bonds was authorized, chiefly to provide funds to retire a portion of the floating debt, as well as previous bond issues, and $23,000,000 worth of these bonds were subsequently sold. This issue was shortly followed on April 1, 1905, by another, the L. & N. executing a mortgage on that date securing an issue of bonds aggregating $50,000,000, bearing four per cent interest due May 1, 1950.

Caboose of the old Louisville & Atlantic Railroad, one of the predecessor lines of the L. & N.'s Eastern Kentucky Division, taken at Irvine, Ky., in 1907. Much of the trackage of the L. & A. has now been abandoned.

One of the last pieces of large-scale construction work undertaken by the L. & N. was its building of the Lewisburg and Northern Railroad, which occurred largely during the period June, 1910, through July 15, 1914. This road was organized by the L. & N. primarily for the purpose of creating a new line between Brentwood, Tenn., and Athens, Ala., a distance of 93.60 miles, by way of Lewisburg, Tenn.

The Lewisburg and Northern also constructed a new line from Maplewood, just north of Nashville, to Mayton, just south of Nashville, a distance of 10.61 miles. This "late-in-the-day" building gave the L. & N. what was, in effect, a second track between Nashville and Decatur since the line between Athens and Decatur, Ala., 12.45 miles, and between Brentwood and Mayton, 4.9 miles, was being given an additional track at the same time. The new line was a low-grade line and with one exception the maximum grade was 0.4 per cent. (Southbound trains encountered a stretch of 6.25 miles of track which had a grade of 0.9 per cent and where it was necessary to use pusher engines.)

This line was completed and placed in operation on July 15, 1914, with the exception of the trackage between Maplewood and Mayton, which because of the conditions created by the first World War was not completed until January 1, 1918.

An integral part of this development was the construction of shops and an extensive yard at Radnor, Tenn., on what is now known as the Radnor Cut-off (Maplewood to Mayton.).

The Tuscaloosa Mineral Railroad was also formed by the L. & N. at about this same time for the purpose of building a railroad from Brookwood, 37 miles southwest of Birmingham, to Tuscaloosa, Ala., a distance of 17.73 miles. This road was completed on August 8, 1912, and added another university town (the University of Alabama) to the L. & N.'s station list. (A branch from Holt Junction to Holt, Ala., 3.09 miles, was also completed at this time and the name of the road was subsequently changed to the Birmingham and Tuscaloosa Railroad, the latter being conveyed to the L. & N. on October 9, 1915.)

The Swan Creek Railway, now quiescent, was completed by the L. & N. on May 20, 1908, it having been built to serve the large phosphate deposits in Lewis and Maury counties, Tenn. It extended from Swan Creek Junction, Tenn., on the Nashville, Florence and Sheffield branch, to Gordonsburg, Tenn., a distance of 17 miles, and old-timers say that the region traversed abounded in rattlesnakes and copperheads, as well as phosphate rock. Tall tales are told of section crews bagging fabulous number of the reptiles between any two given points on the line. Another unusual feature of the Swan Creek Railway was its 59 ("count-'em") curves in its track and it is said that I. L. Chadwell, later a civil engineer at Mt. Pleasant, Tenn., who was resident engineer on the project, always regretted not having put in another curve and making it an even 60. These curves combined to produce a phenomenon when one took a trip over the now defunct line. A start could be made from Swan Creek Junction with the sun in one's face and before Irad, 12 miles away, had been reached, it was at one's back.

The Eastern Kentucky coal fields, to employ a term commonly used, are served by two of the Louisville & Nashville Railroad's operating di-

Freight train of the old Lexington & Eastern Railway, one of the predecessor lines of the L. & N.'s present-day Eastern Kentucky Division, crossing Lollegrod Bridge, Mile 35, in October, 1909.

visions; the Eastern Kentucky and the Cumberland Valley. These two have no direct physical connection, however, although the great bulk of the coal originating on each moves over the L. & N.'s Cincinnati-Atlanta line to the Cincinnati gateway, the most important market for these Eastern Kentucky coals lying north of the Ohio River.

The L. & N. Railroad's Eastern Kentucky Division (later a part of the Cincinnati Division), may be said to have had its inception in the incorporation of the Kentucky Union Railway Company on March 10, 1854, under Special Act of the Kentucky Legislature. It was organized to build a line of railroad from Hedges Station (later L. & E. Junction, 7 miles east of Winchester, Ky.) on the Elizabethtown, Lexington and Big Sandy Railroad, through Powell, Wolfe, Breathitt, Perry and Letcher counties to Big Stone Gap, thence through the Cumberlands to Abingden, Va., located on the Virginia and Tennessee Railroad (later a part of the Norfolk and Western Railway). This ambitious project was not, of course, realized in its entirety. In fact, until the year 1873 the Company contented itself with the acquiring of coal and timber lands in Perry, Leslie and Letcher counties and the making of a number of surveys through that section of Eastern Kentucky, the purpose being, of course, to select a route that would be cheap to construct, economical to operate and yet would reach the maximum number of coal fields.

Actual pick-and-shovel work was not started, therefore, until some time during 1886, during which year the line was completed from Kentucky Union Junction (later L. & E. Junction) to Clay City, Ky., 14.7 miles away. Once commenced the work moved ahead fairly rapidly and by December 9, 1890, had been extended south-eastward to Elkatawa, Ky., some 52 miles distant and northwestward to Lexington, Ky., 28 miles away. The line from Elkatawa to Jackson, 3.07 miles, was completed on July 15, 1891. This descent to the realities of railroading weakened the financial structure of the road and it was placed in the hands of a receiver on February 10, 1891. A subsequent foreclosure sale in March 1894, eventually

This was the common carrier between Hazard and Jackson, Ky., before the building of the L. & N.'s North Fork Extension. The trip usually took all day and required an early-morning start.

resulted in the properties of the Kentucky Union being conveyed to the Lexington and Eastern Railway on October 16, 1894, the latter having been organized for the express purpose of reorganizing the Kentucky Union.

The Kentucky Union seems to have been a fairly well-constructed road for its time. Sixty-pound steel rails were laid in the track and a portion of the track was ballasted. Unballasted track was not uncommon at that time; in fact, a good many of the smaller roads were largely unballasted, the rails and cross-ties being laid directly on the graded right-of-way. There were six tunnels on this line from Lexington to Jackson and some 20 bridges. The foothill country was encountered in the vicinity of Nada, Ky., and it may have been the resultant greater cost of construction that forced the Kentucky Union Railway to establish Jackson, Ky., as its last outpost. (This original line of the old Kentucky Union Railway between Winchester and Fincastle was requisitioned by the War Production Board of the U. S. Government in July, 1942, and removal of the track was completed in November of the same year.)

The L. & N. first became interested in the possibility of developing the Eastern Kentucky coal fields in Perry and Letcher counties, through an extension of the L. & E.'s line from Jackson, Ky., as early as March of 1903. In that month it became curious about the quality and quantities of these coals and it went into the matter with its customary thoroughness. Major R. H. Elliott, of Birmingham, a prominent consulting engineer of the day, was commissioned to not only examine the trackage of the Lexington and Eastern, but to survey all possible routes from Jackson to the headwaters of the North Fork of the Kentucky River and to report on the coal seams in the territory adjacent to the proposed extension. The following is quoted from his report of May 19, 1903, to Milton H. Smith, the L. & N.'s president:

"The coal seams examined in the neighborhood of the towns of Jackson, Hyden, Hazard and Whitesburg, and near Pound Gap, in Letcher County, Ky., are four, and perhaps five in number. They are in general, level, but show local dips, which are very slight and go with the drainage. At only two points were exceptions perceptible; first, the Elkhorn seam dips slightly to the southeast and toward Pine Mountain, and about the head of

Buckhorn Creek in Knott County, there is a dip to the northwest – at both places across the drainage. Necessarily, there are many others which were not seen; but, in general, the coal field is remarkably true and free from geological disturbances."

Major Elliott's report was generally favorable, both as to the feasibility of the proposed extension and the quantity and quality of the coal in the fields to be penetrated. However, Henry Walters, chairman of the L. & N.'s board of directors, did not feel that the time was ripe for further expansion, he also being of the opinion that it would be better for the L. & N. to build its own line into the coal fields aforesaid, rather than to attempt a judicious combination of the old and new, involved in a purchase of the Lexington and Eastern Railway. That line at the time was not in shape to handle a heavy traffic and a financial mishap in 1900 had just stopped short of receivership. In 1903, at the time of Major Elliott's investigations, it was controlled by E. Kennedy Tod, of New York City, and its principal sources of revenue were timber and cannel coal.

Coincidentally enough, the L. & N.'s investigation of the possibilities of an extension into the Eastern Kentucky coal fields in Perry and Letcher counties was initiated just prior to the receipt of a letter from James W. Fox, of New York City and Big Stone Gap, Va. In his communication to President Milton H. Smith, Mr. Fox called attention to the very fine coke which had been produced from coal mined in Pike and Letcher counties, Ky., and suggested that the L. & N. might be interested in building a line to serve this territory. He submitted copies of reports upon coals from the Elkhorn Creek field, which began about five miles northeast of Whitesburg, Ky., as compared with those from other districts in Kentucky, West Virginia and Pennsylvania. They had been prepared by Andrew S. McCreath and John Fulton, mineralogists. These reports demonstrated conclusively that coals from the Eastern Kentucky fields were good coking coals and hence could be utilized satisfactorily in the operation of blast furnaces. The following is quoted from these reports:

"On the whole, I can submit with the utmost confidence that these cokes (that is, those made from coals mined in the Elkhorn Creek field) in their physical property will be found to be very valuable in blast furnaces and other metallurgical uses. I have no hesitation in assuring their successful use in blast furnace practice. From your analyses, as before noted, the sulphur and phosphorus are exceedingly low, lower than the Connellsville. Under these conditions of the physical and chemical properties, especially with very low volumes of sulphur and phosphorus, they are admirably adapted for the use in blast furnaces, producing Bessemer pig iron to be manufactured in the different varieties of steels. If the two samples are fair averages of the product of coal from Kentucky mines, there can be no doubt as to their great value for the uses above mentioned, and I can recommend them with full assurance that they will maintain their place in any market for the uses above mentioned . . . . There is no apparent reason that it should not go into the market, and retain its place firmly, in competition with Connellsville, Pocahontas or other good cokes, **if the cost of production can be secured on equal economies with these noted above.**"

The last sentence from the excerpts quoted above aptly designated the fly in the ointment, however. These hundreds of thousands of acres of coal land had no adequate outlet to the outside world and such coal as was mined reached its markets only after a tortuous trip over crude mountain trails and down winding mountain streams. It was a procedure that was costly, slow, and by the nature of things, highly inefficient. It took seven or eight days, for instance, to make the 86-mile trip from Whitesburg to Jackson, rail transportation's last outpost. "Imports," of course, were subject to the same handicaps.

The crying need and the favorable reports aforesaid, however, were outweighed by the exigencies of the moment and, as stated, Mr. Walters did not feel that the L. & N. would be justified in a penetration of the Eastern Kentucky coal fields at that time. Insofar as the L. & N. was concerned the matter languished until the fall of 1909, when Mr. Smith, as a result of requests from the Northern Coal and Coke Company that the L. & N. extend its line into their properties on the headwaters of the North Fork of the Kentucky River, instructed J. E. Willoughby, engineer of construction, to observe closely the properties of the Lexington and Eastern between Jackson and Lexington as he traveled between those two points by train. Subsequently, Mr. Smith wrote Mr. Walters strongly recommending the purchase of the L. & E. and future extension to Whitesburg, Ky., or vicinity. The following is quoted from that letter and sheds a revealing light upon "M. H.'s" vision and foresight:

"I think it will be well to consider buying the Lexington and Eastern and extending the road from Jackson up the North Fork. The distance from Beattyville Junction (Airedale) via Richmond to Winchester, via the Louisville and Atlantic, is 86.4 miles and from Beattyville Junction via Stanton to Wnchester via the Lexington and Eastern, 50 miles, a difference in favor of the Lexington and Eastern of 36.4 miles. In addition, the length of road to be constructed from Jackson, say to Whitesburg, or to some point on the Rockhouse Branch, would be very much less than the line which Mr. Willoughby is reconnoitering from Heidelburg via Sturgeon Creek.

"We should keep in mind that, aside from forest products, the desirable traffic to be secured (and, in fact, the only traffic that would induce the Louisville and Nashville to construct the road) would be the coke produced from coking coals, or the shipment of coals for coking purposes; that practically all of this will go to and across the Ohio River; that the rates will probably be low; and that the construction of such a line will not produce or create traffic for existing lines, except to a limited extent – say from Richmond or Winchester to Cincinnati or Louisville. At the same time, if a railroad can be constructed with not excessive grades, or with favorable grades on a considerable part of the line, and a large and regular traffic secured, it may, and probably will, prove to be a profitable venture."

Chapter XXVII

North Fork Extension

IN JUNE 1909, just prior to Mr. Smith's recommendation that the L. & N. purchase the L. & E. and extend the line on up the North Fork of the Kentucky River, the L. & N. had purchased all the stock and bonds of the Louisville and Atlantic Railroad, with the apparent purpose of utilizing its lines to reach the coal fields of Southeastern Kentucky. At that time the Louisville and Atlantic extended from Versailles to Beattyville Junction, a distance of 101.10 miles, by way of Nicholasville, Richmond and Irvine, Ky. This line, which was later abandoned between Versailles and Irvine, had its inception on March 30, 1878, with the incorporation of the Winchester and Beattyville Railroad, which by June 1, 1893, had completed and placed in operation the 5.6 miles of track between Beattyville and Beattyville Junction.

Another predecessor line of the Louisville and Atlantic was the Richmond, Nicholasville, Irvine and Beattyville Railroad, which was incorporated on March 10, 1888, and which was organized for the purpose of building a railroad from Versailles to Middlesborough, Ky. The venture had the backing of a number of Louisville capitalists, including Major J. W. Stine, and was constructed principally as a feeder to the Louisville Southern, later a part of the Southern Railway System. The line was completed to Irvine in 1890 from Versailles, but no further construction work was done for a number of years, the railroad being placed in the hands of a receiver in December 1891. It re-

Prior to the building of the L. & N.'s line from Jackson to McRoberts, in 1912, supplies were brought into this mountain territory by push boat from Jackson up the North Fork of the Kentucky River. The accompanying picture shows a North Fork "flotilla" near Lennut, Ky., about two miles north of Hazard, in 1911. The men manning the poles may be seen in the stern of the leading boat.

The first passenger train out of Hazard, shown above, was run on Tuesday, June 25, 1912, and was well patronized. It ran to Jackson, Ky., 45 miles away, and returned the same day. It was said to be the first time that anyone had been able to make this round trip in one day.

mained there until August 19, 1899, emerging from beneath the bar sinister of receivership as the Louisville and Atlantic Railroad, a company which had the backing of a number of Philadelphia capitalists, including Adolph Segal, T. W. Synnott and John Sparhawk, Jr.

They obtained control of the line from Beattyville to Beattyville Junction on July 10, 1900, and, in cooperation with Louisville capitalists, decided to extend the line from Beattyville to Irvine, 33 miles away. This extension was completed in November 1902, and enabled the L. & A. to connect with the L. & E. in the vicinity of Airedale, Ky.

The history of this trackage north and east of Jackson, Ky., has been more or less detailed because of the importance which most of these lines have come to assume in the movement of coal from the Eastern Kentucky coal fields to the Ohio River crossing at Covington and Cincinnati. The line from Irvine to Winchester, for example, is what is known as a low grade line and its construction greatly facilitated the handling of coal. It was, of course, not completed until after the coal had begun to leave its home in the hills in considerable quantities and its construction was typical of the many improvements made by the L. & N. in its pertinent properties once it was established that the coal traffic was even greater than the most optimistic anticipations.

It was from Jackson, however, that the L. & N. began its penetration of the Kentucky coal fields and the implement chosen for this was the Lexington and Eastern Railway. The annual report of the latter for the fiscal year ending with June 30, 1909, reveals that only 8,105 tons of bituminous coal were handled that year, although 57,780 tons of cannel coal were also moved. It might be explained for the benefit of the layman that the word "cannel" is a corruption of "candle" and such coal is so-called because it is highly volatile and burns with a bright flame. That same report reveals that, in all, the L. & E. moved a total of 254,057 tons of freight during the period mentioned and carried 173,000 passengers. For that year, its gross earnings totaled $412,625.65, while its net earnings amounted to $73,136.36.

The L. & E. maintained extensive picnic grounds at Natural Bridge, Ky., and the spot was a focal point for rail excursions.

As a result of its investigations the L. & N. finally purchased the entire outstanding capital stock (5,000 shares) of the L. & E. in November 1910, but even before then it had proceeded with its plans to reach the rich coal lands of Eastern Kentucky.

The first step towards such penetration was the locating of the line and the obtaining of the right-of-way. The first was entrusted to J. E. Willoughby, engineer of construction before mentioned, and the second task was placed under the direct supervision of E. S. Jouett, of Winchester, Ky., who was the Lexington and Eastern's chief attorney, and who later became the L. & N.'s vice president and general counsel. Mr. Jouett appointed right-of-way agents in each of the three counties to be traversed (Breathitt, Perry and Letcher) and the work was commenced on August 29, 1910. The obtaining of a right-of-way in this mountainous section was, of course, more difficult than similar purchases would have been in more effete sections. In a good many sections the natives had had little contact with the outside world and regarded all strangers impartially as "furriners." The locating parties bore the brunt of this suspicion for they were mostly from the "outside" and in many cases were absolutely forbidden to cross certain lands,

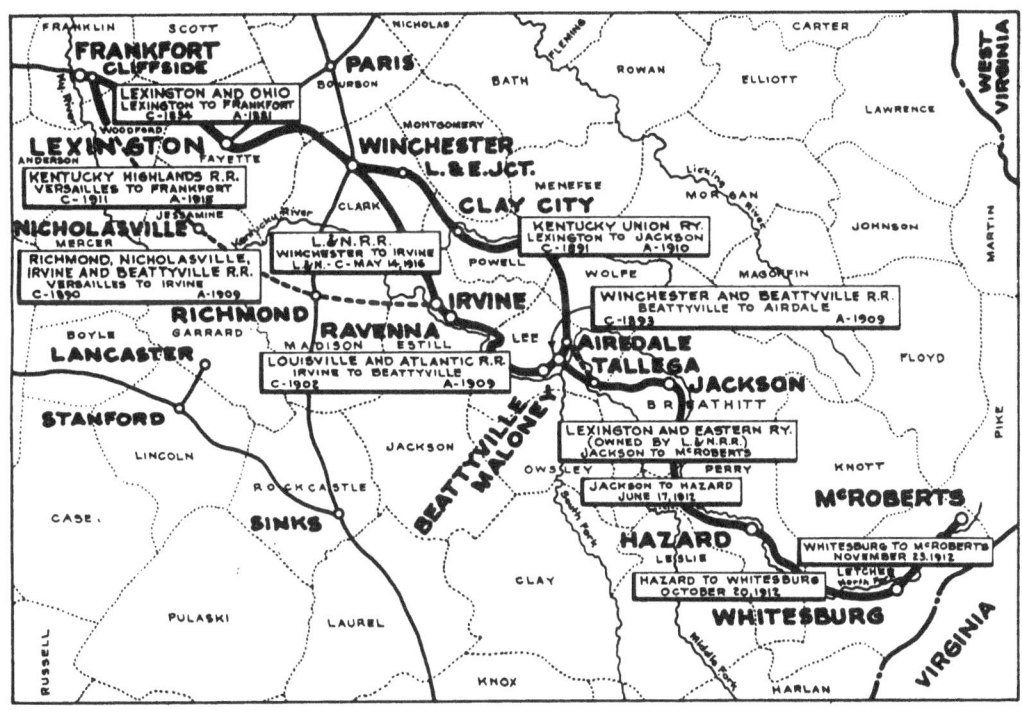

Much of the original track of the old Louisville & Atlantic and Lexington & Eastern railroads was either revised or abandoned following its purchase by the L. & N. This resulted in the abandonment of approximately nine miles of track between Beattyville Junction and Jackson and joined the lines of the L. & A. and the L. & E. at Maloney, instead of Beattyville Junction, now Airedale. (LEGEND: -----Abandoned; C—Date construction completed by predecessor road; A—Date acquired by L. & N.; L. & N.--C—Date construction completed by L. & N.)

This old-time scene at the entrance to the Dave L. Webb coal mine near Seco, Ky., said to be the first coal mine opened in the territory served by our Eastern Kentucky District, is typical of coal mining operations in those early days. The photograph was taken in 1906, but at that time Dr. Webb's famous mine had been operated for about 11 years, or since 1895. The mine was later operated by the Elkhorn Junior Coal Company. In the picture are Dr. Webb's little daughter, Sink Spangler, Matt Webb and Dr. Dave L. Webb, owner and operator of the mine.

these arbitrary edicts against the march of progress being enforced by the owners who sat on their rail fences all day long, rifles in hand. The right-of-way agents, fortunately, were well acquainted in that section, but tactful diplomacy was necessarily a major ingredient in their conduct.

The method employed in obtaining the right-of-way was to first obtain options on the land which might be traversed by the railroad and Mr. Jouett furnished his workers with a plentiful supply of five dollar bills, one of these being given to each owner to clinch the option. An old survey, known as the Walker Survey, was used as a basis for the options, and provided for a route on either side of the North Fork. Later on, one of the two optional routes was selected, those options were exercised, and the L. & N. took deeds to the properties involved. All things considered the work moved along smoothly and by October 1, 1910, 80 per cent of the right-of-way had been obtained. Condemnation suits were necessary in only a very small percentage of the cases involved. The valley of the North Fork is a rather narrow one and the railroad's right-of-way was thus forced to unceremoniously brush aside houses, barns, orchards and gardens. This had a tendency to increase the cost of the properties purchased, but even so, the average price per mile of right-of-way purchased (between Dumont, just south of Jackson, to McRoberts, a distance of 100.55 miles) came to only $2,559.56. Moreover, a certain amount of right-of-way was donated, which had the effect of lowering this figure somewhat. In all, 1,059.497 acres, costing $229,285.46, were purchased for the right-of-way and 112.34 acres were donated, the latter mostly by coal companies. The figures mentioned, of course, refer only to the sums actually paid for the properties and do not include legal fees, traveling expenses and other items.

The following extracts from a letter written by Mr. Jouett at the time, illustrates vividly some of the handicaps under which the railroad labored in obtaining its right-of-way:

"I asked for ten days in which to try the option plan. This was acceptable and I prepared and had printed the necessary blanks and started the work in Breathitt on August 29th, after which I went to Stonega, Va., and struck on horseback through Letcher and Perry. The feeling in Letcher was very hostile, the opinion prevailing that we were simply trying to tie up the available rights-of-way to prevent the building of a railroad by any other company. I argued this with a committee of leading citizens until after midnight before I convinced them of our good faith, by agreeing to a reverter of the parcel involved upon failure to build a road through it within four years. I then awoke the printer, had new blanks printed and was ready in the morning to start out the different forces among whom I had divided the country. I engaged the six leading attorneys, including the commonwealth's attorney and the county attorney, besides acquiring the assistance of the county judge and other court officials . . . .

"I next rode to Hazard, the county seat of Perry, about 43 miles distant, where I made a thorough organization under Wootton and Morgan, our efficient local attorneys, and several other lawyers whom I engaged to help temporarily. Here I held a town meeting and after enlisting the assistance of nearly all the officials, squads were sent out covering the entire line, each accompanied by a special deputy county clerk. I closed up in person nearly all the necessary contracts in and about Hazard.

"From here I rode to Jackson, about 40 miles, where I found that the work had lagged. I got some new men to assist Mr. Pollard, our local attorney, and tried to infuse some new life into that county.

"About a week later I began the retracing of this course, starting at Jackson and traversing the entire length of the line to Whitesburg, in order to close up all the more difficult propositions, my instructions to our right-of-way agents in the first place having been to close nothing when the price demanded was greater than they thought would be given by a jury in con-

Taken at Whitesburg, Ky., in the early part of 1912, this picture shows a number of those who were prominent in the construction of the North Fork Extension from Dumont, near Jackson, to McRoberts, Ky. Those enjoying their day of rest are as follows, left to right: J. E. Willoughby, chief engineer of construction, L. & N.; E. S. Jouett, chief attorney, L. & E., later vice president and general counsel, L. & N.; Mrs. R. W. Warfield; W. S. Morton, division engineer, L. & E.; R. W. Warfield, resident engineer, L. & N.; a Mr. Byers, tie buyer; Resident Engineer Duncan, L. & N.; General Manager W. A. McDowell, L. & E.; J. Coleman Stewart, masonry inspector; R. T. Ewing, masonry inspector.

demnation proceedings."

By January 1, 1911, the right-of-way had been almost entirely secured and the contractors were able to proceed with the building of the line. It, of course, being to the L. & N.'s advantage to do so, it encouraged and aided the contractors in the rapid construction of the line by granting them a flat rate of one cent per mile per person for the moving of labor and by also giving them greatly reduced rates on supplies, materials, livestock, carts, equipment, machinery, etc.

The successful conclusion of the work of obtaining the right-of-way was aided in no small way by the assistance and cooperation of such men as John C. C. Mayo, who was manager of the Northern Coal and Coke Company's properties in Eastern Kentucky, and C. Bascom Slemp, who later became secretary to President Calvin Coolidge. Both of these men had long been active in the development of the Eastern Kentucky coal fields.

The eventual coming of the railroad greatly increased property values throughout all that section of Eastern Kentucky. For instance, in 1910, the property of Perry County, as a whole, was listed at approximately $80,000 for taxing purposes. A little over a decade later this had increased to $23,000,000, and the population of Hazard, the county seat, had increased from 250 to approximately 8,000.

It should be realized, of course, that the lines of the Lexington and Eastern and of the Louisville and Atlantic, as originally acquired by the L. & N., bore faint resemblance to the lines which have later evolved from these properties. Briefly stated, the work undertaken by the L. & N. immediately after acquisition of the two roads just mentioned, may be listed as follows:

1. The North Fork Extension from Dumont, Ky. (near Jackson), to McRoberts; 100.5 miles.

2. The revision of the line and the construction of second track from Paris to Winchester. (This, of course, involved the L. & N.'s own Cincinnati-Atlanta line, but it was an integral part of the development upon which the L. & N. spent millions of dollars for the expedited handling of coal moving between the fields in Eastern Kentucky and the Cincinnati gateway.)

3. The construction of a new line from Winchester to Irvine; 29 miles.

4. The revision of the line from Irvine to Maloney's Bend; 36 miles.

5. The building of a yard at Irvine, Ky.

6. The building of a new line from Maloney's Bend to Tallega; five miles.

7. The revision of the line from Tallega to Jackson; 14 miles.

The cost of this work, exclusive of that of the North Fork Extension, which cost approximately $5.7 million alone, amounted to well over $5 million and resulted in distances being shortened and the subsequent abandonment of a certain amount of track. Although the North Fork Extension was outstandingly the major item of work undertaken by the L. & N. on behalf of the L. & E. and L. & A. it was completed on November 23, 1912, well ahead of some of the other items mentioned. However, all of the other work, with the exception of the new line between Winchester and Irvine, was placed in operation shortly thereafter in 1913 and 1914. The Winchester-Irvine line, owing to certain unfavorable conditions encountered, was not placed in service until May 14, 1916. (The right-of-way ran through a blue clay and

This is the first engine that went through Yellow Rock Tunnel when the Louisville & Atlantic completed its 33-mile extension from Irvine to Beattyville, Ky., in November 1902. The photo was taken at Belle Point, six miles from Yellow Rock Tunnel and four miles from Beattyville. Among those in the picture are: Engineer J. M. Coffelder, Fireman R. Reeves, Conductor D. Minton, Brakeman D. Baker, Construction Foreman H. Wheeler, and Assistant Construction Foreman W. Newman. Evidently it was a gala occasion for all concerned.

soapstone section for a good many miles and it was necessary to drive piling to secure the fills. Moreover, two trestles had to be built which were among the longest and highest on the System. One of these crossed Red River at Sloan, Ky., and was 2,200 feet long and 233 feet high, and the other crossed Howard Creek and was 2,100 feet long and 225 feet high. These heights and lengths compared favorably as engineering feats with the Southern Pacific's Pecos River Bridge which is 1,516 feet long and 321 feet high and which is said to be the second highest structure of its kind in the world.)

In the meantime, the L. & N. had undertaken and completed the reduction of grades and the addition of double track between Covington and Winchester, 91.5 miles, this giving the L. & N., in effect, a low grade line all the way from the Cincinnati gateway to the headwaters of the North Fork of the Kentucky River. In this connection, the following from the Louisville Courier-Journal of December 5, 1913, is of interest:

"The first through passenger train on the new double-track line between Winchester and Cincinnati passed over the new track this morning as far as Renick Station, and in two weeks more trains will be running as far as Austerlitz. Between Austerlitz and Escondida a small gap is yet unfinished, but by January 1, it is confidently expected that all through passenger trains will be routed over the new double-track line all the way from Winchester to Cincinnati.

"It is not generally known that the entire double-track line between Winchester and Paris is a completely new one and built on a grade to conform to the remainder of the line from Winchester to McRoberts, so that there will be practically a down grade haul all the way from McRoberts to Winchester and from Winchester to Cincinnati. By July 1, it is estimated that at least 2,000 cars of coal alone a day will be rehandled at Winchester on the new

This is how Whitesburg, Ky., appeared in 1912, just after the coming of the railroad, whose tracks may be seen at the extreme left.

joint terminals of the L. & N. lines, the land for the terminals having been quietly acquired sometime ago. The L. & N. now owns more than 500 acres for use in yards and terminals in Winchester and the opening of the double-track line to Eastern Kentucky will naturally produce an enormous business for Winchester."

Parallel activity had included the reconstruction of bridges on the old line between Lexington and Jackson and the construction of innumerable spurs and side-tracks to serve the many coal mines, lumber plants and timber operations along the line of road.

Although the L. & E. was not actually conveyed to the L. & N. until October 5, 1915, it had, in effect, owned the road since November 1910. As related, the L. & N. purchased the Louisville and Atlantic in November 1909, and a certain amount of opposition subsequently developed to its control of the L. & E., this being based on the somewhat far-fetched hypothesis that the L. & A. and the L. & E. were parallel and hence competing lines, such ownership being forbidden by Kentucky law. This opposition, however, came to naught. It had a certain limited following in Clay City, Stanton and other towns on the L. & E.'s original line who evidently feared that the new developments would result in a situation to the disadvantage of their communities.

The line from Jackson, or Dumont, was completed to McRoberts on November 23, 1912; a fairly rapid feat of construction. Although the line penetrated rugged country, heavy construction was largely avoided by closely following the valley of the North Fork of the Kentucky River. It was, however, necessary to cross this stream no less than 16 times between Jackson and Millstone, and between Millstone and McRoberts there were a number of crossings of Boone Fork, as the North Fork is known in that territory.

The news that a railroad was to be built through that section of Eastern Kentucky had been news indeed and the far-flung newspapers of that section brought forth from musty retirement their largest fonts of type to herald the new day. Thus, the Mountain Eagle, of Whitesburg, Ky., enthused inkily in its issue of September 15, 1910: " R. R. MATTER SETTLED. WITHIN TWO AND ONE-HALF YEARS THE LEXINGTON & EASTERN RAILWAY IS TO BE COMPLETED FROM JACKSON, KY., TO MOUTH OF BOONE IN LETCHER, COMING VIA HAZARD

AND WHITESBURG. BIGGEST AND RICHEST COAL AND TIMBER FIELDS IN THE WORLD TO BE DEVELOPED. CONTRACT WILL BE LET ON OR BEFORE OCTOBER 15 AND DIRT WILL BE FLYING ALL ALONG THE ROUTE BEFORE JANUARY 1, 1911, MILLIONS WILL BE SPENT IN CONSTRUCTING THE LINE AND WHEN FINISHED LETCHER COUNTY AND THE MOUNTAINS WILL BECOME THE RICHEST SECTION IN ENTIRE SOUTH." An equally enthusiastic story then followed these headlines.

This anticipatory enthusiasm did not wane all during the time the line was being built through Breathitt, Perry and Letcher counties. As the railroad entered the various towns of the region, celebrations were held and each piece of construction work had its perennial audience of young and old. The following is quoted from the Hazard Herald of August 17, 1911, to show how easily the mountain inhabitants adapted themselves to the changing times:

"WILD SCENES AROUND VIPER – ONE HUNDRED KEGS OF POWDER AND FIVE OR SIX CASES OF DYNAMITE LET GO AT NIGHT – PEOPLE FLEE FOR THE MOUNTAINS. The biggest cut on Leighton and Company's railroad contract is just above Mason's Creek. On Friday, the 4th instant, John Woods, a good-natured old gentleman, worked all day filling and stamping several holes with dynamite and powder at this place, where he has faithfully worked since last spring. About 10 o'clock at night he announced ready! All the nearby inhabitants took to the high hills and knobs, carrying with them cows, calves, horses, dogs and probably old hens and young chickens. Those farther away were aroused from their slumbers by the alarm f-i-a-r! f-i-a-r! All the charges were touched off at once by a battery, containing about one hundred kegs of powder and five or six cases of dynamite. Several tons of rock were hurled across the river, filling up the county road and playing havoc with J. S. Combs' fence, barn and corncrib. Those still farther away, sleeping sound, sprang out of bed, ran to the telephone and called his nearest neighbor, saying, 'Hello! Did you hear that big gun – somebody is dynamiting fish!' Mr. Leighton came up the next morning and made all damages satisfactory."

Headlines and phrases like this dotted subsequent issues of the Hazard Herald:

"HAZARD TUNNEL PUNCHED THROUGH." (MARCH 21, 1912) "TRACK LAYING AT THE RATE OF A MILE AND A HALF PER DAY ON HOME STRETCH." (MAY 30, 1912.) "HURRAH! THE STEAM CARS ARE IN HAZARD. COMMERCIAL SERVICE THE 25TH. LARGE CROWD GREETS ENGINE NO. 324 AS SHE CROSSES TRESTLE IN TOWN ACROSS RIVER. BAND PLAYS 'GLORY HALLELUJAH!'" These last headlines headed a story in the June 20, 1912, issue of the Hazard Herald, in which the reporter stated that Monday, June 17, would go down in history of Hazard as a red-letter day, since the first steam horse entered the town at that time. He further said and we quote: "When the track had been laid across the trestle at Messer Branch, a number of the young ladies mounted the engine and track-laying car and, in a short time, had both decorated with flowers, bunting and flags . . . It was intended to have other speeches, but the crowd were too busily engaged in looking at the work of the crew as they put down rail at the rate of one a minute . . . The number of the engine to first come to town was No. 324 . . . Supervisor George Adams said that Monday's work was a record-breaker and thought it would not be a bad idea to have a lot of pretty girls looking on, as the men seemed to work more than they usually did, and he couldn't account for it, other than the crowd looking on . . . A barrel of cider was opened and everybody drank to the future of the town and its people, as also to the railroad . . . In an interview last Saturday, General Manager W. A. McDowell, of the L. & E. R. R. Company, said: "I take great pleasure in announcing that regular passenger service is to be inaugurated over the L. & E. Extension, between Hazard and Jackson, on the 25th of this month . . . The service will be strictly week-end for some time and no trains operated on Sundays.' . . . The steel was brought through Hazard tunnel and up to the edge of town Saturday afternoon, and finished up to Bridge 6, at the upper end of Combs' tunnel, Monday. Preparations for putting in that bridge have been pushed with vigor, and the moving of the heavy timbers necessary therefor, from Bridge 5, employed most of the ox teams in the country for two or three days. The progress of the work opposite town has been very interesting to the people of Hazard."

The great day came at last, as scheduled, and the Hazard Herald's story on the event was titled: "FIRST TRAIN OUT WELL PATRONIZED. NEARLY EVERYBODY WENT TO JACKSON OR SOME OTHER POINT ON THE LINE. ORDERLY CROWD. EVERYBODY HAPPY AND SMILING." The article went on to say that the train, consisting of a combination coach and baggage car, a partition coach for smokers and colored people and a first-class coach, pulled out of Hazard at 7:00 a.m., Tuesday morning, June 25, 1912, Jackson-bound. It was admitted that most of the people were making the trip simply to say that they had been on the first train out of Hazard.

The article casually mentions that several of the passengers had stars on the lapels of their coats and contains this interesting paragraph: ". . . Going through the coaches one found a number of Hazard's leading men and women, all wearing a smile, just like children with a new toy. C. M. Horn, the proprietor of the only theodium in the county, who has been running a picture of his own, said he was going to see what kind of a 'picture show' the L. & E. had. It is possible that in a short time the citizens of Hazard may be able to take a trip over the line at a small price of a dime, as they look at the films shown on the canvas, presenting the scenery all along the line just as seen from the car window . . " (What is referred to here is a bit of vanished America highly popular two generations or so ago. "Passengers" boarded a "train" and the illusion of motion was created by having painted or photographed scenery flap past the car windows at a high rate of speed. - K.A.H.)

The building of the railroad created several amusing incidents. Following the opening of the line to Hazard, the work was pushed forward rapidly, Whitesburg being reached on October 20, 1912, and McRoberts on November 23, 1912. One day a woman living near Neon, Ky., a few miles south of McRoberts, flagged a passenger train and upon being asked what she wanted, asked the surprised train crew to deliver a pail of buttermilk

End of the line. The rail-laying train reached McRoberts, Ky., on the North Fork Extension on November 16, 1912.

to her son at the last mentioned point. One lady, viewing her first train, said: "It had a hard time getting in here and it never will get out I know!"

The naming of Uz (properly pronounced so as to rhyme with "Buzz" but generally called "You-Zee" by railroaders and others), Ky., deserves special mention even in a station list which included such choice nomenclature as Hot Spot, Ice, Trailer, Ermine and Mayking. This station, which is one of the shortest named in these United States, was so designated in honor of Job of the land of Uz, the well-known Biblical character. It was given this appellation by J. E. Willoughby, chief engineer of construction, after he had heard many a hard luck tale from his resident engineer, W. S. Morton, Jr., about his troubles with the natives, laborers, topography, etc., of that section. Uz is about six miles west of Whitesburg, deep in the hills.

The items of trackage previously mentioned may be regarded as the basic structure of the Eastern Kentucky Division. The subsequent years were to see branches constructed up a number of the creeks which are tributary to the North Fork of the Kentucky River. In some cases such construction followed the opening of coal mines in the adjacent hills; in many others it preceded the actual opening of the mines, although obviously the L. & N. was sure that there was coal to haul out before it built its branch.

The more important of these branches, the dates upon which they were placed in operation and the mileages involved, are as follows:

First Creek Branch, Typo to Harveyton, 5.40 miles; completed June 5, 1916.

Rockhouse Creek Branch, Blackey to Duo, Ky., 3.73 miles; completed March 13, 1919.

Lot's Creek Branch, North Hazard to Danfork, 3.19 miles; completed March 13, 1919.

Danger Fork Branch, Danfork to Whitsett, 2.42 miles; completed September 30, 1919.

Jake's Branch Spur, Duane to Hardburly, 2.86 miles; completed September 30, 1919.

Buffalo Creek Spur, Buffen to Diota, 1.31 miles; completed October 1915.

Potters Fork Spur, Wentworth to Haymond, 2.56 miles; completed July 1914.

Yont's Fork Spur, Neon to Hemphill, 2.08 miles; completed July 1914.

Carr's Fork Branch, Jeff to Vicco, 6.46 miles; completed April 15, 1920. (Subsequently extended to Sassafras in 1922.)

Leatherwood Creek Branch, Perry County, Ky., 10.3 miles; completed January 9, 1945.

The Rockhouse Creek Branch Extension, Duo to Deane, Ky., 16.7 miles; completed August 18, 1949.

The Blair Fork Spur, Perry County, Ky., 5.9 miles; completed August 1, 1949.

In addition, private coal companies such as the Chavies Coal Company, the Kenmont Coal Company, the Consolidated Coal Company, the Elkhorn Collieries Company, etc., built roads of their own to connect their properties with the North Fork Extension.

Chapter XXVIII

Harlan County Coal

A PREVIOUS chapter of the History has dealt with the building of the line from Corbin, Ky., to Norton, Va., which was the nucleus for the present-day Cumberland Valley Division. Since the opening of this line to Norton on May 15, 1891, dozens of branches connecting therewith or with tributary branches, have come into being and the hundreds of mines located thereon have poured their millions of tons of coal into the waiting coal cars of the L. & N. Railroad.

Certainly the most important of these branches are those which resulted from the formation of the Wasioto and Black Mountain Railroad Company in 1908. This railroad was originally organized for the express purpose of reaching the immense holdings of T. J. Asher along the Cumberland River, between Yellow Creek and Tom's Creek, in Bell County, and was the instrument whereby railroad lines eventually reached valuable coal properties in Bell and Harlan counties, belonging to such companies as the Harlan Coal Land Company, the International Harvester Company, and its subsidiary, the Wisconsin Steel Company, the American Association and the Kentenia Corporation. A vice-president of the latter corporation was Warren Delano, Jr., a director of the L. & N. Railroad from 1902 until his death in 1920. Mr. Delano was an uncle of President Franklin Delano Roosevelt and it is said that Mr. Roosevelt, as a young man, often accompanied his uncle on horse-back, the only mode of travel at the time, on tours of the Kentenia Corporation's vast acreage of coal and timber lands in Bell and Harlan counties.

Construction of the railroad was started in the latter part of 1907 from a point near what became known as Harbell, Ky., south of Pineville, and on July 23, 1908, Judge Asher formally organized the Wasioto and Black Mountain Railroad. The line, as projected, followed the Cumberland River, as recommended as early as 1887 by Messrs. McCreath and D'Invilliers, mineralogists, to Baxter, Ky. (near Harlan), a distance of 35.59 miles. Thus was remedied, some 20 years later, what Milton H. Smith spoke of as the "monumental and continuing blunder of the C. V.," in referring to the location of the line to Norton, by way of Middlesboro, Pennington, Big Stone Gap, etc., instead of by way of Harlan and Morris Gap. At Baxter, the trackage branched, one line following the Poor Fork branch of the Cumberland River and Looney Creek to Benham, Ky., 24.32 miles distant; the other following the Clover Fork branch of the Cumberland River through Harlan to Ages, 7.22 miles from Baxter. We shall subsequently deal with additions to this trackage, but it might be of interest to first give a bit of the early history of the Wasioto and Black Mountain Railroad.

As stated, part of the trackage mentioned was constructed by T. J.

Asher and Sons, located at Wasioto, Ky., just south of Pineville, who were manufacturers of hardwood and yellow poplar lumber and who had extensive mills, kilns, yards and coal and timber lands in that vicinity. Subsequent to the formal incorporation of the Wasioto and Black Mountain Railroad, the L. & N. advanced Judge Asher some money to assist in the construction of the line and on November 1, 1909, it exercised the right it had obtained at the time of the advancement and the entire capital stock of the W. & B. M. was transferred to the L. & N. At that time the road reached a point about half way between Harbell and Crosby (13 miles) and the remainder of this distance was partially graded. Other railroads were eying the Harlan district at the time and the L. & N. wisely decided to get the jump by procuring something already past the tentative stage. Judge Asher continued on as president of the W. & B. M., however, until August 12, 1915, when the name of the road was changed to the Kentucky and Virginia Railroad Company. From the first the L. & N. operated the line as part of its System, but title was not actually conveyed to it until October 1, 1915.

The Wasioto and Black Mountain Railroad, as originally incorporated, was only empowered to build from a point near Harbell to Tejay (named after T. J. Asher, president of the railroad) where Tom's Creek flowed into the Cumberland River. However, the original articles of incorporation were subsequently amended to read as follows:

"First, the said Wasioto and Black Mountain Railroad Company shall have the right to extend its said line of railroad from its present terminus on Tom's Creek in Bell County, Ky., up the Cumberland River to or near the town of Harlan, in Harlan County; and from thence up Clover Fork of Cumberland River to Morris Gap or the head of said Clover Fork, a distance of about 50 miles, and to construct a branch of said railroad from said town of Harlan, or near thereto, up the Poor Fork of Cumberland River to its head, a distance of about 70 miles, and to construct, maintain and operate the said extension or extensions of said railroad herein authorized and such branches, spurs, switches and side tracks connecting therewith and leading therefrom as may be convenient or necessary, and to construct and maintain and operate, or cause to be constructed, maintained, and opera-

Taken at Harlan, Ky., in 1911, this shows start of rail laying on Martin's Fork Branch; Harlan to Chevrolet.

ted, such telegraph line as may be necessary. The said extension or extensions hereby authorized to extend through portions of Bell, Harlan and Letcher counties in the State of Kentucky.

"Second: The amount of the capital stock of said corporation shall be One Million Dollars, divided into shares of $100 each.

"Third: The highest amount of indebtedness or liability which the corporation may at any time incur shall be $3,000,000, with power to secure any authorized indebtedness by mortgage or deed of trust upon the railroad and other property and franchises of the corporation or to otherwise secure the same."

The purchase of Wasioto and Black Mountain was authorized by the L. & N.'s board of directors on October 6, 1909, and a contract was subsequently awarded the Callahan Construction Company for the building of the extension beyond Tejay. This company was experienced in the building of railroads through mountainous country and had, in fact, constructed about 25 miles of the northern portion of the Knoxville, LaFollette and Jellico Railroad, as well as the L. & N.'s Clear Fork, Oliver Springs and Clear Fork Tunnel branches. Contracts between the railroad and the construction company were executed in February 1910, and the following, which is quoted from the Knoxville Daily Journal of March 4, 1911, is indicative of the speed with which this heavy construction work was prosecuted:

"Officers of the Callahan Construction Company of this city said yesterday that the work of constructing the Wasioto and Black Mountain Railroad in Kentucky would be finished in 30 days.

"The new road is 60 miles long and passes through some of the richest coal and timber lands in the South; it is also said the new line penetrates some of the best iron ore property in this section.

"Since the construction of that railway was started the Wisconsin Steel Company has acquired some valuable property in Harlan County, Ky., and the work of opening the mines on the newly-purchased property of the Wisconsin Steel Company has been started. It will be but a short time until the new coal fields in that part of the Kentucky mountains will be opened and it is said there will be much industrial activity along the new road.

"The new road is the property of the Louisville and Nashville. It has been under course of construction for more than a year and has cost an average of $20,000 per mile for construction . . . .

"During the past few weeks, laborers from all parts of the country have been flocking to the new road, and there will be no trouble in getting men to finish the work within the time stated. It is one of the heaviest pieces of railway work that has been undertaken in Kentucky in several years and the work has been for the most part finished with mule carts and old methods of mountain railway building, as it was impossible to get steam shovel outfits from the railway to some of the mountain districts through which the road extends . . ."

The 60 miles of track referred to in the foregoing extended from Tejay to Benham, with branches to Balkan, Colmar, Amru and Harlan. This trackage, despite the optimistic prediction of the Daily Journal's writer, was not placed in service to Benham until September 4, 1911.

The Middlesboro News-Record of September 2, 1911, had this to say about the opening of the line to Benham: " . . . NEW TRAIN SERVICE MONDAY. Beginning with next Monday a new train service will be established by the L. & N. between Middlesboro and Pineville and points on the Wasioto and Black Mountain Railway, and new daily-except-Sunday passenger service on the Straight Creek Branch. This train is the 'Whirligig' and will leave Middlesboro on the regular schedule at 6:00 a.m., and will arrive at Benham, the latter station 40 miles up Poor Fork Branch to the mines of the Wisconsin Steel Company, at 11:11 a.m., and leave Benham at 11:45 a.m. The lay-over at Harlan is about the same. The new Straight Creek train, which will be put into operation next Monday, will connect with the Harlan train, thus doing away with the 'Whirligig' trip up the Straight Creek Branch, as in the past . . . The opening of the Poor Fork Branch of the Wasioto and Black Mountain Railway marks the completion of the line."

The line into Harlan had been completed somewhat earlier in July 1911 and the July 15, 1911, issue of the Middlesboro News-Record had this to say about the event: " . . . The first regular passenger train will run into Harlan Monday, July 17. Though the station has not been completed and will not be entirely finished for 30 days, trains will come to the depot and temporary offices for the station forces will be established in the building. The Harlan station when completed will be one of the

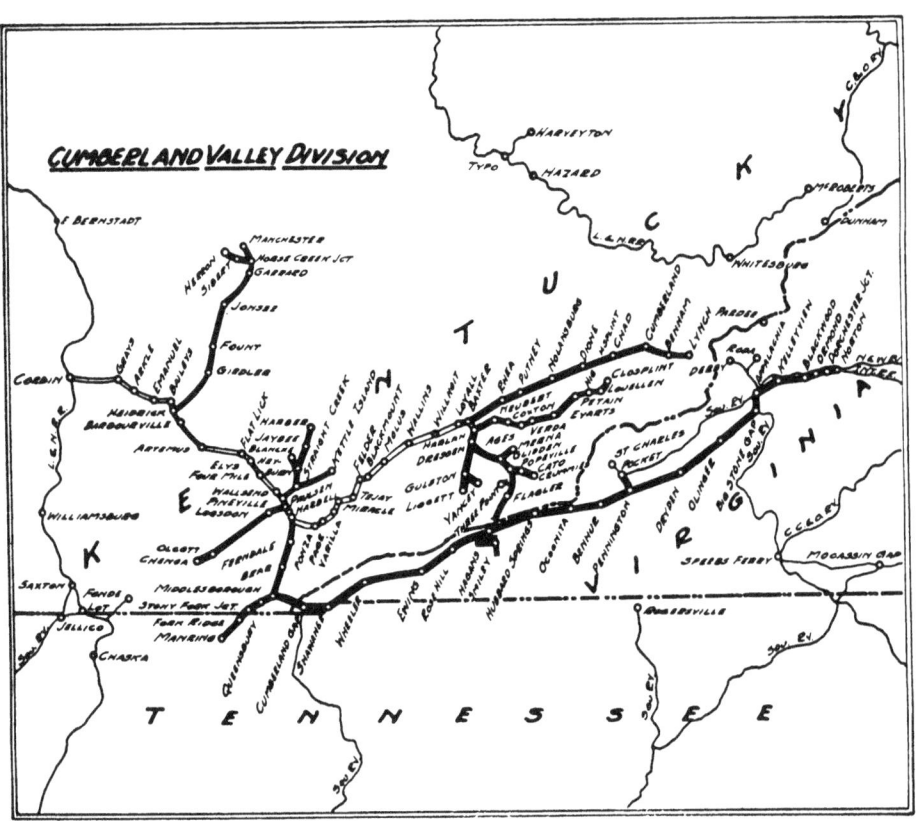

The trackage of the Cumberland Valley Division as it was prior to World War II, and as it evolved from the building of the "main lines" to Norton, Va., and Benham, Ky.

best among the smaller depots on the L. & N. system. W. J. Wilson, who was formerly cashier at Middlesboro freight office, will be agent at this place. He now has charge of the Company's interests at Baxter, the present shipping point for Harlan. (**The line to Baxter, approximately two miles from Harlan, had been opened up in the early part of April of the same year.-K. A. H.**) The old mail route from Hagans, Va., to Harlan has been abandoned and the mail now comes by train. Until the L. & N. runs a Sunday train, the people of Harlan will be without mail. The temporary inconvenience will probably be done away with soon, for, it is understood, the Wasioto and Black Mountain Railway train will run on Sunday in a short time." (**The meaning of this is not quite clear; it may have meant that no mail could be delivered on the following day. - K. A. H.**)

The track from Harlan to Ages, Ky., on the Clover Fork Branch, was surfaced soon after the opening of the line on May 21, 1912, Section Foreman M. S. Harber and his gang doing the work.

A subsequent issue of the News-Record also contains an item of interest. Dated August 12, 1911, it reads: "Sunday train service between Middlesboro and Harlan was inaugurated last Sunday and the train that came into Harlan that morning at 11:00 o'clock brought the largest number of passengers that any train has yet hauled (sic). Four coaches were loaded to the guards and several picnic parties from Pineville, Middlesboro and other points along the line came to Harlan to spend a few hours, eat their lunches in the Court House yard and, incidentally, see the city.

The unusual was frequently the usual thing in the building of the Wasioto and Black Mountain Railroad. An illustrative story was told about one of the track laborers engaged in the construction of the line near Cumberland, Ky. This man was a native of the section and was, of course, not overly familiar with the potency of the Iron Horse. One day he saw a car loaded with ballast rolling down the recently-completed track and headed in his direction. He optimistically attempted to chock the moving wheels with his foot and luckily escaped with the loss of but three toes.

Following the completion of the line to Benham, the board outlines of the Harlan territory trackage were subsequently filled in as follows with the completion of the following trackage:

Harlan to Ages, Ky., 5.07 miles; completed May 21, 1912.

Ages to Kildav, 1.61 miles; completed on or about March 20, 1916.

Kildav to Shields, 6.35 miles; completed October 6, 1918.

Shields to Seagrave (Highsplint), 1.59 miles; completed June 21, 1919.

The line was extended from Benham to Lynch, a distance of about three miles, in 1917, to serve the huge development of the United States Coal and Coke Company, subsidiary of the United States Steel Corporation, centered around Lynch. The L. & N. and the Coal and Coke Company each built a portion of this extension and the coal company's portion was subsequently leased by the L. & N. on May 11, 1929.

That company owned some 42,000 acres of coal land at the headwaters of Looney Creek and in 1917 commenced an intensified development of this property, digging mines, building tipples, installing coal-handling machinery and erecting a complete city to house the miners and care for their needs. This work was started in September 1917, and was thereafter prosecuted with such rapidity that the first car of coal was moved from the mines on November 1, 1917, and by March, 1918, the mines were producing 20 cars of coal per day. (This was gradually increased until at one time they were producing as high as 130 cars per day.)

It might be mentioned at this point that other large industries were quick to realize the economy of having their own "coal bins" in the Eastern Kentucky hills and a number of manufacturers followed the example of the United States Steel Company and purchased holdings in Harlan, Bell, Perry and Letcher Counties.

There were a number of other branches tributary to the line between Harbell and Lynch which were constructed either almost simultaneously, or shortly thereafter. Perhaps the one outstanding item of trackage on the Cumberland Valley Division which the L. & N. subsequently completed was the C. C. & O. Connection, which was also known as the Martin's Fork Branch. This afforded a direct connection between Harlan, Ky., and the main line of the Cumberland Valley Division at Hagans, Va., and its construction followed the joint leasing by the L. & N. and the Atlantic Coast Line of the Carolina, Clinchfield and Ohio Railway on May 1, 1923. This line was acquired to serve as a link between the two railroads, thus providing (with the help presently to be described) a short route for the movement of coal from the Southeastern Kentucky coal fields to the Southeast. This was accomplished by the construction of a 13.6 mile track between Chevrolet, Ky., six miles from Harlan, and Hagans, Va., and the obtaining of trackage rights from the Interstate Railroad between Norton, Va., and Miller Yard, in Scott County, Va., where connection was made with the Clinchfield.

Work on this connection was started in October 1927, and it was completed and placed in service on December 1, 1930, after an expenditure of $5,300,000. Incidentally, the arrangement before mentioned (the use of the Interstate's track, etc.) was originally planned to be only a temporary one, further construction from Hagans, Va., to a connection with the Clinchfield at Speer's Ferry, Va., being contemplated. The latter, of course, would have shortened the route considerably. It was estimated that the total cost of such a line (between Chevrolet and Speer's Ferry, that is) would be in the neighborhood of $16,000,000. Consideration was also seriously given to the construction of a line, estimated to cost around $7,000,000, from Ulvah, Ky., on the Eastern Kentucky to Chad, Ky.,

The first regular passenger train into Harlan was operated on July 17, 1911.

on the Poor Fork Branch of the Cumberland Valley Division, a distance of 18.13 miles. Neither of these projects ever matured, however.

Other branches of the Cumberland Valley Division, in addition to those previously mentioned, which deserve special mention, are the following:

The Cumberland and Manchester Branch, which extends from Heidrick to Manchester, Ky., a distance of 23 miles, with a 3-mile branch from Horse Creek Junction to Heron. (This property was built by the Cumberland and Manchester Railroad and was opened for traffic about January 1, 1917. The L. & N. later became the sole owner of the entire capital stock, but operated the road under lease, effective January 1, 1927.)

The Straight Creek Branch, extending from Pineville to Kettle Island, a distance of six miles. (This was first built in the 'nineties and was subsequently extended to Kettle Island by the L. & N. on September 4, 1911.)

The Left Fork Branch, extending from Straight Creek to Harber, Ky., a distance of 11 miles. (The nucleus of this line was built in 1906 to Griggs, Ky.; the line was subsequently extended from Heyburn, near Griggs, to Harber, Ky., a distance of about eight miles, in July 1930.)

The Chenoa Branch, extending from Paulsen to Chenoa, a distance of 12 miles. (This was completed in October 1893, under L. & N. supervision and was subsequently purchased by the L. & N. in June 1901.)

The Puckett's Creek Branch, extending from Blackmont to Wilfred, Ky., a distance of eight miles. (This line was completed by the Black Mountain Railroad in August 1919. The L. & N. purchased its entire capital stock in May 1923, and the line was absorbed into the L. & N. System on July 16, 1936.)

The Clover Fork Extension, extending from Closplint to Glenbrook, Ky., a distance of 11 miles, was put in service in 1946.

Some of the branches mentioned, as well as other smaller ones, were originally constructed, with L. & N. assistance of varying degrees, by coal operators, or other private industries. The latter generally furnished the right-of-way, did the grading, etc., with the L. & N. furnishing the rail and track fittings, the railroad later leasing these to the coal company, or other, at a nominal rental. (Payment was generally made in "engine fuel," i.e. coal, although the transaction was not on an obvious barter basis.) In this category fell such lines later acquired by the L. & N., as Catron's Creek Branch, Slater's Creek Branch, Lick Branch Spur, Four Mile Branch, etc.

These various penetrations of the coal fields of Eastern and Southeastern Kentucky were paralleled by a constant improvement of the L. & N.'s facilities for handling the steady stream of coal which poured forth from the bosom of Mother Earth. Mention has previously been made of some of the initial expenditures of effort and money on the part of the L. & N. to ready its lines for the expected traffic. Subsequently, it installed a gravity yard at Covington, Ky., strengthened bridges, placed heavier steel rail in the track and double-tracked the Eastern Kentucky Division between Ravanna and Pryse, a distance of six miles, and between Hazard and Perritt, a distance of 18 miles. It also doubletracked the line between Corbin and Harlan, a distance of about 70 miles and by filling in a number of not inconsiderable gaps by the addition of other second track, secured a double-tracked, low-grade line all the way from Covington to Corbin, a distance of 185 miles. Extensive yards to expedite the handling of the coal were also established at Corbin, Crawford, Ravenna, Neon, Loyall and Harlan. Railroad Y. M. C. A.'s were built at Corbin and Hazard in order to provide suitable accommodations for employes.

The various improvements mentioned made it possible for the Louisville & Nashville Railroad to expeditiously handle a coal movement which on the Eastern Kentucky Division alone increased from 341,796 tons (roughly 8,500 cars) in 1913 to a movement of 232,958 cars in 1926. The shipments from the Cumberland Valley increased from 25,841 tons (roughly 600 cars) in 1911 to a total of 356,339 cars in 1928.

As a historical footnote, the first carload (No. 64326) of coal to leave Harlan County was shipped from the Aldrian Mine of the Old Wallins Creek Coal Company on August 25, 1911.

Chapter XXIX

Adjustment to War

SINCE the beginning of the 20th century, the operating costs of America's railroads had steadily increased and their ability to absorb, or rather, to balance such increased expenditures, had been largely enervated by the Interstate Commerce Commission which was given the power to fix "just and reasonable" maximum rates and finally even to suspend rates initiated by the railroads themselves.

The increased expenditures and the inadequate rates, had combined to greatly decrease the earning power of most American railroads by 1914. This had seriously impaired their credit and the outbreak of the World War eliminated one of the chief markets for the sale of their stocks and bonds. At first, too, European orders for American goods slumped heavily with the railroads suffering a resultant loss in traffic.

The case of the L. & N. was not typical of that of most other American carriers, for its conservative management and the certain natural traffic advantages which it enjoyed, had combined to maintain its net operating income at a fairly high level. Thus, in the period embraced by the two dates, June 30, 1906, and June 30, 1914, its net earnings (before dividends had been paid), with one exception, had fluctuated between the approximate figures of six and ten millions of dollars annually. (The L. & N.'s net earnings for the fiscal year ending with June 30, 1908, totaled $2,824,456.42, which was less than 2 per cent upon its investment.)

The Annual Report for the fiscal year ending with June 30, 1915, makes this enlightening comment:

"The decrease in Operating Revenues compared with previous year was $8,300,451.48, equal to 13.85 per cent.

"This great shrinkage was due largely to the effect produced by the war in Europe upon the price and consumption of the products and manufactures of the territory served by the Louisville & Nashville Railroad Company and to the consequent decrease in passenger travel."

The comment referred to then lists the losses, or decreases, by commodities and by freight forwarded from the principal stations, as compared with the previous year, but closes with this significant statement: "Birmingham District is now showing some revival, largely due to orders for Europe."

As intimated in the last sentence of the excerpt quoted, the pendulum was beginning to swing the other way by June 30, 1915. By that time the demands made upon America by the warring nations had completely changed the economic picture and the resultant increase in the operating incomes of the railroads had enabled most of them to successfully bat the wolf away from the front door.

The L. & N.'s Annual Report for the fiscal year ending June 30,

1914 (published several months later), takes cognizance of the first World War in these words:

"Since the closing of the books eight European nations have become involved in a war unprecedented in history. Not less than eight million men at this writing are dead, wounded, prisoners of war, or facing each other in battle. It is evident that for a long time after the close of this war all the surplus money and resources of these countries will be required at home to recuperate from the awful destruction of lives and property, from the dislocation of industry and enormous war debts. At present, neither railroads nor other industries can borrow, anywhere, additional money for new construction or additions, and all such work not already provided for must be postponed for an indefinite period. Fortunately, all important work of this character authorized by the board of directors of the Louisville & Nashville Railroad Company, is practically completed and the cash required to complete payments fully provided. No other important improvements or additions will be authorized until money becomes again available upon reasonable terms."

As revealed by this excerpt, the L. & N.'s house was in very good order. The completion of the North Fork Extension (Jackson to McRoberts, Ky.) and of the line into the Harlan coal fields, had synchronized nicely with the demands that were now being made by American industry for coal to help turn the wheels in filling the requests from abroad for materials and supplies of all sorts. Work upon such projects as the new line from Winchester to Irvine, Ky., and the yards at Radnor, Tenn., proceeded at a snail's pace, but this was not wholly the result of the war, construction difficulties and litigation putting in their two cents' worth. (Radnor Yard was finally completed on March 10, 1919.)

During the period just prior to the commencement of World War I, and shortly thereafter, the L. & N. engaged in a number of activities not connected with the usual day-in-and-day-out routine of running a railroad. It commenced operation of the Tennessee Western Railroad, extending from Iron City to Collinwood, Tenn., a distance of 17½ miles, as con-

Scenes like this were frequently encountered on our lines after America's entrance into the World War as the Old Reliable moved hundreds of thousands of draftees to various training camps.

A scene at the Louisville Union Station during the days of World War I. The Red Cross established a canteen at the location on a 24-hour basis, which was staffed by volunteer women workers. Troops passing through the Station were served coffee, tea, milk, doughnuts, ice cream, sandwiches, soups, etc. A special building, adjacent to the Station, was built for the workers and the food was prepared therein.

tractor for the owners, on March 13, 1913. A connection between the L. & N. and the Tennessee Western at Iron City, Tenn., had been previously completed on February 13, 1913. The Memphis Union Station was completed in 1913, the L. & N. and four other railroads cooperating in this undertaking. It was covered by a bond issue of $2,500,000. An automatic telephone system was installed in the general office building at a cost of $9,128.32 in the early part of 1914. Smoke began to be looked at with a critical eye, but not necessarily because its presence in excess indicated improper firing and hence a waste of fuel, but primarily because it was a civic nuisance. Smoke abatement devices were applied experimentally to locomotives operating in the Nashville Terminals and in the same year of 1915 a number of the L. & N.'s locomotives blossomed forth with such items as glass water gauges, Chicago flange oilers, automatic fire-box doors, super-heaters, electric headlights, etc. More adequate terminal facilities were provided at Lexington, Ky., a result of the increasing coal business being handled over the recently-acquired Lexington & Eastern. And, on March 22, 1916, notice was received from the Interstate Commerce Commission that the property of the Company would be valued as of June 30, 1917.

After the first war year the L. & N.'s gross railway earnings and its net income both increased amazingly, as witness:

Gross Earnings	Year Ending June 30	Net Income (before dividend payments, but after deduction of interest charges)
$51,606,015.39	1915	$ 4,951,763.86
60,317,993.43	1916	14,039,130.09
	Year Ending December 31	
64,928,120.59	1916	16,962,810.62
76,907,387.16	1917	16,464,014.66

Freight traffic, of course, was the major factor in the increased revenues. Raw materials poured into large manufacturing centers and a constant stream of finished products moved northward (mainly) and southward, over the lines of the L. & N. It was a time of great activity and prosperity and the L. & N.'s physical plant was put to it to keep pace with the demands made upon it. Unfortunately, the early war years also saw a renewal of train-robbing and wrecking.

Added to all these troubles was one of the Gulf Coast's most memorable storms, this occurring on September 29, 1915. Damage to property was immense, the gale costing the L. & N. alone, a total of $418,820 for replacement of facilities and equipment. At times the wind reached a velocity of 140 miles an hour and the L. & N.'s service between Mobile and New Orleans was disrupted for 26 days.

After a long period of ever-increasing tension, America entered World War I upon the side of the Allies on April 6, 1917. Just five days later, or on April 11, the nation's carriers established the Railroad War Board. Its purpose and function can perhaps best be explained by the following resolution which was adopted unanimously at that time at Washington, D.C., by a truly representative gathering of railroad executives from all over the country (the L. & N. was represented by Henry Walters, chairman of its board):

"That the railroads of the United States, acting through their chief executive officers here and now assembled and stirred by a high sense of their opportunity to be of the greatest service to their country in the present national crisis, do hereby pledge themselves, with the Government of the United States, with the Governments of the several States and one with another, that during the present war they will co-ordinate their operations in a continental railway system, merging during such period all their merely individual and competitive activities in the effort to produce a maximum of national transportation efficiency. To this end they hereby agree to create an organization which shall have general authority to formulate in detain and from time to time a policy of operation of all or any of the railways, which policy, when and as announced by such temporary organization, shall be accepted and earnestly made effective by the several managements of the individual railroad companies here represented."

These words, eloquently and sincerely spoken, disregarded human nature and the compulsions of long-established habit. Unfortunately, the Railroad War Board, like the League of Nations, did not have a "police force" at its disposal.

That same day of April 11, an executive committee consisting of Fairfax Harrison, chairman, president of the Southern Railway; Samuel Rea, president of the Pennsylvania; Howard Elliott, president of the N. Y. N. H. & H. R. R.; Hale Holden, president of the Chicago, Burlington and Quincy Railroad and Julius Kruttschnitt, chairman of the Southern Pacific Lines, was appointed. Edgar E. Clark, a member of the Interstate Commerce Commission, and Daniel Willard, president of the Baltimore and Ohio Railroad, served as ex-officio members of the committee.

The War Board started to function with high hopes, but the dead hand of the past and the exigencies of the present and future combined

The Memphis Union Station, which was erected in 1913.

to make its task a difficult one. It has been argued pro and con for a number of years as to whether or not the blame for the transportation shambles of the latter part of 1917 should be placed at the door of the railroads themselves, or elsewhere. Sad to relate, the general impression prevails to this day that the carriers were weighed in the balance of the national emergency and found wanting.

This account, with the best intentions in the world, could not qualify as an impartial judge, but when the evidence is all in, it would seem that the fault lay both within and without the railroads, but that circumstances over which the carriers had no control were largely responsible for the car shortages and traffic snarls of America's first war year. There were several reasons for this. In the first place, of course, available equipment was not adequate to transport a freight and passenger traffic which had almost doubled overnight. Julius Kruttschnitt, in a report to the Senate Committee on Interstate Commerce, pointed out that the increase in ton miles alone, handled by the railroads in 1917, over 1915, was greater than the total ton-miles handled in the last previous year of record by all the railroads of Canada, Great Britain, Germany, Russia, France, and Austria combined.

The word "overnight" is thus used advisedly for although the trend since 1915 had been upward, America's entrance into the war meant further sharp increases and the L. & N.'s traffic chart, before indicated, was perhaps typical. That the railroads did not have available sufficient surplus equipment to absorb this increase was again not their fault entirely. Some roads did have a reasonable surplus of locomotives and freight and passengers cars and among these was the L. & N. Railroad. However, the majority of the carriers did not. Equipment costs money and at that time approximately one-sixth of the United States' railroad mileage was in the hands of receivers. The financial situation of most railroads was such that they had very little money to spend for anything other than the bare necessities of corporate existence. The "good" years of 1915 and 1916 had enabled these to make "betterments" but very few "additions."

The L. & N.'s rolling stock had expanded in a normal manner during the decade ending with June 30, 1915, and it had kept a comfortable lead over the demands made upon it. Thus, its motive power had increased from 745 locomotives in 1905 to 1090 locomotives in 1915. During this same period the nember of freight cars increased from 36,633 to 46,710 and the passenger cars from 535 to 659. In this same decade its freight revenues increased from $27,732,625.41 to $36,953,749.28 and its passenger revenues from $8,619,649.59 to $10,859,046.72. Translated into work performed this represented the handling of 27,731,561 tons of freight in 1915 as contrasted to the handling of 24,553,832 tons in 1905 and of 11,849,957 passengers in 1915 as contrasted to 9,573,238 passengers in 1905.

America's entrance into the first World War immediately transferred its men and materials from the seats of the stadium to the badly-scuffed sod of the playing field. The Allies, in desperate straits, sent out an urgent plea for manpower, materials, supplies, food, weapons, ammunitions – the works! This country responded and the railroads poured a steady stream of men and materials into Baltimore, Philadelphia, New York and other ports. And there was where the trouble began. America's merchant marine was being frantically built and that of the Allies had been greatly decimated by the ubiquitous U-boats. There just weren't enough boats to handle the shipments. Loaded freight cars stood idle for weeks and even months at a time on sidings.

Nor was the disparity between America's productive capacity and that of its ships the sole contributing factor to confusion. Red tape did its work too and this by-product of any contact with the bureaucrats, coupled with a system of generously granting priority in handling to any and all Government shipments, rubbed salt in the wounds of a once smoothly-functioning transportation system. The L. & N. by this time, of course, was tarred with the same brush and its fate was the fate of its sister roads, who, generally speaking, had contributed much less to the commonweal. Much of its passenger equipment was constantly being used in the transportation of troops to and from the various cantonments and camps throughout its territory and its armada of over 47,000 freight cars was scattered over the face of the land, some of them being absent from the home rails for months at a time. In 1917, the L. & N.'s credit balance for the hire of freight cars (per diem) amounted to $3,412,525.21, as compared to $1,970,088.17 in 1916 and $764,862.60 in 1915.

Then, too, the railroads in their willingness to cooperate had rerouted much tonnage in a manner to insure its most expeditious handling and this had resulted in a heavy congestion on certain lines, with a corresponding reduction of traffic on others. The efforts of the railroads and the requirements of the War Department were not coordinated and as a result they frequently worked at cross purposes.

And, then, in the latter part of 1917, came the straw which swayed the camel's back to the breaking point, and which was perhaps the one factor chiefly responsible for federal control. This was the collapse of Russia, in the latter part of 1917, which culminated in that country's signing an armistice with the Central Powers at Brest-Litovsk on December 17, 1917, followed by a treaty of peace in the early part of 1918. Sailings of ships for Russia were immediately cancelled and more cars piled up on the sidings. The Allies simultaneously looked to America for additional help to offset this blow and, of course, this took the form of increased production.

So much for the contributing factors which were most responsible, or influential, in causing the so-called "break-down" of America's transportation system. To be honest, there were others, but in comparison, these were mere pin pricks. It has been previously mentioned that in forming the Railroad War Board, the individual roads had been motivated by a sincere desire to render the best service within their power, as well as by the desire to so function that government operation and control (even then discussed as a possibility) would be rendered unnecessary. Unfortunately, however, the element of competition was still present to a certain extent, and the solicitation forces tried to be as helpful to the management as they could. This competition, of course, resulted in a certain amount of duplication of effort and Railroad X frequently handled a movement or shipment that could have been more efficiently or advantageously handled by Railroad Z.

At any rate, the increasing clamor for federal control finally had its effect and at 12 o'clock noon, on December 28, 1917, in accordance with a proclamation of President Woodrow Wilson, the federal government assumed possession and control of all transportation systems located wholly or in part within the boundaries of the continental United States. For accounting purposes the control dated from midnight, December 31, 1917. All of this was in accordance with the authority granted the President by the Army Appropriation Act of August 29, 1916.

(This was not the first time the nation's railroads had been conscripted by the federal government. During the War between the States, the government had taken over about 2,600 miles of railroad, embracing several systems. A director of operations was subsequently appointed, but he resigned very shortly as did his two successors, because of disputes with the military authorities. The resignation of the third director of operations produced this masterpiece of over-statement from the then-Secretary of War, in the form of the following telegram: "Come back immediately. Cannot get on without you. Not a wheel turning.")

CHAPTER XXX

Federal Control

WORLD WAR I and federal control and operation as it affected the Louisville & Nashville Railroad and its employes might be partitioned into three parts: the days prior to America's entrance into the conflict on April 6, 1917, which have already been touched upon; the period from April 6, 1917, to the commencement of federal control on December 28, 1917, also previously mentioned; and the period of federal control from December 28, 1917, to March 1, 1920.

We have already dealt more or less specifically with the first period; business boomed and many thousands of additional employes in all branches of the service were hired. The second period, which might be termed the Railroad War Board period, saw the L. & N.'s conduct of its business handicapped in many ways. Thousands of employes were drafted or volunteered to fight and other thousands accepted employment in the more lucrative "war boom" fields. The movement of troops and of the materials and supplies of the government had to be given preference. Red tape began to cluster around the wheels of the L. & N.'s rolling stock. It was a dramatic time, but since this account does not purport to be a history of America at war, there would be no especial point in describing phenomena which was not essentially peculiar to the L. & N. Its employes were, of course, directly affected by the "meatless" and "wheatless" days observed by the nation and, as a corporation, the L. & N. dutifully cooperated in the observance of such days upon its diners. Generally speaking, only one set meal was available for patrons of our diners during those World War I days (with a choice of fish or meat) and they were rigidly limited to two teaspoons of sugar with each meal and to two ounces of bread made with wheat. The dining car department, as a matter of fact, employed a colored woman in its commissary department at Louisville whose sole duty was to fill little glassine bags with the two teaspoons aforesaid and patrons who were inclined to doubt that they were receiving their two ounces of bread, were confronted with the indisputable testimony offered by a set of postal scales. During World War I the Company operated three "cafeteria" cars for the serving of the selectees moving to army camps and it was no rare thing for 500 men to be served at one meal.

There were, as previously stated, a number of Army camps in L. & N. territory and long trains of 14 or 15 cars, filled with khaki-clad soldiery, became a common sight. One of the largest of these camps was Camp Zachary Taylor, located just outside of Louisville, Ky. There was, as a consequence, a doughnut stand located in the parking lot just across from the Union Station at Louisville, which always did a land-office business whenever a troop train rolled into the station. Service flags were hung in most of the offices and as time passed many of the blue stars were replaced with ones of gold.

During the Railroad War Board period and the period of federal control thereafter passenger business really came into its own and reached a peak that surpassed anything in the railroad's previous history. The following figures tell the story: In the fiscal year ending with December 31, 1916, the L. & N. carried 12,516,777 passengers; in 1917, it carried 14,152,986 passengers and in 1918 it carried 17,086,598 passengers.

(It should be stated at this point that since the L. & N. had been required on November 24, 1916, by the Interstate Commerce Commission to submit annual operating and financial statements for fiscal years ending with December 31, it had decided also to make its Annual Report to the stockholders conform to the calendar years. The 66th Annual Report for the year ending December 31, 1916, was the first of these and contained some duplication of facts and figures since the 65th Annual Report had already covered the first half of the year 1916. At this time the date of the annual stockholders meeting was changed from the first Wednesday in October to the first Wednesday in April. Eight hundred votes were cast against the resolution changing the date of meeting and Alonzo E. Cottier had his written protest spread upon the minutes of the meeting, which was held on April 4, 1917.)

The Railroad War Board period also saw a great increase in the L. & N.'s feminine personnel. The reasons for this increase at that time are, of course, obvious. Manpower was needed upon the battlefield and the womenfolk were an acceptable substitute in many walks of life. It should be explained that manpower never got so scarce upon the L. & N. that women ran locomotives or repaired them; the displacement affected clerical jobs alone, or jobs which were closely akin to clerical work such as those of operators, agents, etc. (This statement applies only to the L. & N.; on some other roads women cleaned engines and did certain types of shop and track maintenance.) Prior to the War the L. & N. had a few women employes, perhaps not over a hundred in all; by the end of 1918, there were thousands of the "weaker" sex upon its payroll. Perhaps this is neither the time nor the place to stress the point, but this wholesale

Letterhead used by Federal Manager W. L. Mapother during the early days of federal control when W. G. McAdoo was director general of railroads.

UNITED STATES RAILROAD ADMINISTRATION
W. G. McADOO, DIRECTOR GENERAL OF RAILROADS

LOUISVILLE & NASHVILLE RAILROAD NASHVILLE, CHATTANOOGA & ST. LOUIS RAILROA
LOUISVILLE, HENDERSON & ST. LOUIS RAILROAD TENNESSEE CENTRAL RAILROAD
BIRMINGHAM & NORTHWESTERN RAILROAD

OFFICE OF FEDERAL MANAGER, LOUISVILLE, KY.

L. MAPOTHER,
FEDERAL MANAGER.

feminine invasion of the profession of railroading improved the appearance of the average L. & N. white-collar worker by about 100 per cent. And, if there be anything to the belief that excessive wearing of one's hat produces baldness, it halted many a receding hairline in its tracks. For witness: this average worker before mentioned, prior to the feminine disruption of the status quo, had generally gone about his duties attired in a derby hat, sleeve garters, and eye-shade (somewhat on the greasy side), and a set of garments purchased long ago and now relegated to that ne plus ultra of sartorial limbos – "good enough to wear to the office."

The change, of course, was a gradual one, and there was even a certain amount of resistance to the new dispensation. Huge quantities of tobacco were still chewed as aggressively as ever and the die-hards refused to make the slightest concession to "co-education." Femininity gradually began to work its insidious miracles, however, and all knew that the battle was lost when the last derby hat began to rest on a hook during the day-time, instead of on the back of a head.

The period of federal control itself might be split into two periods; i.e., the period before the Armistice and the period thereafter. Federal control wrought few changes at first and these were chiefly of a financial nature. The velvet glove effectively sheathed the iron hand of the absentee trustee and the L. & N. continued to operate much as it had always done. It was provided that the federal government would reimburse each individual road for the use of its property and this rental was based on each road's average annual railway operating income for the three years ending with June 30, 1917. This rental was known as the "standard return" and on the L. & N. it amounted to $17,310,494.67 annually. However, the agreement between the director general of railroads and the L. & N., covering the use of the L. & N.'s properties by the federal government, was not entered into until March 14, 1919, after the war had ended, although a tacit agreement along the same lines had been in effect prior to that time. The agreement before mentioned consisted of thousands of words and in addition to its preamble and recitals and the execution, was divided into nine sections, namely, privity, alterations, definitions, etc.; property taken over; acceptance; operating and accounting during federal control; upkeep; taxes, compensation; claims for loss on additions, etc.; and final accounting.

William G. McAdoo, secretary of the treasury, was appointed director general of railroads, simultaneously with the start of federal control. His principal assistant was Walker D. Hines, then chairman of the board of the A. T. & S. F. Railway, and a former L. & N. employe. He subsequently succeeded Mr. McAdoo as director general in the early part of 1919 and it was with Mr. Hines that the Agreement aforesaid was entered into. The Federal Control Act of March 21, 1918, affected a number of changes and the "honeymoon" was over. Perhaps the most important of these was the distinction which was established between the corporate activities of a railroad and its federal activities. The former included such functions as the paying of interest charges, dividends, etc., while the latter, broadly speaking, covered all the phases of actual physical operation.

Scenes like this were familiar ones along the Railroad during World War I as young men answered the call to the colors. This was at Hawesville, Ky., on the old Louisville, Henderson and St. Louis Railway (long controlled by the L. & N. but not formally acquired until April 2, 1929) and shows the first solders-to-be from Hancock County, Ky., en route to camp in the spring of 1917, with family and friends on hand to bid them farewell.

Prior to the passage of this Act the managements had acted as agents for the government, rather than for the stockholders; a change which actually changed very little, save the bookkeeping. On the L. & N. the cleavage at first resulted in this: Henry Walters remained as chairman of the board; Milton H. Smith, president, continued as corporation head and was assisted by a small staff, consisting of the following: E. S. Locke, secretary and treasurer; E. L. Smithers, vice-president; Henry L. Stone, general counsel; William A. Colston, general solicitor; G. W. Wickersham, counsel (later to become famous as the author of the Wickersham Report); H. G. Day, assistant to chairman; C. E. Ambler, assistant secretary and assistant treasurer; W. J. McDonald, transfer agent; Richard Montfort, chief engineer and real estate agent; W. F. Kennedy, auditor; R. J. Wagner, assistant auditor, and a clerical force of about 12. Messrs. Day, Smithers, Wickersham, Ambler, and McDonald were located in New York, the remainder in Louisville. Wible L. Mapother, executive vice-president, was appointed federal manager, not only of the Louisville & Nashville, but of a group of "family" roads, consisting of the N. C. & St. L. and the L. H. & St. L., in addition to the Tennessee Central and the Birmingham & Northwestern. Most of the L. & N.'s official personnel and nearly all of the rank and file served under Mr. Mapother.

At this time, of course, Mr. Smith was advanced in years and he had transferred much of his executive duties to Wible L. Mapother and other trained subordinates. At the time of federal control, Mr. Smith was

Louisville held an Armistice Day parade on November 23, 1918, and L. & N.'s float attracted much favorable attention. With red and white, the Company's colors, predominating, the float was further adorned by a bevy of young ladies from the general office building, each representing a state served by the L. & N.

82 years of age and associates of those days have recalled that the veteran was addicted to catnaps in his office. His mind was as vigorous as ever, however, and he could still deal with a knotty problem with the force and decision of his earlier years or utter a pungent phrase which went to the very meat of the matter. Undoubtedly, federal control was a bitter pill to swallow for one who had always looked with a jaundiced eye upon any attempt of the governing authorities to regulate the conduct of a corporation's business. Now, the dam had burst under the pressure of wartime emergency and the deluge was on. Mr. Smith, however, could accept the inevitable as graciously as the next man. His serene acceptance of the situation is perhaps best summed up in a letter in the files which is entitled: "A communication from Milton H. Smith, president of the Louisville & Nashville Railroad Company, to its officials and employes respecting the government control of railroads." Dated March 29, 1918, it is quoted verbatim herewith:

"The President of the United States having heretofore taken over the control of the railroads of the country and committed their operation to a Director General and the 'Railway Control Bill,' fixing the terms and conditions of Government control, having become a law, I have thought it proper briefly to remind you of some features of the new order of things.

"The property of this Company will belong to the Government as lessee for a period lasting until 21 months after the war ends, unless the President shall see fit to restore it sooner; and every dollar now received or expended is the Government's money. But with the property there passed an asset of equal value the efficiency of a vast army of trained railroad men. Accordingly, the old organization of our Company – its officials and employes – now constitutes a governmental agency engaged for the time being in the operation of this particular railroad system, but entirely subject to the supervision and direction of the Director General, or his duly constituted representatives.

"For convenience, the country has been divided into three territorial districts, Eastern, Western and Southern. Over each of these has been appointed a Regional Director. The lines of the Louisville & Nashville lie within the Southern District, of which C. H. Markham, formerly president of the Illinois Central Railroad Company, is Regional Director, with headquarters at Atlanta, Ga.

"Necessarily, things will not be as they were. Mistakes, too, may occur as heretofore; but let there be no adverse criticism or disloyal spirit. If you have any suggestion which, in your opinion, will improve the service, tell it to your superior officer, who will report it to this department. If meritorious it will be brought to the attention of the Regional Director.

"The Government will doubtless effect combinations of positions and adopt other methods of consolidation and retrenchment, which may necessitate dispensing with the services of some persons now in the Company's employ. Regrettable as this would be, it should be accepted as one of the exigencies of the war, for the winning of which each one of us must make whatever sacrifice is required.

"Let me here say that my chief pride in administering the affairs of this Company in the past has been the splendid loyalty and efficiency of its officials and employes. It is still my earnest desire that, in this new relation, you maintain these distinctive characteristics to the highest degree, for your new position is now more elevated and more important – you are in the direct service of your country in time of war, as much as the Army or the Navy, and in a work almost as important.

"In this, the crisis of our country's history, the one great necessity that stands out pre-eminent above all others at home is an adequate transportation system. In undertaking itself to supply this, the Government has entered upon a huge experiment, the success of which is of vital importance. It **must succeed,** but it can do so only by the complete cooperation, absolute loyalty and devoted service of you and of men like you.

"I have full faith that you will meet this test to the uttermost and will give to the country the best that is in you. Yours very truly, Milton H. Smith, president."

(A sequel to Mr. Smith's letter was a letter from J. D. Keen, veteran Short Line conductor, now deceased, who as chairman of the Employes' Committee on Response, on April 19, 1918, wrote Mr. Smith, assuring him of the loyal co-operation of all employes. Both Mr. Smith's letter and that of Mr. Keen were reproduced in the Louisville Courier-Journal and Mr. Keen's concluded on this note: " . . . We rejoice that we are not saying farewell to you, the genius of our success in the past . . . and we pledge ourselves to make willingly whatever sacrifices are required . . . ")

Just a short while previous, on the occasion of his 79th birthday, Mr. Smith, confined to a sick bed for what is said to have been the first time in his life, answered the joint felicitations of numerous friends, many of whom were heads of other railroads, in the following vein: " . . . I appreciate the kindly remembrances of so many, still active in administering the affairs of beneficent corporations, under the supervision, rules, regulations and control of sundry governmental agencies . . . Existing conditions tend to reconcile me to my practical withdrawal from active participation in conducting the affairs of railway corporations."

The experience of the L. & N. during the period of federal control was, of course, radically different from anything it had encountered in the past. A strenuous rivalry with competing railroads had been its lifeblood; now the lamb and the lion were yoked together and pulled for the common goal. Consolidation was the keynote. Ticket offices, terminal facilities, passenger and freight-train service and other phases of operation were consolidated whenever possible. Solicitation work was abandoned entirely.

Thus, the L. & N. contributed its substantial mite towards the creation of a gigantic transportation system. As previously intimated, the nation, and, as a corrollary, its railroads, were greatly handicapped by having to not only fight a war, but to simultaneously create its men and materials. Some 72 army camps and cantonments were hurriedly erected, necessitating the transportation of huge quantities of lumber and of other supplies. Then, after they were built, they were peopled with millions of men and these huge concentrations of manpower, resulting as they did in a considerable population displacement, radically changed and enlarged the duties of the railroads. The needs of the American Expeditionary Force and those of our Allies were also important factors in the creation of the tremendous tonnage moving over American rails.

The matter of Standard Time also came to the attention of the U. S. Government during the period of federal control and on March 19, 1918, some 35 years after the railroads' adoption of Standard Time, Congress passed the Standard Time Act. This not only sanctioned the four-zone time established by the railroads for this country, but additionally provided for "daylight saving" to conserve current and increase national efficiency. On March 31, 1918, therefore, this latter went into effect and at 2:00 a.m., of that day all trains of the L. & N., in common with those of other American railroads, came to a full stop and watches and clocks were set ahead one hour. National daylight saving was not popular, however, and ended in October 1919, although it had originally been intended for it to be effective during the summer months of each year.

It has been previously mentioned that the L. & N. was paid $17,-310,494.67 annually by the federal government for the use of its properties. This basic income was swelled by additional income from other sources (rents, dividends on stocks, etc.) but it was also considerably reduced by interest charges on the funded debt and by various federal taxes, i.e., the Income Tax, the War Income Tax, and the Excess Profits Tax.

Since the commencement of the war, living costs had steadily mounted and during 1916 and 1917, the employe organizations had asked for increases which would compensate them for the deceased earning power of their dollar. Some of these were granted by the individual railroads, but the situation remained unsatisfactory and several strikes were narrowly averted. Director General McAdoo finally took cognizance of the growing unrest by the appointment of the Lane Commission, which was given the task of investigating railroad compensation, the relation of this to wages paid elsewhere, living costs, etc. It was tacitly understood that any increases recommended would be retroactive to January 1, 1918. After some three months of study and investigation, this committee emerged with its recommendations, these being adopted almost in toto by the director general. The eventual result was the famous General Order 27, dated May 25, 1918, which substantially increased the wages of all classes of employes and which established the basic eight-hour day.

General Order 27 was subsequently amended by a number of supplements thereto, which granted further increases. A discussion of the various ramifications of General Order 27 and its various supplements would not be especially pertinent, but it might be said that on the L. & N. their effect was to potentially increase the road's wage bill by about $16,000,000 annually. The retroactive payments, of course, amounted to several millions of dollars. As originally written G. O. 27 established increases of as high as 43 per cent for the lesser paid employes. These percentages of increase gradually dwindled until they reached whatever per cent was necessary to raise the wages of the higher paid employes ($240 to $249) to the maximum wage of $250 to which the order applied. (The increases were based upon the wage rates in effect in December 1915, and had no application to salaries in excess of $250 per month.)

The brotherhoods, and employes in general, were somewhat disappointed by General Order 27 and this subsequently led to the supplements before mentioned. Such supplementary increases, affecting first one class, and then another, continued throughout 1918 and 1919. Despite these increases, however, there was frequently a disparity between what was asked and what was obtained and the consequent dissatisfaction resulted in a number of isolated strikes, affecting individual railroads. Other strikes had their inception in unsatisfactory working conditions, misunderstandings, etc. These disturbances occurred exclusively in 1919 and afford proof that federal control during war-time and federal control during peace-time were two quite different things.

Other difficulties beset the administration of Director General Walker D. Hines, who had taken over the duties of Mr. McAdoo on January 11, 1919. The railroad managements felt, and it seems rightly so, that freight rates should be increased while the roads were still under federal control, in order that they might be spared the onerous task of "upping" them themselves when the roads were returned to private management. Increases seemed in order, for the first year of federal control (1918) had resulted in a deficit of approximately $245,000,000 and this unhappy trend was continuing, the first six months of 1919 showing a further deficit of approximately $227,000,000. (The total deficit for the entire period of federal control has been placed at various astronomical figures, ranging from $1 billion to $2 billion depending upon the point of view of the writer. If the railroads' claims for undermaintenance are included the deficit is closer to the larger figure than the smaller.) Despite the startling deficit of 1918, however, the trend in 1919 was in the direction of reduced freight rates. (Shortly after the start of federal control, a more or less horizontal increase of 25 per cent was applied to the entire freight-rate structure of the nation, but the additional revenue thereby created had been largely offset by the higher operating costs.)

This step towards reduced rates following the signing of the Armistice, however well intentioned, was unfortunately out of step with the trend of the times. Living costs remained in the stratosphere and gave every indication of mounting even higher. Small wonder then that the railroads pressed for higher rates and Railroad Labor for higher wages. Paradoxically enough, Labor was granted a portion of its demands, but the higher rates were not granted, at least not by the director general. Moreover, the national agreements which were entered into with the various brotherhoods during the waning days of federal control, by shortening hours and setting up a number of restrictions, added to the roads' expenses.

CHAPTER XXXI

War's Aftermath

IT IS not the purpose of this account to discredit federal control of the railroads. Uncle Sam's operation achieved results at a time when they were badly needed, but the feat could be likened to a housewife's opening of a can of beans with a hatchet, when the usual can-opener has been temporarily misplaced. Federal control was a procedure that just wasn't suited to normal times and when the impetus provided by the stimulus of an emergency was lacking, it bogged down badly.

On March 1, 1920, the Louisville & Nashville Railroad, along with the other Class I carriers, ruefully surveyed the damage wrought by its paying guests and started in to keep house again. The transition from federal to private control occurred at a time when business was still on the upgrade and - and this is not generally known - America's roads were shortly to be called upon to handle a volume of business that exceeded even that of the "peak" year of 1918. (However, 1920, eventually tapered off into a depression.) That they handled it expeditiously and well, did much to erase the bad impression created by the unavoidable mishaps of 1917.

As intimated, the L. & N. felt that it had a legitimate claim against the Government, involving the under-maintenance of its properties and such items as the disparity between materials and supplies on hand at termination of federal control and at the commencement thereof. An agreement between the Government and the L. & N. was eventually reached on March 7, 1922, and the former paid the latter a lump sum of $7,000,000.00, in full settlement of all claims having their inception during the period of federal control.

The L. & N.'s financial statement for the year 1920 presents a rather piebald appearance. First, there was the Standard Return (guaranteed by the Federal Control Act for the months of January and February) which amounted to $2,885,082.44; then there was the Railway Operating Income Guaranteed under Section 209, Transportation Act of 1920 (This section provided for a guaranteed income of not less than one-half of the Standard Return for the first six months after the termination of federal control for those railroads which would accept certain conditions and the L. & N. was one of the carriers which did) and finally its own net revenue from railway operations for the months of September, October, November and December, which amounted to $2,736,229.62. Various deductions and increments finally resulted in a net income of $7,863,650.82 for the year.

(It might be stated at this point that the Company's accounting procedure and practice, because of its contract with the Government, at times soared beyond the comprehension of a mere layman. Only expert accountants and other higher mathematicians were at home in a rarefied atmosphere which produced such gems as the following non-stop sentence, which is taken

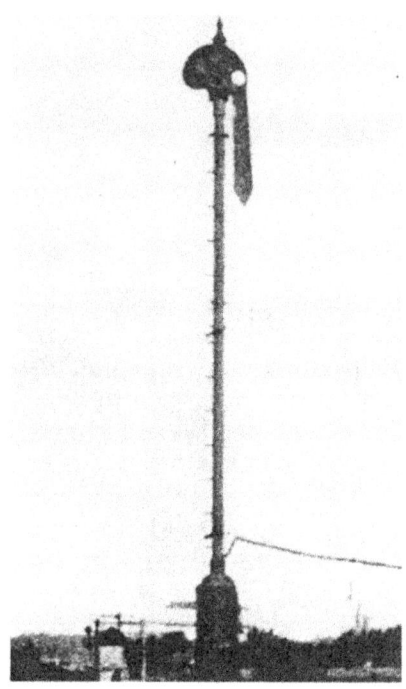

Top: The old "lower quadrant" method of signaling.

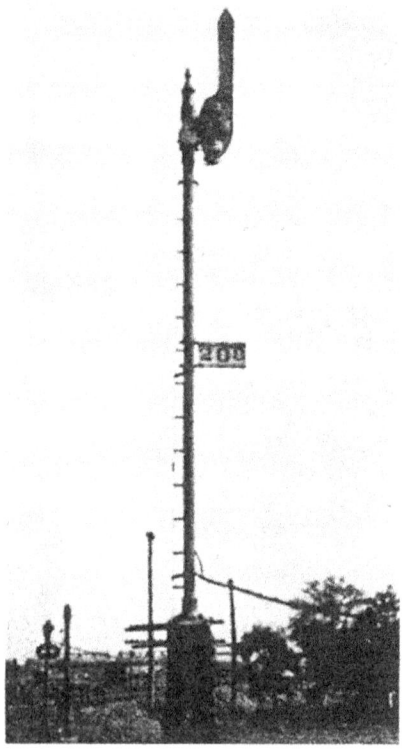

Bottom: The "upper quadrant" method which superseded it in 1918.

from the Annual Report ending December 31, 1918:

"The Director General has agreed to pay currently to the Corporation (The L. & N.) in cash so much of the amounts of accruals from equipment salvage and of the charges to Operating Expenses for equipment depreciation and retirements as do not exceed the cost of equipment acquired since December 31, 1917, either upon its own motion or upon the order of the Director General, provided the Corporation will agree to apply the amounts paid exclusively either to the payment of cash installments or deferred obligations or indebtedness to the Director General for equipment purchased by or on account of the Company during Federal Control, or to the payment of the Company's maturing obligations under equipment trusts made before Federal Control and now outstanding, and also will agree that the amounts of such depreciation, retirements and salvage to be paid over to the Company will be deducted from the amount expended for new equipment on which interest return is to be allowed during Federal Control."

Perversely enough, at the expiration of the guaranty period before mentioned, the traffic the railroads were called upon to handle began to dwindle rapidly and this trend, once established, developed swiftly. The L. & N., at the time, was laboring under an unaccustomed wage load which had increased over 200 per cent since 1916. (In that year its wage bill was $27,279,773; in 1920, it was $86,099,731.) The high cost of corporate existence had been further elevated by an increase in the price of such indispensables as coal and crossties, it being a fact that the road paid $9,790,808 more for coal and $2,140,277 more for crossties in 1920 than it did in 1916.

It is true that this additional expense had been offset to a large extent by the various increases in freight rates which had been

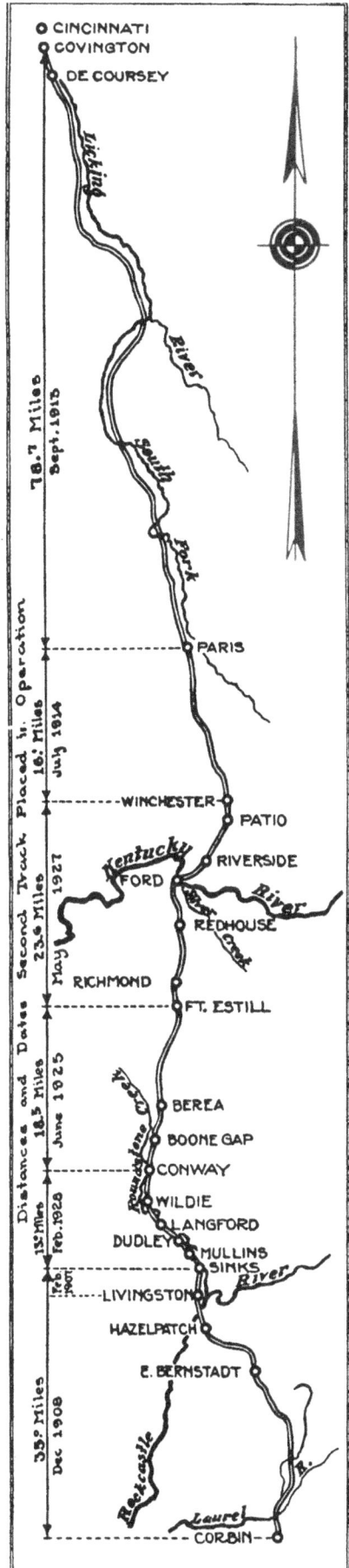

granted and by the greater volume of traffic. Broadly speaking, the increases as they affected the L. & N., were as follows: the 25 per cent flat increase on all freight rates, which had been granted during the early days of federal control, and the 25 per cent increase which was granted to roads in the Southern Region by the Interstate Commerce Commission in August 1920. (At the latter time, railroads in Eastern and Trunk Line Regions were granted an increase of 40 per cent and railroads in the Southern region had their 25 per cent "upped" to 33-1/3 per cent where the freight moved inter-regionally.) These increased freight rates were helpful, as long as there was a sizeable amount of traffic to be handled, but when it began to fall off, as it did during the latter part of 1920, they were not much help to a railroad whose overhead remained more or less constant.

Let us, however, desert temporarily those concerns of the L. & N. which it shared with its sister roads and touch upon matters which concerned the L. & N. alone. During the period of federal control, the Railroad may be said to have been in a state of suspended animation and its individuality was submerged. Not much new work was undertaken, although a few odds and ends, which had their inception prior to the war, were disposed of. Chief among this type of work perhaps was the installation of automatic block signals along various stretches of track where traffic was unusually heavy. This had had its origin in the summer of 1912 and, by the end of 1918, automatic signals governed the operation of trains over 653.89 miles of track.

Another 90 miles of track was so outfitted in 1919 and 1920.

It was during World War I that the old-style "lower quadrant" method of block signaling was discontinued and the "upper quadrant" method was adopted. Radnor

Map of Cincinnati Division's double track, showing the dates second track work was completed.

Yard was completed and placed in operation during the period of federal control, on March 10, 1919, and a certain amount of second track was completed.

An additional yard at Corbin, Ky., to handle northbound business was also placed in operation in November 1919, and at that time the original yard was arranged for the handling of southbound business only. The war years, as previously mentioned, also saw the completion of several small branch lines to coal workings on the Eastern Kentucky and Cumberland Valley divisions, such construction having its inception in the ever-increasing demands made upon the country's coal bins by American industry.

The railroads' problems at the end of federal control were many and vexatious and were intensified by the dwindling traffic of 1920-1921. Some idea of the magnitude of the debacle may be gained from the L. & N.'s statistics for that period. In the first six months of 1921, operating expenses and taxes alone, exclusive of interest charges, etc., exceeded railway operating revenues by $1,138,240.64. The chief reasons for this disparity between income and outgo were two in number: (1) the abnormally high wages of the World War period, which were still in effect and (2) the decreased car-loadings – the hangover which resulted from excess wartime production. Relief finally came on July 1, 1921, when the United States Railroad Labor Board authorized reductions in the pay of employes. (Wages had again been upped 22% for all classified employes on May 1, 1920.) These decreased operating expenses somewhat and the L. & N. was able to make a better showing during the last period of 1921; nevertheless, when the books had received their final audit, a red ink entry of $532,214.69 was revealed – the net loss on the year's operations. (Passengers handled had decreased more than 3,000,000 and freight moved had decreased approximately 10,000,000 tons, when 1921 was compared with 1920.)

This was the first time since 1875 that the L. & N. had experienced a deficit, although it is true that on several occasions in the intervening past the profits had been so slim as to preclude the payment of dividends. (These had been paid each year since 1898, however, none being paid for that year nor for several years previous.) Only twice before in the Company's entire history had the income been less than the outgo; in 1870 when there was a deficit of $522,325.72 and in 1875 when there was a deficit of $7,352.79.

Despite the year's bad showing the Management confidently looked ahead to a day when business would be better, and went forward with its work of revising existing facilities. Much of this centered about the Eastern Kentucky and Cumberland Valley divisions, which were annually being called upon to handle a much larger volume of coal than had been anticipated. Thus, in December 1921, the L. & N. completed a yard at Loyall, Ky., and provided mechanical facilities there in order to remove some of the burden from congested Corbin. A water supply station and reservoir at Dortha, Ky., near Corbin, was also completed in the same month, this being capable of supplying the various thirsty facilities at Corbin with 800,000 gallons of water a day.

The shops at Corbin at this time were undergoing an extensive pro-

A typical construction scene on the old Kentucky Division during the double-tracking of the line from Patio to Sinks, Ky., 1923-1928. The above picture was taken looking north from Langford and shows both the old and new track. The double-track cut eliminated the tunnel.

gram of modernization and enlargement. This work, which was completed in 1921, involved the installation of modern machinery, the construction of a concrete mechanical coaling station, the installation of automatic cinder conveyers and the modernization of facilities in general.

In immediately subsequent years a yard was built at Crawford, Ky., near Hazard, improved mechanical facilities were provided at Hazard, Corbin and Ravenna, Ky., and much second track was constructed on the Eastern Kentucky and Cumberland Valley divisions. The major item in the last mentioned was the building of 40.11 miles of parallel track between Wallsend, near Pineville, and Harlan, Ky. This was completed in May 1926. Other stretches double-tracked included the line from Arkle to Wallsend, 22 miles, completed on July 1, 1924, the line from Pryse to Ravenna, Ky., 5.25 miles, completed in 1922 and the line from Perritt to Lennut, Ky., near Hazard, 15.48 miles, completed in December 1924.

Another "parallelism" worthy of special mention was the double-tracking of the old Kentucky (Cincinnati) Division from Patio, Ky., near Winchester, to Sinks, a distance of 55 miles. For operating reasons, this work was completed as follows: Patio to Fort Estill, May 1927; Fort Estill to Conway, June 1925; Conway to Sinks, February 1928. The revision and double-tracking of this 55-mile stretch of track was started in the fall of 1923 and cost a total of approximately $8,000,000. Incidentally, the line between Sinks and Livingston, a distance of about three miles, had been double-tracked in February 1907, but it had boasted a "double" track of sorts, as early as 1883, which was the date the old Kentucky Central had extended its line south from Richmond to a connection with the L. & N. at Sinks. However, at the time the K. C. had one gauge and the L. & N. another, so a third rail was added to the two already in existence between Sinks and Livingston in order that the K. C. might operate into Livingston, where a car hoist facilitated the removal of freight car bodies from one set of trucks to another set of a different gauge.

The year 1922 fully justified the L. & N.'s optimism and despite the unfortunate nation-wide shopmen's strike which occurred in August of that year, it was able to close out the year with a modest profit. (The shopmen's strike was indirectly a reaction from the boom days of 1918, 1919, and 1920, and was the first nation-wide railroad strike ever to occur in this country. A further wage reduction of 12 per cent was one of its direct causes; the cancellation of the national agreements which had been entered into with the various shop crafts, etc., during federal control was another. In general, 1920 might be described as a year of rising wages and railroad rates, whereas 1921 and 1922 reversed this trend. The wage reductions have been mentioned, they were paralleled by voluntary freight rate reductions in 1921 and 1922.)

Although 1922 was a good year, an ominous cloud, which at first had been no larger than a man's hand, began about this time to assume more threatening proportions. This was the very real and active spectre of bus and truck competition, whose modest beginnings dated back to 1914.

The use of trucks and busses for the hauling of freight and passengers may be said to have received its impetus from World War I with its need for supplementary transport to and from the large army camps and cantonments, but it had its origin in much humbler sources, i.e., the need of the small farmer to obtain ready cash by marketing his surplus products, or livestock, in the distant city, and/or the need of the average merchant in the average small-town for a quicker delivery of his goods. Frequently, the farmers lived in sections remote from a railroad and once their truck was loaded with the produce or livestock, they decided to bring it all the way into the city, even though this might involve a trip of 50 miles, or more, and thus eliminate the expense and trouble of turning it over to the railroad.

Occasionally a farmer would also bring his neighbor's produce, and frequently the neighbor and his family as well, to the distant city, thereby eventually and gradually becoming a carrier for hire. One fine day the thought occurred to this farmer that he could perhaps make more money from the full-time hire of his truck than he could from his farm and the railroads had another potential headache.

In the city, much the same thing was happening. The clerk, or merchant, or small business man with a little money to invest, purchased a truck and began a shuttle operation to the nearby smaller communities. His clients were generally wholesalers, small manufacturers and merchants in adjacent towns, which either lacked railroad facilities entirely or which had very inadequate ones.

All of this competition, at first, was on a very modest scale; the trucks were small, the distances traveled were short and, in general, it might be said that long-distance, large-scale trucking did not become a threat to the railroads until about the middle 'twenties.

Encouraging this process of supplementary transportation, as at first it largely was, were the motor car manufacturers, who began to improve their product, and the various states which entered upon an intensive and extensive program of highway construction, partly underwritten by the tax contributions of the rail carriers. By the 1920s a process which the railroads had more or less ignored – first, because of its comparative unimportance, and, second, because they were engrossed with the problems created by the World War and its aftermath – was brought forcibly to their attention by a few comparative statistics. These revealed that in 1923 alone approximately 2,042,000 motor trucks were registered in this country and that each year saw an increase in their size, their number and the distances traveled. Of course, most of these registrations did not involve carriers for hire, but even so, the truck used by the farmer solely for his own use had some effect on railroad revenues, generally in an adverse direction.

Some idea of the rapidity with which trucking grew into the status of Big Business may be gained from the following: from 1923 to 1925, inclusive, livestock transported by motor truck to 17 selected large markets averaged 5,268,000 head annually. By 1938, this sizeable trickle had grown into a thundering herd of 25,520,000 head. During the same period, unfortunately, rail shipments to the same 17 points declined from 63,860,000 head annually to 21,464,000 head. With a few exceptions, the new carrier made varying gains in all other classes of freight traffic.

In the field of passenger traffic the most formidable competitor was the private automobile, although the behemoth bus was doing its part in decreasing travel by rail. In 1923, the L. & N. alone hauled over 13,000,000 passengers; in 1937, after an intensive battle to reverse the trend through the establishment of cheaper rates, better accommodations, faster schedules, air-conditioned equipment, etc., only 4,133,845 passengers were carried.

The effects of the inroads made by the private automobile and the bus into the L. & N.'s revenues, although smaller, were more noticeable, for the loss of traffic to the trucks had been largely offset by the demands of that boom (which ended with such a resounding crash in October 1929) which had extended through most of the 'twenties.

Other factors, too, had a part in establishing the trend away from the rails, which commenced at the conclusion of World War I. The pipe lines, inland waterways, air lines and the various large-scale hydro-electric developments were also important.

Chapter XXXII

An Era Ends

DEATH struck with heavy hand at the L. & N.'s official personnel during the 'twenties, removing among others, two of its presidents and a former chairman of the board. The entire personnel was saddened by the news of the death of President Milton H. Smith at his home in Louisville on February 22, 1921. Mr. Smith had served the Company continuously as chief executive since March 9, 1891, and as president or vice-president since July 6, 1882, with prior but interrupted service extending back to August 1866, and in recognition of his incomparable services to the road, the stockholders spread the following resolution upon the minutes of their annual meeting, which was held on April 6, 1921:

"The stockholders of the Louisville & Nashville Railroad Company desire in this way to record their profound sorrow at the death of Milton H. Smith, the president, which occurred at his home in Louisville, Ky., on February 22, 1921, in his 85th year, and to extend their sincere sympathy to his family in their great bereavement.

"Mr. Smith gave 50 years of his life to wholehearted, loyal service to this Company and for nearly 40 years was its chief executive officer. During his administration, and due to his rare native ability and remarkable foresight, industry and courageous initiative, the small fragmentary lines that formed the beginnings of the Louisville & Nashville Railroad were wrought into one great homogeneous whole, which was in turn so enlarged and extended as to become one of the most important and valuable transporation systems of the country.

"To the people of the South, among whom he, a stranger, had cast his lot in early life, and to the owners of the great property for whom he always regarded himself as holding the sacred position of trustee, his great abilities were unceasingly and unstintingly devoted.

"The South can never estimate the value of the service he rendered in bringing about its uplift from the depression following the Civil War and in causing the economic development of its vast territory into a wealth greater today than that of the entire Union in 1861.

"Equally impossible is it for the stockholders of this Company to adequately measure their obligations to him for the preservation and enhancement of their investments committed to his keeping.

"He was one of America's great men, and as a railroad executive, in the true and broadest sense, he will ever rank as one of the few great leaders. It has been well said that his genius sprang from an incomparable combination of rugged integrity, love of truth, and extraordinary breadth of vision; and that its proof is written in letters of steel in every county through which the rails of the Louisville & Nashville Railroad pass.

"It is gratifying to his friends that he was privileged to live long enough himself to learn the estimate of his fellowmen and to see the imaginative visions of his early days converted by his efforts into glowing realities. He also saw, it is true, great and unwelcome changes in administrative methods come with the increase of Government regulation, but he did not permit himself to become embittered; he met them as all other conditions, squarely, sanely and successfully.

"The personality of such a man as Mr. Smith is necessarily striking and attractive. In his case it was also paradoxical: Though a giant in wisdom and strength, modesty as to his own attainments was perhaps his outstanding characteristic. Relentless as he was in combat, he fought in the open, never knowingly did an injustice to any man, and in victory was considerate and generous. Subjugating and sacrificing self, he was the embodiment of tenderness and devotion to those he loved. Truly a master mind with a master heart.

"Though his death creates a void that must remain unfilled, the world is better for his endeavors; the example of his life must always remain an inspiration to those who knew him, and the record of his greatness will endure for all time."

On December 10, 1924, Major August Belmont died, after an association with the Company which extended back as far as October 6, 1886. On that date, Major Belmont became a director and was subsequently elected chairman of the board on March 9, 1891. He so served until July 9, 1903, when, as a result of the Gates-Hawley coup of the year before, he resigned as chairman, but continued on as a director until his death. He had been a member of the finance committee ever since March 9, 1891.

Following the death of Milton H. Smith, Wible L. Mapother, first executive vice-president and federal manager of the railroad during the

The Pan-American was one of the first crack trains in the country to have radio. Note the old-fashioned head-sets in use during the early days of this innovation.

period of federal control, ascended to the presidency and under his vigorous and capable leadership a number of radical changes took place. These included the formation of a safety department to better protect and safeguard the health and well-being of employes, the improving of the road's physical plant, and the encouragement lent to the formation of such employe organizations as the L. & N. Cooperative Club, the L. & N. Credit Union, the L. & N. Golf Club, etc. (In fact, Mr. Mapother's interest in better employe and public relations was outstanding.)

In the 1920s there was a certain amount of agitation against railroads and various restrictive measures for their further regulation were in the air. The proponents of government ownership were unusually active, and the railroads decided to take their case to the public. On each road this public relations work took a different form and some railroads even contended that the management should concern itself solely with running a railroad, letting the chips fall where they might. Mr. Mapother, however, early saw the advantages of presenting the Railroad's case fairly and squarely to the public and, in 1923, through a public relations committee, chairmanned by J. J. Elder, executive assistant, Louisville, he took a number of steps towards creating a more sympathetic understanding of the railroad and its problems. The following, and not in order of their importance, are worthy of mention.

In June 1923, the L. & N. commenced the periodic distribution of facts and figures to the people along its lines and to its employes, as well, through the medium of multigraphed circulars. Some of the pertinent subjects discussed were: "Government Enterprise Less Efficient Than Private"; "Shippers of Freight Saved One Billion Dollars in 1923"; "L. & N. Rates and Costs"; etc. Such dissemination effectively supplemented a program of institutional advertising which was carried in the newspapers published in L. & N. territory.

(At the time there was a good deal of confusion in the mind of the people as to the provisions of the Transportation Act of 1920 (which became effective with the transfer of the roads back to private ownership). One of the most prevalent of these misconceptions was that the Act guaranteed the railroads annually a Net Railway Operating Income equal to 6 per cent upon their investment (the value of their properties as determined by the Interstate Commerce Commission). This was, of course, not true; in fact, the so-called "Recapture Clause" of the Act made the individual railroad

Types of L. & N. Service Buttons

15 Years   25 Years   50 Years   35 Years   45 Years

Left: The first issue of the L. & N. Employes' Magazine, which commemorated the 75th anniversary of the founding of the road. Center: Group insurance policy issued as a result of the group insurance plan. Right: Lively Lines, predecessor of the L. & N. Magazine.

turn over one-half of all it earned in excess of six per cent to the Interstate Commerce Commission and retain the other one-half in a special fund for contingencies. As far as most railroads were concerned, however, the Recapture Clause was without application, for they failed by a wide margin to earn 6 per cent upon their investment. This six per cent was later reduced in 1922 to 5¾ per cent and the Recapture Clause itself was finally repealed by Congress in 1933, which directed at that time that all monies thereby paid to the Government be returned, with accumulated interest.)

The L. & N.'s efforts on behalf of an entente cordiale between it and its public included a number of good-will tours by Company officials over the various divisions, during the early 'twenties. Towns all along the line were visited, representative groups of citizens were met and the two groups broke bread together.

In June 1923, H. T. Lively, then freight claim agent, sponsored the publication of a little magazine known as "Lively Lines," which was eventually given a System-wide distribution among employes and others. This could be said to be the predecessor of The L. & N. Employes' Magazine, later to become the L. & N. Magazine, whose first issue appeared in March 1925, in commemoration of the 75th anniversary of the L. & N.

Left: This ad, which was reproduced in the L. & N. Employes' Magazine for June 1925, was originally published in newspapers all along the line and is typical of the institutional advertising of that day.

Right: Sample of multigraphed publicity disseminated to employes and the general public during 1923-1925.

A group insurance plan and the awarding of service buttons and annual passes to those employes who had served the Company continuously for certain periods of time, were three other phases of the L. & N.'s efforts in the 1920s towards a better esprit de corps and a closer understanding with its employes. The group insurance plan which was handled by the Prudential Insurance Company, of Newark, N. J., was inaugurated on July 1, 1925, and the Management defrayed a substantial portion of the premium cost in order that the employes might obtain the insurance at the lowest possible figure. Briefly, it might be said that the master policy, as originally written, provided for the payment of death benefits ranging from $1,000 to $3,000, depending upon the premium paid, which in turn depended upon the compensation of the employe. An additional $1,000 was paid in the case of accidental death and the employe also reaped the benefits of his policy if he became permanently and totally disabled. Exactly 44,203 employes, or more than 86 per cent of those then in service, signed up for the group insurance during the month of July 1925. It was, of course, optional.

The practice of awarding service buttons to employes was adopted in June 1921 and since that time tens of thousands have been issued. Bronze buttons were issued to employes with 15 years of continuous service; silver ones for 25 years; silver and enamel ones for 35 years; gold-and-enamel ones for 45 years and the well-known diamond buttons for 50 years of continuous service. Later on, the employe had his choice of either this diamond button or a watch. Women employes were given service pins, instead of buttons.

Fifty years of continuous service is unusual, of course; however, several L. & N.'ers have exceeded the 60-year mark.

Unfortunately, however, Mr. Mapother was president for but a short time, his death occurring on February 3, 1926, less than five years after that of Mr. Smith. A native of Louisville, Ky., Mr. Mapother had entered the service of the L. & N. in the secretary's office on October 5, 1888, when but 16 years of age. He transferred to the executive department the next year and in the short space of 16 years he advanced to the position of first vice-president, this elevation becoming effective February 16, 1905. He was elected president on March 17, 1921, following the death of Mr. Smith. Whitefoord R. Cole, president of the N. C. & St. L. Railway, was elected president of the L. & N. on March 23, 1926 to succeed Mr. Mapother.

No mention of the highlights of the early 1920s would be complete unless it included the fact that The Pan-American was inaugurated on December 5, 1921. This train, which came to be the symbol of the L. & N.'s passenger service, proved popular with the traveling public from the very start.

Mention has previously been made of some of the outstanding additions and improvements which the L. & N. made to its plant in the early 1920s. Huge expenditures were also made for locomotives and other rolling stock during the period 1920-1925, which increased the road's ownership of locomotives from 1,209 in 1920 to 1,344 in 1925; of its freight cars from 52,462 to 65,025; and of its passenger cars from 683 to 925. These sizeable increases, necessitated by the Company's booming business, do not tell the

Rigolets Bridge as it appeared on July 29, 1925, just after its completion.

whole story for much obsolescent equipment was either sold or destroyed during the same period, thus balancing a portion of the purchases. Such additions to the L. & N.'s motive power and other rolling stock were paralleled by corresponding additions and betterments to other portions of its physical plant and in order to obtain the wherewithal for these huge expenditures the L. & N. was forced to increase its funded debt from $183,266,-170.00, as of December 31, 1920, to $237,842,835.00, as of December 31, 1925, an increase of $54,576,665. This had been created through the issuance of a series of equipment trust bonds and the usual mortgage bonds upon the road's properties.

Because of the increasing value of its physical plant, the L. & N. saw fit in 1921 to make application to the Interstate Commerce Commission for permission to issue an additional $53,000,000 of capital stock, to be distributed as a stock dividend to the stockholders. The Commission deferred action until February 24, 1923, when the L. & N. was authorized to issue $45,000,000 of additional capital stock, subject to certain conditions. The L. & N.'s capitalization was thus increased from $72,000,000 to $117,000,000.

After an interim of some three years, work was commenced again on the installation of automatic block signals and by the end of 1925, 1,093.19 miles of L. & N. track was so protected. Automatic train control also made its appearance upon the L. & N. in 1924 and 1925, in accordance with orders issued by the I. C. C. on June 13 and December 26, 1922. The first installation was made between Etowah, Tenn., and Corbin, Ky., a distance of 162 miles and was completed in December 1926. Another installation was subsequently made between Mobile and New Orleans, a distance of 140 miles, with completion in the early part of 1927.

We have already told of the disastrous experience of the L. & N. in the year 1921, which showed a big red deficit. In 1922 it earned 4.78 per cent upon its investment; in 1923 5.17 per cent and in 1924 5.29 per cent. Moreover, these per cents were based on the road's original investment and did not take into account such factors as good will, replacement cost, etc. They were not based on the valuation eventually decided upon by the railroad and the I. C. C.; hence they were much higher than they would have been had they been based on the finally determined value.

Those two "problem children" of the engineering forces, the bridges over Rigolets and Chef Menteur, also figured in the "news" in the 'twenties. These two structures had been buffeted considerably by wind and water ever since their completion in the 1870s by the old New Orleans, Mobile and Chattanooga Railroad Company, the predecessor road of the present-day New Orleans-Mobile line and on a number of occasions the gales and waves wreaked such havoc that the structures had to be partially re-built. Finally, in order to avoid the past interruptions to traffic caused by damage to the structures, authority was given for the construction of entirely new bridges across the two bodies of water. That for Rigolets was granted in September 1922, and that for Chef Menteur in March 1924. Both of these new bridges accommodated a single track line of railroad and were built to withstand any wind velocity, or water pressure resulting from the wind, that might be expected or that had theretofore been experienced. The bridge over Chef Menteur, 19 miles east of New Orleans, which was placed in operation in February 1926, consisted of two 270-foot through truss fixed spans and one 279-foot-8 inch through truss draw span, with 143 feet of trestle and 3,894 feet of fill on the east approach and 143 feet of trestle and 4,188 feet of fill on the west approach; total cost $954,664.

The bridge over Rigolets, 30 miles east of New Orleans, which was completed in June 1925, consisted of eight 330-foot fixed spans and one 414-foot through truss draw span, with a western approach of 254 feet of trestle and 4,189 feet of fill and an eastern approach of 1,246 feet of trestle and 3,648 feet of fill; total cost $2,304,109.

The construction of the bridges just mentioned occurred at a time when the L. & N. was re-building a number of its bridges between Nashville and Louisville in order to permit the use of heavier motive power and trains, and while it was also engaged in the re-construction of its Tennessee River Bridge at Knoxville, its Licking River Bridge between Newport and Covington and its Alabama River Bridge north of Montgomery.

Chapter XXXIII

We Mend Our "Ways"

THE L. & N.'s 76th birthday (March 5, 1926) found the road enjoying good financial health and going a land-office business. Indicative of the increasing traffic which the road was being called upon to handle was the fact that during 1926, 417.90 miles (net) of industrial track were added to the System total to provide service to the many new industries which had opened up all along the line.

The Cumberland & Manchester Railroad, before mentioned, a hill-country "pike", joined the family at the close of that year and for some time thereafter residents of sections quite remote from C. & M. trackage were mystified by the sight of locomotives labeled "Cumberland & Manchester" operating over L. & N. tracks. The Cumberland & Manchester Railroad, although it penetrated only Knox and Clay counties, Ky., also served portions of the counties of Leslie, Owsley, Jackson and Laurel, by reason of its proximity to Richland Creek and the South Fork of the Kentucky River. These streams were the originating common carriers for large timber operations in the counties mentioned and, in many cases, the stations on the C. & M. were the nearest railroad shipping points, as neither Owsley, Leslie or Jackson had any railroad trackage worth mentioning. There were also a number of coal mines located on the Cumberland & Manchester and coal and lumber had always been the branch's chief revenue producers.

The construction of 14.1 miles of double track between Lebanon Junction and Parkston, Ky., two miles south of Elizabethtown, was authorized in July 1926, and was completed about one year later. What might have been a routine piece of second-track construction was given especial interest by the elimination of the old tunnel at Muldraugh's Hill, over which the founders of the road had labored so long and arduously back in the 1850s and which had left a string of headaches all the way from Louisville to Nashville. This tunnel, a 2,000-foot affair and one of the road's ante-bellum prides and joys, was not completed and placed in service until January 1, 1860, which was after the running of through trains between Louisville and Nashville. Prior to its completion, Muldraugh's Hill was ascended by means of a temporary track.

The second-track work mentioned, involving as it did considerable right-of-way revision at Muldraugh's Hill (originally spelled variously as both Muldro and Muldrow), eliminated the tunnel by the construction of a cut 4,600 feet in length. This cut was 70 feet deep at the deepest point, was 40 feet wide at the bottom, 75 wide at the top and cost approximately $450,-000. The work at Muldraugh's Hill also involved the elimination of Bridges (really trestles) .Nos. 14 and 15 through the creation of fills with the limestone rock removed in making the big cut. These were about 400 feet west

Muldraugh's Hill, on the main line a few miles south of Louisville, in 1893. From a painting by A. F. LeGros, master painter, L. & N. shops.

of the original bridges, the stone abutments of which were still standing in 1963. During the War between the States the superstructures of these bridges or trestles, were twice destroyed by the Confederates. After their first destruction during the early days of the War, and after they had been re-built by the L. & N., the North erected fortifications in their vicinity for their protection. This seems to have been "scare-crow" protection, i.e., more implied than actual, and for a short while was effective. On December 28, 1862, however, General John Hunt Morgan, in the course of one of his daring raids upon L. & N. property, forced the garrison of these fortifications to surrender and, in the words of Superintendent Albert Fink, ". . . They (the trestle-works) were immediately reduced to ashes."

Other historical land-marks felt the march of progress also shortly thereafter. In October 1927, Bridge No. 193 over the Mobile River was completed and the re-building of Bridge No. 188, over the Tensas River, was completed in May of the following year. The bridge over Green River, near Munfordville, Ky., previously mentioned in this account, was rebuilt, the work being completed in June 1926. Such construction work permitted the use of heavier motive power with a consequent expediting of freight and passenger schedules.

The year 1927 also witnessed the inception of a grade separation project at 4th and G streets in Louisville, an outstanding example of the work of this nature which the Company was doing all over the System. The 4th and G separation, which was begun in August 1927, and completed in November 1928, was followed by another of equal magnitude in Louisville at 3rd and K streets. This latter project, which was commenced in December 1929, was completed in October 1930, the City of Louisville and the L. & N. cooperating to bring about these desirable civic improvements.

The grade crossing situation had long been a troublesome one in Birmingham also and on October 31, 1928, the L. & N. became a party to an agreement with the Southern Railway, the City of Birmingham and the Alabama Great Southern Railroad Company to reconstruct the viaduct at 22nd street, and to construct underpasses at 14th, 18th and 20th streets. This work, which was actually begun in December 1928, and which also involved a re-arrangement of the L. & N.'s passenger station facilities at Birmingham, was not completed until April 7, 1933; the magnitude of the project being such that a mere listing of its outstanding items does not suffice to indicate its scope. The work was, of course, complicated by a successful effort not to interfere with the normal operation of trains and, in general, to permit them to run quite as if nothing was happening, which, as implied, was far from being true.

Grade separation work was also subsequently performed in the Greater Cincinnati area shortly thereafter, the 19th Street viaduct at Covington, over the Cincinnati Division tracks, being opened on October 2, 1931, and the 40th Street underpass at Latonia being opened on October 12, of the same year. Both of these projects were commenced during the latter part of 1930.

One of the chief sufferers from the Gulf Coast's "big blow" of September 1926, a 120-mile an hour gale, was the L. & N.'s coaling plant at Muscogee Wharf in Pensacola, Fla. Here wind and water had combined to do their worst, not only to the coaling station, but to other L. & N. properties in that vicinity. Their little unexpected call, in fact, caused a loss at that location alone which approximated $800,000 and which cancelled service for about 12 days between Pensacola and points east. On November 12, 1927, or a little over one year after the visit of the storm, a new $350,000 mechanical coaling plant was placed in service at Muscogee Wharf. At the time of its construction it was referred to as one of the most modern coaling plants in the world. Its use was later discontinued and it was subsequently dismantled.

July 14, 1927 witnessed the inception of a giant project, in which the L. & N. had a direct interest, and which had a gestation period of nearly six years. The Cincinnati Union Terminal Company was formed on the date mentioned and thereafter for several years, or until the dedication of Cincinnati's magnificent Union Station on March 31, 1933, seven railroads, including the L. & N., labored long and arduously, through the instrument they had created, to bring to completion this $41,000,000 transportation marvel. The center-piece of this project was, of course, the Union Station aforesaid with its magnificent mosaic murals, its spacious

The mechanical coaling plant at Muscogee Wharf, Pensacola, after its completion on November 12, 1927.

and elaborate accommodations, conveniences, etc., but its cost – about $6 million – was obviously only a small part of the total cost. Other items which contributed to the $41 million total were the obtaining of additional right-of-way and land for expansion; the demolition of some 276 structures; the erasement of several streets at grade; the construction of the gigantic Western Hills viaduct; the construction of some 21 buildings, besides the station, including a handsome railway mail post office, and the installation and revision of some 94 miles of track. All L. & N. trains entering Cincinnati began using the new station following its completion, resulting in the abandonment of the use of three other stations by the trains of the Railroad. These three were the Pennsylvania Station at Pearl and Butler streets, built in 1880, which had been used by the L. & N.'s Short Line trains; the Central Union Station at 3rd and Central streets, built in 1884, which had been used by the old Kentucky (Cincinnati) Division trains and a small wooden station at 4th and Smith streets, belonging to the Cincinnati Inter-Terminal Railroad Company, which was formerly used by the L. & N. "shuttle" train, operated for employes between Newport, Covington and Cincinnati for a number of years. This "shuttle" train, because of its unceasing labors, was descriptively known as "The Doodle-Bug," and its operation was discontinued some time prior to the dedication of the new Union Station.

The use of the New Union Terminal by all L. & N. trains and the abandonment of these three stations, necessitated some revision in the L. & N.'s routes into the Queen City. After March 31, 1933, both the Short Line and Cincinnati Division trains entered Cincinnati via the C. & O. Bridge and the C. & O. tracks on the north side of the Ohio River, eliminating the running of Short Line trains through Newport, Ky., and the use of the N. & C. Bridge. The highway portion of this bridge was subsequently sold to the Commonwealth of Kentucky, but freight trains continued to run between Latonia and Cincinnati, by way of Newport and the N. & C. Bridge.

Sibert Yard, Mobile, as it appeared on August 6, 1929, two months before its formal opening.

A section of the line on Muldraugh's Hill after the completion of the construction work in 1927. Note the stone piers that supported the original line.

The total of the L. & N.'s expenditures for improvements in 1927 amounted to $16.4 million, a substantial part of the $175 million which the L. & N. spent for improving its properties during the period 1920-1927, inclusive. The railroad track, the keystone of railroad operation, felt especially the effects of the march of progress. On its main line the L. & N. began to gradually replace the lighter types of rail with 100-lb. rail. In 1927, 70,890 tons of rail, none of which was lighter than 100 pounds to the yard, costing nearly $3,000,000, was purchased and laid. Four hundred and forty-three miles of main line track were involved in this replacement program, which was paralleled by an expenditure of approximately $5,000,-000 for various types of rolling stock of improved design, capacity and power.

The year 1927 has been singled out for especial mention, in the direction of a recapitulation of expenditures, etc., because it was a typical year of the "Coolidge Prosperity" era of the 'twenties. Business was good and the net income for that year – $16,726,241.26 – struck an average between the especially good years of 1926 and 1925, with net incomes of $19,422,111.37 and $18,700,710.86 respectively, and the somewhat leaner years of 1929 and 1928 with net incomes of $14,323,219.55 and $13,726,542.34 respectively. In 1927, 9,438,696 passengers were carried and 63,898,695 tons of freight were moved.

The net incomes for 1925, 1926 and 1927 were also a convincing answer to those critics who had claimed that the L. & N.'s Guaranteed or Standard Return ($17,310,494.67 annually) during the period of federal control was excessive and was beyond the average annual earning capacity of the road, even though it was based fairly and squarely enough on the L. & N.'s average annual railway operating income for the three years ending with June 30, 1917. Even the figures mentioned do not tell the whole story

Top left: The old Central Union Depot at Cincinnati; top right: The old Pennsylvania Station. Bottom: Air view of the Cincinnati Union Terminal taken shortly after completion of the project. Approach used by trains of the L. & N. is at extreme lower right.

for the 1925-1929 totals are net income after the deduction of interest charges, while the Guaranteed or Standard Return was based on net railway income, before the deduction of interest charges, and the L. & N. paid such charges out of the $17,310,494.67 mentioned.

The years 1928 and 1929 saw a continuation of the widespread program of improvement and addition to the properties of the Railroad. Bridges and trestles on the Louisville-Lexington line were reconstructed to permit the use of heavier power. The grade separation work at Louisville and Birmingham, which had its inception in 1928, has been previously mentioned. August of that year also saw the start of the work at Sibert Yard at Mobile,

The row of telegraph poles in the upper left background indicates the location of the L. & N.'s line into Mobile as it was prior to 1926.

Ala., and an 11-story annex to the general office building at Louisville, Ky., was also authorized in 1928, although no actual work was done in that year.

Sibert Yard was a most ambitious project and was an integral part of the L. & N.'s long-range program of expansion on the "southern end" of its properties. Mention has been made previously of how the reconstruction of various bridges on the old N. O. & M. Division, including those over the Mobile and Tensas Rivers, had permitted the use of heavier power. Sibert Yard, which was formally opened on October 6, 1929, cost over one million dollars to build and its 14 storage tracks provided for the chambering of 900 freight cars. The providing of adequate mechanical department facilities was also an integral part of the Sibert Yard project, enabling the L. & N. to abandon the use of its Choctaw yards and shops at Mobile. Sibert Yard was located adjacent to the $10,000,000 Alabama State Docks, completed the year before and from the very first it has worked in close conjunction with this huge instrument of import and export, its switch engines having easy access to its properties. As a matter of fact, about three miles of the L. & N.'s old main line into Mobile from the north ran through the properties to be occupied by the Alabama State Docks. Before the Docks could be built it was necessary for the L. & N.'s line to be moved back from the Mobile River in a westward direction and for the L. & N. to deed to the State Docks a substantial block of its property in that vicinity. The L. & N. abandoned its old line and accepted the new line from the State Docks Commission on February 15, 1926.

The annex to the general office building was authorized in the latter part of 1928, although no work was done that year. The first shovelful of earth was turned on July 1, 1929, and thereafter the work proceeded rapidly, the building being ready for occupancy by the early part of February 1930. The completion of the annex increased the general office building's Broadway frontage to 368 feet and gave it the distinction of being one of the largest structures in the country occupied exclusively by the offices of one railroad. It is 368 feet wide, 60 feet deep and 161 feet high.

The building of the annex had been necessitated by a constant increase in the road's clerical personnel; a result of the boom days of the "Coolidge Prosperity" era. Prior to the completion of the annex, the Company's clerical forces at Louisville were housed in several buildings in the central part of the city in addition to the general office building itself. For example: A portion of the car accountant's force was located at various times in three different buildings at 9th and Broadway; the auditor of freight accounts' force was positioned on three floors of the Gibbs-Inman Building at the southeast corner of 9th and Broadway; the freight claim department had been in the Board of Trade Building at 3rd & Main; a portion of the auditor of disbursements' force was in the Union Station; the general development department was in the Urban Building on Fourth Street, near Main; the auditor of passenger accounts had been in a building at 8th & Broadway, and the tie inspector's force of the chief engineer's office was located in a small cottage which stood on the site of the annex.

The year 1928 was also highlighted by the disastrous floods which inundated L. & N. lines in Southern Alabama and Northern Florida during April and which caused great damage in the vicinity of Garland, Evergreen, Castleberry and Brewton, Ala., on the M. & N. O. Division and at various points on the Alabama & Florida Branch and on the Pensacola Division. Train service on the main line between Montgomery and Mobile was cancelled from April 23 to April 26. With the resumption of operations, slow orders were the rule and the trains ploughed along through stretches of the line which were under as much as 30 inches of water.

These floods, while they set several new records of their own, were but mild spring freshets compared to the floods which ravaged the Deep South and Southeastern Kentucky and Northeastern Tennessee in March 1929, seriously interfering with the operation of trains on a number of divisions and causing much damage. Chronologically, and "Systemically," the deluge occurred in this wise: In the early part of March a three-days' steady downpour in Southern Alabama caused rivers and creeks to overflow their banks and flood the surrounding terrain to a depth of several feet. Roughly, the flooded area extended from Montgomery south to Mobile, with the towns of Brewton, Garland, Castleberry, Pollard, Geneva, Selma, Georgiana and Evergreen being especially hard hit. Train service was, of course, annulled while the flood waters covered portions of our track for miles and miles and even after the waters receded operation was not immediately possible for many fills had been washed away and much track had been twisted askew by the turbulent streams.

In Florida, it was the same story with McDavid, Molino, Milton and Caryville, on the Pensacola Division, bearing the brunt of the attack.

Somewhat later in the same month, the generally tranquil forks, branches, rivers and creeks in the Cumberland Mountain area went on a rampage, inundating considerable stretches of our Eastern Kentucky, Cumberland Valley and Knoxville and Atlanta divisions and doing great damage to the towns of Barbourville, Pineville, Williamsburg, and Ravenna, Ky., and Harriman, Tenn., all on the L. & N.

A check for $1,741,000 is unusual, even in the financial circles to which the L. & N. is accustomed, but on March 27, 1929, it was the recipient of just such a check. The story behind this is an interesting one and involves a phase of railroad operation not heretofore mentioned. Briefly, the facts were as follows:

For many years the Western Union Telegraph Company had maintained on the L. & N.'s right-of-way pole lines which were constructed after the building of each section of railroad. During that era it was the practice of the commercial wire companies, for obvious reasons, to construct communication lines adjacent to railroads; in most instances upon the railroad right-of-way and, in consideration of this privilege, would set aside certain wires for the exclusive or joint use of railroads for the purpose of dispatching trains and general message work.

On May 31, 1876, the L. & N. Railroad and affiliated railroad companies entered into an agreement with the Western Union Telegraph Company, superseding all previous contracts between the respective interests. This agreement, like that of its predecessors, was drawn on the basis of an exchange of services and facilities and without any rentals or cash being involved.

The contractual arrangement mentioned was renewed from time to time, and continued amicably until August 17, 1912, the Western Union having advised the L. & N. a year previous that it desired to terminate the contract. The telegraph company then filed condemnation suits to acquire a right in perpetuity along the railroad's property, the L. & N. meanwhile notifying the Western Union to vacate its right-of-way and station premises. This the latter refused to do and subsequently obtained injunctions restraining the L. & N. from ejecting it. In 1911, however, following its recipiency of the Western Union's notification of termination one year thence, the L. & N. proceeded to construct its own pole lines and telegraph and telephone wires and equipment. This work was done under the direction of the late R. R. Hobbs, then superintendent of telegraph. As each section of this work was completed the railroad discontinued the use of the Western Union's facilities. It took several years to complete the job. (A short while prior to 1911 the L. & N. had commenced the dispatching of trains over certain of its lines by the use of telephone and practically all of the construction mentioned involved the providing of telephone communications.)

The legal maneuvers mentioned resulted in some 17 years of litigation, involving 44 appeals to the state and federal appellate courts, seven of them going to the Supreme Court of the United States. The L. & N. succeeded in defeating nearly all of the condemnation suits previously mentioned, the Western Union being successful only in condemning a small portion of the road's right-of-way in Mississippi and Louisiana. Finally, in July of 1928, the L. & N. and the Western Union entered into an operating contract under which the remainder of the Western Union's poles were removed from the railroad's property, except for the short section between New Orleans and Mobile, and the telegraph company was permitted to rent attachment space for its wires upon the railroad pole system. On March 27, 1929, the Western Union in compromise settlement for the rent claimed by the Railroad for the telegraph company's occupancy of its right-of-way and for other facilities furnished during the long-drawn-out litigation turned over to the L. & N. the check in the amount of $1,741,000 before mentioned.

CHAPTER XXXIV

Belt-Tightening

THE waning days of 1929 found the L. & N. looking ahead to the early part of 1930 when funded obligations, represented by the Company's bonds in the amount of $13,000,000, would mature. In order, therefore, to reimburse its treasury for the money expended in retiring these bonds, as well as to obtain the cash to permit it to pay for extensive improvements to roadway and equipment, the L. & N. made application to the Interstate Commerce Commission for the authority to sell bonds aggregating $20,000,000. Such sale was subsequently authorized by the Commission on February 21, 1930, and the bonds were sold on February 27, yielding $18.5 million.

L. & N. trains into Cincinnati have entered the Queen City via several structures spanning the Ohio River and on April 3, 1929 another of these was placed in service. This was what was known as the C. & O. Bridge and began to be used by all L. & N. passenger trains entering Cincinnati. As the bridge's name would imply, it was not owned by the L. & N., but it occupied a strategic position in the operation of its trains and was perhaps its most important link with other rail carriers of the nation.

A brief recapitulation of the L. & N.'s "bridgeways" into Cincinnati reveals three such structures: the N. & C. Bridge, between Newport and Cincinnati, completed on or about April 1, 1872 and used by Short Line passenger trains until the opening of the Cincinnati Union Terminal in April 1933; the old C. & O. Bridge between Covington and Cincinnati, just upstream from the new bridge, completed on Christmas Day, 1888, and used until the opening of the new C. & O. Bridge on April 3, 1929, by the trains of the Cincinnati Division; and, of course, the new bridge itself.

The story of the L. & N. in the Cincinnati area has been dominated by the tendency elsewhere apparent on the System to continually outgrow facilities and/or arrangements once considered adequate. When the old Louisville, Cincinnati and Lexington Railway, or Short Line, entered Covington in 1869, it at first remained on the south bank of the Ohio River, utilizing the facilities of the Kentucky Central in Covington. It soon became ambitious to enter Cincinnati, but the city of Covington objected vigorously, being loath to relinquish its terminal status and become a mere way station. Tangible direction to its protests was given by its refusal to grant a right-of-way for a bridge approach. The status remained at quo for a while until the neighboring city of Newport, seeing in this difference of opinion an opportunity to obtain a railroad, offered the L. C. & L. the necessary right-of-way. This offer was accepted and in 1872 the L. C. & L. laid its tracks from Milldale, later Latonia, through the heart of Newport and simultaneously undertook to complete the Newport and Cincinnati Bridge, which had been projected as early as 1868. However, the major share of the credit for the completion of this bridge goes to the Little Miami Railroad, later leased to the Pennsylvania Railroad, which at the time was desirous of obtaining connection with a Southern carrier. As previously mentioned this bridge was completed on April 1, 1872 and the L. C. & L. subsequently used the terminals of the Little Miami in Cincinnati.

C. & O. Bridge as it appeared during the false-work phase of its construction in 1929.

The new and old bridges at Henderson, Ky., shortly after the completion of the former (on the left) in the latter part of 1932.

Bridge across the Tennessee River at Danville, Tenn., shortly before its completion in November 1932.

Following its disputed passage across the Ohio River the L. C. & L. still had no direct physical connection with railroads in the western portion of the city and carload freight for the C. H. & D. and the Erie was set off at Walton, Ky., where it was turned over to the Southern for delivery. Carload freight for other west end lines was delivered over a street connection track. At that time the L. C. & L.'s yard and roundhouse were located at Wilders, Ky., and remained in use until 1891 when the yard at Latonia was built.

The L. & N. obtained the L. C. & L. in 1881 and the purchase of the Kentucky Central in 1891 gave it another entrance into the Queen City. The resultant use of the C. & O.'s terminal facilities on the north side of the river made it possible for the L. & N. to discontinue the arrangements previously mentioned for the delivering of freight to lines in the west end of Cincinnati. Later on, to facilitate its exchange of business with these west end lines, the L. & N. built what was known as the Cincinnati Inter-Terminal Railroad, which extended from the Cincinnati approach of the C. & O. Bridge to a connection with the C. H. & D. and the C. & O. of Indiana and other railroads in the west end of Cincinnati. (See map.) This connecting line was completed in 1904.

In order to obtain additional terminal facilities in Cincinnati, the L. & N. in 1904 also purchased the N. & C. Bridge from the Pennsylvania Railroad,

The Plum Street Produce Yards at Cincinnati.

which had, in turn, obtained it from the Little Miami Railroad, and acquired property along the river front from the N. & C. Bridge to Plum Street, with the immediate intention of building a freight depot and team tracks between Plum and Vine streets. It was the intention to reach this property by building a viaduct from the N. & C. Bridge, but the city of Cincinnati ruled against such construction. The L. & N. then abandoned its plans for a depot, but constructed team tracks and a drive-way between Plum and Vine streets south of Water Street. This yard was served by delivering cars to the Pennsylvania Railroad for placement and this to some extent prevented the L. & N. from realizing the full potentialities of the location for the handling of perishables into the Cincinnati area.

However, in 1926, the L. & N. completed additional tracks just west of the East End Station and on July 18, 1932, opened the new Plum Street Yard, which at that time had five tracks and two drive-ways. On April 5, 1933, the L. & N. secured trackage rights from the Pennsylvania on Water Street from Smith Street to Walnut Street, east of the C. & O. Bridge to the yard with L. & N. engines and crews. This was a big improvement and the yard was subsequently enlarged that year and in 1934 to a capacity of approximately 150 cars. It was thoroughly modern in every respect. A $125,000 fruit and vegetable shed, which was steam heated and which housed 20 cars was completed in March 1938.

The C. C. & O. Connection, previously described, was very probably the outstanding piece of construction work undertaken by the L. & N. in the decade or so prior to World War II. While its length and its importance entitle it to this distinction, the building of the 7.69-mile extension from Heyburn to Harber, Ky., in 1929-1930 should not be overlooked.

This Left Fork Branch (C.V.) tapped vast tracts of timber; and following its building, a number of coal mines were also developed in that territory. Much of the acreage served was owned by the Asher Coal Mining Company.

In 1930, the effects of what was generally known as "The Depression" began to be felt by American railroads and the L. & N. was no exception. Its net income, despite some retrenching, dropped dizzily from $14,323,-219.55 in 1929 to $6,605,936, which was alarming as a trend, if not especially so when considered as the net profit from one year's operation. Worst of all, however, this trend showed every sign of accelerating its pace and 1930, which was not so fine, by contrast with 1931, and even 1934 and 1935, could well have been referred to as the good old days. The following tabulation tells the tale succinctly, if sadly:

Year	Net Income
1931	$1,039,946
1932	2,108,875 (net loss)
1933	1,795,716
1934	2,967,385
1935	4,128,943

Although the times were thus dubious, the Company proceeded with the various projects which had had their inception in more prosperous

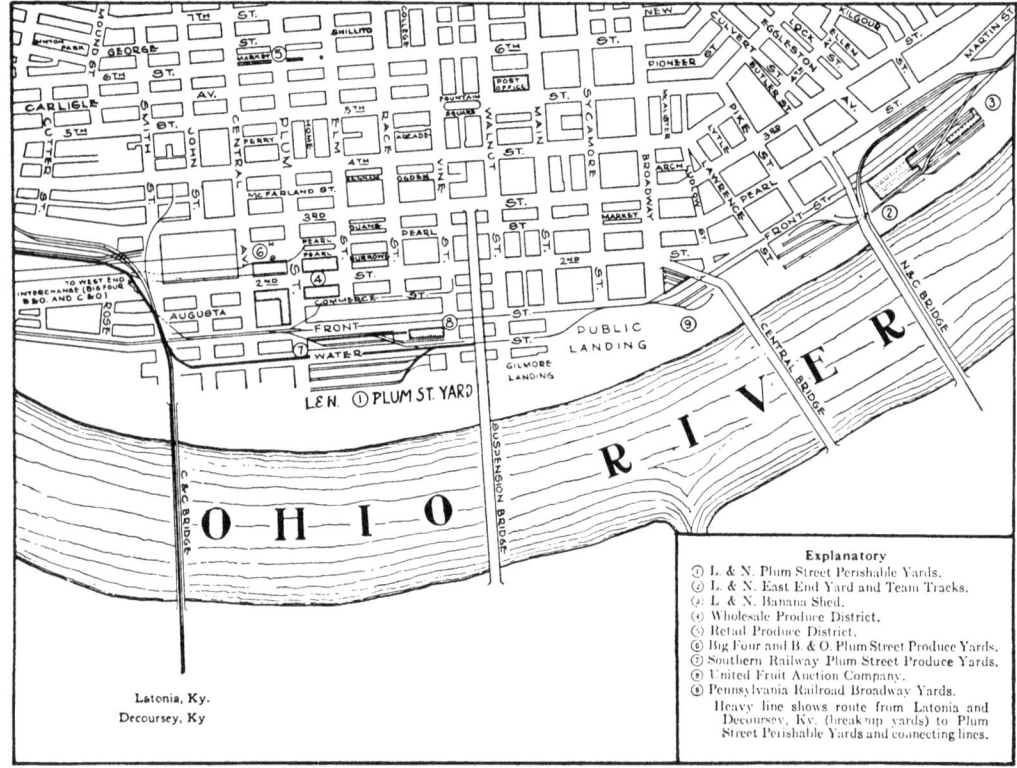

Map showing location of Plum Street Yard, Cincinnati, and route from break-up yard.

days. These included the building of branch lines in Southeastern Kentucky, participation in the building of a new union terminal at Cincinnati, grade separation work at Louisville, Covington and Birmingham, and the re-construction of various bridges.

Despite the curtailing of expenditures in 1930, an even more strenuous program of retrenchment was necessitated in 1931 and 1932 and the Company, struggling to keep its corporate head above the water, was forced to take a number of drastic and mutually distasteful steps, involving the furloughing of thousands of employes and substantial reductions in the pay of those remaining in service. These reductions and the subsequent restorations are such an adequate index to the ebb and flow of the Railroad's fortunes during the decade of the 'thirties that their effective dates are listed herewith. First to feel the repercussions occasioned by the deceased revenues were the officials and supervisory officers of the Company, whose salaries were reduced 10 per cent effective January 1, 1932.

One month later, or effective February 1, as a result of agreements with the various brotherhoods, representing all classes of employes, a reduction of 10 per cent was made in the pay of all employes, other than those previously mentioned, for a period of one year. By mutual consent, this agreement was extended from time to time until July 1, 1934, at which time a restoration of 2½ per cent was made. An additional 2½ per cent was restored on January 1, 1935, and the remaining 5 per cent on April 1, 1935. The original 10 per cent reduction in the salaries of officers, effective January 1, 1932, had been followed by another 10 per cent reduction – amounting to 9 per cent of the basic rate – on July 1, 1932 and this latter was restored along the lines of the restoration of the 10 per cent to the rank and file of employes.

An agreement had been reached with the clerical and station forces of the Company for a monthly two-day lay-off without pay, effective July 15, 1932. This agreement was continued until May 1, 1937, when the two days were restored. A reduction of 10 per cent in the amount of pensions granted retired officers and employes, which became effective May 1, 1932, was restored in 1936, and the original 10 per cent reduction in the pay of officers and officials was also restored in 1936. One or two of the general offices at Louisville took as many as four days off a month without pay, in addition to the 10 per cent cut, during the period 1932-1936.

Death, which is proverbially no respecter of personages, took no holiday as far as the L. & N. was concerned in 1931, but removed two of its veteran high-ranking officers. The first of these two to feel Death's heavy hand was George E. "Boss" Evans, executive vice president, who died at his home in Louisville on January 7, 1931, after a brief illness. Mr. Evans, at the time of his death, had been with the L. & N. for over 57 years, having served it continuously since 1873. Mr. Evans had achieved his eminence through promotion from the ranks and had been a vice-president of the Company for the last 26 years of his life.

Henry Walters, the chairman of the L. & N.'s board of directors, also passed away in 1931, his death occurring on November 30 in New York City. Mr. Walters was 83 years of age at the time and had been connected with the L. & N. as chairman of its board of directors since July 9, 1903. A native of Baltimore, Mr. Walters had also been chairman of the board of the Atlantic Coast Line Railroad. While Mr. Walters' energies were primarily occupied by the demands made upon him by the affairs of these two great railroad systems and those of other railroads with which they were closely affiliated, he still found time to indulge in his avocation of art and to devote himself to many philanthropies. Lyman Delano, executive vice president of the Atlantic Coast Line and a member of that same Delano family who had taken such an active part in the destinies of the Atlantic Coast Line and Louisville & Nashville systems, was appointed chairman of the board following Mr. Walters' death.

Train No. 92, engine No. 1080, emerging from the north end of Hagan's Tunnel on December 1, 1930. This was the first train to pass through the 6,215-foot tunnel under Cumberland Mountain on the C. C. & O. connection.

Despite the parlous times, the L. & N. in January 1931 authorized the construction of a new bridge across the Ohio River at Henderson, Ky., to replace the one dedicated in 1885, which was no longer equal to the demands of traffic. Actual work was started in May of the same year and thereafter moved along rapidly, with a dedication of the structure occurring appropriately enough on December 31, 1932, for it was a large-scale dramatization in steel and concrete of "off with the old – on with the new!" The new bridge, including the new approaches, had a total length of 12,123 feet, and its cost was over $3 million. The removal of the old bridge, as ordered by Uncle Sam's War Department, was completed on December 11, 1933, a fire of undetermined origin expediting the work, but reducing the value of the material salvaged.

Although there was thus a span of some 47 years between the dedications of the two bridges spanning the muddy waters of the Ohio, eyewitnesses who were contemporary to both occasions were not lacking. Frank Krug, the fireman on the first train to cross the old structure, was present as an honored guest on December 31, 1932, as were Vice-President T. E. Brooks, an operator at Henderson, Ky., when the first bridge was dedicated; and W. H. Courtenay, chief engineer, under whose direction the new bridge was built, who, as assistant to the resident engineer, had played a big part in the construction of its predecessor.

Henderson, Ky., within whose corporate limits the new structure was located almost in its entirety – for the town's city limits extend to the low-water mark on the Indiana shore – celebrated the dedication enthusiastically and vociferously. Church bells rang, whistles blew and "vox pop" made itself heard in a number of ways as No. 54 from the north made the inaugural trip over the new bridge.

The building of the Henderson Bridge was paralleled, on a somewhat smaller scale, by the building of a bridge over the Tennessee River at Danville, Tenn. Work on this structure was commenced in July 1931, and the bridge received its baptism of fire by the trains of the L. & N. for the first time in November 1932. It cost a total of $706,432.

By the latter part of 1931, after some two years of the Depression, many of America's railroads were facing disaster and to grant them relief the Interstate Commerce Commission in that year approved certain small increases in freight rates and charges. The I. C. C. then suggested that the revenues which resulted from these increases be pooled by all the railroads and used as a fund for the benefit of those carriers who failed to earn their fixed charges. This was done and resulted in the organization by the railroads of the Railroad Credit Corporation which loaned money thus available to needy carriers who qualified with certain formulated rules. (Fortunately, the L. & N. was never forced to avail itself of the resources of the R. C. C. and, as of December 31, 1940, had a credit to its account of $328,396 with that organization.)

The L. & N., in common with other carriers, attempted to counterbalance the effects of the Depression by the obvious methods of curtailing outgo and increasing income. In the field of freight revenues, it felt, along with the other carriers, that the best way in which to do the latter was by increasing the freight rates. In the field of passenger traffic, however, it differed from most of its contemporaries in that it felt that passenger revenues could be increased by reducing the existing rates, and it was one of the first railroads in the country – the first major system – to put this theory into actual practice. Passenger travel on the L. & N. had been tobogganing rapidly for a number of years and 1931 and 1932 with only 3,008,217 and 2,149,692 revenue passengers carried, presented a sad contrast to even so recent a year as 1927, when the comparable figure was 9,438,696. In 1927, for instance, the L. & N.'s passenger train mileage amounted to 12,631,333 miles, while in 1932, only five years later, this figure had dwindled to 9,706,935 miles, a decrease of 23.15 per cent. Prior to April 1, 1933, passengers on the L. & N. were carried for 3.6 cents per mile, regardless of the type of accommodation used.

The L. & N.'s experimentation with reduced passenger fares was of vital interest, not only to the management, but to employes, too, for the latter would receive direct benefits in the form of increased employment through the re-instatement of trains. It is, in fact, no exaggeration to say that the nation-at-large manifested a keen interest in the L. & N.'s experiment which, as implied, had its inception on April 1, 1933, in the dark days of a depression whose gloom was just beginning to lighten perceptibly. At that time the rate for day coach travel was reduced to two cents per mile and the rate for Pullman travel was reduced to three cents per mile. The Pullman surcharge was eliminated on all parlor and sleeping-car travel on L. & N. lines, reducing the charge for Pullman space occupied by one-third.

The L. & N., in its experiment with reduced fares was joined by three family railroads, i.e., the N. C. & St. L., the A. & W. P., and the Western Railway of Alabama, and by the Mobile and Ohio. The reduced fares were originally placed in service for only six months' time, with their retention beyond that period depending upon the public's response to the innovation.

It would not be true to report that the reduced fares were a spectacular success from the very start and that the countryside thereafter was strewn with the wreckage of abandoned buses. Despite an intensive and extensive campaign of enlightenment, folks in general were slow in learning of the new dispensation and its implications. The fares, however, did reverse the unfavorable trend of the past few years and the number of passengers carried showed a commendable increase, even though the revenues decreased slightly. Most encouraging was the fact that even though passenger revenues had decreased insofar as the year 1933 itself was concerned when compared with 1932, each month the new fares had been in operation showed a lessening of this decrease and September, October, November and December, 1933 had shown nice increases, in revenues and passengers carried, over the same months of 1932.

Moreover, it was felt that by increasing the number of passengers carried the fares had justified their further retention and on September 30, 1933, therefore, with some slight change, they were extended for another six months. (Pullman fares were then reduced to two cents per mile for distance traveled on round-trips.)

A glance at the record reveals that 2,505,823 passengers were carried by the L. & N. in 1933, as contrasted to 2,149,692 passengers in 1932, even though passenger revenue dropped slightly from $5,176,918.01 to $4,531,424. The reduced fares were continued for six months, dating from September 30, 1933, but, on December 1, 1933, the L. & N. in common with most other Southern carriers, further reduced its fares to one and one-half cents per mile for coach travel, with Pullman fares ranging from two to three cents per mile, depending upon the nature of the trip. This latter step, which brought the Company's fares more in line with those of its non-railroad competitors, was even more successful than the first reduction had been and 3,809,205 passengers were carried in 1934, with passenger revenues totaling $5,306,214.32. The fares last mentioned remained in effect until October 15, 1937, when round trip fares in Pullman cars were increased from two to two and one-quarter cents per mile. One month later the coach fare was increased from one and one-half cents to two cents per mile. This upward adjustment proved unsatisfactory, however, (coach passenger revenues decreased 22.4 per cent in 1938, compared with 1937) and on January 15, 1939, coach fares were again reduced from two cents to one and one-half cents per mile. On June 1, of the same year, round trip coach fares were further reduced to 1.35 cents per mile for each mile traveled.

Nor was the lowering of passenger fares the only break which the L. & N. made with the procedures of the past. Simultaneously, it largely nullified one of the strongest arguments of the trucking interests with its inauguration of pick-up and delivery service on less-than-carload shipments on March 15, 1933. It had long been claimed by truckers and their supporters that the truck was a much happier medium of transportation than the railroad, because it could with equal facility pick-up a shipment, transport it and deliver it to consignee at destination, whereas the railroad's function was confined to carrying the shipment between the railroad freight stations. The Louisville & Nashville Railroad was not the first railroad in the country to realize that this supplementary service could be utilized by the rail carriers, as well as by the truckers, but it was one of the first, and its adoption of the practice on the date mentioned, enabled it to regain much of the less-than-carload business that had been lost to the trucks.

As originally constituted, the L. & N.'s pick-up and delivery plan affected nearly 500 stations on its lines and on the lines of seven other Southern carriers who adopted a similar plan. The provisions placed in effect on March 15, 1933, were admittedly experimental and probably erred on the side of conservatism. The P. & D. service was free only on shipments moving within a radius of 230 miles and there were a number of restrictions on the size, weight and type of freight to which the plan applied. In general, the reaction to the new innovation was a favorable one and the subsequent adoption of a similar service by virtually every large railroad in the country, greatly enhanced its value to the average shipper. The L. & N.'s experience was such that it soon realized that a liberalization of the service was requisite to its success and accordingly on May 10, 1933, extended the 230-mile radius to 360 miles and on January 20, 1936, commenced the free pick-up and delivery, with some slight exception, of all less-than-carload freight shipments originating at or consigned to agency stations on its lines, regardless of the distance involved.

CHAPTER XXXV

Water on the Track

THE early 1930s witnessed the establishment of a trend on the L. & N. Railroad, which was the direct result of the Depression and which offered a sad contrast with the days of less than 30 years or so previous when the Railroad was busily engaged in building new trackage or in acquiring that which was already built. This trend was the increasing abandonment of branch lines, whose operation was no longer profitable.

Prominent among the abandonments in the decade mentioned were those of 76 miles of the old Louisville & Atlantic line, from Cliffside, near Frankfort, Ky., to Irvine, Ky., removal of which was authorized August 17, 1932; 32 miles of the Clarksville & Princeton Branch, Princeton Junction, Tenn., to Gracey, Ky., which removal was authorized on March 27, 1933; the 9½-mile Gate City Branch, Ruffner Mine No. 2 to Trussville, Ala., removal authorized March 9, 1933; the 10½-mile Prattville Branch from Prattville Junction to Prattville, Ala., removal authorized October 31, 1933; the 11½-mile West Point Branch from Iron City to Pinkney, Tenn., removal authorized November 27, 1933; the 23-mile Richmond Branch, from Fort Estill to Lancaster, Ky., removal authorized December 1, 1933 the 5½-mile South Branch, from Redding to Readers, Ala., removal authorized March 17, 1934; the 11-mile Napier Branch from Napier Junction to Napier, Tenn., removal authorized February 19, 1934; the 31-mile Clarksville Mineral Branch, extending from Hematite through Van Leer to Pond, Tenn., and its 6-mile spur from Van Leer to Cumberland Furnace, Tenn., removal authorized November 1, 1936; and the 12-mile Adairville Branch, from Russellville to Adairville, Ky., removal authorized in the fall of 1938.

A number of somewhat smaller branches were also abandoned in the 'thirties and in nearly every case the discontinuance of freight and passenger service followed by a few weeks the granting of the authority to abandon. The actual removal of the rails, crossties and other appurtenances of the line generally took place soon afterwards.

The trackage specifically mentioned totaled approximately 224 miles, and, as an interesting coincidence, this was only slightly less than the L. & N.'s trackage at the outbreak of the Civil War (269 miles). When the smaller abandonments are included the discarded trackage of the 'thirties exceeded the Civil War figure.

Roughly parallel to the abandonment of branch lines no longer profitable to operate was the dismantling of obsolete equipment. In July 1933, the L. & N. authorized the scrapping of 251 locomotives, all over 30 years of age, 3,671 small capacity wooden freight cars and 368 units of work equipment. This rolling stock (original cost – $7,000,000) was sold "on the hoof" to David J. Joseph Company, of Cincinnati, which completed its dismantling at Boyles and South Louisville in April of the following year.

As indicated in an earlier installment a major headache of the L. & N.'s personnel for a number of years was the federal valuation of the Company's properties, as of June 30, 1917, which was carried out under the aegis of the Interstate Commerce Commission. This huge task, dealing as it did with almost astronomical sums, as well as with other mathematical niceties, was at once the auditors' despair and delight. It was primarily undertaken in order that a logical keystone for the making of rates might be established and that, as a corollary, the roads might be permitted to earn a fair return upon their investment. It was originally estimated that the total cost of this stupendous task, involving as it did every steam railroad in the country, would not exceed $5,000,000, but this guess fell woefully short of the mark, and the final figure was in the neighborhood of $200,000,000, divided in a three-one ratio between the individual carriers and the government respectively.

Extremely capable and well-informed men have differed widely in their interpretation of what really constitutes a road's "value" and such terms as "capitalized income," "market value of securities," "original cost," "reproduction cost," "cost less depreciation," "prudent investment," and the like were bandied back and forth with fervor. In brief, it was a moot question and when the I. C. C. emerged in March 1932, with the figures that they said represented the final value of the L. & N.'s properties, as of June 30, 1917, for rate-making purposes, the Company immediately took exception to them and the manner in which they had been derived. As established by the Commission at that time these figures were as follows:

$300,275,000 - Property owned and used for common carrier purposes.
   7,827,269 - Property owned but not used.
  25,004,103 - Property used, but not owned.

The resultant figure of $308,102,269 for owned property was in excess of the Company's investment in road and equipment as of June 30, 1917, this latter figure being slightly less than $300,000,000. However, even though the federal valuation and the Company's investment were thus sur-

Typical abandonment scene on the L. & N. This is how a portion of the Adairville Branch looked, following the removal of the track. Red Oak station is in distance.

Advertisement of the National Life and Accident Insurance Company, owners of Station WSM, advertising the daily-except Sunday broadcast of The Pan-American. This was issued during the time the program went on the air at 5:08 p.m.

prisingly close, there were, of course, obvious adjustments necessary, not to mention those which were debatable, before the I. C. C. figure could be regarded as an equitable one for rate making purposes. There was the cost of the betterments and additions which the L. & N. had made to its properties since 1917. And then, in the disputed category, was the value of the Louisville & Nashville Railroad as a "going" concern, the "appreciated" value of its properties and the reproduction cost of same, as factors to be considered.

As mentioned in a previous chapter, in no year subsequent to the enactment of the Transportation Act of 1920 and the "recapture clause" of Section 15a thereof, did the L. & N. earn the "fair return" of 5⅔ per cent (originally 6 per cent) permitted it by law. The valuation of the road fluctuated from year to year, of course, and in most of the years the net railway operating income fell far short of a figure which could be correlated with the per cent permitted, using the road's valuation (as amended) as a basis. The Louisville & Nashville, in common with other rail carriers, felt that the "recapture clause" of the Transportation Act was an unfair one and there was not a "wet eye" in the house when it was repealed by the Emergency Railroad Transportation Act of 1933, which directed that the money already paid in by certain more affluent carriers be refunded to them with accumulated interest.

Mention has already been made of some of the steps which the L. & N. took in the 'thirties to combat the pernicious anemia of dwindling freight and passenger revenues. It was in May 1934, that that great boon to the traveling public, air conditioning, made its bow upon the lines of the L. & N., as a strictly "home-grown" product, when authority was given in that month for the air-conditioning of eight dining cars. At that time a few air-conditioned and pre-cooled Pullmans had been operating over the lines of the L. & N. for a short while. This air-conditioned equipment proved to be so popular that in 1935, 1936 and 1937 a large number of the day coaches, dining cars and Pullmans operating over the lines of the L. & N. were also air-conditioned. By July 1937, practically all of the Company's main line trains, except a few locals, were completely air-conditioned from "stem to stern." This large-scale program, involving approximately 150 dining cars and coaches, cost the L. & N. more than a million dollars and paid dividends in the form of a satisfied and comfortable traveling public.

The year 1933, which saw the inception of lower passenger fares and the introduction of a modified free pick-up and delivery service on the L. & N., also witnessed the inauguration of The Pan-American broadcast over Station WSM, Nashville, Tenn. This was extremely popular with radio tuners-in following its inception on August 15, 1933, when The Pan-American roared by the 878-foot tower of WSM, a few miles south of Nashville, and its sounds and that of its whistle were picked up by a microphone placed beside the track and broadcast. The time was 5:39 p.m. C.S.T. This unique program remained on the air for more than a decade and it was a tribute to The Pan-American's personality that it was able to hold its audience day after day, except Sunday, for so long a time. Fan mail was received from every state in the Union and from many countries abroad.

On July 1, 1931, the L. & N. took the first of a number of steps which it was subsequently to take in the consolidation of its operating divisions and terminals, and which eventually reduced their number by about one-half. On that date the New Orleans and Mobile and the Mobile and Montgomery divisions were consolidated into the Montgomery and New Orleans Division and the Owensboro Division was discontinued as an operating unit, with its trackage being divided between the Evansville and Memphis divisions. Then, shortly thereafter in the same year, the Knoxville and Atlanta divisions were consolidated into the Knoxville and Atlanta Division, the name of the Kentucky Division was changed to the Cincinnati Division and the old Cin-

Mechanized hoisting equipment which was purchased by the Company in 1937 for use in the handling of stores at South Louisville.

cinnati (L. C. & L. or Short Line) and Louisville divisions became the Louisville Division.

No other changes of moment were made until June 16, of the following year, at which time the Cincinnati Terminals vanished to become a part of the Cincinnati Division and the Louisville Terminals met the same fate, becoming a part of the Louisville Division. Then on January 1, 1934, the Nashville Division was merged into the Louisville and Birmingham divisions and a few weeks later the Memphis Division, or Line, was discontinued as an operating unit, its trackage being divided between the Evansville and Louisville divisions, with the latter getting practically the lion's share. To keep the Louisville Division from becoming an unwieldy one, the trackage from Latonia, Ky., into Louisville, was assigned to the Cincinnati Division and various other stretches of trackage which the former had inherited from the old Short Line were assigned to the Eastern Kentucky Division, as was the line between Paris and Lexington, formerly a part of the Cincinnati Division. The Pensacola Division was subsequently made a part of the Montgomery and New Orleans Division, leaving eight divisions and two terminals.

Whitefoord R. Cole, the L. & N.'s 16th president, died on November 17, 1934, while en route from Nashville to Louisville. As previously mentioned, Mr. Cole had succeeded Wible L. Mapother, following the latter's death on February 3, 1926. He was president during some of the Company's most trying times and it is a tribute to his leadership that it weathered these storms better than most. The Louisville & Nashville was not alone in feeling his loss keenly. Mr. Cole's valuable work as a member of the advisory committee of the Association of Railway Executives, as a director of the Association of American Railroads and as chairman of the Southeastern Presidents' Conference, made his passing a blow to the other rail carriers of the nation as well. James B. Hill, president of the N. C. & St. L. Railway, succeeded Mr. Cole as president of the L. & N. on November 27, 1934. Mr. Hill, a native of Spencer, Tenn., in Van Buren County,

Stores department storage yard at South Louisville Shops, showing concrete walks constructed in 1937.

The Breckinridge Street underpass crossing Beargrass Creek; a part of the East Louisville grade separation project which was completed on October 4, 1937.

entered the railroad field in August 1898, as relief agent for the N. C. & St. L., at Bon Air, Tenn., after a previous informal relationship with the "Dixie Route's" agency at Doyle, Tenn., where he studied telegraphy and learned the duties of a station agent. Mr. Hill's subsequent association with such rail leaders as Wible L. Mapother and Whitefoord R. Cole gave him valuable experience and his election to the presidency of the N. C. & St. L. on March 23, 1926, gave him the opportunity to make practical application of this stored knowledge.

The year 1934 also witnessed the passage on August 1 of the first Railroad Retirement Act, which called for a monthly contribution from each employe equal to two per cent of each month's salary and a corresponding four per cent contribution from the Company, for the creation of a fund to provide for superannuated employes. This Act was subsequently declared unconstitutional by the Supreme Court on May 6, 1935, and the money paid in by the employes was refunded to them. Shortly thereafter, or on August 29, 1935, Congress enacted new railroad pension legislation by the passage of two bills; one of these provided a pension system for employes and the other by levying a payroll tax of $3\frac{1}{2}$ per cent on employes and Company alike provided the wherewithal for the payment of the pensions. Following a series of appeals, negotiations and revisions the two Acts were subsequently supplanted by the Railroad Retirement Act of 1937, and the Carriers Taxing Act of 1937, which have since remained in effect. Here, once again and subsequent to their enactment, a portion of the money previously paid in by employes was refunded to them.

Briefly described, the Acts mentioned provided for the payment of annuities to employes after they have reached the age of 65 or after the completion of 30 years of continuous service. The annuities were based on years of service multiplied by basic units representing average monthly salary earned.

The years 1935, 1936 and 1937, generally speaking, were good ones; that is, as compared with those of the prior 'thirties, although the last quarter of 1937, showed a trend that was later to become solidified into the "recession" of 1937-1938. Many of the highlights of this trio of years have been previously mentioned and such efforts to regain traffic lost, or to secure the traffic still held, as air-conditioning, lower passenger fares, free pick-up and delivery, faster schedules, etc., were supplemented by an intensive program of additions and betterments to the road's physical plant. Among the outstanding phases of this was an expenditure of approximately $500,000 for the purchase and installation of new mechanical repair facilities, principally at South Louisville; an expenditure of $102,625 to improve the states department "transport" system at South Louisville by the construction of concrete roadways and the purchase of tractors and trailers; an expenditure of over $100,000 for mechanized tools and machinery for the maintenance of way department; an expenditure of nearly $250,000 to equip certain locomotives with boosters, feed water heaters and stokers; an expenditure of approximately $77,000 for the installation of the Evans automobile loading device on 200 freight cars and last, but obviously not least, an expenditure of $6,626,792 for 2,700 new steel A. A. R. design hopper cars, 327 new Rodger type ballast cars and one Dynamometer car for checking the efficiency of the road's engines.

A number of grade crossings on the lines of the L. & N. were also eliminated in 1936, and thereafter, through the cooperation of the federal government, which underwrote the major portion of the costs involved.

The car repair tracks and east yard at DeCoursey, Ky., on January 23, 1937, during the Ohio River Valley flood.

In all, 92 such separations were made prior to World War II, through the medium of underpasses or overhead bridges. These were of varying magnitude with the palm undoubtedly going to the East Louisville project, which was completed on October 4, 1937, and which gave the L. & N. over a mile of "elevated" track in the Kentucky metropolis. Five streets pass beneath this gigantic structure of steel and concrete and the construction of a new station at Baxter Avenue was an integral part of the project, which cost approximately $1,500,000, this being borne by the L. & N., Uncle Sam and the city of Louisville.

Overshadowing all else, however, and indisputably so, in the middle 'thirties, at least insofar as its L. & N. repercussions were concerned, was the Ohio River Valley flood of 1937, which dumped billions of tons of water into the laps and front yards of residents of that section in late January and early February. In making this large-scale uncalled-for donation the Ohio River, and its tributaries, covered nearly 200 miles of L. & N. track, curtailed operation on the northern end of the System for two weeks or longer,

This is how the right-of-way south of Howell, Ind., looked after the 1937 flood waters had subsided. The track at the right was a temporary one.

The old Water Street freight station at Louisville during the height of the 1937 flood. The station was later leased to the Joseph Denunzio Fruit Company; has now been removed. Note the empty tank cars floating around.

Trains operated by the L. & N. from Louisville, and elsewhere, played an important part in the evacuation of refugees from flooded areas.

and did property damage which nicked the L. & N.'s pocketbook to the tune of $730,965.

A philosopher has said that we find pleasure in the recollection and discussion of past misfortune, the pleasure being in direct ratio to the extent of the original calamity. Understandably this is so and the 1937 flood was to give L. & N. employes and others many pleasurable moments in the years to come; at the time, however, just the reverse was true, of course. Although badly handicapped as a servant of the people by the rising waters, the crippled L. & N. fought back gamely and rendered invaluable service to numerous inundated, or partly inundated, communities in Indiana, Illinois, Ohio and Kentucky, evacuating refugees and bringing in food, medicine, coal and clothing, as well as relief workers.

The flood waters, which first invaded L. & N.-territory around January 20, at Maysville, Ky., were not long in attacking the vital nerve centers of the railroad. By January 21, the Railroad's approaches into Cincinnati were covered at English and Eagle, Ky., on the Louisville-Cincinnati line and at Demossville and Falmouth, Ky., on the Cincinnati-Atlanta line. The yards at DeCoursey were completely inundated, as were the East End and West End stations of the L. & N. in Cincinnati. Moving on south the flood waters struck one of their severest blows at Louisville and vicinity, curtailing operation in and out of the city, as early as Sunday, January 24. There the water rose to a height of nearly three feet above the level of the first floor of the general office building, forcing employes out of the building for some 11 days or from January 23 to February 2. The shops at South Louisville and the Union Station were partially flooded, and, as stated, train operation in and out of the city was cancelled, not only because of flooded approaches, but additionally because much of the trackage within the city itself was under water, which ranged in depth from several inches to 15 or 20 feet.

Despite the fact that much of its Louisville Terminal trackage was flooded, the L. & N. was able to operate trains over portions where the water was not too deep and in the early days of the flood, when refugees were still pouring from the city, it operated shuttle trains between the Union Station and South Louisville and between the head of Jefferson Street and Crescent Hill. Thousands of persons were evacuated to safety in this manner. There were countless incidents centered in a flood locale, in which the L. & N. played an important part; it turned over its depots in many cities to the homeless, it brought in badly-needed cars of coal, food and medical supplies, it donated large quantities of supplies such as caboose stoves, caboose lamps, candles, copper wire, lamp bulbs, water kegs, etc., from its stores department and it evacuated refugees. At Evansville, also hard hit, much of its rolling stock equipment was used as headquarters by the military and the Red Cross and as homes for the homeless and its three-mile approach on the Indiana side of the Ohio River to its Henderson Bridge came in handy as a route to high ground.

An outstanding example of the succor which it brought to excessively dampened communities was its cooperation with the Southern Railway to bring a 45-ton transformer from Lexington to Lyndon, Ky., a suburb of Louisville, in order that the eastern section of the city might have power and light and thus lessen the burden of caring for the sick and distressed. This was not the simple feat that it might sound and involved, among other things, the change of a crossing of the L. & N. and Southern at Shelbyville, Ky., into a connection which was achieved in a surprisingly short time by swinging the tracks of the L. & N. and the Southern around at acute angles to their former positions. Ere long the transformer was at Lyndon where power from the line of the Kentucky Utilities Company was "stepped down" and the eastern portion of the city was soon enjoying the boons of electricity. The L. & N. recovered from the flood in a surprisingly short time. By February 17, normal operation of trains had been completely effected, subsequent to the re-building of the track and restoration of the fill south of Howell, Ind., and the flood itself and its depressing aftermath of discomfort and inconvenience were gradually forgotten.

CHAPTER XXXVI

War Again!

JAMES B. Hill became president of the L. & N. on November 24, 1934 and under his leadership and guidance, there were a number of innovations directly concerned with the creating of a better esprit de corps among employes and the furthering of the road's service to the public. Perhaps the initial step taken by Mr. Hill was the inauguration of the "President's Page" in the L. & N. Magazine which he used for nearly 16 years, or until his retirement, for keeping in touch with employes and in discussing with them matters of common interest. Then, in the spring of 1935, Mr. Hill inaugurated the policy of holding family rallies at various strategic points on the System. The first of these was held at Louisville on the night of July 10, in the Jefferson County Armory and immediately achieved distinction as the largest crowd ever seated indoors at Louisville. In the following months these rallies were eventually supplanted by the Friendly Service movement, which had its inception in the spring of 1936. Friendly Service aimed at creating a better understanding between the road's employes and the public they serve, as well as among the employes themselves.

Interest was kept alive through the medium of meetings held periodically at various points on the System. They combined instructive talks on L. & N. policy with high-grade entertainment, the talent generally having been recruited from the ranks of employes or from among those in their families.

A suggestion system, which was inaugurated on January 1, 1937, was

The South Wind (left) and the Dixie Flagler (right) powered by streamlined L. & N. locomotives, made their inaugural bows in L. & N. territory in December 1940.

President James B. Hill addressing the crowd of 20,000 members of the L. & N. family who attended the first Family Rally at Louisville on July 10, 1935.

another innovation pioneered by Mr. Hill.

Highlights of the year 1937 also included the granting of wage increases to the non-operating and operating employes of the Company, the former having their wages upped five cents an hour and the latter five and one-half cents per hour. These increases became effective August 1, 1937, and were the result of agreements entered into nationally between the various brotherhoods and the member roads of the Association of American Railroads. The Louisville & Nashville's wage bill was increased approximately $290,000 per month by these raises.

In general, 1938 was a rather undistinguished year, the reasons for this being found in dwindling freight and passenger revenues. By the end of that year a reversal of the trend had set in but final figures showed that freight revenues had decreased $9,258,267, or 12.0 per cent compared with 1937, and passenger revenues had decreased $1,009,509, or 14.0 per cent.

The fall of 1938 witnessed the inauguration of a fast freight service between Cincinnati, Louisville and the Gulf ports of New Orleans, Mobile and Pensacola, in the shape of a pepped-up No. 71, which came to be known as The Silver Bullet. This new service, which was typical of the strenuous efforts which the L. & N. was making at the time to combat competition, permitted second morning delivery of merchandise moving from Cincinnati and Louisville to the Gulf ports mentioned, and elsewhere. Although, in actuality, only $10\frac{1}{2}$ hours were sheared from No. 71's schedule, in effect, it gained 24 hours for the receivers of the freight, since it permitted early morning delivery, whereas prior to that time, No. 71 arrived too late in the afternoon for delivery of its merchandise during the business day. Thus, No. 71 was rescheduled to leave Covington, Ky., across the river from Cincinnati, at 5:15 p.m. after the late afternoon depot delivery of less-than-carload freight and by dawn of the second morning, its freight was on hand at the various depots along the Gulf coast.

This big improvement in No. 71's schedule was achieved by giving it a clear track, employment of night warehouse forces, faster preparation of waybills, alert dispatching of trains, reduction of stops for coal and water and by the close cooperation of all employes. Improvement in a number of other fast freight schedules was subsequently made.

The war clouds, which had gathered ominously over Europe in the fall of 1938 came at a time when the L. & N., along with other American railroads, was enjoying a period of comparative prosperity. In 1939, for example, its total railway operating revenues increased $8,953,696, or 11.3 per cent over 1938. A greatly augmented freight tonnage contributed the major portion of this increase. Very little of this burgeoning prosperity could be attributed to the war abroad and, as a matter of fact, any influence the latter may have had was preponderantly in an adverse direction due to the closing of certain ports to American shipping. In this period of comparative quiet which extended from the close of the war in Poland in September 1939, to the invasion of Denmark and Norway in March 1940, the L. & N., as if possessed by some sixth sense, began to place its house in order and remove a certain amount of dead wood from its field of operation. The latter step involved the abandonment of branch lines no longer profitable to operate and included the removal of the 17.91 mile line from Morganfield to Clay, Ky., the discontinuance of trains thereon being effective December 18, 1939, the termination of train service on the Swan Creek Branch, Swan Creek Junction to Gordonsburg, Tenn., 17.04 miles, effective December 30, 1939, and the abandonment of operation on the Tennessee Western Railroad (leased by the L. & N.), extending from Iron City to Collinwood, Tenn., a distance of 16.64 miles, which became effective February 12, 1939.

In the sphere of constructive endeavor, its major improvements to its property, all authorized during the waning days of the year 1939, included the purchase of 1,200 all-steel hopper coal cars, costing $2,217,694,

The "Silver Bullet," or No. 71, fast freight train, whose schedule was streamlined in 1938.

the purchase of two 600 H.P. diesel electric switching locomotives – the L. & N.'s first diesels – the rebuilding and modernization of 1,000 freight cars, the re-conditioning and modernization of a number of passenger coaches and an expenditure of $71,783 for new machines and tools for the maintenance of way department.

Perhaps one of the biggest jobs undertaken by the Management in 1939 was the re-financing of $69,243,000 Unified 4% bonds, issued in 1890, which became due on July 1, 1940. Various problems were confronted by the Company in the execution of this re-financing, it being its desire both to reduce the bonded debt and obtain a good price for the new issue of bonds. Minority stockholders, not in full possession of the facts and prodded into action by selfish outside interests, came forth to protest the ultimate re-financing decision, but eventually re-considered when the situation was explained to them in its entirety.

Briefly, $9,243,000 of the Unifieds were paid off in cash from the treasury and $60,000,000 worth of Collateral Trust Bonds were issued and sold. One-half of these bonds were 10-year 3½% bonds and the other half were 20-year 4% bonds. This re-financing was approved in its entirety by the Interstate Commerce Commission on January 30, 1940, and the selling of the bonds for cash in advance of the maturity date of the Unified 4%'s on July 1, 1940, and the other advantageous features of the plan, enabled the Company to reduce its annual interest charges by $519,720.

The successful blitzkriegs against the Low Countries and France in May and June 1940, brought home to Americans forcibly and for the first time the gravity of the Nazi menace and the words "National Defense" began to be heard with ever-increasing frequency. Spurred on by the emergency, Congress passed legislation after legislation, involving the expenditure of billions of dollars. These huge sums were subsequently spent in the construction of army camps, powder and munition plants, airplane factories, shipbuilding facilities, etc. Such an expedited program of construction placed an enormous job of hauling upon America's railroads and the movement of hundreds of thousands of selectees about the country each month (a result of the passage of the National Selective Service Act) did nothing to lighten this burden. However, the railroads had profited by the lessons of

Some of the several hundred boxcars which were rebuilt at the South Louisville Shops in 1940.

Nos. 10 and 11 were the first Diesel electric switch engines purchased by the Company and were placed in service in the yards at East Louisville in the fall of 1939.

the former World War and this time a weighing in the balance did not find them wanting.

The railroad had prepared for just such an emergency ever since 1918 and the evolved 1940 model transportation plant was vastly superior to the 1917-1918 one. Train speeds, tons handled per train hour, and car and locomotive capacities had all increased considerably, permitting a more efficient execution of the work to be done. Important, too, was the change in the organizational setup. The Association of American Railroads, streamlined and efficient, cooperated to the fullest extent, and successfully, with the 13 Shippers' Advisory Boards, with the port transportation committees and with the Government's manager of military transportation, in avoiding traffic snarls and congestion.

On the Louisville & Nashville Railroad, the freight traffic handled increased from 42,093,172 tons to 49,429,151 tons, when 1940 was compared with 1939. Passenger traffic, after a slow start, was stimulated late in the year (1940) by the passage of the Selective Service Act.

Many of the industries and army camps and training centers, which either came into existence or were expanded as a result of the National Defense program, were located on the lines of the L. & N., or were well within its sphere of influence. Due the distinction of especial mention, among several dozen such projects, were the 24,000 acre shell-loading plant at Milan, Tenn., known as the Wolf Creek Ordnance plant, the Westinghouse Naval Gun Mounting plant at Louisville, Ky., the Southeastern Army Air Depot at Mobile, Ala., the Gadsden Ordnance plant at Ord, Ala., and the Vultee Air Corporation's huge factory near Nashville, Tenn.

The L. & N., to handle its booming business, intensified its program of addition and improvement begun during the closing days of 1939. During 1940, it authorized the purchase of an additional $9,318,246 worth of equipment, receiving in exchange for this tidy sum the following items:

100 all-steel box-furniture cars.

25 cement cars

Car retarders were placed in service at the northbound classification yard, DeCoursey, Ky., in the fall of 1940, at a cost of approximately $200,000.

    50 70-ton mill type gondolas
3,500 50-ton all steel hopper bottom coal cars
  100 50-ton all-steel double-door, end door box cars
    50 70-ton all-steel mill gondolas

Other large sums were spent for the modernization of coaches, the installation of "AB" standard air brakes, the re-building and modernization of 900 boxcars, the improvement of motive power through the installation of stokers, super-heaters, reverse gears, etc., the construction of additional trackage, the installation of car retarders at DeCoursey, Ky., and the purchase of numerous items of equipment, tools and machinery for the mechanical and maintenance of way departments.

The year 1940 also saw an amendment of the various land grant acts through the medium of the Transportation Acts of 1940. The pertinent section provided that railroads which had been constructed with the aid of land grants and which had been reimbursing the Government through the medium of reduced rates on all Government traffic throughout the subsequent years, could henceforth charge the full tariff rates for the movement of all persons or property for the United States, except military or naval property moving for military or naval and not for civil use, or military or naval personnel traveling on official duty. The compensating proviso was that the railroad should file a release of any claim it might have against the Government for land due it under the original land grant or grants.

The L. & N. filed its release on November 6, 1940, thus relinquishing a valid claim to over 1,100,000 acres of land, but obtaining in return tariff increases on the traffic previously mentioned which were expected to increase its annual earnings by about $350,000.

The L. & N. itself, of course, was not a land grant railroad and the acreage involved was part of that donated by the Government to the states of Alabama and Florida as grantors to four railroads, which were later absorbed by the L. & N. The trackage of these four included the line from Decatur to Montgomery, Ala.; from Montgomery to Flomaton, Ala.; from

Once again, in the fall of 1940, soldiers began to move to camp over the L. & N. lines.

Flomaton to Pensacola, Fla., and from Pensacola to Chattahochee, Fla., a total distance of 505 miles.

The arrangement mentioned was concluded with the U. S. Department of the Interior on November 27, 1940. The Government was still given a preferential rate of 50 per cent less than regular rates on military freight and passenger traffic and the increase, of course placed non-military governmental traffic on a par with non-governmental traffic.

Although the year 1940 was a fairly prosperous one, it was not without its vexations. Taxes continued to mount and those paid in 1940 - $10,-304,935 - increased $2,169,235 over those paid in 1939.

Moreover, busses, trucks, pipe lines, airplanes and inland waterways continued to make drastic inroads on traffic. Indicative of the seriousness of the competition and of the Company's determination to combat the same is the following from the 1940 Annual Report:

"All possible effort is being made to meet this competition, both by rate adjustments and by improved service. All-commodity rates have been established for traffic now handled in carloads that formerly moved in less-than-carload lots. This, coupled with faster schedules and more prompt placement of cars for unloading, has been helpful."

The year 1940 passed without a fatality to a passenger in a train accident - the 23rd consecutive year in which this commendable record had been achieved by the L. & N.

The South Wind and the Dixie Flagler also made their bows in L. & N. territory during 1940, their initial jaunts occurring on December 19 and 17 respectively. These streamlined all-coach passenger trains which traveled between Chicago and Miami, used the lines of the L. & N. between Evansville and Nashville (Dixie Flagler) and between Louisville and Montgomery (The South Wind). The L. & N. cooperated in the streamliner motif by streamlining two of its Pacific type locomotives, Nos. 277 and 295, at its South Louisville shops. It also subsequently streamlined another Pacific-type locomotive, the No. 275, which replaced the No. 295 in pulling

The spur line to the Wolf Creek Ordnance Plant at Milan, Tenn., was completed in March 1941 and cost approximately $75,000.

The South Wind between Louisville and Montgomery. No. 275 was equipped with a supertank which had a capacity of 27½ tons of coal and 20,000 gallons of water and this "camel's hump" permitted The South Wind to run non-stop between Louisville and Nashville and between Nashville and Birmingham. The last mentioned was a distance of 205.4 miles and was believed to be the longest non-stop coal-powered run in the United States at that time. It was the original intention to operate these all-coach streamliners only as winter season trains, but they proved to be so popular that they were retained in service as year 'round trains and were made coach-Pullman. The Dixie Flagler was subsequently discontinued in 1954; its successor, The Dixieland, made its last run in 1957.

Chapter XXXVII

World War II Years

BY the beginning of 1941, the national scene had vastly changed within the span of one year. In that time America's industrial plant had greatly expanded as a result of the intensified national defense effort and was busily engaged in producing the sinews of war. The effects of the passage of the National Selective Service Act and the Lease-Lend Act were more and more noticeable. Carloadings and, to a lesser extent, passenger loadings, too, were climbing steadily upward and this trend continued throughout 1941.

Thus, the L. & N. moved 58.5 million tons of freight in 1941 as contrasted to 49.4 million tons in 1940 and 3.6 million passengers as compared to 3.1 million.

Even prior to Pearl Harbor many army camps and other military establishments had been located in the South, on or near the lines of the L. & N., and many huge defense projects had been constructed and placed in operation. Some of these installations covered thousands of acres and the L. & N. was kept busy hauling construction materials and finished products alike. There was a constant movement of troops between homes, induction centers and training camps.

But all this activity was just a "drop in the bucket" compared to what took place after the Japanese had bombed the American fleet and military installations at Pearl Harbor on that historic December 7, 1941.

Fortunately, the L. & N. had wisely cleared its decks for action some time before Pearl Harbor. It had scrapped a number of obsolete freight cars and worn-out locomotives during the latter part of 1940 and throughout 1941, but had more than balanced this destructive activity by the purchase of 5,300 new freight cars, 14 steam freight locomotives, 12 Diesel electric switchers and eight Diesel electric passenger locomotives. Much of this new equipment was delivered in the latter part of 1941, or the early part of 1942, and all of it was in service by late fall of the latter year.

The Railroad's first centralized traffic control installation – between Brentwood, Tenn., and Athens, Ala., a distance of 96 miles – was completed in June 1942 and made a valuable contribution to the war effort.

The L. & N. abandoned considerable unprofitable trackage in 1941 and 1942, this including 63 miles of Evansville Division track in Kentucky, the 5.28 mile O'Fallon Branch in Southern Illinois, and 47 miles of the Winchester and Maloney Branch between Winchester and Fincastle, Ky. The latter line, in fact, was requisitioned by the U. S. Government for its metal in late July 1942, with removal being completed by December 1, 1942. Approximately 8,840 tons of rail, track fittings and bridges were thereby released for Government use, most of the rail being further utilized as relayer rail in the construction of war plant layouts and military camps.

The L. & N., along with the nation's other railroads and employers generally, was somewhat handicapped in the performance of its duties throughout the conflict, not only by the difficulty – and often impossibility – of obtaining needed material and equipment, but also by the drain upon its manpower for the armed forces.

In fact, as of January 1, 1946, a total of 6,936 L. & N. employes had been furloughed to the armed forces and of these 112 had made the supreme sacrifice.

The extent of the L. & N.'s contribution to the war effort is best conveyed by the following traffic statistics for the seven-year period, 1939-1945, inclusive:

Years	Passengers	Tons of Freight
1939	3,202,442	42,093,172
1940	3,140,586	49,429,151
1941	3,589,198	58,504,412
1942	6,421,218	71,021,454
1943	11,905,645	72,607,969
1944	12,440,022	73,374,452
1945	10,074,128	70,235,764

As indicated, this increase of nearly 300 per cent in its passenger traffic and of almost 70 per cent in its freight traffic was successfully handled with comparatively little over-all addition to either the rolling stock or the personnel. (Actually, the L. & N. had fewer passenger-train cars in 1944 than in 1939.) Thus, at the end of 1939, the L. & N. had 28,000 employes, compared with approximately 34,200 at the end of 1944, when the war effort was at its peak, and had 947 locomotives, 58,328 freight cars and 589 passenger-train cars at the end of 1944, as compared with 942, 52,196 and 704 respectively at the end of 1939.

The answer to this modern miracle of the "loaves and fishes" lay, of course, in greater efficiency of operation. The cooperation and loyalty of employes, coupled with improved methods and a physical plant in A-1 condition, due to the millions of dollars which had been spent for improvements just prior to Pearl Harbor, formed a potent team which produced results. Working together, they enabled the L. & N. to haul more tons per car, more cars per train and more gross ton miles per train hour than ever before.

(The figures previously listed on passengers and tons of freight carried during the war years, while impressive, do not tell the whole story. Thus, while the 12,440,022 passengers moved in 1944 fell short of the 17,482,098-figure for the peak year of 1920, passenger-miles – the real yardstick – in 1944 was 2,517,875,634 as compared to 884,142,595 in 1920. Correspondingly, the nearly 64 million tons of freight hauled by the L. & N. in 1927 amounted to approximately 13.5 billion ton miles; the 73,374,452 tons hauled in 1944 amounted to 17.4 billion ton miles.)

To the extent possible, each department of the railroad refined and improved its operations, always keeping in mind the vital importance of conserving essential material. Thus, in the shops, there was a greater utilization of welding for the restoration of worn parts; iron or steel was substituted for the more critical copper in maintenance and repair wherever

When America went to war, the L. & N., along with the other railroads of the country, was called upon to move huge quantities of war material, including such items as the tanks, scout cars, etc., shown.

possible; grease and packing were reclaimed, and old axles, journal box wedges and the like were re-forged. In short, conversion, reclamation, substitution and protection went hand in hand and united to release vast amounts of critical materials, even though many of the wartime procedures would not have been normally followed because of the expense involved.

The activities of the roadway department were especially varied and numerous. Despite the war, there was grade reduction at several points on the L. & N., allowing a heavier tonnage to be moved, thus relieving congestion and permitting the freight to be moved quicker to destination.

In addition to the C. T. C. installation between Brentwood, Tenn., and Athens, Ala., three other such installations on the L. & N. were "war babies" and each made a real contribution to expediting the movement of traffic. These were between Mobile and Montgomery, 172 miles; between Irvine and Patio, Ky., 25 miles; and between Lebanon Junction and Sinks, Ky., 107 miles. A start upon a fifth installation – between Strawberry and Henderson, Ky., 137 miles – was also made in the closing months of the war.

Many miles of additional track had to be constructed during World War II to serve the military camps and war plants adjacent to, but not always **right on** the L. & N.'s lines. Dozens of passing tracks all over the System were also lengthened so that the longer trains operated could be accommodated. The line between Gentilly and Higgins, La., 7½ miles, was doubled-tracked in the summer of 1942.

War plants directly served by the L. & N. included the vast Milan Ordnance Center, Milan, Tenn., the Bluegrass Ordnance Depot, near Richmond, Ky., the Higgins Boat Works, Higgins, La., Ingalls Shipbuilding Corporation, Pascagoula, Miss., and outstandingly, the Clinton Engineering Works, Oak Ridge, Tenn., home of the atomic bomb.

There were, of course, hundreds of war plants in the larger cities which the L. & N. also served, either directly or through switching arrangements.

There were dozens of military establishments directly served by the L. & N. and worthy of especial mention were the unique Barrage Balloon Training Center at Camp Tyson, near Paris, Tenn., and huge Keesler Field, Biloxi, Miss., where so many Air Force technicians were trained.

As the nation's war effort intensified and oil and gasoline became more "precious," coal assumed increasing importance. Thus, the L. & N. received permission in the latter part of 1943 to build its 10.32-mile long Leatherwood Creek Branch in Perry County, Ky., to tap hitherto inaccessible coal fields containing many millions of tons of coal. This line was completed and placed in operation January 9, 1945. Shortly thereafter the Railroad commenced the construction of another branch of equal importance – the 10-mile Clover Fork Extension in Harlan County, Ky., which was completed in May 1947. Four smaller branch lines in West Kentucky – totaling about 10 miles of track in all – were also completed during the closing months of World War II.

Improved interlocking plants were installed at several key locations; bridges and trestles were strengthened, a large amount of heavier (132-lb.) rail was installed and several hundred spring switches were placed at strategic points, eliminating time-consuming stops and starts.

Closer on-the-ground supervision was also given to the operation of trains by the appointment of additional trainmasters and assistant trainmasters and facilities, long idled by the preceding Depression, were placed in service. Outstanding, in the latter connection, was the re-opening of Strawberry Yard (then known as Mapother Yard) just south of Louisville in July 1941. At that time it had a capacity of 1,765 cars.

A major contribution of the L. & N. to the war effort was its operation of the so-called "symbol" freight trains and of the "mains" for handling troop movements. Generally speaking, the symbol trains were fast through freights which handled only terminal business between such points as Cincinnati and Mobile, Louisville and Mobile, Cincinnati and New Orleans, Louisville and Memphis, East St. Louis and Birmingham and so on. They were assigned numbers, or symbols, such as LN-1, LN-7, SK-1, ED-7, etc.; hence the designation as "symbol" freights. They were operated in advance of their schedules whenever possible. Of course, the shipments they handled, almost without exception, were directly related to the war effort. Careful attention was given to every detail of their operation so that they could roll over the line at passenger-train speed.

The symbol oil trains were closely akin to the other symbol freights except that they handled gasoline and other petroleum products exclusively and made no stops for tonnage while on the L. & N. They moved by certain assigned routes between the producing centers in Louisiana, Texas and the Southeast to the Eastern Seaboard. When Hitler's submarines during the early part of World War II effectively cancelled coastal and inter-coastal shipping, the L. & N. – along with a number of other railroads, of course – for a long time bore the brunt of moving the badly-needed oil and gasoline formerly hauled by the tankers. These symbol oil trains did much to keep folks warm and the wheels – either in war plants or on the streets and highways – turning.

In this connection, the following statistics are enlightening. In 1940, the L. & N. carried approximately 1,200,000 tons of crude petroleum and refined petroleum and its products. In 1943, when the operation of the symbol oil trains reached its zenith, the comparable figure was over 3,000,000 tons. To help the reader better visualize this tonnage, the increase amounted to approximately 18,000 tank cars. Following the completion of the Big Inch and the Little Inch pipe lines, the movement of crude petroleum by rail fell off somewhat in 1943 and 1944, but in the latter year the refined petroleum movement soared to a new high on the L. & N. – 2,875,153 tons – giving it a ranking second only to King Coal, as far as specific commodities were concerned.

A more intensive loading of cars, both for carload and less-than-carload freight, the operation of second sections of passenger trains for the handling of mail and express and the cooperation of shippers and receivers of freight in promptly releasing rolling stock were also important factors in keeping the traffic moving.

Much of the tremendous increase in the L. & N.'s passenger business was caused by military movements handled en masse, via the "mains" previously mentioned, and by the sizable furlough travel, or by smaller groups of service men, traveling as a unit, but not handled in the mains, nor in extra cars in regular trains.

Serving as many military establishements as it did, the L. & N. played an important part in the logistics of the armed forces. The invasion of North Africa, for instance, in November 1942, involved the moving

The L. & N. Railroad made a major contribution to the nation-wide scrap drive with its donation of an old abandoned railroad bridge across the Kentucky River at Irvine, Ky. The bridge was scrapped by blasts of dynamite on November 17, 1942, the work of demolition being done by the 387th Engineer Battalion (Separate) from Fort Knox, Ky. Some 186 tons of metal were thereby salvaged for the war effort.

of some 22 million pounds of food, 38 million pounds of clothing and equipment and 10 million gallons of gasoline, among other things, to ports of embarkation. Of course, many other railroads also had a hand in moving these mountains – and lakes – of war materiel.

The Home Front had its casualties, too, during World War II. The L. & N.'s outstanding record of not having a passenger killed in a train accident since December 20, 1917 – the date of the Shepherdsville wreck – came to a disastrous end on July 6, 1944. At that time several cars of a long troop train were derailed at Highcliff, Tenn., killing 35 and injuring 91.

The following figures for the peak wartime years of 1943 and 1944 include only the cars handled by the L. & N. for the armed forces in mains or as extra cars in regular trains:

	1943	1944
Pullmans	36,110	33,624
Coaches	11,482	4,359
Baggage	3,280	3,040
Kitchen	3,985	3,076
Diners	1,904	2,244
Freight cars	9,927	3,066

Involved in the movement of this sizable fleet was the transportation of 1,744,582 members of the armed forces in 1943 and of 1,254,292 in 1944.

In order that this military traffic, as well as the related booming civilian business (caused in large part by travel to and from the army camps) might be handled as satisfactorily and as expeditiously as possible, a number of revolutionary changes were made early in the war.

The seating capacity of a number of diners and passenger coaches was increased; in the first case by adding additional tables and in the second by eliminating the lounge rooms. Additional personnel was hired and trained by the dining car department, whose business increased by leaps and bounds with the result that 2,264,489 "meals on wheels" were served in 1944, for instance, as contrasted to a pre-war peak (in 1926) of 642,433 meals. Seats in lounge and observation cars were sold, thereby utilizing all space possible; and many off-line freight and passenger offices were closed in order that personnel might accompany the military movements as troop escorts. Ticket forces were increased in towns and cities near the large army camps and at the large terminals.

One of the most revolutionary changes in the L. & N. "landscape" during the war years involved its personnel. Many of the younger employes were furloughed to the armed forces; many older persons, including a number who had actually retired, again became active employes. Outstanding, however, was the increase in the number of women employes and the nature of the tasks they performed. Many were hired as stenographers and clerks, of course, but there were also women ticket sellers, messengers, agents, operators, "draftsmen," and "shopmen." The "L. & N. Wacs," as the "lady shopmen" came to be called, worked as cleaners, sweepers, material handlers, rivet catchers and handlers, turntable operators and as engine cleaners. More than 200 were employed at South Louis-

Left: When Uncle Sam took over nation's railroads December 27, 1943, to avoid a threatened interruption to rail transportation, War Department assigned Lieut. Colonel J. H. Veal, seated, to L. & N. as its official agent. He is shown with two members of his staff. Seizure terminated at midnight, January 18, 1944. Right: In the early days of World War II, as each L. & N. employe entered the armed forces, his name was placed on star on board in lobby of general office building. Practice eventually had to be discontinued because of great number called to colors.

ville alone (in the shops and roundhouse) at the peak of the war effort in 1943 and 1944.

In all, of the some 35,000 employes which the L. & N. had at the war's end, approximately 10 per cent were women.

Throughout World War II, the trafic department understandably placed its emphasis upon service rather than sales and freight was solicited only to balance freight-train operation. Passenger soliciatation was, of course, "out" for the duration and the day was to come that once would have been considered a wild impossibility, i.e., the L. & N. began to periodically advertise in newspapers throughout its territory asking people not to travel except in case of absolute necessity.

A complete recapitulation of the L. & N.'s contribution during World War II would be much longer than the foregoing. Above all, the L. & N. kept the wheels rolling and the home fires burning. These home fires were stoked by it, both corporately and by its individual employes. These employes purchased $25,255,000 worth of War Bonds through payroll deduction from July 1, 1941 to June 1947 (and, of course, many employes otherwise purchased a large number of Bonds); they donated thousands of gallons of blood and took part in the various scrap drives and otherwise served in their communitites as air raid wardens; by joining car pools, by working with the U. S. O. and by doing without many things once considered vital necessities.

Worthy of special mention, too, is the 728th Railway Operating Battalion, which was officered predominantly by L. & N. employes and had many of the L. & N.'s other employes as enlisted men. It made a creditable contribution to final victory, serving overseas with distinction in Great Britain, France and Germany.

The L. & N.'s performance in World War II was in vivid contrast to that of World War I. In the last named conflict it was so entwined in the red tape of Federal Control, it was so hamstrung by a lack of locomotives and freight cars, and so many shippers were uncooperative in the prompt loading and unloading of cars, that it is understandable that at times the L. & N. figuratively coughed and spluttered, as did the nation's other railroads for the same reasons.

During much of World War I, the L. & N. paid no taxes, of course; that is, during the period of Federal Control. In fact, Federal Control of the L. & N. and the nation's other railroads resulted in a $2-billion deficit which had to be met largely by the taxpayers. During World War II (or more exactly during the four-year period, 1942-1945, inclusive) the L. & N. paid a total of **more than $165 million** in various Federal taxes (normal, surtax and excess profits) and spent approximately $50 million in improving and enlarging its transportation plant so that it might operate at maximum efficiency during the national emergency.

As a historical footnote, there was also a brief period of Federal Control during World War II. At 6:00 p.m. C.S.T., December 27, 1943, to forestall a threatened strike, Uncle Sam took over the nation's railroads. The reins rested lightly, however, and control was terminated at midnight, January 18, 1944, after the differences between the railroads and the brotherhoods had been resolved.

CHAPTER XXXVIII

The First Century Ends

VE-DAY and VJ-Day came in sudden and unexpected close succession, eliminating many problems and anxieties, but creating others, admittedly not as urgently important, but vexatious just the same.

In some quarters there was considerable pessimism about the nation's economy in the months and years ahead and it was predicted that "grass would grow in the streets" of many communitites which had had phenomenal growth because of the wartime boom. The Saturday Evening Post, as a matter of fact, in an issue published in the early part of 1944, selected Milan, Tenn., as a typical "horrible example," with the author drawing certain gloomy conclusions concerning the Milan Ordnance Center's and the town's future when the war was over.

The L. & N. Magazine, in a modest way in its issue of May 1944, sought to refute the Satevepost's views. Over-all, it can be said – also modestly – that its more optimistic predictions were closer to the mark than those of the older publication. The L. & N. Magazine based its views in large part on the comparative ease with which such wartime facilities as the Center, for instance, could be converted to peacetime production and on the big backlog demand for consumer goods which had been snowballing ever since Pearl Harbor.

Naturally, the nation's conversion of the proverbial swords into ploughshares did not take place overnight nor did it occur without some unemployment and economic hardship. Nevertheless, it took place with a comparative ease which confounded the pessimists.

Carloadings on the L. & N. were an apt reflection of the national economy. In 1946 they fell off to 65,465,893 cars; then in 1947 climbed to a new high of 75,229,437, exceeding even the peak war year of 1944. In 1948, a new plateau was reached, exceeding the 1947 total by several hundred thousand cars. The 1948-1949 "recession" dropped loadings back to 58,793,961 cars, but the forward motion resumed in 1950, rounding out the L. & N.'s first 100 years with a creditable figure of 68,283,021.

The L. & N.'s passenger traffic was something else again and was a continuation of a trend which had been very much in evidence prior to World War II; that is, a trend away from the railroads and to the highways and airways.

The following statistics tell the story:

Year	No. of Passengers Carried by L. & N.
1945	10,074,128
1946	7,014,547
1947	5,558,518

1948	4,069,565
1949	3,224,876
1950	2,624,736

The L. & N. was not, of course, resigned to this trend; it made a valiant attempt to reverse it through providing faster and otherwise improved service, in the purchase of new equipment, the modernizing of older equipment, and various intensified promotional activities.

Looking ahead, the L. & N. had during the closing months of World War II placed an order for 28 modern lightweight, aluminum-alloy cars, consisting of 20 coaches, four tavern-lounge cars and four diners. They were eventually delivered in the late fall of 1946 at a cost of approximately $2.5 million. They were placed in service November 17, 1946 as two complete new trains. One, The Humming Bird, operated originally between Cincinnati and New Orleans; the other, The Georgian, between St. Louis and Atlanta. At first, all-coach, or more properly non-Pullman trains, sleeping cars were ultimately added to each and their routes were changed and extended as will be described later on.

Both The Humming Bird and The Georgian received their names as the result of a contest which attracted nearly 300,000 entries. A total of $3,500 was distributed in prize money to the winners as follows: First prize - $1,000; second prize - $500; and third prize - $250 (in each case). As a matter of fact, each winning name was submitted by a number of contestants (671 for The Humming Bird; 1009 for The Georgian) but the awards were given on the basis of the best reasons for the name submitted with the entry. Other award-winning (second and third prizes) names were The Magnolian, The Thoroughbred, The Dixiana and The Aristocrat, each of which was also popular with the contestants.

In 1946, in cooperation with other railroads participating in the through passenger service provided by The Crescent between New York and New Orleans, the L. & N. ordered, as its "share" of new equipment needed, 11 passenger-train cars costing approximately $1.2 million. These consisted of three coaches, one diner, two mail-baggage cars and five sleeping cars, all of stainless steel construction. Thus proudly gleaming, The New Crescent made its inaugural run March 11, 1950.

To supplement the purchase of this new equipment, the L. & N. concurrently carried on a program of modernizing older passenger-train equipment in the years immediately after VJ-Day. Outstanding was the conversion of 27 coaches into modern, de luxe equipment and of three diners.

On July 1, 1949, the L. & N. also acquired 57 conventional-type sleeping cars from the Pullman Company. These were purchased in accordance with the plan whereby the nation's major railroads acquired the stock of the Pullman Company from Pulman, Inc. This action resulted from the ruling that Pullman must either separate itself from its carbuilding activities or the providing of sleeping-car facilities for the railroads. It chose to remain in the carbuilding business.

Further to attract passenger traffic back to the rails and to retain that which it still had, the L. & N. speeded up the schedules of a number of its passenger trains and changed and/or extended the routes of both The Humming Bird and The Georgian. The extent to which The Georgian

Typical of transitional period on L. & N. when the diesel-electrics were replacing steam power is this scene in late 1948 at Gentry, Ky., on Eastern Kentucky Division. Steam engine, hauling long string of empties, heads south for mines, as pusher-service diesels on rear of heavy coal train wait for main to be cleared so they can assist train on climb up Elkatawa Hill.

was patronized between St. Louis and Atlanta proved to be a big disappointment. After a series of studies it was determined that its best potentialities lay in making it primarily a Chicago-Atlanta train and this was done June 1, 1948, sleeping cars also being added at that time. Service continued to be provided between St. Louis and Atlanta via a connection with The Georgian at Evansville. Following the re-routing The Georgian proved to be one of the most popular of L. & N. trains.

In September 1948, sleeping cars were also added to The Humming Bird between Cincinnati and New Orleans and in April 1949, a new sleeping car line for the train was established between New Orleans and Chicago.

In reality, thereafter, The Humming Bird had a "dual personality," operating as separate trains between Chicago and Nashville and Cincinnati and Nashville, combining at Nashville southbound to form one train and, of course, separating at Nashville northbound. The train was handled by the C. & E. I. between Chicago and Evansville, as was The Georgian.

Another "name" train joined the L. & N.'s passenger-train fleet on July 31, 1949, with the inauguration of The Gulf Wind between New Orleans and Jacksonville. Utilizing the rails of the L. & N. and Seaboard Air Line, it provided convenient, overnight service – the fastest yet – between the two cities, clicking off the 612 intervening miles in approximately 15 hours.

Simultaneously, the L. & N. was intensifying its efforts to introduce the comfort and convenience of travel by rail to the public and especially to the younger generation. A program which began modestly in 1948 with "nine-cent" train rides for youngsters in the Louisville area – usually between Crescent Hill and the Union Station – snowballed in succeeding years. As a result, at the end of the Railroad's first 100 years, thousands of grade-school and kindergarten students were annually making trips of varying lengths in L. & N. trains.

Following VJ-Day the L. & N. was able to intensify many activities which had their inception during the early days of World War II and, in some cases, even before.

Outstanding were increasing dieselization, the installation of additional centralized traffic control, and the building of new branch-line trackage.

Here are the pertinent figures on dieselization for the five-year postwar period, 1946-1950, inclusive, these reflecting in the earlier years a continuing uncertainty on the L. & N.'s part in the steam vs. diesel controversy then perplexing railroad management:

Year	Diesels Installed
1946	9
1947	None
1948	6
1949	29
1950	99

During this same period, it is interesting to note, the L. & N. had secured 22 steam locomotives, all of the M-1 class, the most powerful it had ever acquired.

The L. & N.'s first diesels for freight service were ordered in 1949 as the result of the experience derived from the operation of diesels in yard and passenger service. The economies proved to be so great that they could not be disregarded even though the L. & N. as a road which derived considerable revenue from the hauling of bituminous coal was loath to take a step which would further reduce the coal industry's markets. But it was a step which had to be taken if the L. & N. were to survive in the fiercely-competitive postwar transportation world. It was a step which was taken only after careful thought and consideration.

The installation of centralized traffic control also received renewed impetus at the end of World War II. The installation between Strawberry

Much branch-line construction highlighted the last years of the L. & N.'s first century. This was chiefly in Eastern Kentucky and West Kentucky to reach, develop and serve new coalfields. Shown are the concrete piers for one of the bridges on the 16-mile long Rockhouse Creek Branch extension in Letcher County, Ky., which was completed in 1949.

and Henderson, Ky., 137 miles, was completed in July 1947; followed by installations between Irvine and Blackey, 125 miles, exclusive of seven miles of double tracking. A start was also made upon the 145-mile installation between Henderson, Ky., and Amqui, Tenn., in 1950.

James B. Hill, who was president of the L. & N. from November 27, 1934 until his retirement on July 1, 1950, often referred to the construction of new trackage to serve coal fields in Eastern and West Kentucky as the outstanding achievement of his administration which covered nearly 16 years. Certainly, this construction helped appreciably to keep the L. & N.'s coal cars loaded in years to come.

Mention has been made of the Leatherwood Creek Branch and the Clover Fork Extension in Eastern Kentucky and of the construction of four smaller branches in West Kentucky during World War II. These were followed by the Homestead Spur, 4.78 miles, and the Marigold Spur, 2.36 miles, both in West Kentucky, in 1947; by the Rockhouse Creek Branch Extension 16.7 miles, and the Blair Fork Branch, 5.68 miles, and the Camp Branch, 2.52 miles, all in Eastern Kentucky, in 1949; and, in the same year, in West Kentucky, by the Pee Vee Spur, 2.46 miles, the Vogue Zeigler Spur, 1.69 miles, and the Fies Spur, 1.65 miles.

A personnel development program was inaugurated in 1947 to teach employes more about themselves, their country and the world they live in. Several thousand employes completed the training, taught by the conference method.

A closely-related highlight of the postwar years which rounded out the L. & N.'s first century, was the increasing industrialization of the South. World War II, of course, gave a tremendous impetus to the rediscovery of Dixie. Factories producing a great variety of war materiel and in vast quantities, sprang up almost overnight and on every hand. Airplanes, chemicals, explosives, ships, synthetic rubber, shells, tanks – and even the atomic bomb – rolled off the assembly lines or the equivalent thereof and made a valuable contribution to final victory.

Wartime operation in the South proved so successful that many plants readily converted to more peaceful production; Dixie's increased purchasing power, in turn, led to the establishment of other factories which wished to be closer to consumer markets. Thus, at long last, the South was taking fuller advantage of its great natural resources, its abundant water supply, its favorable climate, its ample labor force and adequate transportation facilities. All of these had now been supplemented by a trained labor force which had the requisite know-how, gained in the crucible of war, to use the tools and machinery of production.

The L. & N.'s consciousness of industry's trend toward Dixie was

What a way to ruin a railroad! On September 19, 1947, one of the worst hurricanes ever experienced hit the Mississippi Gulf Coast and adjacent territory. "Emma," as the hurricane was tagged by the Weather Bureau, did great damage to the L. & N.'s track, bridges and other facility all the way from Ocean Springs, Miss., to New Orleans, La. Worst damage to track was done between Pearl River Bridge and Higgins, La., a distance of 28 miles. Shown is the station and track at English Lookout, La., after the gale had struck. The line was reopened for traffic between Ocean Springs and Gulfport, Miss., October 7. Complete service was restored October 24. Total cost to L. & N. was in excess of $2 million, exclusive of loss of traffic.

illustrated by its freight car acquisitions during the period 1946-1950. Here's the five-year record:

Year	Freight Cars Acquired
1946	1,850
1947	4,669
1948	4,781
1949	4,000
1950	1,100
Total	16,400

The approximate cost of this sizable addition to the rolling stock was $61 million. The acquisitions included automobile cars, boxcars, hoppers, covered hoppers, gondolas and flatcars. Contemporaneously, the L. & N. was engaged in converting 500 older-type freight cars (gondolas, coke cars and boxcars) into flatcars with bulkheads for the handling of pulpwood, which was making an increasingly heavy contribution to the L. & N.'s loadings.

At the close of the war, the L. & N.'s traffic department's promotional set-up was still more or less geared to the South's agricultural economy. For various reasons, agriculture had decreased in importance, traffic-wise, even before Pearl Harbor. A chief reason was that agricultural products were being diverted in large volume to motor vehicles which were exempt from regulations which applied to the railroads; hence could more successfully compete for the traffic.

Accordingly, on June 6, 1949, the L. & N.'s traffic-development staff, which had spent much time in furthering agricultural pursuits in the areas served, was reorganized with the accent on promoting and locating diversified industry in L. & N. territory.

The L. & N.'s operations were disturbed by strikes and the threat of strikes on several occasions during the immediate postwar period. Federal control, to avoid a threatened interruption to transportation, foreshadowed by an impending strike of two of the railroad operating brotherhoods, again became an actual fact at 4:00 p.m., May 17, 1946. This seizure was a brief one, however, and lasted only until 4:00 p.m., May 26. The strike of the United Mine Workers in the spring of the same year also hampered operations considerably because at that time the L. & N. was still largely dependent upon coal as fuel for its motive power. In fact, at the end of 1946, it still had 893 steam engines in service, as contrasted to only 59 diesels.

Again, in 1948, at 12:00 noon, E.S.T., May 10, to forestall a disruption of the nation's transportation system, threatened by a strike of three of the railroad brotherhoods, the Army, at President Harry Truman's direction, took "possession, control and operation" of America's railroads. This seizure lasted until 3:00 p.m., E.S.T., July 9.

Giving a fillip to the running of the Railroad throughout 1950 was the L. & N.'s celebration of its 100th anniversary. The actual anniversary date was March 5, when it had been granted its charter by the Commomwealth of Kentucky 100 years before. All things considered, the anniversary observance was a modest one. There were no elaborate reenactments of the past, but historians of the future will find many mementoes of the occasion, chiefly in the form of commemorative printed matter. The latter included 200,000 copies of a handsome, full-colored 24-page illustrated brochure, which told the story of the L. & N.'s growth and of the role it played in the development of the South; a special 100th anniversary edition of the L. & N. Magazine (which was also its own 25th anniversary edition); various advertisements; 175,000 copies of a billfold calendar; a 104-page rotogravure edition of the Louisville Courier Journal and Times (in whose preparation the L. & N. cooperated) entitled "The L. & N. Story"; a special edition of Modern Railroads, devoted to the L. & N. (also with the cooperation of the L. & N.); a philatelic cachet posted March 5, 1950 on the Cincinnati-Nashville R. P. O. route; and decks of playing cards with the Centennial insignia.

Perhaps the most heart-warming and dramatic observance of the L. & N.'s 100th anniversary, however, occurred June 7, 1950 when a huge Family Rally was held at the Jefferson County Armory in Louisville. More than 15,000 employes, their families and friends attended for an evening of fellowship and fun. The occasion had a saddening note, however, with the announcement by A. L. M. Wiggins, the L. & N. chairman of the board, that James B. Hill, who had headed the Railroad for the past 16 years, was resigning as president effective July 1. Mr. Wiggins said, however, that Mr. Hill would continue as a director and that he would also serve as chairman of an advisory committee which had just been created by the board of directors.

Mr. Wiggins also made another announcement that evening which was to cast a long shadow. He said that the directors at a meeting that afternoon had elected John E. Tilford, executive vice president, as president to succeed Mr. Hill, also effective July 1.

The Newcomen Society of North America also honored the L. & N.'s 1st 100 years as a "Private Builder and Public Servant" with a dinner at the Pendennis Club, Louisville, February 1, 1951. President John E. Tilford was the principal speaker and spoke for some 45 minutes on the history of the L. & N. and its present status. His remarks were subsequently incorporated by the Society into an attractively-designed booklet and distributed to some 12,000 members in this country, Canada and Mexico.

CHAPTER XXXIX

First Ten – Second Hundred

MANY worthwhile things had been accomplished during Mr. Hill's administration and many innovations inaugurated. The L. & N. had successfully weathered the "Great Depression" and made a notable contribution to final victory in World War II. Passenger-train equipment had been air conditioned: a suggestion system for employes had been established; pick-up and delivery of less-than-carload freight (instituted in 1933) had been broadened; dieselization had made its bow, as had centralized traffic control; new coalfields were reached by branch-line construction; the Friendly Service movement had been inaugurated and Family Rallies held at many points all over the System; and freight yards had been modernized and enlarged.

As a result of these things and many others the L. & N. had constantly set new records in the efficient handling of traffic and had had net income during the 15-year period, 1935-1949, inclusive (roughly corresponding to Mr. Hill's term of office) of more than $188 million.

During the decade of the 1950s, many other changes took place.

The L. & N., as a major coal-carrying railroad, had been extremely reluctant to change its motive power from steam to diesel-electric. Such dieselization at first was on a very modest scale. However, the diesel was so much more efficient than the steam engine that the savings implicit in complete dieselization could not be disregarded. In 1950, the L. & N. crossed the Rubicon with its acquisition of its first diesels for general freight service (five units had been previously used in helper service on the Eastern Kentucky Division) and thereafter dieselization proceeded at greatly intensified tempo. The following figures tell the story.

Year	Diesels Acquired
1950	99
1951	116
1952	74
1953	75
1954	49
1955	20
1956	60
1957	138*
1958	None

*These were acquired with the merging of the N. C. & St. L. on August 30, 1957.

The L. & N. became completely dieselized November 3, 1956, the total cost of the program approximating $90 million.

Some idea of what this meant in greater efficiency may be best ob-

Waving a farewell for posterity are the train and engine crew who participated in the last "official" steam-powered run on the lines of the L. & N. The date was January 28, 1957; the place, Worthville, Ky.; the run from that point to DeCoursey, Ky., with Local Freight No. 86. Although the L. & N. had been completely dieselized since November 3, 1956, Engine No. 1882 had been on "lend-lease" to the Carrollton Railroad. When its tour of duty expired, it "worked its way" back home and eventually to the scrap-pile — the fate of many another once powerful L. & N. steamer in the 1950s.

tained by referring to that well-known railroad "yardstick" – gross ton-miles handled per freight train-hour. In 1949, the figure for the L. & N. was 30,756. By 1957, it had increased to 50,892. In 1958, it was 52,312.

The installation of centralized traffic control also was pushed. At the end of the L. & N.'s first century it had had 625 miles of this. By the end of 1958, it covered 1,772 miles of main-line operation, with work well along on the installation between Mobile and New Orleans. In one instance, that of the installation between Corbin and Loyall, Ky., a distance of 68 miles, it thereafter became possible to remove the second track between those two points. (The merging of the N. C. & St. L. into the L. & N. had added 522 miles of the total mentioned.)

The 1950s were also featured by the continued modernization and enlargement of existing freight yards and by the construction of three entirely new yards – Radnor Yard, Nashville; Tilford Yard (originally Hills Park, but re-named in honor of Mr. Tilford), Atlanta; and Boyles Yard, Birmingham.

At each of these the classification of freight cars was accomplished by gravity, with the momentum of the cars controlled by retarders. At Tilford Yard and Boyles Yard, the retarding and classification was done electronically, with radio, automation, radar and television being utilized to the fullest extent practicable. The total cost of these three yards alone approximated $34 million.

Still other modern yards were planned and developed. Ground for Wauhatchie Yard, Chattanooga, Tenn., was broken March 12, 1959. It was a part of a $4.8 million relocation plan at Chattanooga, which also involved the building of new freight and passenger stations, the relocation of considerable main-line trackage and the elimination of several grade crossings. This relocation was planned to make available for industrial use a sizable area in downtown Chattanooga.

When the L. & N. re-commenced construction of branch-line trackage in 1944, an activity which had been dormant throughout the Depression and necessarily much of World War II, the emphasis at first was upon the reaching, developing and serving of new coalfields. Such construction continued in the 1950s but other construction was closely allied to the intensified industrialization of the South. Outstanding was the so-called General Electric Spur at Louisville, 5.77 miles in length, which was completed in 1952.

This was constructed primarily to serve General Electric's huge $200 million Appliance Park, but because of foresight in acquiring valuable acreage nearby for industrial sites, it became an important source of other tonnage. The Ford Motor Company was the next major industry to locate thereon and many others followed.

Other outstanding "spurs to business" construction in the 1950s included the 2.37-mile long Doe Run Spur (completed in 1951) to serve the Olin-Mathieson Chemical Corporation at Brandenburg, Ky.; the 2.55-mile long Gonzalez Spur (1952) to serve Chemstrand's huge $86.5-million plant near Pensacola, Fla., for the making of nylon fibers; and the 3.12-mile Maxine Spur (1953) to reach and serve a new coal mine of the Alabama By-Products Corporation a few miles northwest of Birmingham.

Several additional small spurs were also constructed during this decade in West Kentucky to reach new coalfields.

The results from this new construction and the South's boom generally were extremely gratifying. During the 10-year period, 1949-1958, inclusive, more than $1 billion was spent by new industry in locating on L. & N. tracks; almost as much by existing industry for the expansion of facilities.

Cars handled by the L. & N. during this period (with some inevitable waxing and waning) reflected the South's "New Look."

Year	Revenue Freights (tons)
1949	58,793,961
1950	68,283,021
1951	70,713,204
1952	66,755,771
1953	67,615,831
1954	60,598,936
1955	61,068,625
1956	71,895,518
1957	73,440,828
1958	71,958,502

A "by-product" of the L. & N.'s dieselization and the consequent scrapping of its steam locomotives was the Railroad's donation of engine bells to small, needy churches in rural communities. Shown are several en route to a new sphere of usefulness. In all, nearly 400 locomotive bells were so donated.

The "Kiddie Special" was first operated from Louisville to Lebanon Junction, Ky., and return, in March 1951. Including the 1961 operation, some 100,000 youngsters from schools in Louisville and Jefferson County and in New Albany and Jeffersonville, Ind., "across the river," had made the 60-mile round-trip. For many it had been their first trip by train. Teachers and some parents accompanied the children.

During the period, 1940-1949, inclusive, cars handled on the L. & N. averaged approximately 67 million tons a year. This period, of course, includes the abnormally high traffic of World War II, but even so, the yearly average for the period, 1949-1958, exceeded the average for the earlier period by more than one million tons.

Another reflection of the increased traffic which the L. & N. was called upon to handle during the 1950s was its purchase of new freight cars.

In all, between the beginning of 1950 and the end of 1958, the L. & N. purchased 20,000 new freight cars of the most improved construction and design. Of these, 17,000 had actually been delivered during that period and the remaining 3,000 cars – all 70-ton hoppers for the hauling of bituminous coal – were placed in service in 1959.

In spite of a continued valiant effort, passenger traffic continued its downward spiral in the 1950s. The nature of this to some extent is conveyed by the following figures:

Year	Passengers Carried
1950	2,624,736
1951	2,682,736
1952	2,322,291
1953	2,096,449
1954	1,763,462

1955	1,263,021
1956	1,418,016
1957	1,287,822
1958	1,097,384

There was some consolation in the fact that while the number of passengers had fallen off by almost six million annually within the span of 12 years (1946 compared with 1958), the average passenger traveled a much greater distance on L. & N. rails. In 1946, for example, the average passenger traveled only 188.13 miles; in 1958, the comparable figure was 273.76. Thus, the decline in passenger-train **revenues** is not reflected proportionately by the above figures. In 1958, these revenues (including mail and express) amounted to approximately $20.9 million. In 1946, the comparable figure was $29.8 million.

A. L. M. Wiggins, elected chairman of the board of directors, September 1, 1948.

The decreasing patronage accorded many of the L. & N.'s trains – chiefly locals, but also some of more impressive status – made it necessary for the Railroad to discontinue in the 1950s no less than 74 passenger trains and to eliminate the passenger service provided on 34 mixed trains. This program encountered opposition in many quarters; ironically enough in some cases from the very communities whose lack of patronage had forced the train or trains to operate at a deficit.

However, the program had two beneficial results. It brought about an estimated aggregate annual savings of $5.7 million and it enabled the L. & N. to concentrate on improving the service and equipment of its remaining trains which were better patronized. Thus, in the early part of 1953, the Railroad placed in service in The Humming Bird, The Georgian, The Pan-American, The Flamingo and The South Wind 22 lightweight sleeping cars which embodied the latest innovations in "horizontal"

Left: Air view of the $16 million Passenger Terminal at New Orleans, showing proximity to business district. Terminal was dedicated April 16, 1954. Arrow points to old Canal St. Station.
Right: The $¾ million Mobile Passenger station was dedicated February 8, 1955.

The L. & N.'s version of "piggyback" was first known as TOTE—Trailer-On-Train-Express. It was activated on a modest scale in the summer of 1955 and was subsequently greatly expanded.

train travel.

Shortly thereafter another lightweight sleeping car and 13 lightweight coaches were secured for placing in the various "name" trains.

Simultaneously, the L. & N. intensified its program of educating the younger generation in the comfort and convenience of travel by train. The most spectacular outgrowth of this was the "Kiddie Special," operated each March between Louisville and Lebanon Junction, Ky., for a number of successive week days. The first of these specials was operated in March 1951. Including the 1959 operation, approximately 75,000 youngsters had made this 60-mile round trip between Louisville and Lebanon Junction. In March 1959, for instance, on each of 13 successive week days more than 1,000 junior scholars rode an 18-car Special and spent an eventful and hilarious two hours on the rails, temporarily freed from classroom cares, if not from their watchful teachers.

A complete listing of the many new departures embarked upon by the L. & N. during the 1950s might make for rather tedious cataloguing, but at least a passing mention should be made of the following:

End-to-end communication for freight trains via two-way radio; the teletyping of train consists; the greater mechanization of both roadway and shop maintenance; an intensified replacing of lighter rail in mainline track with 132-lb. rail; the strengthening and modernization of bridges; the first laying of welded rail (in 1958); the adoption of trackside electronic "hot-box" detectors to help solve one of the railroads' perennial problems – the overheated journal, which can cause a derailment; considerable research, undertaken either independently or in cooperation with the Association of American Railroads; the building of modern freight stations at Radnor and Tilford yards for handling less-than-carload shipments; and the air conditioning and remodeling of the general office building at Louisville and of other structures elsewhere on the System.

In fact, the activity of the L. & N. throughout the 1950s might best be described as kaleidescopic. Faced by subsidized competition on many

Welded rail moves through Nashville en route to being placed in Evansville Division track. First installation was on M. N. O. & P. Division in latter part of 1958.

fronts, and handicapped by restrictive legislation, it still found time to consider and then implement a large-scale merger and to improve and modernize every facet of its operation. These latter included, in addition to the others, the inauguration of TOTE (piggy-back) or Trailer On Train Express, in 1955; the building of a new $1 million passenger station at Mobile, and co-operation with other railroads at New Orleans in a $41 million terminal-improvement project there; and the completion of a new $1 million bridge across Pearl River some 40 miles east of New Orleans.

In the latter part of 1959, work was started on a new passenger station at Birmingham; on a new division office building at Boyles and permission was sought for the joint use by the Atlantic Coast Line and the L. & N. of the latter's yards at Boyles, Montgomery and Atlanta.

Two major happenings of the 1950s had sharply contrasting attributes. One was the strike of 10 non-operating brotherhoods against the L. & N. and certain affiliated railroads, which lasted for 58 days

Against typical "Magic City" background, visiting financiers, who had arrived aboard Financial Inspection Tour Special, inspect site for new $10 million Boyles Yard. Tour was on L. & N. lines, September 21-24, 1954; moved from Cincinnati to New Orleans.

or from March 14 to May 11, 1955. Four of the five operating brotherhoods were subsequently to join in this work stoppage which was marked by some violence and destruction of property and by considerable disruption of normal service.

Basically, the strike resulted from a disagreement between the L. & N. and affiliated railroads and the brotherhoods over a recommendation of the Emergency Board, appointed by the President of the Untied States, concerning a health and welfare plan. After the L. & N. and brotherhoods had originally disagreed over how the cost of this should be underwritten, the Board recommended that such a plan should be made **available** to employes, with the cost equally divided. Most of the nation's railroads subsequently signed an agreement which made the health and welfare plan **compulsory** for every non-operating employe covered, with the cost equally divided.

The L. & N. felt that no employe should be forced to take this insurance if he did not wish to. After months of discussion, the L. & N. and affiliated lines and the non-operating brotherhoods were unable to reach any sort of agreement and the strike was called on March 14, 1955.

Finally, following prolonged and unsuccessful mediation at Washington, the National Mediation Board, at the request of both the Railroad and the brotherhoods, appointed an arbitrator. Both sides in the dispute agreed to accept his decision in the controversial health and welfare matter as final and binding, all the other issues having been resolved by stipulation agreement between both parties to the dispute just prior to the arbitration.

The arbitrator's decision, in essence, was that the L. & N. was permitted to retain its own health and welfare plan and not become a party to the so-called National policy; however, he ruled that the L. & N. must pay the entire cost of this insurance for its non-operating employes. Although the arbitrator's decision was not announced until May 20, 1955, by mutual agreement the work stoppage had come to an end May 11, 1955.

Left: Air conditioning of general office building, Louisville, was completed in summer of 1955; modernization and relocation of various offices got under way in spring of 1956. Right: Accounting, bookkeeping and payrolling became increasingly mechanized during the 1950s.

Typical of the modern freight houses which were built in the 1950s is the one shown at Radnor, Tenn., adjacent to Radnor Yard. Here an endless underfloor conveyor is one of the many up-to-the-minute installations which speed the less-than-carload freight between shippers and receivers.

The merging of The Nashville, Chattanooga and St. Louis Railway into the L. & N. - the second major event - was admittedly on the more constructive side, although even it met with considerable opposition and aroused much bitterness. The path to culmination on August 30, 1957, was, in fact, a long and tortuous one, beset with legal obstacles and various delaying tactics provided by proponents of the status quo, whose sincerity is not doubted or impugned.

Of course, after the merger had become a fact the task was not done - it had just begun. The absorbing of another Class I railroad - the largest such merger in railroad history in many years - posed many problems but most were successfully resolved. As an immediate result, the L. & N. became the third largest railroad in the South and the 16th largest in the nation. It was placed in a much better position to compete for available traffic, not only in its own territory, as an originating carrier, but in a wider segment of off-line territory, too.

These were the L. & N.'s vital statistics, immediately following the merger:

It then had 5,697 miles of main track, or approximately 9,300 miles of all track.

It had 734 diesel locomotives, 593 passenger-train cars and 67,336 freight cars, with 2,000 new cars on order.

It had approximately 25,000 employes and over 16,000 stockholders, some of the latter residing in every state in the Union.

The combined gross investment in property devoted to public service, plus working capital and material and supplies, approximated $907 million, divided 83 per cent L. & N. and 17 per cent N. C. & St. L.

To introduce the "New South" and the service provided to a large part of it by the L. & N., a Financial Inspection Tour was held in September 1954. This was rather unique in that it was on L. & N. rails for four days, September 21-24, inclusive, moving from Cincinnati to New Orleans, via Corbin and Louisville, with several stops en route.

Aboard were some 65 leading financiers, bankers and industrialists, largely from the North, East and Midwest, who were the Railroad's guests on this tour of its territory. Traveling in a 15-car "Financial Inspection Tour Special," these were able to see for themselves the results of the phenomenal shift of industry to L. & N. territory within the past several years. And, of course, simultaneously, the visitors saw the impressive strides made by the L. & N. in improving its physical plant to more effectively serve the South's expanding industrial might.

It is worthy of emphasis that this industrialization continued unabated thereafter. Indeed, had a comparable tour been conducted in September 1959, and had it been possible for the same guests to participate, it would have been well worth their while to "retrace their steps." A comparable tour was to take place in October 1962.

Much had happened in the intervening five years, that is, between 1954 and 1959. Many hundreds of millions of dollars had been spent upon new plants producing a wide variety of products: air conditioners, automobile glass, rubber, paper, fibreboard, chemicals, lumber products, foodstuffs, automobile parts, synthetics, building materials, poultry feed, pencils, baseballs . . . to name a few. Correspondingly, an equal or even greater sum had been spent by existing industry (some of it a comparative newcomer to Dixie) for the expansion and modernization of facilities.

"Industrial parks" had also been created at several localities; in the Pinson Valley east of Birmingham; in the area adjacent to the 5.77-mile "G.E." spur at Louisville; and in areas at or near Frankfort, Ky., Edenwold, Tenn., and Jackson, Tenn. For these "parks" or subdivisions, the L. & N. acquired land for subsequent resale to industry and worked closely with local authorities to make these sites attractive through adequate water supply, other

Top: To better acquaint patrons and employes with L. & N. and territory served, a movie, "The Old Reliable" was filmed in 1954. The picture, in sound and color, ran for 25 minutes. Shown is a "Lights, Action, Camera!" bit aboard a tavern-lounge car. Bottom: L. & N. was host to many special "intracity" movements in 1950s. Here group from Louisville Chamber of Commerce, aboard specially-outfitted gondolas, inspect industrial areas served by L. & N.

utilities and proper zoning.

Industry and consequently traffic thus became gratifyingly diversified and the traffic flow north and south became better balanced. While the L. & N. was once and had been for many years regarded primarily as a coal-hauling railroad, by the end of 1958 it could no longer be so considered. In that year the major traffic classification "manufactures and miscellaneous" provided 42.6 percent of the L. & N.'s gross revenues from freight traffic, whereas in 1938 it had provided only 26.3 percent and in 1948, 37.2 percent.

"Mountains" of coal, however, continued to be moved by the L. & N. and in spite of the somewhat troubled waters of the coal industry and an increased use of other fuels, loadings of this commodity remained commendably high. (In 1947, for instance, the L. & N. moved approximately 38.2 million tons of bituminous coal; for 1958, the comparable figure was 33.4 million.)

The centralized hiring of employes was another great forward step taken during the 1950s. It was activated in 1955 at Louisville, with branch offices subsequently established at Birmingham, Mobile, Nashville and Latonia, to insure the hiring of personnel best qualified for the many tasks to be done.

It is worthy of mention, too, that commencing in 1956, supervisory personnel on the L. & N. were given the opportunity to take selected courses in adult education at the college or university of their choice, with the Railroad paying the cost of tuition.

Long aware of the importance of good employe relations, the L. & N. intensified many of its activities in this field during the 1950s. The L. & N. Cooperative Club and the L. & N. Veterans' Club, which had come into existence in the 1920s, continued to promote fellowship among employes. The L. & N. Fishing Club was established in 1955 at LaGrange, Ky., and in 1956 the L. & N. Golf Club moved to its new home at Coral Ridge, Ky., complete with a handsome clubhouse, a swimming pool and a nine-hole golf course. The Tilford Bowling Tournament and the Tilford Golf Tournament at Louisville (extended under the name and sponsorship of William H. Kendall after he was elected president) became institutions.

A considerable sum was spent by L. & N. in 1950s in equipping through freight trains for end-to-end communication via two-way radio. By 1959 most cabooses and locomotives in main-line service had been so equipped.

During period, 1949-1958, more than $1 billion was spent by new industry in locating on L. & N. tracks; almost as much by existing industry for expansion of facilities. Plant shown is typical of many huge installations which were built by L. & N. tracks — or reached by spurline construction — during this era. As a result L. & N.'s traffic became more diversified and traffic flow, north and south, better balanced, making for more efficient operation.

Stock-option and stock-purchase plans, and insurance and comparable benefits for officers and other employes, were inaugurated. An "Employes' Handbook" was prepared in 1959 to help all employes – particularly new employes – to become better acquainted with the Railroad and their role in its operation.

Shortly after the L. & N. passed its 109th milestone a change occurred in its top leadership. On April 1, 1959, John E. Tilford retired as chief executive. The directors elected William H. Kendall, vice president and general manager, to succeed him the same date. Mr. Kendall had been a director since October 17, 1957.

Mr. Tilford continued as a director and was appointed chairman of the advisory committee. Here he dealt largely with various corporate aspects of the Railroad's operations.

A statement made by President William H. Kendall at the end of 1959 seems appropriate to conclude this chapter. He said, in part:

"The most important problem of the L. & N. is still that of reducing costs so we can stay competitive. Everything we're doing is aimed at effecting economies and getting business back. It's difficult to say whether we'll gain on the problem or just hold our own. For the years immediately ahead, however, the prospects, taken as a whole, are encouraging, indicating increased responsibility and opportunity for a time-tested public servant and a plant adequate to the many tasks to be done."

Air view of Boyles Yard taken shortly after its activation December 2, 1958, looking north toward classification yard. In foreground at right are main yard office and retarder tower, with master retarder and group retarders to left. Lead from receiving yard is in center foreground. Structure at extreme left is car service building. Main line is at extreme left to west of classification yard and departure yards.

Top: The nerve center of centralized traffic control — the control board — whereby dispatcher can govern movement of trains many miles away by signal-light indication and power switches, eliminating necessity for written train orders and strict adherence to time table operation. C.T.C. is sometimes called "phantom double track" because, in effect, it doubles amount of traffic single track can handle. Bottom: Retarder operator keeps watchful eye on flow of cars through retarders, but retardation and classification are done automatically by VELAC — Automatic Retarder Control System.

Chapter XL

Into the Space Age

UNDER President William H. Kendall, the Louisville and Nashville inaugurated a vigorous modernization program to keep abreast of the Space Age.

It was a commitment to evolutionary change which affected every phase of the Railroad's operations and which resulted in a greatly improved plant.

Some indication of the effectiveness of this program may be gained from that key statistic of railway operating efficiency – gross-ton-miles-per-freight-train hour. In 1959 this was 54,713; in 1963 it had increased to 55,019, which compared with 48,531 for even so recent a year as 1955.

Historically, the needs and possible needs of traffic had largely shaped expansion and manner of growth of the Railroad. As a result of its intensified commitment to keep pace with the times, the L. & N. gave new importance to a parallel precept that the Railroad could influence the growth of its traffic by its **own** planned growth and development.

It was realized that the nation's economy was expanding rapidly; that traffic which should be moving by rail had been lost to competition; that traffic which had never moved by rail **could** be moving by rail, and that the L. & N. could improve its handling of the traffic it already had.

Accordingly, the L. & N. made every effort to better market its product – transportation.

Its **primary** tool was a carefully trained traffic-sales force, working out of 51 offices strategically located throughout the country, with close supervision and direction, both on and off the line of road, and from headquarters in Louisville.

The program to back up this customer-oriented effort called for more powerful diesel locomotives, the procuring of larger and more dependable freight cars, especially designed in many cases to serve a specific need, considerable roadway, freight yard and terminal improvement, and an increasing utilization of automation largely made possible by the tremendous progress registered in the field of electronics.

Industry Moves South

Highly important to the L. & N.'s commitment to this evolutionary change and to its traffic requirements was the South's changing economy. It was a development which resulted in the establishment in Dixie of hundreds of new, large industries, each representing investments aggregating millions of dollars in structure, machinery and equipment, and in an extensive expansion of existing industry.

For instance, Standard Oil of Kentucky's new petroleum refinery at Pascagoula, Miss., represented an investment of $125 million; duPont's titanium oxide plant at New Johnsonville, Tenn., $75 million, and Consolidated Aluminum's plant there, $28 million; the Chrysler Corporation's and Boeing's N. A. S. A. Saturn Rocket project, New Orleans, $150 million; American Cyanamid's synthetic fibre plant, Pensacola, $27 million; and Ford Motor's automotive-glass factory, Nashville, $50 million. Also, a huge export grain elevator, costing $4 million, was erected at Pascagoula. This was the source of thousands of carloads of traffic annually.

These are just a few examples of the major developments in L. & N. territory after 1958, but they illustrate the magnitude of the South's industrail growth. Hundreds of other manufacturing facilities, distribution warehouses and mineral and forest projects likewise materialized, helping greatly to further diversify the economy along the L. & N.'s lines.

As for decades past, the L. & N. continued to play an important role in the location of much of the South's new industry. Frequently, when the L. & N.'s existing railhead was several miles distant from the considered site of a new plant, spur lines were built to provide service. The Railroad also was able to assist in the location of many projects through its ability to furnish a wide variety of data about resources, labor, sites, cultural advantages, taxes and transportation services, to name only a few.

One major development, which may be said to have matured during the early 'sixties, also was very helpful in the obtaining of new industry. This was an intensified cooperation with local authorities in the establishment of so-called industrial districts, or sub-divisions.

Standard Oil of Kentucky's new refinery at Pascagoula cost approximately $125 million.

The L. & N. reached the Bowaters Southern Paper Corporation at Calhoun, Tenn., in June 1962, with its construction of a 9.2-mile long branch line, the longest piece of construction undertaken by the L. & N. since 1949. L. & N's line and Hiwassee River are in foreground.

For instance, at Louisville, with the cooperation of local authorities, 300 acres of land were obtained for the Derby City Industrial District on the southern edge of the city. Another 98 acres were subsequently purchased nearby. Then, in the summer of 1963, the Louisville Space Center, of which the L. & N. was one of the organizers and investors, procured another 300 acres which had formerly been occupied by an Army medical depot. The property had nine huge warehouse structures, containing over 1,700,000 square feet of floor space, all served by rail sidings. Comparable developments occurred at such L. & N.-served points as Nashville, Atlanta, Knoxville, Chattanooga, Montgomery, New Orleans, Decatur and Lexington.

During this five-year period, at least 1000 new plants, warehouses and other permanent industrial-type operations were located on line, representing an investment of more than $1.1 billion, and with an estimated normal traffic potential of 287,000 carloads annually. This paralleled an expenditure of nearly $800 million for the expansion of existing industry, estimated to produce some 73,000 carloads annually.

One "new" industry in the sense that it was **new** to the L. & N., which reached it in June 1962, was the plant of the Bowaters Southern Paper Corporation at Calhoun, Tenn., already in operation for several years and previously served only by the Southern Railway. This required the construction of a 9.2-mile long line, the longest stretch of track which had been built by the L. & N. since 1949. This new construction provided an important access to pulpwood supplies in 22 counties in Kentucky, Tennessee, North Carolina and North Georgia.

Another 11.8-mile long spur was completed in Eastern Kentucky in the summer of 1963 to serve new coal-mine operations, and a three-mile long track was built at New Johnsonville, Tenn., in the fall of 1963, to serve the plants previously mentioned. In the spring of 1963 the L. & N. also acquired a five-mile, privately-owned stretch of track known as the Century

The L. & N.'s Derby City Industrial District, on the southern edge of Louisville, provides an attractive site for any industry seeking a location favored by excellent transportation facilities, adequate public utilities and closeness to consumer markets.

Branch and connecting with the L. & N. six miles west of Columbia, Tenn. It had been under lease for some time to provide service to the Monsanto Chemical Company and to other large phosphate mining and processing industries in the area.

A 300-car hold yard was built at Pascagoula in connection with the grain elevator just described.

Other important industrial trackage was built at Louisville, Owensboro and Carrollton, Ky.; at Cartersville, Atlanta, and Marietta, Ga.; Nashville, Jackson, Chattanooga, Pulaski and Murfreesboro, Tenn.; New Orleans and Pascagoula, and Montgomery, Birmingham and Florence, Ala.

There was some abandonment of existing trackage—notably that of the 12 miles of branch line from LaGrange to Eminence, Ky., whose complete removal occurred during the latter part of 1960. The original line had been completed as early as 1851 by the former Louisville and Frankfort Railroad.

Some 21 miles of the 28-mile branch from Lewisburg to Fayetteville, Tenn., a part of the former N. C. & St. L., were also removed.

Piggyback Booms

Especially spectacular was the development of piggyback during 1959-1963, after it had played a minor role in the L. & N.'s traffic parade for several years following its activation in the summer of 1955.

In the early 'sixties, however, as the result of the providing of new equipment and facilities, piggyback really came into its own. Combining many of the advantages of both rail and truck transport, it obtained for the L. & N. new types of business until then largely beyond its reach. One of the most important of these newcomers was the automobile which "returned" to the Railroad at that time. We quote the world "returned" since the L. & N. had long handled automobiles. Prior to 1960, however, they moved rather cumbersomely – and hence infrequently – in boxcars.

In the summer of 1960 the L. & N. placed in service its first bi-level rack cars for the piggybacking of automobiles. These made such a hit with the industry that the Railroad soon obtained others; then, shortly thereafter made its first purchase of tri-level rack cars, each capable of carrying 12 standard-size automobiles; or 15 "compacts." These also proved popular; as a result, the L. & N. scheduled its first all-automobile piggyback train in October 1961 (Nashville to Atlanta) and soon became one of the principal rail carriers of automobiles in the nation.

Less-than-carload merchandise freight joined the piggyback parade in the fall of 1963, with door-to-door pick-up and delivery at point of origin and destination provided by contract carriers. As a historical footnote, U. S. mail was also piggybacked (for the first time) between Chicago and Atlanta during a seven-weeks' experimental period in the spring of that year. The piggybacking of express commenced in 1962 and piggyback trailers became a common sight on certain passenger trains at about the same time.

Resurgent piggyback necessitated many additions to and betterments of the L. & N.'s physical plant. This involved the improving of clearances along the line of road, the obtaining of equipment, and the installation of loading and unloading facilities and marshalling yards at Louisville, Memphis, Atlanta, New Orleans, Nashville, Birmingham and other major points. By the end of 1963, the L. & N. had piggyback facilities in 32 cities. Others were in the blueprint stage, and portable ramps, which could be moved as required, povided service where it was needed temporarily or on short notice.

By 1963 the L. & N. was leasing from the R E A Leasing Corporation, operators of a nation-wide trailer-and-container pool, more than 800 units of piggyback equipment. Many of these had been owned by the L. & N. itself, but it was found advantageous to sell the trailers to R E A Leasing (a subsidiary of R E A Express) and then to lease them back.

The L.&N. also was a participating member of the Trailer Train Company, owner of a national pool of flatcars, especially adapted to the handling of piggyback shipments. The L. & N. had, at the end of 1963,

Train watching once again became a popular sport as the L. & N. wheeled the long auto-rack trains over its lines.

Piggyback ramps such as this portable one at Louisville helped speed union of trailer and flatcar.

more than 1,100 flatcars of its own.

Specialized sales and service departments also were established to deal solely with the obtaining of piggyback traffic and to deal with its problems.

Comparative figures give some idea of piggyback's amazing, jack-and-the-beanstalk growth on the L. & N. Only 2,037 trailerloads were handles in 1959 and no automobiles (in piggyback service) at all. By 1962, piggyback traffic proper had jumped up to 15,695 carloads and automobiles had very definitely moved into the traffic picture with 16,144 carloads.

The upward surge continued in 1963 when 24,850 carloads were piggybacked and 23,595 carloads of autos were carried.

The L. & N. at the end of 1963 was offering shippers a highly flexible piggyback service consisting of what the trade termed Plans I, II, III, IV and V. Without going into too great detail, these gave the shipper the choice of having his shipment carried in regular highway trailers on flatcars; or the Railroad provided the trailers and pick-up and delivery service; or it carried the shipper's own trailers at a flat rail rate either on its own flatcars or those of the shipper; or the shipment was handled by the Railroad under joint-motor rail rates and arrangements with a trucking company.

New King Coal

Other segments of the L. & N.'s traffic, in addition to piggyback, had obvious importance, too. The L. & N. continued to move a sizeable tonnage of bituminous coal throughout 1959-1963. The 32.4 million tons transported in 1962 represented an increase of 1.4 million tons over 1961; this further increased to 33.7 million tons in 1963.

Much of the L. & N.'s coal tonnage in 1962 and 1963 was consigned to electric utility generating plants located in the South and Midwest; some of it moved from on-line mines to off-line points as distant as Tampa and Sutton, Fla. The latter movement resulted from the historic I. C. C. decision in the Tampa-Sutton Fine Coal Case – a decision which recognized the reasonableness of permitting the L. & N. to grant reduced rates for the movement of fine coal from Eastern Kentucky to those Florida points. Part of the justification for these rates was the L. & N.'s ability to use covered hopper cars which otherwise would have returned south empty after moving phosphate rock north from Florida. Some 300,000 tons of coal per year were involved.

There were a number of factors which contributed to coal's continued importance for the L. & N. in spite of the competition provided by other producers of heat, light and power. These included the Railroad's own improved methods for speeding the product from mine to consumer through the use of better yard facilities and equipment.

In the latter category was the L. & N.'s purchase or upgrading of many thousands of coal cars and its developing of a special hopper car with a 100-ton capacity, capable of being unloaded automatically in less than 30 seconds, thus permitting a faster turn-around and greater utilization of equipment.

This quickened transition from loads to empties permitted the inauguration of the solid or **unitized** coal train.

As an example, the first of these unitized trains, started in the fall of 1951, moved 38 carloads of coal in 70-ton hoppers each week day from the West Kentucky coalfields to a T. V. A. steam plant in Alabama, some 250 miles away, every 24 hours. Comparably, a later unitized train also made its round trip of 470 rail miles in 24 hours, moving 5,000 tons each week day in 70-ton hoppers (usually 70 or more cars to a train out of a pool of 128 cars) from a mine in Western Kentucky to another T. V. A. plant near Bridgeport, Ala.

With complete delivery of its new 100-ton automatic cars on order at the end of 1963, the L. & N. planned to go a step further and inaugurate a unitized train which would move this 5,000 tons of coal with a single 50-car set of equipment. Other trains of a similar nature also were scheduled.

At the end of that year the L. & N. was operating eight unitized trains which handled with slightly less than 3,000 cars a volume of coal which

"Pants-Leg" chutes at end of conveyor poured coal into hopper cars at rate of 35 tons a minute; did much to make possible successful operation of unitized coal trains. Train never came to complete stop; could be loaded in two and one-half hours.

Coal regained its importance in the L. & N.'s traffic picture in the 1960s, with some 33.7 million tons handled in 1963, moving largely from mines in Eastern Kentucky and West Kentucky.

formerly had required the use of more than 4,000 cars.

Developments within the industry also made the use of coal more attractive and competitive and in many instances these were aided or encouraged by the Railroad which implemented a rate structure keyed to volume and which lent encouragement to expansion of existing facilities or even new construction.

In the majority of cases, of course, the L. & N.'s improvement of its plant, which resulted in a betterment of the handling of its coal traffic, also benefitted other segments of traffic.

Bigger and Better Yards, Too

The L. & N.'s intensified yard improvement and expansion program which had its inception in the 1950s, with the building of new facilities at Boyles (Birmingham), Hills Park (Tilford Yard, Atlanta), and Radnor (Nashville), continued unabated throughout 1959-1963.

The largest single investment was $11.5 million for the **new** automated DeCoursey Yard, completed December of 1963. This retarder-equipped classification yard, long so important to the movement of traffic – and particularly coal – to and from the South and Eastern Kentucky through the Cincinnati Gateway, as improved and enlarged, had a total of 89 tracks, capable of holding 7,370 standard-length freight cars. Its maximum daily working capacity of 7,000 cars was roughly double that of the old yard. Its modernization and enlargement made it one of the most outstanding in the nation.

Another phase of this work was the modernization and expansion of the new Atkinson Yard, which was activated in August 1963 and which replaced three smaller yards. Located just north of Madisonville, Ky., it was one of the major steps taken by the Railroad in that year to relieve con-

There was considerable yard improvement and expansion on the L. & N. during 1959-1963. **Left:** The new DeCoursey Yard, across the Ohio River from Cincinnati, was completed in the latter part of 1963. **Right:** Wauhatchie Yard, seven miles southwest of Chattanooga, was completed in the summer of 1961.

gestion and to speed the flow of coal between mines and consumers. Some 2.7 miles long, it contained 16 miles of track, accommodated 1,334 freight cars and occupied a key position in much of the coal movement from the West Kentucky fields. This district, which is also served by the Illinois Centrail Railroad, produced some 32 million tons in 1963 alone, a good part of which moved by rail.

Leewood Yard, at Memphis, was also expanded and modernized in 1963 and eight classification tracks were added at Tilford Yard (Atlanta) at a cost of more than $400,000.

Earlier, Wauhatchie Yard, seven miles southwest of Chattanooga, Tenn., was completed in the summer of 1961. It replaced Cravens Yard in the central part of the city and had 18 tracks, accommodating 1,444 freight cars, with a maximum working capacity of 2,500 cars per day. It was part of the L. & N.'s $4.5-million modernization program in that city, a program which involved relocating some 17,000 feet of main-line track, eliminating several grade crossings, and which was to give Chattanooga new freight and passenger stations.

Right-of-way Improved For Bigger Shipments

The $1.5 million tunnel-and-bridge clearance project on the L. & N.'s so-called "second main line" between Cincinnati and Knoxville was another forward step taken to meet changing needs. Many clearances were too low to permit the desired movement of tri-level auto-rack cars and the increasing over-all size of freight cars made it desirable to increase clearance widths also at many points. Thus, the minimum height clearance for this trackage was set at 19 feet, seven inches – the minimum width clearance at five feet, eight inches – up to seven feet for certain curved tunnels. Practically all of this work was completed by the latter part of 1963 and involved the raising of nine highway bridges and the remodeling of no less than 18 tunnels.

In addition, three other tunnels – between Louisville and Cincinnati – aggregating 900 feet in length, were eliminated as part of the program to provide increased clearance for the Space Age's over-size shipments.

The roadway was otherwise improved throughout 1959-1963 by an increasing use of 132-lb. welded rail, by better ballasting and by research and development which introduced more automation to track maintenance, thus enabling the work to be done better and faster and minimizing interference with train operation.

New Uses Found for Electronics and Automation

The L. & N., in fact, continued to make an increasing use of both electronics and automation. Each played an important role in the operation of the new, freight-car classification yards and the application of C. T. C. concepts.

Centralized traffic control, as mentioned in previous chapters, was first used by the L. & N. in 1942. By the end of 1963 the movement of trains was controlled in this way over more than 2,000 miles of main-line track, permitted by signal-light indication and power-controlled switches operated by a train controller, and eliminating the need for train orders. The $2-million installation between Winchester and Corbin, Ky., was to utilize both microwave and ground wires, with completion of the project permitting the removal of 49 miles of second track. Similarly, 114.6 miles of second-main line track was removed between Calera and Athens, Ala., following a C. T. C. activiation between Athens and Birmingham.

In August 1961, a C. T. C.

Extensive tunnel clearance permitted the operation of trains with bigger freight cars. Huge undercutter (in background) helped to speed the necessary work of enlargement.

installation for the track between Mobile and New Orleans, 135 miles, was placed in service, followed by the activation of the comparable one between Athens and Birmingham, 98 miles, in the summer of 1963. This put the entire main line between Cincinnati and New Orleans under centralized traffic control.

The placing in service of electronic, data-processing equipment in freight yards at Louisville, Birmingham and Chattanooga in 1962 did much to improve record-keeping and car-data transmission and this worked in close conjunction with the modern electronic computers installed in July 1962 in the L. & N.'s data-processing center at Louisville. These computers were used not only to speed the flow of information requisite for prompt car tracing and accounting, but also gave a valuable assist to payrolls, operations analyses, equipment control and to many other things.

During the 1959-1963 period the equipping of locomotives and cabooses with radio (permitting two-way conversation between crews on freight trains) continued.

Communications generally received the L. & N.'s close attention throughout this five-year span and it further improved its approximately 3,000 miles of teletype circuits and its 10,000 circuit miles of carrier telephone facilities. Outstanding was the superimposing of an additional 2,000 miles of telephone circuits on existing wire and cable lines.

At the end of 1963, the L. & N. had one of the largest completely independent railroad communication systems in the nation, and this had had inter-city dial circuits since 1928. When the renewal and expansion of its dial switchboard at Louisville was completed in 1963, it became one of the largest owned by any railroad in the country.

Hotbox detectors, for electronically revealing heated journal boxes on

The data-processing center at Louisville, following its completion in July 1962, made a valuable contribution to the L. & N. in car tracing and accounting; in payrolling; in equipment control and in other ways.

freight cars, were first installed on the L. & N. in 1959; at the end of 1963 the Railroad had 28 of these.

Electronics also began to be used in 1962 to help expedite mail handling at the Nashville Union Station. Several million pounds of sacked mail (chiefly outbound religious periodicals) normally move each month through this station.

Motive Power and Rolling Stock Evolved, Too

The L. & N. became completely dieselized in the early part of 1957; thereafter, for several years its stable of diesels was sufficiently powerful and efficient to meet traffic demands. However, time began to exact its inevitable toll in the early 1960s; as a consequence, the L. & N. obtained its first new replacement diesels in 1962.

These were 29 in number and were the first of their kind in the South. Designated as GP-30s (general purpose), each had 2,250 h.p., and were 50 per cent more powerful than the F-3 and F-7 units (1,5000 h.p.) which they replaced.

Intensifying its replacement program in 1963, the L. & N. ordered an additional 53 new replacement diesels, many of which had been delivered by year's end. Of these, 29 had 2,250 h.p. and 24 had 2,500 h.p., the latter becoming the most powerful in the L. & N.'s ownership when they were first placed in fast freight service between Cincinnati and New Orleans in August 1963.

It was anticipated that these new units would be able to haul fast freights at higher speeds and on less fuel.

During the same year the L. & N. also purchased (second-hand) from

This hotbox detector at Paris, Ky., is comparable to 27 others which the L. & N. had at the end of 1963 for electronically detecting heated journal boxes on freight cars. **Inset:** Close-up of the detector in action.

The L. & N.'s newest "home away from home" for its trainmen was attractive and contains many comforts and conveniences. The L. & N. had a number of these in service at the end of 1963 — in all, planned to have 100 on the rails by some time in 1964.

the abandoned Rutland Railway nine 1,600 h.p. road switchers and 25 units of various types from the Lehigh and New England Railroad, also defunct.

At the end of 1963, less than a quarter of a century after the L. & N. had rather experimentally placed its first diesels (switchers) on the job at Louisville, it owned, or had on order, a total of 776 diesel units of all types.

At the other end of the L. & N.'s train, the term, "little red caboose," was rapidly becoming non-descriptive. In the latter part of 1963, 100 new cabooses were authorized to be built at the South Louisville Shops and some of these were actually rolling by the end of that year. They were both to supplement and to supplant older cabooses, of which 536 were in service at the end of 1962.

Externally, these new cabooses featured a color scheme of distinctive gray, with yellow trim and red lettering, to match that of the diesels; internally, the walls were painted a light blue, with floors maroon and upholstery in brown and black.

They incorporated many improvements, both in their construction and in their installations. Each had a bay window on each side, long-travel draft gear (to cut down jolts and jars), "Ride-Control" trucks (ditto), full-length adjustable passenger-car type seats, conveniently positioned handrails, electric lights, clothes lockers, an oil stove and heater, an ice cooler with compartments for food storage, a radio telephone, a lavatory and running water.

The evolution which took place "in between" the head end and the rear end of the L. & N.'s freight train of this era was no less impressive and was an intensification of a trend which had its inception in the early postwar years.

Mention has previously been made of the 100-ton automatic unloading hopper and of the equipment used in various extensions of the piggyback service. In the 'sixties thousands of other freight cars with a very definite new look appeared on the L. & N. These were bigger, sturdier and smoother riding. The larger proportion of this newly purchased or rebuilt equipment had roller bearings; some had cushioned-underframes; others, special load-retaining devices; still others had special features to permit a quicker loading or unloading, or the handling of certain commodities.

The L. & N. itself rebuilt 5,000 of its 50-ton hopper cars during 1960-

1962, increasing the capacities in many cases, and continued this program through 1963. In 1962 and 1963 it "stretched" - at its South Louisville shops - 1,200 of its boxcars, increasing their lengths from 40 to 50 feet.

In the five-year period ending 1961, the L. & N. purchased over 8,000 hoppers rated at 70 tons; then expanded this and other segments of its fleet by additional purchases throughout 1962 and 1963.

The year 1963 was an especially important one in the growth of the L. & N.'s rolling stock. At various times throughout this 12-month period it purchased 100 quick loading and unloading **covered** hoppers of 100-ton capacity, 431 cars of various types and capacities for the hauling of grain, assorted bulk commodities, trucks, automobiles and wood products, 1,425 80-ton hoppers and 825 100-ton hoppers, 400 covered hoppers, 125 bulkhead flatcars, and 100 jumbo boxcars. Just at year's end it authorized the purchase of 20 cushioned underframe boxcars, equipped with 70-ton trucks. These had a 10,000 cubic-foot capacity, were 17 feet high and had an inside length of $86\frac{1}{2}$ feet and were higher and longer than any then currently in use on U. S. railroads. They were to be used for carrying automotive stampings.

During this same year the L. & N. commenced to build 50 of the 100-ton fast-unloading coal hoppers at South Louisville and ordered another 150 of the same type from an outside builder. A start was also made by the L. & N. on the rebuilding of 3,150 older units of equipment.

The L. & N.'s new 150 "Boca Grande" covered hoppers, of either 70- or 100-ton capacity, proved especially helpful in the moving of silica sand, grain and cement. The full-length longitudinal trough hatch on top permitted bulk loading in one continuous flow; hence the name "Boca Grande" - "Big Mouth." The L. & N. was the first in the nation to put this type of car into service.

The bulkhead flatcars, some with 70-ton capacity and others with 100-ton capacity, proved to be very helpful in the moving of lumber, tube panels, and other bulky loads. There were also 50 of the 100-ton, 60-foot "Cushioned Cargo" boxcars on the rails at the end of 1963, used to haul a wide variety of commodities. The L. & N., as one of the owner roads of Fruit Growers Express, was also operating, under lease, 100 of the 70-ton insulated, bunkerless refrigerator cars, with the need for recurrent icing thus eliminated. More than 1,600 boxcars, usually referred to as "DFs" - for

Smaller hopper at right has a capacity of 50 tons. The jumbo wood-chip car beside it has a capacity of 7,000 cubic feet, or 100 tons. L. & N. placed 50 of the latter in service in 1963.

Dunnage or **Damage Free** – were equipped with load-retaining devices and were moving considerable less-than-carload freight.

A number of gondolas had been converted into coke carriers, each equipped with 11 separate containers, each with a capacity of 300 cubic feet. More than 200 standard 70-ton open-top hoppers, with rust-resistant lining and with built-up sides, were expediting the movement of wood chips, as were 50 of the 100-ton capacity. Many other cars had been especially adapted for the hauling of soil pipe, coiled steel, automotive castings, ferro alloys, pitch, plate glass, pulpwood, heavy machinery and a host of other things.

To conclude this section, here's a brief break-down, without mention of specialized function or capacity, of the L. & N.'s 58,304 revenue producers which were actually in service April 1, 1963:

Open-type hoppers – 33,336; covered hoppers – 1,487; boxcars – 14,239; gondolas – 6,170; flatcars (special) – 27; flatcars (bulkhead) – 309; flatcars (regular) – 1,129; pulpwood cars – 1,380; and chipwood cars – 227. More than 7,000 of these cars were equipped with roller bearings.

As a result of this activity, the L. & N. had in 1963 the youngest car fleet in the South and one of the youngest in the nation, with an average age at the end of that year of approximately 12 years, compared with a national average of a little over 18 years.

Since much of the work of modernizing the L. & N.'s freight-car fleet was done at the Railroad's own shops at South Louisville this necessitated a parallel modernization of car-repair facilities there. Work was begun in 1962 on a $5-million mechanized car-repair shop and on a $1-million automated wheel-and-axle shop. Re-tooling also permitted the assembly-line technique to be applied successfully to the repair of hopper cars, commencing March 1, 1960, and to locomotives, commencing in the fall of the same year.

Fast Freights Rolling

The obtaining of new rolling stock and of more potent motive power were important factors in enabling the L. & N. to inaugurate several fast freights in the early 1960s. The unitized coal trains have already been mentioned, as has the all-piggyback auto-racker moving between Nashville and Atlanta. (The run of the latter was subsequently extended to Louisville and to East St. Louis, the two sections combining at Nashville to continue south to Atlanta.)

The acquisition of the GP-30s enabled the L. & N., in the summer of 1962, in cooperation with the Pennsylvania Railroad, to place on the rails a pair of speedsters known colorfully along the line as the Dixie Jets; more prosaically, by time-table designation, as Nos. 72 and 73. They operated between New Orleans and New York via Montgomery, Birmingham, Nashville, Louisville and Cincinnati. They did much to expedite the movement of freight between cities in the Deep and Central South and New York and other Eastern points, shaving hours off the previous fastest time and providing shippers in the Central South and East with third-morning delivery. More specifically, for instance, in the case of No. 72, northbound, it was scheduled to make the 1,677-mile trip in 78 hours.

Air view of the South Louisville Shops taken in the latter part of 1963. At center (right) is new $5-million mechanized car-repair shop, then still under construction.

The operation of these trains — and of "tributary" trains — helped serve the L. & N.'s important export and import traffic, moving through the ports of New Orleans, Gulfport, Pascagoula, Mobile and Pensacola. At each of these cities extensive port-improvement programs were under way.

Then, in the early fall of 1963, as a result of the completion of its Cincinnati-Knoxville clearance improvement project, the L. & N. inaugurated two fast freights known as the "Auto Vans." These were operated jointly by the L. & N. and the Atlantic Coast Line between Cincinnati and Jacksonville, via Knoxville and Atlanta, making the trip in about 27 hours' time and permitting second-morning delivery in the Florida metropolis. Southbound, the train carried only automobiles from Northern assembly plants, and piggyback trailers; northbound, perishables and piggyback traffic.

These were the more spectacular aspects of the L. & N.'s fast freight service; there were dozens of other trains whose performance, compared with that of even so recent an era as the 1950s, was equally noteworthy.

The L. & N. also had the honor, in the spring of 1963, of handling the largest single shipment ever to move over an American railroad up to that time. It consisted of a refinery reactor vessel, having a gross weight of over 1,330,000 pounds and moved from Combustion Engineering's Chattanooga Division plant to Pascagoula, Miss., where it was installed at the new refinery of Standard Oil of Kentucky.

Passengers, Mail and Express Handled, Too

While understandably freight continued to receive the major share of the L. & N.'s attention during this era, passengers, mail and express, those three passenger-train standbys, were not overlooked. The number of passengers carried apparently had leveled off at about the one-million level and the "average passenger" continued to travel a greater distance, year by year. Thus, in 1959 he journeyed 276 miles; in 1963 this had increased to 286.4 miles.

A number of units of passenger-train equipment were renovated during 1961 and 1962 and this refurbishing and modernization continued throughout 1963. Two diner-lounge cars which were introduced in January 1960 became especially popular with patrons.

In June 1960 a new $500,000 passenger station was dedicated at Birmingham. Of modern architectural design and embodying every comfort and comvenience for passengers, it was a two-story structure, brick-faced, and with a striking tiled mosaic adorning its front. Passenger traffic facilities were on the first floor - railroad offices on the second. (In conjunction with the construction of this building, a new $250,000 division-office building was erected at nearby Boyles Yard.)

A new passenger station was to be built at Biloxi, Miss. Many special movements were handled by the L. & N. during 1959-1963. The Railroad operated a Financial Executives' Inspection Tour in October 1962 to afford a first-hand introduction to the L. & N. and the resurgent South to some 50 men representing some of the nation's top investment houses, banks and insurance companies.

The L. & N.'s "Snowball Special" - operated on March 9, 1960 as an emergency measure - enabled the Railroad to rescue several hundred basketball fans who were marooned at various points between Louisville and Bowling Green, Ky., by a heavy snowfall. These Western Kentucky State College students had hopefully elected to make the trip (to a basketball game at Lexington) in chartered buses.

Wind and Water...

Generally speaking, the elements were kind to the L. & N. in the 1960s. There was an exception or two, however. For instance, there was the tornado which struck Ravenna, Ky., June 9, 1961, doing great damage not only to the Railroad facilities, but to the city in general. Our roundhouse there was almost completely demolished, as was the steel footbridge across 12 yard tracks, and the division office building.

In all, this high-wind visitation, which lasted but a few minutes, cost the L. & N. approximately $130,000.

In March 1963, weeks of snow and ice, followed by heavy, early-spring rains, produced considerable high water in Eastern Kentucky and Tennessee, affecting portions of four of the L. & N.'s divisions - the Chattanooga, the Knoxville and Atlanta, the Cumberland Valley and the Eastern

This Boca Grande — "Big Mouth"— covered hopper car was so-called because the full-length trough on top permitted bulk loading in one continuous flow. It was used for the moving of silica sand, grain or cement and was of 70- or 100-ton capacity.

"America's heaviest rail shipment" moved over the lines of the L. & N. in the spring of 1963, traveling from Chattanooga to Pascagoula. A refinery reactor vessel, with a gross weight of 1,330,000 pounds, it was installed at the new refinery of Standard Oil of Kentucky.

Kentucky. This inundation of trackage was followed by rock slides and parts of the line were out of service for varying legnths of time – in the majority of cases, however, for not longer than two days.

This flooding and its aftermath cost the L. & N. about $500,000.

The General Once Again Makes History

While devoting most of its attention to the present, the L. & N. did not overlook the past, relating this to its present and future. This occurred with its revitalization of the famous old locomotive General which dramatically appeared at Kennesaw, Ga., to commemorate the 100th anniversary of the Andrews Raid, which took place on April 12, 1862.

The Raid was one of the most blood-tingling episodes of the War between the States. It has long had a particular interest for railroaders as it not only had a railroad background, but underscored the importance of railroads and a belief in that importance by the military as early as a century ago.

In brief recapitulation before proceeding with the latter-day activities of the General:

The Raid involved the capture of the General at Big Shanty (Kennesaw) Ga., by a party of 19 Union soldiers disguised as civilians and headed by the noted Union spy, James Andrews. So manned, the little engine, and three boxcars detached from its train, headed north over the Western and Atlantic Railroad (now operated by the L. & N. under lease from the State of Georgia) with the intention of destroying bridges and track all the way to Chattanooga, 105 miles away. It was the thought that such destruction would seriously disrupt the South's flow of men and materiel – might even shorten the war.

However, due largely to the quick-wittedness, daring and determination of Conductor William A. Fuller, the purloined locomotive was so closely pursued that the damage done was slight and it was abandoned at Ring-

The L. & N.'s passenger station at Birmingham, completed in June 1960, was modern in every respect; cost some $500,000 to build.

gold, Ga., 22 miles from Chattanooga. The raiders took to the woods, but were eventually captured. Eight, including Andrews, were hanged as spies, but the daring of all was recognized by the United States, through awards (in some cases posthumously) of the first Congressional Medals of Honor ever presented.

The General, rescued from the scrap-heap, eventually arrived in Chattanooga in 1891 and was placed on display in the Union Station there, so remaining until its reactivation on April 14, 1962, a reactivation which restored it to all its steam-powered glory of yesteryear.

When the little engine "re-appeared" at Kennesaw – re-named Big Shanty for the day – it was greeted by a throng of some 10,000 persons, many of whom were colorfully garbed in Civil-War-era costumes. Two special excursion trains were operated from Atlanta by the local chapter of the National Railway Historical Society. There were scores of newspaper reporters and photographers present and many dignitaries, including President William H. Kendall, of the L. & N., Daniel P. Loomis, president, Association of American Railroads, and Governor Ernest Vandiver, of Georgia.

The ceremonies concluded at Kennesaw, the General rolled north towards Chattanooga, making various stops en route. At Ringgold, where it had been so unceremoniously abandoned 100 years before, it was greeted by a crowd of more than 12,000 people. This time the engine "made it" to Chattanooga and here again cheering throngs were on hand and special ceremonies were held, including the paying off of the General's crew by President Kendall with Confederate money.

This was just the "opening gun" in its commemorative campaign; subsequently it was to travel extensively and to be greeted by enthusiastic crowds wherever it visited – New Orleans, Cincinnati, Birmingham, Atlanta, Louisville, Knoxville, St. Louis – and many points in between.

In its travels the General was accompanied by a faithful companion, Coach 665, a museum car, which contained many relics of the Raid, either authentic or restorations. On the contemporary side, model displays and photographs of L. & N. rolling stick and motive power, C.T.C., passenger stations, yards and so forth, helped give visitors a very good idea of the present-day railroad.

Special guests invited to ride in Coach 665, were given the opportunity to actually witness the L. & N. in action through tours which eventually covered most of the System and which were usually tied in with Civil War Centennial programs or with other events suitable for the General's participation.

During 1962, its peak year of performance, the General and Coach 665 visited 12 states, involving 9,000 miles of travel under the engine's own power and 5,000 miles piggybacked because of the distances involved.

Following its reactivation in April 1962, the General received an excellent press, as illustrated by this sampling of newspaper and magazine clippings.

In all, 42,500 invited guests rode the train in 1962 and another 640,000 persons went through the coach.

The comparable figures for 1963 were 11 states visited, some 7,100 miles of travel (approximately 2,200 under its own power) 44,582 invited guests and 340,795 museum-coach visitors.

The L. & N. received several awards from national organizations for the effectiveness of its use of the General in telling the Railroad's story specifically and that of the railroad generally.

Retirements and Appointments

A number of changes took place in the L. & N.'s official family at the top level during 1959-1963.

On April 18, 1961, A. L. M. Wiggins stepped down as chairman of the board of both the Louisville and Nashville and Atlantic Coast Line railroads, thus relinquishing an important post he had held for more than 12 years.

Mr. Wiggins continued as a director and chairman of the L. & N.'s advisory board until the early part of 1963 when he resigned both posts,

When the General made its initial appearance on April 14, 1962 at Kennesaw, Ga., re-named Big Shanty for the day, it was greeted by a crowd of more than 10,000 persons, many of whom wore Civil-War era costumes. It then moved north, making stops, to Chattanooga.

but retained an association as director emeritus.

New directors elected during 1959-1963 were W. S. Cutchins, president, Brown and Williamson Tobacco Corporation, Louisville; Lucien E. Oliver, vice president, Sears, Roebuck and Company, Atlanta; C. R. Yates, vice president – finance, L. & N., Atlanta; John L. Christian, vice president – manufacturing, Monsanto Chemical Company, St. Louis; James R. Crist, executive vice president, the Southern Company, Atlanta; and J. Crossan Cooper, Jr., attorney, Baltimore.

Directors they replaced were: William J. McDonald, retired vice president – finance, L. & N.; A. J. Moses, retired vice president, Combustion Engineering, Chattanooga; John E. Tilford, former President, L. & N.; Alexander E. Duncan, founder chairman, Commercial Credit Company, Baltimore; H. Lane Young, retired vice chairman of the board, Citizens and Southern National Bank, Atlanta; and Mr. Wiggins.

Mr. Duncan and Mr. Young each continued as a director emeritus.

Four appointments made by the L. & N. during 1962-1963 recognized the importance of four major cities and their adjacent industrial areas. These involved the creation of the post of resident vice president at Atlanta, Nashville, Birmingham and New Orleans.

In each case, the resident vice president was to be chiefly concerned with industrial development and community-and-customer relation matters.

Organizational Set-up Revised

The L. & N.'s "re-tooling" also involved the reorganization of a number of existing departments, and the creation of other new positions (in addition to those just mentioned) and departments to better cope with the problems posed by a rapidly evolving railroad. Some of these changes had to do with industrial-development and community-development and public relations; others with a better utilization of motive power and rolling stock; others with accounting, data processing and taxation; others with piggyback; still others with marketing.

Manpower in the Space Age

The improvement of the L. & N.'s personnel during this five-year period was just as important as that of its physical plant and occurred at an accelerated rate.

There were many facets to this evolution. One was that new employes were potentially better employes to begin with than were their predecessors. The L. & N.'s standardized employment program, initiated in 1956, by its careful recruiting, screening and testing, eliminated as far as was humanly possible, the filling of round holes with square pegs.

Morale was better, too. The average L. & N. employe in 1963 had many advantages – life, disability and unemployment insurance . . . free hospitalization for himself and members of his family . . . vacations and holidays with pay . . . good working conditions and prospects for advancement . . . wages which compared favorably with those of other industry – among others. In addition, many employes were provided with opportunity to supplement their education by special studies at the school of their choice, with the Railroad paying the tuition. A number took ad-

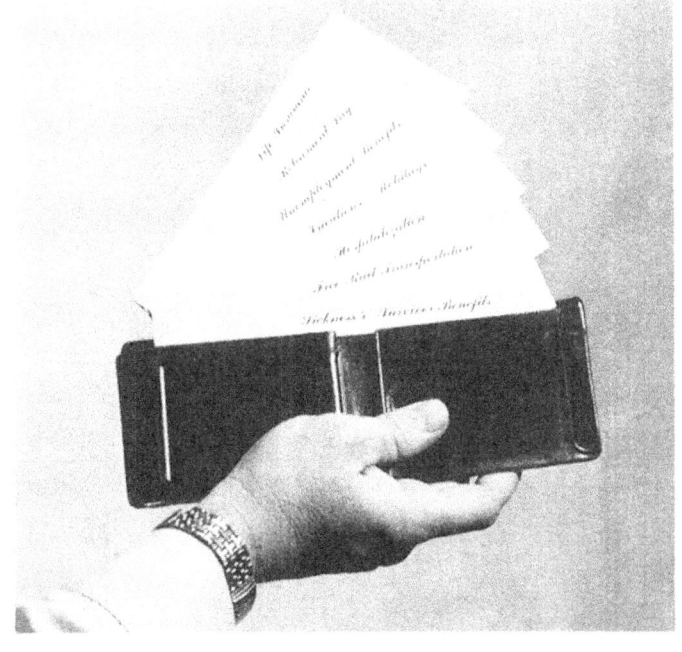

The "dividends" from the L. & N.'s "invisible paycheck" include those shown: **sickness and survivor benefits; free rail transportation; hospitalization; vacations and holidays with pay, life insurance,** and others.

vantage of this offer for self-improvement.

L'Envoi

In this chapter we have attempted to give a picture of five eventful years in the history of a 113-year old railroad. Necessarily a number of happenings had to be omitted in the history proper and many of these are dealt with in the appendices. The L. & N. was a railroad that, as indicated, was still growing and continually finding new fields of usefulness. Its top management and its some 17,000 employes hope to add to that usefulness in the years to come.

– March 5, 1964

The Louisville & Nashville Railroad

1850-1963

Appendices

Appendix I

From Wood to Steel

IT IS, of course, fairly obvious that the keystone of railroad operation is the railroad train and the track upon which it operates, even though such items as passenger stations, rate structures and stocks and bonds occasionally have a tendency to obscure this dominant importance. In the history proper the emphasis was placed mainly upon the "external" aspects of the railroad, to the comparative neglect of its "internal" development and evolution.

But the history of the Louisville & Nashville Railroad has thus not been alone a history of the acquisition of other roads, of the construction of new lines, or of the developing of cities and industries. Its story is also the story of the gradual evolution of the steam engine, its replacement by the diesel and, more broadly, of the development and improvement of the freight and passenger train from northernmost tip of cowcatcher to southernmost tip of caboose, or observation car, as the case might be. Closely paralleling this development has been the one of the railroad track and its various adjuncts.

Perhaps the greatest change in the L. & N.'s physical plant occurred during the two decades or so that followed the close of the War Between the States. It is perhaps unnecessary to describe the external aspects of an L. & N. passenger train of that era. The wooden coaches, the small engine with its more than generous portion of smokestack and cow-catcher, and all the rest of it, are familiar to us all. The interior of the typical coach of the 'sixties deserves extended mention, however. Once within the average day coach the traveler was confronted with almost Spartan simplicity. The seats made no concession to comfort, being austere and uncompromisingly straight. The Victorian fecundity of ornamentation which was later to bedazzle the eye was still a number of years distant.

These earlier coaches were lighted by candles and a big headache of the L. & N.'s purchasing department of the day was the procuring of candles which would burn satisfactorily and give the road its money's worth. Heat was supplied by large stoves placed at each end of the coach and on cold days the passengers had an understakable tendency to congregate around these dispensers of warmth. Since the vestibuled coach had not yet come into use, each opening of the door brought in a generous blast of cold air from the outside.

Water was carried in tanks suspended beneath the coaches and whenever a passenger had a desire to remove some of the grime of travel he elevated this water up into a basin by means of a hand pump. And should he be otherwise urged he could avail himself of facilities which were extremely simple, but which afforded a fine view of the roadbed beneath.

The evolution of passenger equipment on the L. & N. **Top:** This woodburner, complete with wooden coaches, makes a stop at the woodyard, Livingston, Ky., in 1870. **Second from top:** This open-vestibule passenger train was more or less standard on the L. & N. in the 1900s. **Third from top:** The stream-lined Dixie Flagler, a pride of the L. & N. in the 1940s. **Bottom:** The Humming Bird of the 1960s — sleek and shining.

Freight equipment, understandably, has shown a considerable evolution in the past 100 years. **Left:** Various types of freight cars in the yards at Nashville during the Civil War. **Right:** Many "Cushioned Cargo" boxcars, of 100-ton capacity, were added to the Louisville & Nashville's rails in the 1960s.

Along about 1868, however, progress began to invade the precincts of the day coach. Hot water heaters replaced some of the stoves, ornate kerosene lamps took the place of candles and a gravity-principle water system was made possible by providing overhead tanks for the water supply.

Then, in 1887, and for a number of years thereafter, several American railroads, including the L. & N., tentatively experimented with the application of a narrow enclosed vestibule to passenger coaches. This had certain impracticable features and was not wholly successful, and, in 1893, a wide vestibule, somewhat similar to that in use today, was first applied. An anti-telescoping feature was incorporated in the wide vestibule, and is still an important feature in passenger car construction. The L. & N. gradually adopted this type of coach, it eventually becoming standard equipment, although a few of the old "open-air" type were still in service at so recent a date as World War II.

Gas lighting made its bow in 1887, along with the heating of coaches by steam, the latter being generously supplied by the locomotive ahead. These, too, were gradually adopted by the L. & N., and just about the time they had completely replaced their predecessors, i.e., the kerosene lamps and the hot water heaters of one sort or another, they, in turn, were brushed aside by the march of progress. In 1899, the first axle generators and storage battery systems for car-lighting came into use and in 1903 the heating of coaches was first done by what is known as the vapor system of steam heating. The basic principle of this system is that it converts the locomotive's high pressure steam to steam at atmospheric pressure. It thus affords a relief from the uncontrollable high temperatures generated by pressure steam and eliminates the hazards of scalding, which was always a possibility with high pressure heating due to broken pipes and connections. A number of improvements have been made on the original patent since 1903, one of the most important of these being the thermostatic control of vapor heating, which was introduced in the early 1920s.

In the meantime, the method of supplying water to the coaches had also undergone a change. Air pressure water systems were first installed in 1893 and were modified and improved as they continued in use.

That passenger-car comfort and design continued to improve was evidenced by air conditioning and streamlining, two radical innovations of the 1930s. Several streamlined passenger cars made their bows upon the L. & N. in that era; many more made their appearance in 1946 with the inauguration of The Humming Bird and The Georgian. Air conditioning was introduced upon the L. & N. in May 1934 and within the next seven years $1 million was so spent on 150 coaches and diners.

So much for the improvements in the passenger coach most apt to be noticed by the casual passenger. There were a number of more important mechanical changes which took place, many of these involving the passenger coach, either directly or indirectly. Outstanding, of course, was the gradual emergence of the all-steel car. The typical L. & N. passenger coach of 1870, or thereabouts, was about 50 feet long, ten feet wide and seven feet high. It was built entirely of wood, weighed about 50,000 pounds and seated 60 persons. The various improvements that were made in connection with the passenger coach at first tended to increase its weight and, of course, the change from wood to steel construction contributed substantially to this trend. In the early days, the wheels of the passenger coach were about the only part of it that were made of metal. These were of cast iron and it was 1879 before steel-tired wheels replaced the less durable ones of cast iron. Shortly before that time trucks with six wheels replaced those with four wheels and in 1900 some experimentation

At right, top: This 100-ton capacity, quick-unloading coal hopper can be unloaded in less than one-half a minute. **Bottom:** Bulkhead flatcars, such as this one, have proven very effective in the handling of lumber, tube, panels, piping, poles and brick. Each made its bow upon the L. & N. in the 1960s. Coal hopper was built at L. & N.'s own South Louisville Shops; bulkhead flat by Thrall.

Coach travel by rail has changed greatly since the days of the war between the States. **Left:** Unionists on their way to prison camp under Confederate guard. This graphically depicts the Spartan simplicity of the average day coach of that era. **Center:** A day coach interior of the Gay Nineties. Note the oil lamps and the elaborately ornamented ceiling. **Right:** Daycoach travel on the L. & N. in the 1960s was made in air-conditioned comfort amid pleasant surroundings.

was done with all-steel under-framing. This type of construction was gradually adopted and the first all-steel cars followed in 1908 as a natural outgrowth of the trend to increase the safety of travel by rail. The use of the solid wrought steel wheel in place of the cast iron wheel with the steel tire was first commenced in 1912.

The L. & N., following a long-established practice of immediately utilizing worthwhile and practical innovations, placed its first all-steel coaches in service in 1913, and thereafter gradually retired the obsolete wooden ones.

The passage of the Federal Safety Appliance Act in 1893 made it mandatory for all railroads to equip their trains with automatic couplers and automatic air brakes. As has been previously mentioned, the link-and-pin method of coupling cars together was the one most generally used prior to the invention of the automatic coupler, although some experimentation had been done with a combination of vertical hooks and links. The latter, however, was not generally satisfactory and the link-and-pin method was most widely used. This latter was simplicity itself, although responsible for a number of four-and-even-lesser-fingered brakemen, since it obviously did not operate automatically. Both the link and the pin were removable and a lack of uniformity in height of the holders for the links, called "drawbars," increased the danger to the brakeman.

The evolution from simple link and pin to patented automatic coupler varied widely on each railroad and it has been stated that at one time more than a thousand different types of "Lincoln pin" couplers were in use in this country. As indicated, the passage of the Federal Safety Appliance Act hastened this evolution. Prior to its passage the various individual railroads had made some progress with automatic couplers of one sort or another and the Louisville & Nashville had experimentally applied a few of the Janney type, which radically revised previous concepts of car coupling. It was an improved version of this device which was later adopted by the L. & N.

Much of the credit for the development of a practical and efficient automatic coupler belongs to the Master Car Builders' Association, formed in 1867, as does indeed comparable credit for the development and standardization of passenger and freight cars and their parts. In 1885, this Association authorized a public trial of 42 of the over 3,000 couplers for which patents had been issued. As a result, the Janney type, with the swinging knuckle, was finally selected. By 1902, all L. & N. rolling stock was equipped with automatic couplers.

Air brakes made their appearance upon the L. & N. somewhat earlier than the automatic couplers and the record shows that the Company made its initial purchase of straight air brake equipment in 1871. Prior to that time all brakes on all L. & N. rolling stock were set by hand. In cold or rainy weather brakemen generally carried a supply of salt or sand to improve their traction on the icy or slippery tops of the freight cars, and many a brakeman was "grounded" permanently because he lost his footing. The job thus called for a keen eye, an iron nerve and a nimble foot and when the engineer whistled for "brakes!" the brakeman (there were generally three to each freight train, which in those days only averaged about 18 cars) had to concentrate a lot of hard and dangerous work within a comparatively short time.

The L. & N.'s experience with the air brake, reduced to the dry statistics, reads as follows: 26 sets of straight air brake equipment for locomotives and 94 sets for cars were purchased in 1871, only two years after George Westinghouse, "the damn fool who thinks he can stop a train with air," had brought forth his invention, and in December 1880, the first automatic air brake equipment was purchased and installed. Thereafter, the L. & N. adopted the various improvements and refinements

Below, left: Most rolling stock was coupled together by the link-and-pin method before the advent of the automatic coupler. The switchman was forced to stand between the rails so as to guide the link into the opposing slot. **Bottom, right:** Close-up of the modern-day coupler. Couplers are securely fastened together upon impact of the cars.

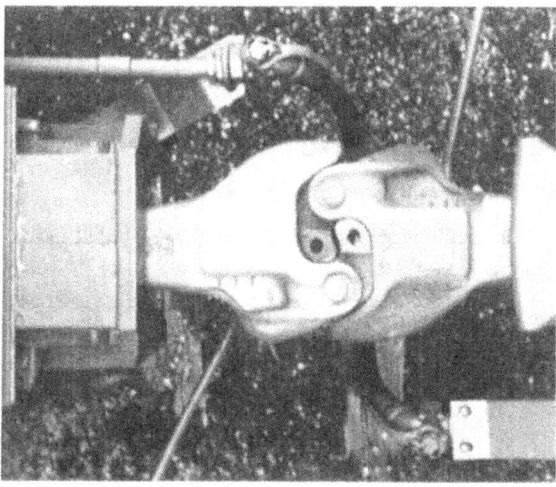

of the device as they were made available, and by 1914 all of its rolling stock was equipped with this boon to the safe and efficient operation of trains. Although it was thus 1914 before complete uniformity was achieved, as early as 1905 all of its rolling stock, with the exception of 4.06 per cent of its freight car ownership, was equipped with air brakes.

In order that L. & N. employes might be made thoroughly familiar with the workings and principle of air brake equipment, the Westinghouse Company sent an instruction car over the lines of the L. & N. in the year 1893. This proved so worthwhile that subsequently, in 1899, the L. & N. fitted up a similar car of its own in its old shops at Tenth and Kentucky streets, Louisville, and sent it over the System in charge of the late Frank Sherman, who pioneered in air brake instruction on this railroad. For many years Mr. Sherman and his car, No. 360, were a familiar sight along the line of road and thousands of employes learned the mysteries of the air brake under his tutelage.

The evolution of the freight car, of which there are some "57 varieties," has been as pronounced as that of the passenger car, but was not as spectacular until the 1950s and 1960s. The first freight cars were understandably crude affairs and the term "boxcar" adequately described them, but from the very first railroad men seemed to have realized that different commodities required different types of transport. Thus, on the L. & N., the early Annual Reports of the 1850s, even before the road was completed to Nashville, make frequent mention of such types as "rack, platform, boarding, hand dump, stone and sawyer (wood) cars." They were of wooden construction and even as recently as the 'eighties had very small capacities, 10 or 15 tons being about the average. Their evolution into the all-steel boxcars of today with capacities ranging from 50 to 100 tons, has thus been highlighted by a constant decrease in the amount of wood used in their construction and its replacement by iron, steel or aluminum and by a constant enlarging of their capacities. This evolution, both strengthened the car and greatly reduced the loss and damage of freight. The accompanying increase in its load capacity greatly enhanced the railroad's ability to handle the available traffic in an efficient manner.

(It is not known when the first hobo made his initial appearance upon an American railroad, but it must have been well before 1874, which is the year when steel or iron was first used in the underframes of freight cars. Such construction signified the beginning of the end of the practice of "riding the rods," i.e., the steel rods which were placed beneath the cars to strengthen the wooden underframing. When steel underframing was used, there was no place for the hobo to rest his weary head beneath the car.)

The freight car with the steel-framed superstructure did not come into use until around 1908, but was not long in proving its worth. At that time the L. & N. was manufacturing a goodly part of its motive power and rolling stock at its South Louisville Shops and subsequently, in 1914, a modern steel car shop at South Louisville for the construction and repair of steel passenger and freight cars was built.

Two outstanding varieties of freight cars are the tank car and the refrigerator car and, oddly enough, these have been in use, in one form or another, almost since the dawn of railroading. The railroads were anx-

Coke-container cars were also an innovation of the 1960s. Gondolas were equipped with 11 separate containers (each of 300-feet capacity), which are lifted out of car by crane.

ious to prove that they could excel the canal boats and the wagon freighters at anything and everything in the way of hauling freight and the refrigerator car afforded them an excellent opportunity to show what they could do with the handling of perishables, a type of traffic which the canal boats and freighters aforesaid had handled gingerly, if at all, depending upon the comparative perishable nature of the product. One of the first "refrigerator" cars consisted merely of a boxcar with several goodish-sized chunks of ice placed on a platform in its interior. No attention at all was paid to such factors as insulation, air circulation, etc. Somewhat later, or in 1857, some experimentation was done with a boxcar with double sides and floors, the interstices being packed with sawdust to provide insulation. Ice, placed in a large box which was positioned in the doorway after loading, provided the refrigeration. The familiar arrangement of installing ice bunkers in the ends of the cars was not introduced until about 1871, although the first patent for a refrigerator car was obtained in 1867.

The arrangement of ice bunkers, once accepted and improved, proved to be the answer to the handling of perishables and revolutionized the eating habits of a nation, creating greater markets for the farmer, packer and grower and a more abundant life for ultimate consumers everywhere.

The insulated, bunkerless refrigerator car made its appearance in the early 1960s, operating on somewhat the same principle as the electric refrigerator.

The tank car has also been around for quite a while and has come a long way from the crude affairs of yesteryear, which consisted of wooden or steel tanks cradled on the top of the flat cars to which they were more or less securely fastened. Most of the tank cars of today are privately-owned and while most of them are used in the transportation of oil and gasoline, a great number are also used for handling milk, molasses, vinegar, tar, acid and various other liquids.

There are, of course, many other types of freight cars, other than those specifically mentioned and the L. & N.'s ownership also includes stock cars (first introduced in 1861), automobile cars, gondolas, hoppers, flats, dump cars, pulpwood cars, chipwood cars, depressed-center flats and covered hoppers.

For many years, the 50-ton boxcars or hoppers were the largest owned by the L. & N., but they lost that distinction in the postwar era. In 1954, for instance, 250 specially-designed hopper cars, of 95-ton capacity, were obtained for the moving of Venezuelan iron ore from the Port of Mobile to U. S. Steel at Birmingham. Shortly thereafter, the 70-ton hopper also became a principal workhorse of the L. & N.'s fleet for the moving of bituminous coal. The first 2,000 of these were bought from Pullman-Standard in 1957-1958 and an additional 3,000 were delivered in 1959 by the same manufacturer.

The L. & N. also had a number of 70-ton covered hoppers, used for the handling of such commodities as talc, dry phosphate rock, alumina and the like, and of 70-ton gondolas used for handling both steel and coal. In 1957, the L. & N. placed in service its first DF ("Damage Free") boxcars and its first Airslide cars, the latter being especially adapted to haul such bulk commodities as flour and sugar. TOTE, or Trailer-On-Train-Express, later known as piggyback, requires specially-outfitted flatcars and trailers.

As mentioned in Chapter 40 – "Into the Space Age" – the early 1960s witnessed further revolutionary change in the L. & N.'s freight-car fleet. That era was featured by the introduction of the bi- and tri-level auto rack car, the 100-ton fast-unloading hopper car, the 70- or 100-ton "Boca Grande" covered hopper, with its full-length longitudinal through-hatch on top, the bulkhead flatcar, the 100-ton, 60-foot "Cushioned Cargo" boxcar, the coke-carrying gondola, with its separate containers, the two-story (built-up) open-top hopper, for handling wood chips, the 70-ton (10,000 cubic foot capacity) 86½ foot jumbo boxcars, and many another freight car especially adapted for the hauling of soil pipe, coiled steel, pitch, plate glass or a host of other commodities.

APPENDIX II

"Varnish" Train Ensemble

PASSENGER train equipment, of course, includes many items of rolling stock other than the passenger coach discussed in a previous installment, notably the dining car, the railway mail post office, the baggage and express car and the Pullman.

Let's take these up for some detailed discussion in the order of their listing. Thus, we deal first with the dining car, which is a fairly late arrival on the lines of the L. & N. The record shows that the Railroad's dining car department came into existence in 1901. In that year the Company purchased three dining cars from the Pullman Company and these were subsequently placed in service in October. Prior to this time some meals had been served on Pullmans but it had been the usual practice to provide meals for patrons by stopping trains at certain established stations long enough for passengers to appease their hunger at a restaurant located in or near the station. As a matter of fact, this practice was continued to a limited extent, with certain trains, even as late as the 1940s.

The first dining cars purchased, which were of wooden construction, and each of which had a seating capacity of 30, were placed in service between Lebanon Junction and Cincinnati on Nos. 4, 7, 8 and 1 and between Birmingham and New Orleans on Nos. 1 and 4. L. M. Hill, formerly with the Chicago and Eastern Illinois Railroad in the same capacity, was the first superintendent of dining cars. Some 56,908 meals were served on L. & N. diners in the department's first year of existence, with a resulting revenue of $47,425.34. These cars were manned by a steward, two white cooks and three waiters.

The L. & N. subsequently purchased, or built in its own shops at South Louisville, a number of other diners, chiefly during 1906, 1913,

At **left** is interior view of L. & N. dining car in use in the 1900s. At **right** is scene in diner-lounge car obtained by the L. & N. in 1960.

This stainless steel R.P.O. car was placed in The Crescent in March 1950.

1915 and the decade of the 'twenties. The Company's first all-steel diner – No. 2700 – was acquired in 1914 and all diners subsequently obtained were of all-steel construction. Commencing with the acquisition of No. 2707 in 1921, the seating capacity was standardized at 36 persons. (Following the inauguration of the country's National Defense program in 1940, a few of the diners were changed so that they could accommodate 48 people at one time. They were used when there was a large movement of selectees, soldiers, sailors and marines, etc., traveling over our lines and served regular meals to as many as 200 persons in about three hours' time.)

The cafeteria car has also been an item of L. & N. rolling stock on various occasions in the past and was used on the road during World War I. A complete meal was served cafeteria-style in such cars to troops carrying their own mess kits and the food available was not confined to sandwiches, pies and the like. Thousands of doughboys were served in this manner. Shortly after the inauguration of the dining car department in 1901, four cafe cars (Nos. 1013, 1014, 1015 and 1016) were placed in service. Such cars were very popular during their brief existence on our lines (they were converted into diners in 1905) and were generally used in accommodating travel to and from the Louisiana Purchase Exposition, held at St. Louis, Mo., during the greater part of 1904. They were similar to the buffet cars now in operation on many American railroads.

At the end of 1963, the L. & N. had 15 all-steel dining cars; also seven tavern-lounge cars, all of which were air conditioned. Ten diners and four of the tavern-lounge cars were in regular service, the other cars being used for special service and relief purposes. Five of the diners were 48-seat and the remainder 36-seat.

The number of meals served in L. & N. diners fluctuates from year to year, of course, and is an index to the national economic picture. In 1943, during World War II, a total of 2,380,547 meals was served, with revenues amounting to $2,701,794.49 At that time, every dining car available was placed in use to take care of the heavy demands of the different branches of military service. In 1958, for instance, only 352,154 meals were served, with revenue amounting to $893,344.74.

In October 1957 rolling buffet service was inaugurated on the Memphis Line Section of The Pan-American. The rolling buffet was designed for more economical operation on trains not heavily patronized, as it can be operated from one of the coaches, eliminating one car, as well as terminal expense. Coffee, milk, sandwiches and comparable items are peddled from the cart which is taken through the coaches by an attendant. Coach service, consisting of coffee, sandwiches, milk, etc., served by waiters, was also available on other trains.

In the latter part of 1959, the L. & N. obtained two diner-lounge cars from the Chicago and Eastern Illinois Railroad. After considerable modernization and renovation these were placed in service on The Pan-American between Cincinnati and Montgomery in the early part of 1960. Each of these cars had 28 seats in the diner section and 18 seats in the lounge section, with a bar serving as a divider. They specialized in serving beverages, full-fledged meals and snacks for the traveler who was watching his calories or who just didn't "feel real hungry" and operated with a somewhat smaller crew than the standard diner.

L. & N. diners, throughout the years, have gained quite a reputation for their food and service. Old Hickory Smoked Country Ham, cured especially for the L. & N.

Left: Interior and exterior views of the first railway post office car, which made its initial trip on August 28, 1864, between Chicago and Clinton, Ia., on the C. & N. W. Ry. Below: Interior views showing both ends of an R. P. O. car operated by L. & N. in the 1950s.

on a farm in Kentucky, attracted an unusually large following.

A diner's kitchen is a miracle of compact efficiency and this, too, has evolved with the times. Every inch of space is utilized to the best advantage and, although the space is not as large as the kitchen in the average home, and is shared by the chef and one or two cooks, the food is expertly prepared within its narrow confines.

In March 1957, the L. & N. completed a program of modernizing its diners, including the kitchens, and most of the latter were equipped with gas ranges and mechanical refrigeration. Prior to that time, these kitchens had coal-burning ranges and broilers and coffee urns using charcoal.

The dining car crew, on a heavy run, will consist of a steward, a chef, two cooks, a pantryman and four waiters. Each diner is stocked with approximately 1,000 napkins and 325 table cloths and the value of each diner's silverware, glassware, chinaware, kitchenware, linens and other fittings was approximately $4,000, based on prices prevailing at the end of 1963.

Much money is invested, too, in the Company's commissary department which keeps the diners and tavern-lounge cars stocked with a large variety of provisions, liquors, soft drinks, beverages, cigars and cigarettes and which also furnishes replacements of linen, silverware and other items as needed.

L. & N. diners, throughout the years, have had as guests several presidents of the United States, as well as high-ranking dignitaries from foreign lands. Many celebrities partake of L. & N. dining-car cuisine on their visits to the Kentucky Derby and the extra or "standby" diners are always pressed into service to accommodate the heavy travel to and from this famous sporting event.

One postwar development in dining-car modus operandi was the providing of dormitory cars for dining car crews when the tours of duty involve overnight travel. At the end of 1963 there were three straight dormitory cars in the L. & N.'s ownership and three combination dormitory-baggage cars.

The Railway Post Office

The records are rather obstinately obscure as to the exact date of the operation of the first railway post office car over the lines of the L. & N. At the onset, of course, a distinction should be made between the **railway post office car** and a car used simply for carrying mail. The records show that as early as 1858 the L. & N. entered into a contract with the U. S. Government for the transportation of mails at the flat rate of $100 per mile per annum, weight or quantity not entering into this original agreement. At this time, a stage coach line collaborated with the railroad in carrying the mail between Louisville and Nashville, the latter's line between these two cities having not as yet been completed.

Railway Mail Service, as such, did not make its bow until 1864 and prior to that time no worthwhile attempt was made to utilize a railroad car as a branch of the post office, it being regarded almost solely as a medium for the **transportation** of the mail. For instance, the mail

At Right, Top: Engine No. 7, complete with the type of baggage car used prior to the turn of the century. **Center:** Loading a baggage car at Louisville in the 1920s. **Bottom:** Interior of a steel, 3-door baggage and express car sometimes used for horses.

for the towns along the L. & N. between Louisville and Nashville would be placed in the mail car of a certain train and this would be sorted on the car en route and put off at the various stations. However, no attempt was made to sort the mail which was destined for points beyond Louisville or Nashville. Such mail was consigned to certain designated post offices, known as "distributing post offices" and was there sorted and re-forwarded. Thus, mail originating in the South or Middle West and consigned to New England points might pass through two or more distributing post offices. The postal clerk at point of origin noting a letter's destination, in accordance with existing instructions, would place it with others headed that way and mail the lot to Pittsburgh. At Pittsburgh, all this mail would be distributed and re-forwarded, with some of it being again distributed and reforwarded upon arrival at New York. Such a procedure, obviously, greatly delayed the mail and was an expensive one.

As stated, Railway Mail Service made its bow in 1864 and was inaugurated shortly thereafter on the lines of the L. & N. The theory of Railway Mail Service, as intimated, was that sorting or distribution could be done on the train **en route** and it was designed and executed to do just

Railway Express Agency operations at Louisville, here shown, are typical of those in the many large cities served. Motor vehicles, for intracity pickup and delivery, team up with railroad rolling stock and motive power, to offer convenient and reliable service for handling of shipments.

that in the most efficient and expeditious manner possible. Such a radical departure involved a corresponding change in the design and construction of railroad cars used in the carrying of U. S. Mail and at first the L. & N., in common with other American railroads, merely re-modeled certain cars already on hand. Such makeshifts proved increasingly unsatisfactory, however, with the amount of mail handled increasing each year. The records show that the L. & N. placed its first postal cars in service in 1869, these being three in number. These were undoubtedly made-over cars, fitted out with the requisite racks, pouches, pigeon-holes, etc., to handle the required sorting. Early day postal cars were known by name instead of number and the records contain mention of the "Kentucky," "Nashville," "Memphis," "Evansville," "Louisville," "Columbia," and many others. By the turn of the century the L. & N. had 66 full postal and R.P.O. apartment cars in service.

At the end of 1963, postal clerk service was being performed on a number of L. & N. trains, including practically all through trains. It is estimated that at that time postal clerks were distributing or re-distributing over one million pieces of mail of all sorts (letters, newspapers, parcel post) per day on L. & N. trains alone.

The L. & N.'s ownership then embraced 22 full 60-foot all-steel railway post office cars (including six acquired at the time of the N. C. & St. L. merger) and 30 R. P. O. apartment cars with 40- or 30-foot compartments for the distribution of mail. All the R. P. O. cars were all-steel construction. Two of the 60-foot R. P. O. cars mentioned were stainless steel, streamlined cars especially built for service in The Crescent. These cars, Nos. 1120 and 1121, actually have an inside length of 81 feet, each having a 21-foot baggage apartment, in addition to the 60-foot R. P. O. apartment.

Several of the railway post office cars were built at the Company's own South Louisville Shops. After 1912, however, all such cars were purchased and were of all-steel construction. With the exception of Nos. 1120 and 1121, which were built by Pullman-Standard, these were obtained from the American Car and Foundry Company.

The Express and Baggage Car

The railway express or baggage car, although operated as passenger train equipment, is, in reality, another variety of the freight car. This is rather self-evident when its particular function is examined. When used as an express car, for instance, it handles less-than-carload freight for which an expedited handling is required and when used for baggage it transports the individual "freight" of the passengers, i.e., trunks, suitcases, boxes, etc.

The baggage car has been an item of L. & N. rolling stock since the first train was run and its function has changed very little since that time. It has evolved in the same manner as the passenger coach, the passing years having seen its wood gradually replaced by steel and a gradual increase in its capacity.

At the end of 1963, the L. & N. had some 160 straight baggage or express cars (excluding partitioned cars).

While there are several different varieties of the railway express car, such as the box express, the horse car and the refrigerator car used in the handling of perishables, etc., which are used exclusively for express, the type most commonly encountered on the lines of the L. & N. is the baggage or express car previously mentioned, which is generally 70 feet long and is of all-steel construction.

The express business in this country has an interesting history and its highlights are perhaps familiar to most of us. It progressed from a carpet handbag, carried for certain patrons by an obliging railway conductor, to an extensive use of canal boat, stage coach, pony express and railroad alike, and finally, in the 20th Century to the utilization of the airplane. At first many companies were attracted to this field by its possibilities, but by the beginning of 1918, their number had been reduced to seven, of which four, Adams, American, Southern and Wells-Fargo & Company, operated over 92 per cent of the existing railroad mileage and transacted about 95 per cent of the business done annually. The Adams and Southern express companies operated over the lines of the L. & N. under a joint contract whereby our railroad agreed to carry their packages, etc., for a certain stipulated compensation. The records show that one of the L. & N.'s first express contracts was executed with the Adams Express Company on July 1, 1865, superseding the "Army Freight Line" which was operated over our line by the Adams people between Louisville and Nashville during the War between the States. The Army Freight Line used its own express cars. The contract called for the L. & N. to

Old-time print showing interior of a sleeping-car in use on lines of New York Central in 1869.

furnish the Express Company with an express car on each of its daily passenger trains between the two cities last mentioned for the transportation of "express goods, merchandise and smalls," and provided for the accommodation of express shipments in the baggage cars of trains operating over the road's branches.

Subsequently, a contract was entered into jointly between the L. & N. and the Adams and Southern express companies on December 28, 1880, which gave these latter companies the privilege of handling express shipments over the Railroad's lines. The two companies divided the L. & N.'s express business between them; Adams continued to handle the traffic on the original main line (Louisville to Nashville) and on branches in Kentucky, Tennessee, Indiana and Illinois, while the Southern did the same for lines south of Nashville. (Prior to the execution of this contract the Company handled the express business itself on its road south of Nashville and under the terms of the 1880 contract sold all of its wagons, safes, horses, etc., used in the conduct of such business, to the Southern.)

The contract just mentioned, with some modification from time to time, continued substantially in effect until the inception of Government ownership during World War I, at which time the express transportation services of the seven companies before mentioned were merged into the American Railway Express Company which began operation on July 1, 1918. It was succeeded on March 1, 1929, by the Railway Express Agency, Inc., a joint facility of all the railroads of this country. In 1960, its name was changed to REA Express.

Railroad's Land of Nod - The Pullman

Probably no single innovation so revolutionized travel by rail as the introduction of the sleeping car. It greatly increased its possibilities and blazed the trail in comforts subsequently to be adopted by other types of passenger train equipment.

Outstandingly, it made possible the operation of equipment from one line to another, without the necessity of the passenger changing cars en route. All this, of course, did not happen overnight.

When railroads first appeared on the American scene and for some few years thereafter, the theory of rail travel was to get the traveler between point of origin and destination without visible damage or destruction. His comfort en route was purely incidental and most railroads were smugly complacent about accomplishing the feat at all. Of course, people have slept in railroad cars since the very dawn of railroading, but at first they did so at their own risk and with no assistance from the management. The records show that George M. Pullman, whose name has since come to be synonymous with the railroad sleeping car, was not the first and hence not the only citizen to have the idea of a railroad car adapted to the slumber of its passengers. As early as 1836 the Cumberland Valley Railroad (of Pennsylvania) proudly placed a sleeping car at the disposal of its public. This was a made-over coach and would almost suffer by comparison with one of the L. & N.'s present-day cattle cars. Four compartments, each containing three bunks, were positioned on each side of the coach. Mattresses were furnished, but other bed clothing was not and the patrons went to bed and awoke fully clothed. Many other railroads soon copied the idea and some furnished bed clothing, but because of failure to launder it occasionally the results were not entirely satisfactory.

In 1859, George M. Pullman, who was in the cabinet-making business with his brother, introduced the first sleeping cars roughly corresponding with those of the present day. At that time he remodeled two coaches of the Chicago & Alton, Nos. 8 and 19, both 44-footers, incorporating many new ideas of his own, then deemed radical, into such reconstruction. For instance, he introduced his idea of an upper berth, constructed so that it might be closed during the daytime and used as a receptacle for bed clothing. It was suspended by an elaborate arrangement of ropes and pulleys. The lower berths were so constructed that an adjustment or two changed them into comfortable seats and vice versa. It was the first serious attempt to utilize a car both as a sleeping car and a coach for comfortable daytime travel. In common with their contemporaries these first Pullmans were heated by wood-burning stoves and were lighted by candles. There were 10 uppers and 10 lowers in each car.

During the troubled years of the War between the States, Mr. Pullman perfected his plans for a

Top: Interior of "The Pioneer," first all-Pullman built car. Center: The interior of Pullman car "Titania," typical of elaborate decoration of 1880s. Bottom: Interior of Pullman which was standard in sleeping car service for many years. In postwar era it was replaced by Pullmans with bedrooms, roomettes and sections.

more modern Pullman car and one that would be built new from the ground up. Such a car was completed in 1865, its total cost, including fittings, etc., being in the neighborhood of $20,000. This car was called "The Pioneer" and Mr. Pullman, cannily looking ahead to the future, added the serial letter "A" in confident expectation that others of its ilk would soon be forthcoming. Like many trail-blazers, Mr. Pullman could not adequately foresee a future which would outstrip his wildest dreams and which would contain some 8,000 (1940) Pullman cars, whose naming alone would constitute somewhat of a problem. In later years and particularly just before World War II, Pullmans were named so as to have some identity with the railroads over which they operated or the territories served. Thus, at one time or another, cars were assigned to the L. & N. with such names as "Milton H. Smith," "John James Audubon," "Stephen Collins Foster," "Sidney Lanier," "George Rogers Clark," and "James Guthrie."

Top: Exterior view of one of 22 "Pine" sleepers placed in service by the L. & N. in 1953. (They were so termed as each was named after a species of pine found in L. & N. territory. Three others were obtained following N. C. & St. L. merger.) Each had six sections, four bedrooms and six roomettes. Botton, left: The double bedroom (resulting from operation of folding-sliding partition when it was desirable to combine bedrooms) was easily made ready for nighttime occupancy. Convenient ladder provided easy access to upper bed. Bottom right: Bedrooms were just as easily re-converted to daytime occupancy, permitting the occupant to get much more work done enroute.

Interior of a Pullman parlor car in use in 1876.

"The Pioneer-A" was a foot wider and two and one-half feet higher (because of its hinged upper berth) than any passenger car in service and many clearances along the line of road had to be changed to permit its passage. This car was soon followed by other Pullmans, these being changed and improved from time to time and the first vestibuled sleeping car was placed in service in 1888. Both the dining car and the parlor car were offshoots of the sleeping car idea.

At first Pullman did not monopolize the sleeping car field, but his competitors were subsequently absorbed by his organization. These competitors, of one era or another, whose very names have now been almost forgotten, included the Gates Sleeping Car Company, the New York Central Sleeping Car Company, John B. Anderson & Company, Paine Harris & Company, the Wagner Palace Car Company, the Monarch Sleeping Car Company, the Knight Cars, the Woodruff Sleeping and Parlor Coach Company, and the Mann Boudoir Car Company. Many of these came into existence subsequent to the close of the War between the States and all flourished but a comparatively short time, absorbing each other and in turn being absorbed by the Pullman Company prior to the beginning of the Twentieth Century.

The records show that John B. Anderson & Company entered into a contract with the L. & N. on September 2, 1864, for the operation of sleeping cars over its lines. This contract was later transferred to Paine Harris & Company, and was subsequently superseded by a contract entered into between the L. & N. and the Pullman Southern Car Company (just then organized) on June 19, 1872. Under the terms of this latter contract the Pullman Southern Car Company took over all of the physical assets of Paine Harris & Company and its numerous affiliates (E. H. Paine & Co., Paine Wang & Co., Paine & Co., Inc.) consisting of some 18 sleeping cars and an interest in two others. Paine Harris' operating company was known as the Crescent City Sleeping Car Company and had such privileges over the lines of the L. & N. and one or two other railroads. The Crescent City Sleeping Car Company was the result of the amalgamation of the Harris Sleeping Car Company, the aptly named Rip Van Winkle Sleeping Car Company and the Paine, Wang and Shelton Sleeping Car Company, all of which were controlled by E. H. Paine, a sleeping car tycoon of the day. The contract mentioned gave the Pullman Southern Car Company the exclusive drawing room or parlor and sleeping car privileges on the lines of the L. & N. for a period of 15 years.

Interesting eye-witness descriptions of the old Rip Van Winkle sleeping cars have been left by former employes of that company. In the daytime passengers faced each other upon longitudinal sofas. At night, the sofa became the lower berth, its lowered cushioned back permitting double occupancy. A partially permanent partition separated the sofas by day and this was made a complete headboard at night by extracting from under the cushions a hinged portion that made a solid wall. There were also upper and center berths, but these were for single occupancy only. The porter pulled out the center berth from **above** the upper berth, which was hinged, and the former was held in position by slots in the uprights that supported the curtain rods between sections. Both of these berths were "staggered" with relation to each other and the lower berth and it was thus possible for the occupant of each berth to partially see his neighbors. Thus, the center berth was positioned above the half of the lower berth next to the car aisle while the upper berth was above the half of the lower berth next to the side of the car. The conductors of that day insisted that the occupants of the three levels invariably minded their own business.

The Pullman Southern Car Company was subsequently amalgamated with Pullman's Palace Car Company in 1882 and the latter, in turn, was succeeded by The Pullman Company in 1899, following the acquisition of the Wagner Palace Car Company.

For many years thereafter The Pullman Company operated practically all of the sleeping cars on American railroads. Then, in 1949, Pullman, Inc., had to "divorce" itself from the sleeping-car business and the stock of The Pullman Company was acquired by a number of the nation's major railroads, including the L. & N. As a result of this, the Railroad acquired 57 conventional-weight sleeping cars on July 1, 1949.

In the 1950s, however, this conventional-type sleeper, usually with one drawing room and 12 sections (12 uppers and 12 lowers), began to be replaced with sleepers which offered the traveler a wider choice of accommodations – bedroom, roomette or section. In 1953, the L. & N. itself placed in service 22 lightweight sleepers, each containing six sections, four double bedrooms and six roomettes. Three others were obtained through the N. C. & St. L. merger in 1957.

Appendix III

L & N Motive Power

THE old Lexington & Ohio (later to become a part of the L. & N.) after experimentation with both steam engines and horses as motive power, finally decided that the latter were more satisfactory and reliable. The L. & N. itself never used horses as motive power.

The records show that the L. & N. purchased its first locomotives from Niles and Company, of Cincinnati, in July 1855. These were two in number and were of the 4-4-0 type with driving wheels 60 inches in diameter. They were a vast improvement over the first locomotives to appear on the American scene 25 years earlier.

Prior to the completion of the line between Louisville and Nashville in 1859 other locomotives had been obtained in September 1856 from Fairbanks, of Taunton, Mass.; in September 1857, from Moore & Richardson, of Cincinnati, and in June and October 1858, from M. W. Baldwin. The Baldwin locomotives were five in number and, as a gesture of appreciation to certain counties and individuals, who had contributed so much to the road's success, they were named as follows: "James Guthrie," then vice-president of the road; "Sumner" and "Davidson," after the counties in Tennessee; "Warren County" (in Kentucky) and "George MacLeod," then chief engineer of the L. & N. The six engines previously obtained had been similarly designated and this practice of honoring individuals or localities by naming locomotives for them was continued for a few years. L. & N. engines were also assigned numbers, of course, from the very first.

The five Baldwin engines were small, weighing only about 40,000 pounds and, with the exception of the "Sumner," their wheel arrangement corresponded to the C or B class switch engines long used on the L. & N. (See accompanying chart) The "Sumner" was a 4-4-0 type and its wheel arrangement was similar to the Class D engines, of which, as recently as 1941, only five were in service. The tender had eight wheels and each tank had a capacity of only 1,500 gallons of water. Cabs were of walnut wood and the engines were decorated with much brass work and fancy painting. Their innards were quite different from those found in the L. & N.'s latter-day locomotives and externally, too, they bore little resemblance. The stack was of the so-called "Yankee" pattern, shaped like a truncated cone and was a little over seven feet tall and six feet in diameter at the top. The opening at the top was covered with a wire-netting to serve as a spark arrester.

No. 8 was built by Baldwin in 1858, had flexible-beam truck, was named Davidson. Engine was used in construction, freight service, wound up career as yard switcher.

Moore & Richardson delivered No. 20 to L. & N. in 1859. Engine was taken south by Rebels in Civil War, was recovered in 1865. No. 20 was passenger engine with 66-inch drivers, ran until 1885.

No. 38, was another engine stolen by Rebs during Civil War. Built by Baldwin in 1860 as Mogul-type for freight service, it was converted to the 4-6-0 type in 1871.

This beautiful engine, No. 77, was one of several American or 4-4-0 types designed and built by Thatcher Perkins at 10th and Kentucky Shops, Louisville, in 1870-71.

The locomotives previously mentioned were chiefly used in freight and construction service and were supplemented in 1859, just prior to the opening of the road, by additional purchases from Moore & Richardson. At the time the road was opened for traffic between Louisville and Nashville the L. & N. had a pool of 18 locomotives at its disposal. Five additional locomotives – one from Moore & Richardson and four from the Schenectady Locomotive Works – now American – were purchased in 1860 and the Company placed its first "homemade" locomotive – No. 30 – in service in that year. This was built at its shops at 10th and Kentucky streets in Louisville, Ky. It has been claimed that No. 29, or "The Southern Belle," was the first locomotive built south of the Ohio River, but this seems to be in error since "The Southern Belle" was not built by the L. & N. at Louisville until 1871. The original No. 29, which was built by the Schenectady Locomotive Works, was re-numbered a few years after being placed in service.

The L. & N. re-numbered its locomotives on several occasions, this being done because of duplication, resulting when locomotives were acquired with the purchase of other railroads, and because of the desirability of having all locomotives of the same class consecutively numbered. The last large-scale re-numbering took place on July 1, 1897, and involved 549 locomotives. Only 20 engines retained their former numbers at that time; No. 14, Nos. 411-414, inclusive, and Nos. 860-874, inclusive.

The War between the States, of course, placed a heavy burden upon the little road's motive power and it was augmented from time to time during that conflict in order that the increased traffic might be handled expeditiously and to replace engines borrowed by other roads or destroyed by the Confederates. The majority of these new locomotives were obtained from either the Schenectady or Baldwin people, although there were isolated purchases from William Mason, of Taunton, Mass., and Rogers & Company, of Paterson, N. J. At the end of the war the L. & N.'s motive power roster listed 61 locomotives, most of which were described as being in good, or running order. No. 6, however, was listed as being "blown-up" and No. 58 as being "burnt by guerrillas." This tabulation, which was for the year ending June 30, 1865, revealed that in that year L. & N. locomotives had run a total distance of 983,047 miles and that the total expense involved was $413,473.62. This covered operating and maintenance costs, including charges for fuel, water, labor, etc. The voracious Iron Horse consumed some 41,076 cords of wood in that fiscal year, the check for this termite-like appetite coming to $153,968.31. However, even at that early date a few of the locomotives were coal-burners.

Surprisingly enough, from the close of the War between the States until 1870, only one new locomotive was placed in service. This was built by the L. & N. itself at Louisville and made its bow in 1869. The '70s, however, were to witness many additions to the L. & N.'s motive power. Many of these were purchased, some were built by the L. & N., and a number were obtained when the L. & N. acquired the Nashville & Decatur and the South & North Alabama in 1871.

During 1870, 15 locomotives of the 4-4-0 or American type were placed in service. These were obtained from Baird & Company, of Philadelphia, a subsidiary of the Baldwin Locomotive Company and all were coal-burn-

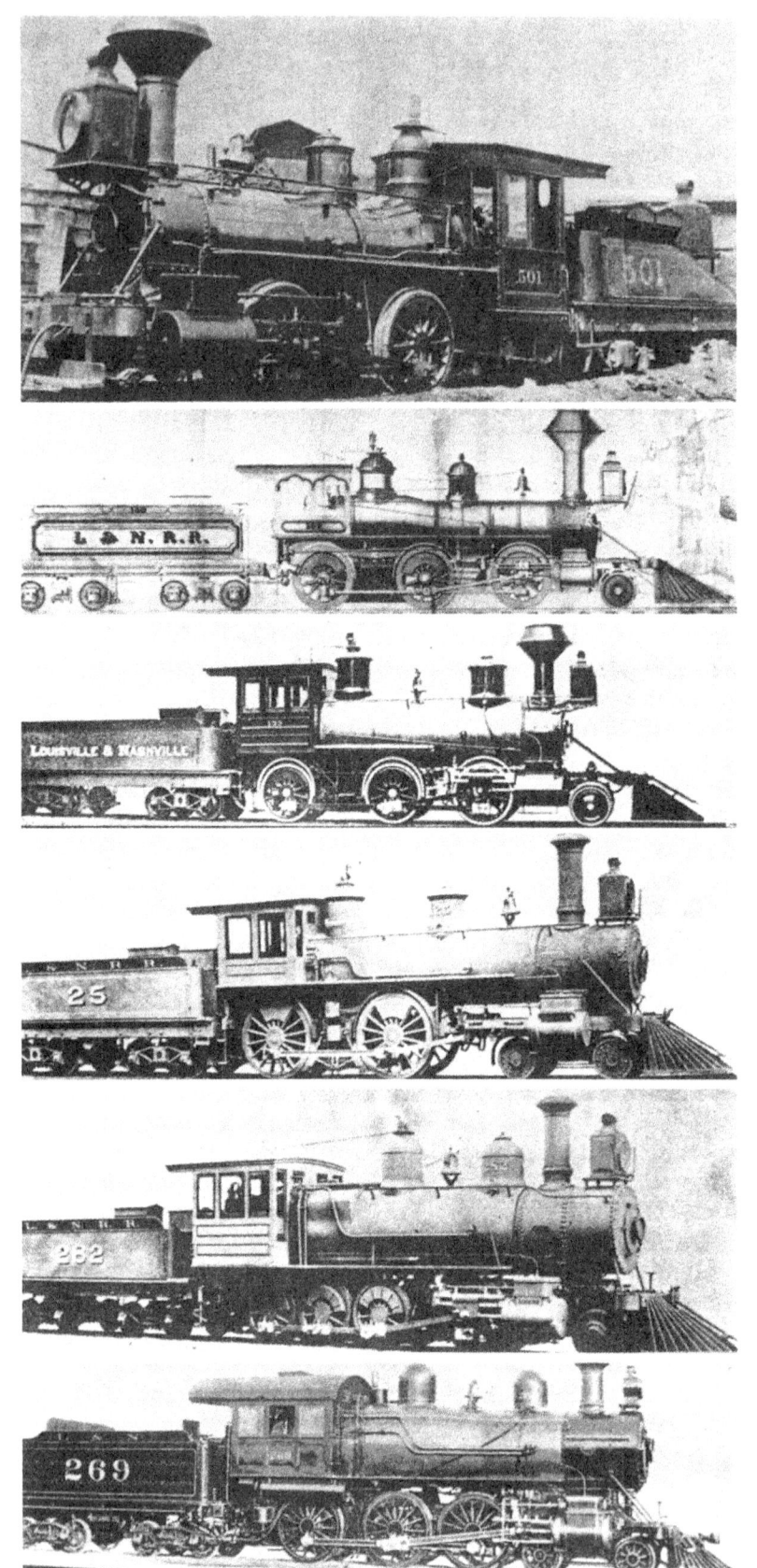

No. 501 was typical of "yard goats" of 1865-1900 period. An 0-4-0 type, engine was turned out by Baldwin in 1867 for old Evansville, Henderson & Nashville Railroad.

As L. & N.'s superintendent of machinery from 1869-1879, Thatcher Perkins designed many new engines for Road, including Mogul No. 102, built by L. & N. shops in 1873. Original painting owned by J. B. Speed Museum, Louisville.

Success of Perkins-designed No. 102, **above**, led Road to buy over 40 larger 2-6-0s in next decade. No. 133 was built by Rogers in 1881, had 55-inch drivers.

Standard passenger power of 1880s was 4-4-0 like No. 25, turned out by Rogers in 1886. Many 4-4-0s were rebuilt with new boilers by Company's own shops in 1920s.

Consolidation, or 2-8-0 type, made bow on L. & N. in 1883. Subsequent orders included No. 282, Rogers, 1889. Road pioneered application of Belpaire fireboxes in 1880s.

Prized passenger power of early 1900s was Class G-13 ten-wheelers, built by Baldwin in 1903. Class represented ultimate development of 4-6-0 type on road.

ers. Four of these locomotives had diamond stacks and eleven of them had the Laird type of balloon stack. Their wheels were painted red and they were adorned with a profusion of brass, at once the despair and delight of firemen. They were used in passenger and fast freight service. The brass mentioned was a distinguishing charasteristic of L. & N. locomotives for a number of years and it is said that when Col. Edward H. Green was president of the road for a brief spell in 1880 and 1881, that his wife, famed Hetty Green, chided the management severely for what she thought an excessive use of this commodity in the trimming of locomotives.

By the early '70s the road's management was firmly convinced of coal's superiority over wood as a fuel and optimistically estimated that when coal could be used exclusively its fuel bill would be reduced 25 per cent or about $45,000 per year. To that end all locomotives ordered new, or built in its own shops at Louisville – the L. & N. had purchased the shops of the old Kentucky Locomotive Works (Olmstead, Tennys & Peck) at 10th and Kentucky streets in 1858 – were coal-burners and the wood-burners on hand were being converted as rapidly as possible.

The improvements which were constantly being made in locomotive construction and design, coupled with the fact that the L. & N.'s motive power was frequently supplemented by locomotives obtained when other lines were acquired, prevented for a good many years the adoption of standard types for the moving of passenger and freight equipment. Several of the lines taken over by the L. & N. in the '70s, '80s and '90s had some rather unusual types of motive power and during those decades the L. & N. was a sort of railroad melting pot for many dissimilar classes.

Many of the L. & N.'s early-day locomotives were built in its own shops at Louisville, as mentioned, and the guiding genius behind such construction was Thatcher Perkins, who was superintendent of machinery from 1869 until his retirement in 1879. A "Yankee From Down East," Mr. Perkins, prior to his L. & N. connection, had served the Baltimore &

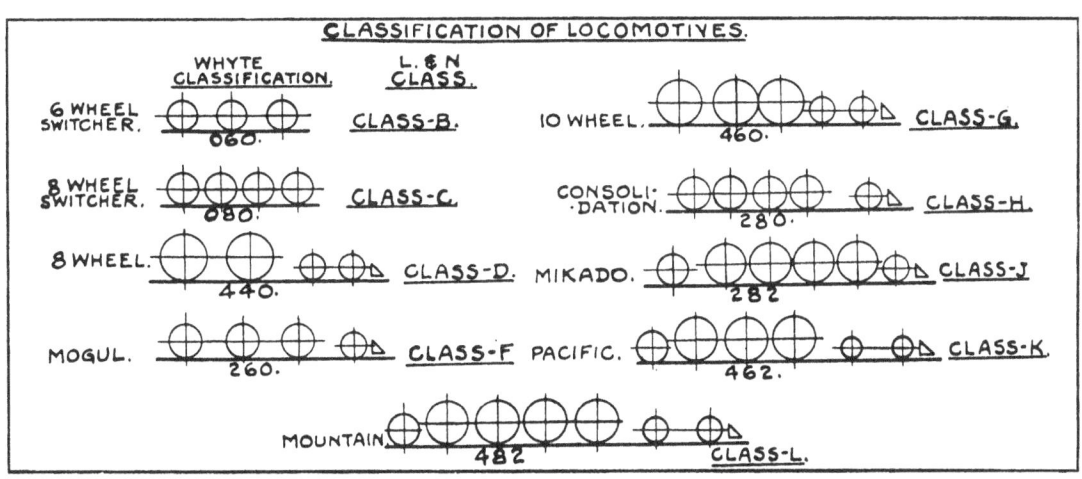

This chart will assist the reader in identifying the locomotives reproduced in the accompanying pages and in giving him a better conception of the various types of steam locomotives referred to in the text. This chart does not include the M-1, or 2-8-4 type which was the last steam motive power obtained by the L. & N.

Baldwin outshopped No. 500 in 1897 especially for display at Tennessee Centennial Exposition. Later rebuilt and renumbered, engine ran in local passenger service until 1937. Crews dubbed No. 500 "Queen Lil!"

Highly successful Class H-23, 2-8-0 types, represented by No. 989, were standard freight power in early 1900s. Baldwin, Rogers, L. & N. Shops built 200 H-23s.

L. & N's first Pacifics or 4-6-2s, Nos. 150-154, were delivered by Rogers in 1905. Company shops duplicated design with 40 more Pacifics from 1906-10. No. 152 is preserved for posterity by Kentucky Railway Museum.

No. 1200, Class H-25, improved version of Class H-23, came equipped with piston-valves superheater. Rebuilt with power reverse, many of this type operated until 1950s, dieselization.

No. 1281, Class H-28, was ultimate in Consolidation or 2-8-0 type on road. L. & N. Shops designed, built 94 H-28s and H-29s (improvement of H-28 Class) from 1911 - 1914. Many were later rebuilt with automatic stokers.

Ohio on two occasions as its "master of machinery" and had obtained practical knowledge of locomotive construction as a member of the firm of Smith & Perkins (Virginia Locomotive Works) of Alexandria, Va. A natural-born mechanic, Mr. Perkins had a flair for locomotive design and construction and his "Southern Belle" was widely acclaimed as one of the most beautiful engines of the day. It was immortalized by the song, "No. 29," composed by Will S. Hays, of Louisville, then river editor of The Courier.

During the '60s the great majority of the locomotives purchased or built had four drivers. From the very first there was a gradual increase in the weight of the engines and whereas the ante-bellum models had weighed around 50,000 pounds, or even less, subsequent acquisitions in the '60s and '70s tipped the beam by as much as 71,000 and 80,500 pounds.

In 1871 and 1872, the Company placed in service five locomotives which it had built itself. Each of these had six drivers and weighed 80,500 pounds. They were used in heavy freight service and proved so satisfactory that subsequently in 1872 and 1873 the L. & N. purchased 41 locomotives from Rogers & Company of this 2-6-0, or Mogul type. It also purchased 10 locomotives of the 4-4-0, or American type, during that period from the same company and, as a matter of fact, Rogers & Company obtained most of the L. & N.'s locomotive business during the decades of the '70s and '80s. A number of Rogers' locomotives were also added to the L. & N.'s motive power roster with the acquisition of the Mobile and Montgomery Railway, the Mobile, New Orleans and Texas Railroad, the St. Louis & Southeastern Railroad and the Louisville, Cincinnati and Lexington Railway during the '80s.

In 1873, the L. & N. purchased a number of switch engines from the Baldwin Locomotive Works, subsequently designated as Class A, which were unique in that they had a 0-4-0 wheel arrangement and extremely small fire-boxes. The last of these was retired from service on September, 30, 1911.

The number of iron horses in the L. & N.'s stable was thus constantly increasing and by 1882 these numbered 368, most of them having been built by the L. & N., or Rogers & Company.

During the '80s, however, despite the fact that the volume of freight and passenger business increased tremendously, the L. & N. built or purchased new, comparatively few locomotives, the total increase being less than 100 for the 10-year period. There was a very good reason for this. The acquisition of such roads as the M. & M., the M. M. O. & T., the L. C. & L., and the St. Louis and Southeastern added many locomotives to the roster and since the operation of these lines was thereafter integrated with that of the L. & N., it meant that a fewer number of locomotives could henceforth do the same work.

In the '80s, the L. & N. placed its first Consolidation type locomotives in service. These had a 2-8-0 wheel arrangement and developed a tractive force about 10 per cent greater than that of the Moguls (2-6-0), the respective ratings being approximately 25,000 pounds and 22,000 pounds. These Consolidations were used in heavy freight service and were characterized by their long fire-boxes and comparatively short boiler barrels. This type of locomotive was manufactured by several builders and the L. & N. turned out a number itself in its shops at 10th and Kentucky, Louisville. These Consolidations were said to be among the first in the United States which used the Belpaire fire-box, which, in turn, was replaced by the radial stay type along about 1903.

The chief factor, which influenced L. & N. locomotive design and construction, was the work to be done and this, in turn, was conditioned by such factors as America's industrial expansion, its constantly increasing population, its agricultural growth, the development of its raw materials and the nature of the competition provided by other carriers. Alone, or in combination, these necessitated greater speeds in the moving of passengers and freight and the moving of greater loads at one time. Thus, the capacities of freight cars were increased, more cars were hauled in a train and schedules were speeded up. As it became evident that existing motive power could not handle the traffic, new engines, either bought or built, were designed to remedy the deficiency between load and tractive force. At even so late a date as the '80s and early '90s, however, the average freight

---

The Louisville & Nashville Railroad's Annual Report for the year ending October 1, 1860, shows it was the proud possessor of 30 locomotives. Sixteen of these seem to have been obtained from Moore & Richardson during the period 1859-1860. After it had purchased 19 locomotives the Company evidently decided to number future acquisitions exclusively, instead of assigning them both names and numbers. The names of the 19 locomotives mentioned, their builders, and the dates purchased, were as follows:

Name	Builder	Date
Ben Spalding	Niles & Company	July, 1855
Hart Company	Niles & Company	July, 1855
Governor Helm	Fairbanks	Sept., 1856
Louisville	Fairbanks	Sept., 1856
New Haven	Moore & Richardson	Sept., 1857
Marion	Moore & Richardson	Sept., 1857
Muldraugh	Baldwin	June, 1858
Davidson	Baldwin	July, 1858
Hardin County	Moore & Richardson	July, 1858
Green River	Moore & Richardson	Sept., 1858
George McLeod	Baldwin	Oct., 1858
James Guthrie	Moore & Richardson	Dec., 1858
James E. Gamble	Moore & Richardson	Jan., 1859
Edmonson	Moore & Richardson	May, 1859
Barren	Moore & Richardson	May, 1859
Warren	Moore & Richardson	June, 1859
Simpson	Moore & Richardson	June, 1859
Quigley	Moore & Richardson	Aug., 1859
Newcombe	Moore & Richardson	Sept., 1859

The names of these locomotives and their builders do not quite coincide with information obtained from other sources and it is probable that some re-naming of locomotives had already been done at the time the above list was compiled, in much the same manner as the L. & N. was subsequently to re-number its locomotives.

train consisted of only about 18 cars, whose capacities ranged from 10 to 15 tons.

The Consolidations were the first radical departure from the colorful museum pieces of the earlier days of railroading. They were not especially handsome engines and their smoke-stacks and cow-catchers were strictly utilitarian, but they were the answer, at least for a brief space, to the problems mentioned.

In 1890, the L. & N. purchased a group of 10-wheeled passenger locomotives from the Rogers Locomotive Works. These represented an increase in tractive force of approximately 33-1/3 per cent over the heaviest American (4-4-0) types and their 67-inch-in-diameter driving wheels permitted them to maintain the fast schedules then established. Having proved their worth these 10-wheelers (4-6-0) were made the standard for subsequent purchases of this sort, with various modifications being made from time to time. These were secured from various builders and their peak development was represented in the purchase of eleven in 1903 from the Baldwin Locomotive Works. These were subsequently designated as Class G-13 and, re-built, some of them still gave good service as late as 1942. They had a tractive force of 25,000 pounds. (It was one of these locomotives, built for the L. & N. by Baldwin in 1897, which was exhibited at the Tennessee Central Exposition.)

At the beginning of the 20th Century the L. & N.'s most powerful freight engines were the Consolidations, while the 10-wheelers represented the apex in passenger power. Around 1900 the Consolidations began experiencing growing pains. Twenty locomotives of this type, designed for especially heavy freight service, as then constituted, were built by the Baldwin Locomotive Works for the L. & N. in 1903, and this class was subsequently built in large numbers by the Baldwin people, by Rogers and by the L. & N. itself. They were blood brothers to the 10-wheel (G-13 class) passenger locomotives and had many points of similarity, even though used in dissimilar service. Some 300 Consolidations (including Class H-25 and H-27's, improved versions of H-23) were built between 1903 and 1910 and many of them, rebuilt and outfitted with Walschaerts valve gear and other improvements, still gave good service as late as World War II.

Modifications of the basic design were made from time to time, such as increased length of piston stroke, increased diameter of cylinders, etc. The outstanding variations, and for many years the most powerful "hogs" in the L. & N.'s ownership, were the H-28 (later converted to H-28A), H-29 and H-29A engines, all of which were built at the Company's own South Louisville Shops during 1911-1914. They had superheaters, developed tractive forces varying from 47,000 to 49,000 lbs., had Walschaerts valve gear and carried 18 tons of coal and 8,500 gallons of water. Ninety-four of these were built and placed in service in the period mentioned. In the '30s a program was adopted of equipping all H-29 and H-29A engines with stokers at the rate of 14 per year.

The need for power of materially increased capacity in the handling of passenger traffic at high rates of speed led to the adoption of the 4-6-2 or Pacific type passenger locomotive in 1905. These were the L. & N.'s first Pacific locomotives and they soon displaced the 10-wheel G-class engines theretofore used for the same type of work. They had a 10 per cent greater tractive force than the 10-wheelers and a total of 45 were placed in service between 1905 and 1910. With the exception of the first five, which were built at the Rogers Works of the American Locomotive Company, all were built at the Company's own South Louisville Shops. These K-1's, K-2A's and K-2B's were subsequently supplemented in 1912 and 1913 by 17 other locomotives of the same class designated as Class K-3 and still later by 46 locomotives of the K-4, K-4A and K-4B classes, which were built at South Louisville between 1914 and 1922.

Additional Pacific type engines, Classes K-5 through K-8, were later built by Baldwin and by American. In more recent years stokers were applied to all K-5 and K-7 engines.

World War I was responsible for a great many changes in L. & N. motive power. At gradually increasing tempo the L. & N. began to handle a traffic that was larger than anything it had theretofore experienced, or even dreamed of. This called for a motive power with a greater capacity and one that was capable of performing efficiently at higher sustained speeds. Some solution, in the case of passenger motive power, was achieved by modification and improvement of the Pacific or 4-6-2 type of engine. At that time the Consolidation H-29A's were the L. & N.'s most powerful freight engines.

The first year of World War I, however, saw the introduction of a new and more powerful type of freight engine upon the L. & N. This was the Class J-1 Mikado engine, with a 2-8-2 wheel arrangement, the first of which developed a tractive force of 57,000 pounds, or an increase of 16 per cent over the Class H-29A Consolidations. Sixty-two of these were built at the South Louisville Shops between 1914 and 1918. One of the locomotives of this class was subsequently equipped with an auxiliary locomotive, or tender booster, for hump yard service at DeCoursey, Ky., which increased its maximum tractive force by 12,600 pounds, making it the most powerful locomotive then in L. & N. service. In 1918 and 1919 the Company built 18 J-1A Mikado type locomotives at South Louisville which had greater capacities than the J-1's. All of the J-1A's and a majority of the J-1's were subsequently equipped with stokers. Sixteen more

Until advent of M-1 Berkshires, No. 1906 and Class J-4A sisters were L. & N.'s most powerful locomotives. All J-4As were equipped with boosters. Class J-4 and J-4A Mikado or 2-8-2 types served as standard main-line freight power from 1920-1950.

From 1911 - 1923, South Louisville Shops designed, built 400 engines of four different types, including 34 Class C-1 eight-wheeled heavy switchers like No. 2101 here shown.

4-6-2 Type, No. 266 and handsome Class K-5 sisters powered L. & N.'s fastest expresses for nearly three decades (1920-1950).

South Louisville outshopped 95 heavy Mikados, Class J-1 and J-2, (like the J-2 1480 pictured) from 1914-1921 for use in Eastern Kentucky coalfields. Js were ideal powerful, low-speed pullers.

locomotives of a class designated as J-2A were built by the L. & N. in 1921, and were the first L. & N. locomotives built at South Louisville with stokers.

Following the inauguration of federal control on December 28, 1917, the L. & N.'s motive power was augmented by a number of locomotives assigned to it by the United States Railroad Administration. These engines and a number of others were subsequently purchased from the U. S. R. A. by the Company from 1918 to 1922, the following engines being involved: six yard engines of the C-2 type, Nos. 2118-2123; six passenger engines of the K-5 type, Nos 240-245; 18 freight locomotives of the J-3 class, Nos. 1500-1517, and 20 freight locomotives of the J-4 class, Nos. 1750-1769. The last mentioned locomotives, which were built by Brooks, were placed in service in the early part of 1918 and were promptly nicknamed "McAdoos" after W. G. McAdoo, the director general of the U. S. R. A. They were originally designated as J-3's and were numbered Nos. 1550-1569, inclusive. The Mikado type engines furnished by the U. S.R.A. were of two designs, light and heavy, and the Company subsequently purchased 75 of the light design (tractive force, 54,700 pounds), in addition to the 18 J-3 class engines mentioned as having been secured from the U. S. R. A., from Richmond, Schenectady and Brooks in 1920, 1922 and 1923. All were equipped with stoker, superheater and power reverse gear.

Those of the heavy design, or J-4 class, were all obtained from Brooks or Richmond (both of which were later taken over by the American Locomotive Company) and the record reveals that 141 such engines, including the 20 of the J-4 class obtained from the U. S. R. A., were placed in service during the period 1918-1927. The J-4's were also equipped with stoker, superheater and power reverse gear. The J-3's had a tractive force of 54,700 pounds and weighed 292,000 pounds, while the J-4's had a tractive effort of 63,000 pounds and weighed in the neighborhood of 323,000 pounds.

A slightly more powerful Mikado type locomotive, No. 1999, a three-cylinder engine, designated as Class J-5, was built by the American Locomotive Company for the L. & N. in 1924, and subsequently, in 1929, 24 locomotives of the J-4A Class were obtained from the Baldwin people. These had stoker, syphon, power reverse gear, superheater, feedwater heater and booster and for many years had the distinction of being the most powerful locomotives on our road. Their tractive effort was 66,150 pounds, but the boosters, increased this tractive effort by 12,075 pounds.

However, the J-4A's lost the distinction mentioned in the summer of 1942 with the delivery of 14 new freight locomotives which had been ordered in the fall of 1941 from the Baldwin Locomotive Works. These new locomotives were of the 2-8-4 class, the first of this type the Company had ever owned, and had greater capacities than any ever placed in service on the L. & N. Their starting tractive effort, including that of the trailer booster, was 79,300 pounds; also their tractive effort at running speeds was appreciably greater than that of the J-4A's because of greater boiler capacity and more efficient utilization of steam in the cylinders. Their larger drivers admitted of high speeds. These engines had roller bearings on all driver, trailer, engine and tender truck journals and had a total weight, with tender loaded, of 824,500 pounds. The tender carried 24 tons of coal and 22,000 gallons of water. The original 14 engines of this class, known as M-1's, were supplemented by the delivery of six additional in 1944 and 22 more in 1949, the last mentioned built by the Lima Works.

During the two decades between the two world wars (roughly 1920-1940), the L. & N.'s passenger motive power fleet saw the addition of larger and heavier locomotives of both the Pacific (4-6-2) and Mountain (4-8-2) types. Previous mention was made of six Pacific-type engines, Class K-5, designed and assigned to the L. & N. by the United States Railway Administration. As compared with the next largest passenger engine then in service (Class K-4), the new K-5's represented an increase in starting tractive force of 22 per cent and in total weight of 19 per

Lanky Class L-1 4-8-2s like No. 409 (Baldwin, 1926) were largest steam passenger engines owned by L. & N., powered Pan-American, Azalean, Southland, Flamingo and Dixie Flyer trains. L-1s had 70-inch drivers.

Mighty M-1 Berkshires such as No. 1960 ruled Cincinnati, Eastern Kentucky and Cumberland Valley divisions for comparatively brief time before dieselization. Baldwin and Lima built 42 M-1s from 1942-1949. M-1's clean lines were created by concealing piping under boiler jacket. Huge tenders held 20,000 gallons of water, 27 tons of coal. M-1s were last new steam engines bought by L. & N., were also Road's largest.

cent. They did admirable work and were followed in 1923 and 1924 by 20 additional locomotives of closely similar design from the Baldwin and American Locomotive people.

A most satisfactory engine mechanically, the K-5 Pacific (together with the Class L-1, 4-8-2 or Mountain types) served as the Railroad's standard "fast" or "express" passenger locomotive for many years, being so used on the swiftest main-line trains as well as handling, in later years, more important secondary main-stem and branch line runs. Two K-5's, Nos. 275 and 277, were streamlined by South Louisville Shops forces in 1940-41 to pull the Chicago-Florida Dixie Flagler and The South Wind streamliners.

Mention should also be made of an experimental three-cylinder Pacific-type passenger locomotive purchased in 1924 from the American Locomotive Company. This engine, No. 295 (Railroad class K-7) was similar in design to the Class K-5 engines except for the addition of a third and larger cylinder between the two smaller cylinders. Mechanically, No. 295 was never too successful and in 1940 was rebuilt at South Louisville as a conventional two-cylinder locomotive. It was also streamlined for service on The South Wind. With an oversized tender that held for $27\frac{1}{2}$ tons of coal and 20,000 gallons of water, No. 295 reeled off the 392 miles from Louisville to Birmingham at the helm of the Wind with only one stop at Nashville. The big tender enabled the locomotive to establish the 205-mile Nashville-Birmingham dash (spun off at 55 m.p.h. average) as the longest non-stop, coal-powered run in the country at the time.

The ultimate development attained in passenger steam motive power on the L. & N. came with the purchase of 22 Mountain type or 4-8-2 locomotives, (Railroad class L-1) from the Baldwin Locomotive Works in 1926 and 1930. The design of the L-1 engines was based directly on the United States Railway Administration's standard mountain type, although a number of new features were incorporated into the L-1's.

struction.

With a tractive power much greater than the heaviest L. & N. Pacific-type engines, the L-1's became ideally suited to heavy passenger service on the more hilly divisions of the railroad, particularly between Cincinnati and Nashville and Cincinnati and Atlanta. Later, they found wider use over much of the system.

The evolution of the passenger locomotive, after a comparatively static period extending from the acquisition of the L-1's, resumed its forward motion with the purchase in the fall of 1941 of eight diesel-electric passenger locomotives from the Electro-Motive Division of General Motors. These eight locomotives (in reality, two separate units of 2,000 horsepower each) were delivered in the spring of 1942, with four additional two-unit engines delivered in 1945 and two more in 1949.

These diesels were placed in service on fast passenger runs between Cincinnati and New Orleans; between Cincinnati and Atlanta; and between Nashville and East St. Louis, releasing a number of steam-powered passenger engines for other use.

The "yard goat," or switch engine, being a more prosaic member of the L. & N.'s motive power family, did not receive quite the attention accorded its more powerful kin, but this "stay-at-home" also evolved with the times. Here, too, dieselization, has had its impact, with the result that as early as April 1, 1953, the L. & N. had only 19 C-Class (0-8-0) steam-powered switch engines still in service, along with 34 Consolidation (2-8-0) engines used in switching service.

At one time, the L. & N. utilized a number of B-Class (0-6-0) switchers, but all had been scrapped after World War II. Some of these had been converted from older Consolidation types, this work having been done at the Company's South Louisville Shops. These converted engines had been originally built for heavy freight service by Rogers prior to the turn of the century. The C-Class switchers were built by the L. & N. and the American Locomotive Company, or its subsidiaries, during the period

Below left: 660 h.p. switcher No. 10, Alco 1939, was first diesel-electric on L. & N. Unit operated mostly in Louisville Terminals, was retired in 1963. **Below right:** An experimental three-cylinder Pacific-type, No. 295, was built by Alco in 1925. Middle, or 3rd cylinder, was removed in 1940 when engine was streamlined to pull The South Wind, Florida streamliner. Big tender helped No. 295 to reel off 205-miles from Nashville to Birmingham non-stop, set long-distance record for coal-powered trains.

L. & N.'s first road-passenger diesels were 16 2,000 h.p. units delivered by Electro-Motive in 1942. No. 450, **above**, leaves Louisville with The Pan-American on maiden run, May 18, 1942. Sixteen additional 2,000 and 2,250 h.p. units came in 1945 and 1949 to augment original diesels in main-line service.

1915-1925 and were built especially for switching service. Both the 6- and 8-wheel switchers were distinguished externally from road freight and passenger motive power, not only by their unusual wheel arrangement, but by the comparative smallness of their driving wheels as well. These had driving wheels which were only 51 inches in diameter, speed not being an essential of their function, as compared to diameters of 70 and 63 inches, for instance, found in the Mountain and Mikado types, respectively.

In the fall of 1939, the L. & N. placed two diesel-electric switch engines in service at its East Louisville Yards. One was obtained from the American Locomotive Company and the other from the Electro-Motive Division of General Motors and each was 600 horsepower. Later, in the fall of 1941, the Company ordered 12 additional diesel-electric switchers of the foregoing capacity; four each from American, Baldwin and Electro-Motive. These were all placed in service at Louisville. Later on, during World War II, a number of other diesel switchers were obtained from the various manufacturers and were assigned to various points on the System.

Like the economical housewife who remodels papa's pants to fit a long succession of growing youngsters, the L. & N. has always endeavored to obtain the maximum of service from its locomotives. To that end, as age would begin to exact its inevitable toll, it has transferred locomotives to branch lines after they have become inadequate for main line service; it had judiciously shifted engines from freight service to yard service, and in the days of steam rebuilt a number of engines at its South Louisville Shops.

Much of the effort of the Railroad's mechanical department dating from the early 1930s was expended upon not only making the coal-burning locomotive a more efficient piece of machinery, but also one that would be less of a civic nuisance, i.e., one that would produce the irreducible

Freight diesels made bow on L. & N. in 1948 with arrival of five EMD 1500 h.p. F-3 units including No. 2500. Units were first used as helpers in Eastern Kentucky, were later tested system-wide to pave way for dieselization.

Full freight dieselization program brought on purchase in 1950 of 37 1500 h.p. F-7 units. Freighters were both "A" or cab-types, like EMD No. 801, and "B" or boosters.

minimum of black smoke. To that latter end, greater care was taken in the selection of coal, improved and more scientific methods of firing were adopted and outstandingly, in 1944, there was the over-fire steam air jet which was just what had long been needed to eliminate black smoke. The device, in fact, proved so effective that eventually practically all of the Railroad's steam engines were equipped with it.

However, the intensified dieselization of the L. & N.'s motive power, dating from 1950, soon, of course, removed much of the emphasis formerly placed upon the performance of the steam engine. For instance, by April 1, 1953, the Railroad had 315 steam engines still in service, as compared to 443 diesels. The steam engine's most important use at that time was in moving loads and empties between the coalfields of Eastern Kentucky and the Cincinnati Gateway, the M-1's being used almost exclusively and all of them being so utilized.

Mention has previously been made of the L. & N.'s first purchase of two switchers. In succeeding years and prior to 1950, dieselization was largely confined to yard engines, although, as recorded, sixteen 2,000 h.p. passenger engines were placed at work in the spring of 1942, followed by eight in 1945 and four in 1949. In August 1948, the Railroad secured five 1,500 h.p. units from Electro-Motive and these were put to work in helper service on the Eastern Kentucky Division, pushing the long coal trains up Elkatawa Hill.

However, it was in 1950 that dieselization of the Railroad's motive power began in earnest. In that year, as the result of intensive studies,

"Second generation" diesels made debut on L. & N. in 1962-63, with acquisition of high-horsepower, all-purpose units from EMD and General Electric, like No. 1600, 2500 h.p. U25B type. Road also introduced new gray, yellow color scheme in 1962.

Versatile road - switcher units were acquired from 1951 on, could be operated in either direction, in line-haul or yard service. EMD GP-7 No. 500 was one of group of "Geeps" equipped with steam generators for passenger service.

the L. & N. obtained its first diesels for use in freight service – 37 of them. In all, during that year, the L. & N. ordered 181 new diesels, most of them earmarked for freight service, although some passenger, switching and general purpose units were also included.

This intensified dieselization, which continued throughout 1951, 1952, 1953, 1954 and 1955, reached its ultimate and destined conclusion in the early part of 1956 when the L. & N. authorized the purchase of 56 additional diesels at a cost of some $9.3 million. It announced at that time that the delivery of these engines – scheduled to be completed by April 1, 1957 – would enable it to completely dieselize its operations.

Actually, complete dieselization, as far as the L. & N.'s own operations were concerned, became a fact on November 3, 1956. On that date, its freight, passenger and yard operations became 100 percent dieselized for the first time. It then still owned 36 steam engines of the J-4 and M-1 classes (these were soon white-leaded and subsequently scrapped), but only one of these was still in active service. It had 598 diesels then on its rails and four on order and these latter were delivered shortly after the first of the year. Total cost of dieselization – at the beginning of 1957 – $87 million.

The lone exception mentioned was Engine No. 1882 on "lend-lease" to the L. & N.'s affiliate, The Carrollton Railroad. It, too, bowed out of the picture on January 28, 1957, and had the distinction of being the last steamer to run on the L. & N. Railroad. At that time, it hauled Local

Freight No. 86 from Worthville to DeCoursey, writing finis to an era.

Dieselization placed many a problem in the lap of management and necessitated a radical revision in maintenance, servicing and repair practices. Additionally, training programs for employes had to be set up, passing tracks lengthened (to accommodate the longer trains that the diesels can haul), bridges strengthened, fuel stations provided and roundhouse and shop facilities converted.

As the diesels were delivered and put to work, the older types of steam power were retired and eventually scrapped. One interesting by-product of the scrapping of this older steam power was the Railroad's subsequent donation of the removed engine bells to small rural churches along its lines. In all, nearly 400 bells were so donated.

Complete **dieselization** greatly lightened the L. & N.'s burden, making it unnecessary to provide dual facilities such as water tanks, coaling stations and repair facilities for both steam and diesel power.

The L. & N. purchased no diesels in either 1957, 1958, 1959, 1960 or 1961. However, it did acquire 138 "new" diesels at the time the N. C. & St. L. was merged into it on August 30, 1957. Then, during 1962 and 1963, it purchased 116 additional diesels. These included 34 obtained second-hand from two other railroads. The 82 new diesels had either 2,250 or 2,500 horsepower – the most powerful in the L. & N.'s ownership.

At the end of 1963, the L. & N. had in service, or on order, 769 units of all types.

Powered by a GP30, an L. & N. freight train rolls through the night.

Appendix IV

L & N Roadway and Track

THE Louisville & Nashville's "railroad" has undergone many changes since the first stretch of track was laid in July 1855. The gauge of its track was gradually lessened many years ago, steel has replaced the original iron rail and the rail has constantly increased in weight and improved in quality, crossties are now creosoted and the number of track fittings and accessories had greatly increased. There have been equally important changes involving other parts of the right-of-way.

Insofar as the original lines of the L. & N. are concerned, the track which was constructed in 1855 bore some resemblance to the track in use today and basically its construction was identical. The same could not be said, however, for the track of some of the railroads which are now a part of the L. & N. and which came into existence at an earlier date than the L. & N. Take, for example, the track of the old Lexington & Ohio Railroad, between Lexington and Frankfort, which is now a part of the L. & N.'s Cincinnati Division. When that road was first constructed in 1831, iron strap rail was inbedded in limestone sills, which were laid in the direction of the track instead of at right angles to it. In the wintertime, the intense cold often caused the iron strap rails to break. The loose ends, known as "snake heads," would frequently curl up and poke through the flooring of rolling stock, causing great damage and confusion, and occasionally injuring the occupants. As might be imagined, this track was far from satisfactory, although its lack of crossties did make the work easier for the horses which the L. & O. used as motive power for a few short years. Finally, the maintenance of the L. & O.'s track became such an expensive nuisance that the limestone sills and strap rail were removed and a more orthodox track substituted.

There were other types of track construction, at one time in more or less general use on American railroads, which were never utilized by the L. & N. One of these formed the track by spiking strap rail to wooden stringers, which supported it longitudinally, and these stringers, in turn, were fastened to or imbedded in wooden "sleepers" or crossties. However, by the time the L. & N. commenced the construction of its track in July 1855, the practices previously mentioned had almost entirely disappeared from American railroad construction and the L. & N.'s first chief engineer, L. L. Robinson, gave a great deal of thought and study to the type of roadbed and track which would be best suited to the projected Louisville & Nashville Railroad.

Morton, Seymour & Company, prominent contractors of the day, obtained the original contract for the construction of the line between Louisville and Nashville and of the Lebanon Branch, extending from

Lebanon Junction to Lebanon, Ky. They optimistically opined that they could finish this little chore in in two and one-half years' time, dating from May 2, 1853, and their reward for such honest endeavor was to be at the the rate of $35,000 per mile. Unfortunately, however, finance went hand in hand with construction and when, in May 1854, there was a shortage of ready cash, empire-building on the L. & N. ceased abruptly. Construction done was largely represented by a right-of-way between Louisville and Nashville which was partially graded and by partially completed bridges, masonry work and trestling. No rail had been laid at that time although some 156 tons of iron were on hand for the job.

Subsequently, in the early part of 1855, Justin, Edsall and Hawley took over the contract from Morton, Seymour & Company, and the first rail was laid in July of that year. Thereafter the track penetrated the rugged country south of Louisville slowly, with local farmers and the slaves of the more affluent of these, doing much of the grading that remained to be done. ("All trees, bushes and roots shall be cut and grubbed up," said the chief engineer.) Simultaneously, the track was pushing north from the north side of the Cumberland River at Nashville, and slowly, but surely, the gap was lessened. At last, the two prongs of iron were joined at a point north of Bowling Green and the first through train between Louisville and Nashville was operated on October 27, 1859, as related in one of the early installments of this history.

Two of the chief obstacles to the operation of through trains had been the crossing of Green River, near Munfordville and the ascent of Muldraugh's Hill, north of Elizabethtown. The resultant 1200-foot bridge across Green River and the tunnel through Muldraugh's Hill were undoubtedly the two chief engineering feats performed upon the little road.

The tunnel through Muldraugh's Hill was not completed until after the line between Louisville and Nashville was in operation and prior to such completion, the Hill was negotiated by means of a temporary track, which on the north side had an incline of 190 feet to the mile, which almost put it in the "roller coaster" class. The incline on the south side was 88 feet to the mile.

Another of the engineering feats worthy of especial mention was the tunneling exactly halfway between Fountain Head and Gallatin, Tenn. In penetrating the barrier imposed by Tennessee Ridge, the railroad constructed twin tunnels near the summit of the Ridge, both of which were located on curves. The first of these encountered on a trip south from Louisville was 945 feet long and 85 feet below the summit; the second, which was encountered 388 feet farther south, was 600 feet long and 165 feet below the summit. The rock cuttings for some three and one-half miles of this portion of the road cost the Company in the neighborhood of $200,000.

As originally planned, the L. & N.'s track had a gauge of six feet, but this was changed to five feet before hardly any construction worth mentioning had been accomplished. Some rolling stock with a gauge of six feet had been purchased, however, before the decision to change to the narrower gauge was made, and some of this could not be utilized on the new track, its construction being such that its gauge could not be lessened

The accompanying illustration is taken from Harper's Weekly of April 7, 1860, and shows the Cumberland River Bridge at Nashville, Tenn., as it appeared shortly after completion. At that time it was used jointly by the L. & N. R. R., and the Edgefield & Kentucky Railroad, the latter being subsequently acquired by the L. & N. Harper's Weekly described the bridge as one of the finest structures of its kind in the country and stated that it had an extreme length of 700 feet, made up of four spans, two fixed, one on each side, and two draw spans in the middle. They were said to be the largest railroad draws in the world. The entire cost of the bridge was approximately $200,000. The structure shown was destroyed by General Floyd when the Confederates vacated Nashville in February, 1862, and the one which replaced it was built by engineering forces of the U. S. Government under General Don Carlos Buell. The L. & N. subsequently paid the Government $33,000 for this new bridge, but had to replace it in 1868 with a structure which cost approximately $70,000.

by as much as one foot. The road's first crossties were of either white oak, cedar or black locust and were laid about 2,700 to the mile. They were approximately nine feet in length, about six inches wide and about six inches thick. It was stated in the chief engineer's report for 1854 that 60 lb. rail would be placed in the track, but 54 lb. rail, and somewhat lighter weights, seem to have been used instead. Each rail was spiked to its crossties with 16 spikes, each of which weighed eight ounces. Wrought or cast iron "chairs" were used to support the rails at the joints. The ballast generally used was gravel or broken stone spread one foot in thickness over a space 10 feet wide.

Much careful attention was given to the original right-of-way and the various adjuncts of the track such as bridges, trestles, cuts and tunnels. Due to the rugged nature of much of the country between Louisville and Nashville, the line as originally constructed had a number of cuts and trestles, but the latter were soon replaced, in most cases, by bridges or embankments. The principal bridges were constructed across Salt River, Rolling Fork, Nolin River, Big Run, Sulphur Ford, Green River, Barren River, Station Camp Creek, Drake's Creek, Mansker's (Manscoe's) Creek and Cumberland River and there were smaller bridges across a number of lesser streams.

The original line between Louisville and Nashville had 4,140 feet of bridges and 3,956 feet of trestles and was served by nearly 13 miles of tributary track in the shape of sidings and switches. Less than one-fourth of the 185 miles of the Main Stem was curved track and very few sharp curves were encountered. Some 45 miles of track were on level grade, while on 100 of the remaining 145 miles the incline did not exceed 50 feet per mile.

Little more than one-half the line was ballasted at the time of the road's opening on October 27, 1859. At that time there were stations at a number of points along the line, as well as culverts, cattle-guards, water stations, section houses, turn-tables, sand houses and the like. In connection with the depot situation the Annual Report for the fiscal year ending with June 30, 1860, stated that a general design had been prepared for second-class stations, providing for freight, store and passenger rooms and that parties desiring depot conveniences were permitted to construct same on Company property at their own expense. It further reported that at that time such stations had already been constructed at Rowletts, Woodland, Rich Pond and Woodburn, Ky., and at Mitchellville, Richland, and Fountain Head, Tenn. Company-built and more commodious stations were located at Bowling Green, Horse Cave and Franklin, Ky., and, of course, at Louisville and Nashville.

The total cost of the main line, as of February 1, 1860, just after the opening of the road, including interest paid and discount on bonds sold, was $6,607,245.77.

As mentioned, much of the trestling used in the construction of the orig-

This reproduction of a sketch appearing in Harper's Weekly, February 20, 1864, depicts a railroad accident common to that time. The iron rails, made brittle by cold weather, frequently snapped off and broke through the floor of the car.

inal line was of a temporary nature and was soon replaced by bridges or fills. Several types of trusses were used in supporting the first bridges on the main line, these including the Beam Truss, the McCallum Truss, the Howe Truss and the Fink Truss. The latter was the invention of Albert Fink, a young German immigrant, who became the L. & N.'s engineer and superintendent of machinery and road department shortly after the completion of the line between Louisville and Nashville. Subsequently most of the bridges were equipped with his truss. The truss principle in bridge construction was just then coming into general use. Previously most bridges had been constructed with stone arches or with girders of wood or iron.

A comparison of the L. & N.'s original line with that of the Memphis & Ohio Railroad, which was completed in 1860, and which was later acquired by the L. & N., is rather interesting. The Memphis & Ohio was 130 miles long and extended from Memphis to Paris, Tenn. In 1868, the L. & N.'s main stem had 6,724 feet of bridges and only 912 feet of trestles, despite the rugged nature of the terrain and the many creeks, forks and branches which the line crossed. At that time, the Memphis & Ohio, a shorter road and one which traversed the comparatively level countryside of Western Tennessee, had 563 feet of bridges but had 25,677 feet of trestlework, due to the many small streams which were crossed.

Some other facts about the original construction of the L. & N.'s line between Louisville and Nashville: Rock excavations were 18 feet wide at grade and the sides had a slope of one foot horizontal to every five feet vertical. Earth cuts were similarly formed, except they were 20 feet wide at the grade line. All embankments, or fills, whether of rock or earth, were 16 feet wide at the grade line for the single track line. At those points along the line where the base of an embankment was faced with the periodic threat of high water, it was lined with rock to the proper height. Those man-made caverns known as tunnels also felt the touch of early-day standardization. Those that were cut through solid rock were 12 feet wide at the grade line, the tops of the vertical sides being 12 feet above grade. The peak of the tunnel's arch was 18 feet above the track. Tunnels cut through earth were securely shored and arched with protecting timbers.

The L. & N.'s track suffered much damage during the War Between the States and there was scarcely a mile of it that escaped unscathed. Green River Bridge, the tunnel at Muldraugh's Hill and various other bridges and tunnels felt the heavy hand of the god of war, along with stations, roundhouses, water tanks, wood piles and other facilities of the railroad. A favorite divertissement of raiding Confederate cavalrymen was to uproot the track and then warp the iron rails by heating them over a roaring blaze of crossties.

The L. & N. emerged from the war, however, in fairly good physical condition. This was due to a number of reasons. Principally: (1) it had prospered financially during the war; (2) the M. of W. forces of the L. & N. under the alert and able leadership of Albert Fink, engineer and superintendent of machinery and road department, repaired the damage and reconstructed the road in a surprisingly short time; (3) the engineering forces of the U. S. Army lent valuable assistance in the work of reconstruction and (4) the damage done during the closing years of the war was com-

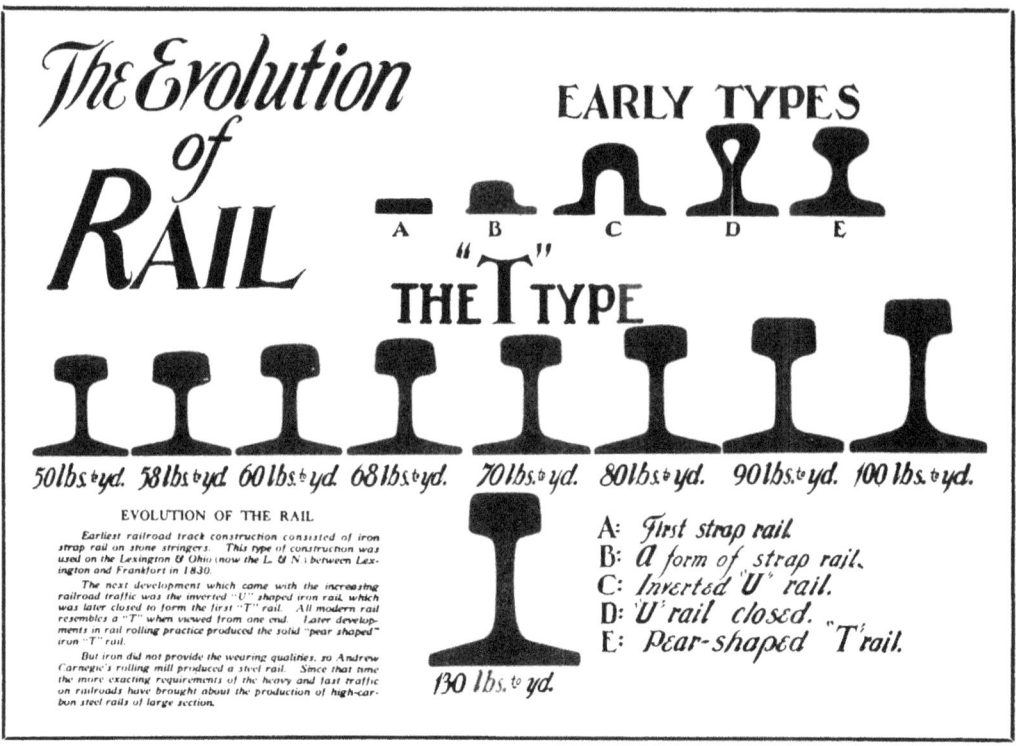

Chart showing the evolution of rail and comparative sizes.

paratively light, permitting the railroad to largely replace the makeshift repairs which had been necessitated during the early days of the conflict in order that train operation might be resumed as soon as possible.

As the little road's business increased so did the wear and tear on its rail and the pertinent statistics cast an interesting side-light on this phase of its operations. For instance, during its fiscal year ending with June 30, 1860, the L. & N. placed 109 tons of new iron rail in the track – the road, in fact, was still being built – and 113 tons of repaired iron. During 1860-1861, no new or re-rolled iron was added, but 516 tons of repaired iron were. Then, in 1861-1862, 463 tons of new iron, 32½ tons of re-rolled iron and 143½ tons of repaired iron were placed in the track. In 1862-63, the figures were: new iron, 433 tons; re-rolled iron, 95¼ tons; repaired iron, 558 tons. In 1863-'64, the figures were 2,933½ tons, 471 tons and 1,104 tons and in 1864-'65, 2,268 tons, 491 tons and 1,000 tons.

During this period the number of new crossties placed in the track annually, most of which were hewn to the railroad's specifications by farmers living adjacent to the right-of-way, fluctuated back and forth. In the fiscal year ending with June 30, 1860, 16,672 new ties were placed in the track. This dropped to 10,082 ties the next year, rose to 27,752 ties the following year, then dropped to 16,871 and thereafter soared dizzily to 96,709 new ties and 112,479 new ties in the fiscal years ending in 1864 and 1865 respectively.

In those halcyon days of running a railroad the cost per mile of road for maintenance averaged only $1,544.24 annually, based on the six-year period of 1859-1865. The figure mentioned was much higher than it would have been during more normal times, of course, but even so compares favorably with the figure for 1962 which was approximately $4,000.

Ballast, in those early days, due to the comparative lightness of engines and equipment, did not play as important a part in the roadbed as it does today. Thus, at the close of the fiscal year ending with June 30, 1866, nearly seven years after the completion of the road, only 146.3 miles of the main line were completely ballasted. At that time five miles were ballasted with sand only, 13.2 miles were partly ballasted and 20.5 miles had no ballast at all. Some 25 miles of the road's 47-mile Lebanon Branch had nothing at all to cement the union of Mother Earth and L. & N. track, and 28 miles of the 46-mile Memphis Branch were also similarly unadorned.

In fact, ballast in those days was really just what its name implied in more ways than one. It was the first thing to go "overboard" when times were bad, and when times were good the Company treated itself to a few miles of nicely ballasted track.

By the end of the fiscal year closing with June 30, 1867, the Company's roadbed and track were in such excellent condition that it was able to proudly boast that although some of its passenger trains were running at a scheduled time of 26½ miles per hour, the actual running time being more than 30 miles an hour in many cases, that no accidents had resulted from defective track.

By 1869, the Company was handling such a heavy volume of traffic that the management was seriously considering the feasibility of building a second track from Louisville to Lebanon Junction, Ky. The increased volume of traffic, creating as it did the use of heavier and more powerful equipment with a consequent increase in the wear and tear on the railroad track, necessitated the use of heavier and improved iron rail. Finally, during the latter part of 1870, the L. & N. placed its first steel rail in the track and the records show that during the fiscal year ending with June 30, 1871, some 998 tons of steel were laid on the main stem. The management defended this radical step with these prophetic words:

"Under our heavy traffic iron rails of the best manufacture now last but a short time and it was therefore considered more economical to use steel rails though their first cost is about 60 per cent in excess of iron rails."

Despite these stirring words, however, the railroad continued to place new iron rail in the track for some years thereafter, although the disparity between purchases of steel and iron rail constantly increased in favor of the former. Moreover, for a good many years this steel rail was placed almost exclusively in main stem trackage. The Annual Report for the fiscal year ending with June 30, 1876, shows that of the 185 miles of the main stem, 4.07 miles still had the original iron rails laid in 1857-1859; 21.43 miles had iron rail with chair fastenings; 37.26 miles had iron rail of the "fishbar" type (so called because the rails were secured at the joints by iron "fishes" or splices) of Johnstown, Guest, New Albany or Rhymny manufacture and 122.24 miles had fishbar steel rails of English, French, Cambria or Edgar Thomson manufacture.

The evolution of the railroad rail for such a simple-looking object has been a highly involved one. The iron strap rail previously mentioned, which was used on the old Lexington & Ohio, and which in itself represented quite an advance over the first types of rails used, was soon replaced, on most roads, by an iron rail which was T-shaped. It seems probable that this type of rail has been used almost exclusively on the L. & N.'s own lines from the very first. Undoubtedly, some of the lines acquired were originally laid with different type rail and some pear-shaped rail was found in an old track near the freight house at 9th & Broadway in Louisville, some years ago. It may have been released from the track of some acquired line.

The rail which was secured at the joints by means of the chair fastenings had a tendency to become loosened and bruised at the ends by the blows of the wheels, and it was to eliminate this that the "fishbar" type of track construction was introduced.

These chair fastenings, which on the L. & N. seemed to have been used solely to support the rails at the joints, were used on some roads, notably in England, to secure the rails to each crosstie and, however used, were the forerunners of the present-day tie plates which help to securely anchor steel to wood. It cannot be ascertained just when tie plates were first used on the L. & N., but it must have been subsequent to May 30, 1886, when the gauge of most of the L. & N.'s track was changed from five feet to four feet, nine inches. The existing accounts of that stirring bit of L. & N. history contain no mention of tie plates and since their presence would have undoubtedly complicated matters we may assume that at that time they were not a part of typical L. & N. track construction.

In the 'seventies and 'eighties of the 19th Century, much additional trackage was either acquired or built by the L. & N. Railroad. Trackage constructed was invariably laid with steel rail and the Company boasted as early as 1877 that the Main Stem from Louisville to Nashville was virtually laid with rail of this metal. As a matter of fact at that time some 35 miles of main stem track still had iron rail and it was 1880 before all of it disappeared. Most of the remaining System trackage was still laid with iron rail. (In 1880, the L. & N. was operating some 1,840 miles of first main track.)

Many of the roads acquired by the L. & N. were in poor physical condition and it was many years before their construction could be improved to the point where their track compared to that of the original line or to other L. & N.-built portions of the System. The Mobile and Montgomery Railway, for instance, which was acquired on January 15, 1880, had no less than 17 different makes of iron rail in its track at that time, some of it being extremely light in weight.

In 1856, Henry Bessemer, an English ironmaster, in searching for a better iron for use in cannons, discovered a commercially feasible way of converting iron into steel. It was this discovery that made it possible for the L. & N. and the other railroads of its day to procure the longer-lasting rails of steel for laying in their track. Even so, the steel originally laid in the L. & N. track was far from satisfactory. It was greatly inferior in quality to the steel rail in use today and in the 'seventies and 'eighties much of it was very light, being either of the $58\frac{1}{4}$ lb. or 67 lb. or 68 lb. types. This early steel rail was rather low, with a thick base and a relatively thin head and as a consequence the railroad was frequently troubled with broken rails. As traffic increased, so did the weight and power of the road's rolling stock and motive power, and the track and roadbed were considerably strengthened during the decades mentioned to support these increased loads.

As the century grew older, more and more of the heavier or 68 lb. steel rail was placed in main line trackage, many more miles of road were ballasted and bridges and trestles were strengthened. Much of the removed rail was re-laid on portions of the line less heavily traveled, a practice that continues to this day. The great majority of the bridges and trestles which were replaced or improved could have been reasonably expected to give many more years of service had not the increased weight of equipment ruled otherwise.

Much trouble was experienced by the L. & N. and other American roads, by rail breakage, and in 1874 a number of prominent engineers convened with the purpose of holding a clinic on the troublesome steel

PATENTED MARCH 26, 1872.

Even early-day track maintenance was featured by many labor-saving gadgets. The inventor of the one here pictured claimed that it could straighten out crooks (in the track) at the rate of over 50 to the hour. As far as is known this device was never used on the L. & N., although the "Jim Crow" rail bender was used to straighten or curve rail out of track.

rails of the day. Nothing much developed from this meeting except the recommendation that the bulk of the rail's metal be transferred from the base to the head. This, however, merely transferred the seat of the trouble and for a number of years thereafter American railroads were troubled with rail failures originating in the base. While the design and lightness of the typical rail sections then in use had a great deal to do with the aforesaid breakage the main contributing cause, of course, was the quality of the steel itself, which lacked stiffness, toughness and hardness, as compared with the steel commonly in use today.

In 1885 approximately 123 miles of new steel was added to the track. Some 108 miles replaced iron rails, while 15.45 miles replaced steel rails. These replaced steel rails, at the most generous estimate, couldn't have been in the track for more than 14 years and while this was good performance, it lacks quite a bit of being permanence as we mortals judge it.

For many years the management had wistfully discussed the possibility of constructing second track and finally, in 1888, its traffic had increased to such an extent that a certain amount of such construction became imperative. This building has been previously dealt with in the History proper but at this point it seems appropriate to record that the Company's first second track was authorized in 1888 and involved those portions of the line between East Louisville and Anchorage; between South Louisville and Shepherdsville; between Edgefield Junction and East Nashville; between Birmingham and Boyles and between Birmingham and Oxmoor. All of this work, totaling 43 miles of second track, was completed by 1890 and 68 lb. steel rail was used exclusively.

In the late 'eighties the L. & N. began to lay more and more of the 68 lb. steel rail annually in its track and in the fiscal year ending with June 30, 1891, laid nearly 100 miles of track with a somewhat heavier rail of a 70 lb. pattern. As of June 30, 1892, here's how the L. & N.'s main stem's 185 miles of steel were allocated: 58¼ lb. - 73.62 miles; 67 lb. - 6.80 miles; 68 lb. - 61.07 miles; 70 lb. - 43.74 miles. The majority of the remaining System trackage was constructed with either 58¼ lb. or 68 lb. steel rail.

(The records of the chief engineer's office, which are still extant, show that 8,000 tons of 50 lb. steel rail was purchased from the Lackawanna Iron & Coal Company on July 20, 1881. This must have been used in side or yard tracks for at that time the Company was placing more and more of the heavier patterns of steel rail in its track. The first 68 lb. steel rail was included in a purchase of 20,000 tons from the Bethlehem Iron Company on March 14, 1885, the remainder being 58¼ lb. steel rail. The last 58¼ lb. steel rail was purchased from Carnegie Bros. Co., Ltd., on June 13, 1891.)

The Company's policy of rapid-fire acquisition of other lines made it somewhat difficult for it to completely eliminate iron from its trackage until after the turn of the century. Each year it replaced many miles of the remaining iron rail with steel rail, but each year its acquisitions of other railroads, or stray bits of trackage, would add more iron to its System. It was, in fact, not until 1924 that the Company was able to announce that the last vestige of iron had disappeared. As a matter of historic interest it should

The East Louisville grade separation as it appears at the Baxter Avenue Station. This was completed in October, 1937.

be recorded that the L. & N.'s last iron was found in some .61 miles of track on the Birmingham Division's five-mile Shelby & Columbiana Branch, which stubbornly lingered on in service long after the rest of the track had been changed to steel. (However, the .61 miles mentioned had been the only stretch left with iron since 1909.)

The first 80 lb. steel rail was placed in L. & N. track during the fiscal year ending June 30, 1898, about eight miles being laid at that time. This heavier steel proved to be just what the doctor ordered and thereafter it was placed in the track in ever-increasing quantities. Thus, at the end of the fiscal year ending with June 30, 1906, of the System's total of some 4,016 miles of main track, approximately 1,189 miles were laid with 80 lb. steel rail. At that time the majority of the L. & N.'s track contained either 58¼ lb. or 70 lb. steel rail and about 13 miles of the recently acquired A. K. & N., was laid with 85 lb. steel rail. Steel rail of a 141 lb. pattern made its appearance on .51 miles of the New Orleans and Mobile Division and .20 miles of the Pensacola Division in the fiscal year ending June 30, 1910. This was a special girder or street car track rail and was used in paved streets at Pensacola, New Orleans and Mobile. Some of it was later installed at Birmingham and Louisville; in the latter city in the track at Third and Gaulbert on the so-called "Gaulbert Street Cut-Off."

Rail of the 90 lb. pattern made its first appearance in L. & N. track in the fiscal year ending with June 30, 1912, and also proved very satisfactory as the Company's traffic, with some ebb and flow, constantly increased and as the roadbed began to be called upon to support still heavier loads. In the year just mentioned the lighter steel rail began to disappear from the L. & N. track at a more rapid rate. Thus, at the end of the fiscal year ending with June 30, 1913, there were 350 miles of 90 lb. steel rail in main track; at the end of 1914, 625 miles; at the end of 1915, 1,050 miles and at the end of 1916, 1,314 miles. In 1916, the L. & N., at the instigation of the I. C. C., commenced the present-day practice of having its fiscal year conform to the calendar year and at the end of that year the figure for the 90 lb. rail was 1,437.48 miles. In 1918, it was 1,791 miles. It was not until 1922 that 100 lb. rail made its appearance in L. & N. track. In 1921, the L. & N. laid about one-half mile of track with a special girder rail weighing 159 lbs. to the yard. And by the close of 1925 it had 2,220 miles of the 90 lb. rail in its track and some 721 miles of the 100 lb. rail.

At the end of 1930, 1,622 miles were laid with the 90 lb. rail, 2,193 miles were laid with 100 lb. rail and a little over 1,000 miles with rails of lighter patterns. This trend toward heavier rail continued and thus by the end of 1939, 2,713 miles were laid with the 100-lb. rail and 1,278 miles with the 90-lb. rail. At the end of 1941, the Company had 2,827 miles of first main track laid with 100 lb. rail and 1,189 miles laid with 90 lb. rail. Some 6,600 miles were laid with lighter rail, chiefly of the 80-lb. and 70-lb. patterns. In 1941, the Company placed 7,295 tons of 131-lb. rail (about 31 miles) in service for the first time.

During World War II some new rail, mostly of the 100-lb. type, was placed in the track. In the postwar years, the L. & N. standardized on 132-rail for its replacements in main line track and each year thereafter a considerable quantity of this was installed. Thus, at the end of 1958, the L. & N. had 1,955 miles of first-main track laid with 132-lb. rail, 435 miles with 115-110-lb. rail, 2,251 miles with 100-lb. rail, and 1,497 miles with 90-lb. and lighter weights.

The L. & N.'s track was developing in other ways too while iron was giving way to steel and while the steel itself was becoming bigger and better. Unballasted track began to disappear from the L. & N.'s main line as the importance of ballast began to be more fully appreciated. As previously noted, the first L. & N. track was ballasted with either stone or gravel, when it was ballasted at all, but as the road expanded and as the number of its locomotives increased, it became more economical to use other material. Thus, prior to the turn of the century, many miles of L. & N. track were ballasted with cinders from its own Iron Horses, or from the industries along the line of road; with slag from the roaring furnaces of the Birmingham district or with copper slag from the mines at Copperhill, Tenn.; with chatt (metallic ore and rock) and with sand. Even to this day these different types of ballast are widely used in L. & N. track, with slag and rock and gravel predominating, however.

The crosstie's development remained static for a number of years and prior to the turn of the century not much change occurred in this part of the track. As mentioned, the crossties were originally laid about 2,700 to the mile of single track and as the traffic increased the space between the ties was slightly lessened to give the rails a firmer foundation. Today (1963) there are about 2,800 crossties to each mile of L. & N. single track, and the average crosstie in main line track is slightly wider and thicker than its 19th Century predecessor, but not quite so long. White oak, cedar and black locust were first used exclusively in the hewing of the crossties, but the Company later found that other woods, more plentiful along its lines, were almost equally as satisfactory and soon began the use of red oak, sap pine and cypress. Despite the fact that the L. & N. was one of the first railroads in the country to chemically treat its bridge timbers it was 1912 before it began to similarly treat its crossties in order to protect them from decay and thus lengthen their life.

Multiple tampers, such as this one, help speed the work of track re-surfacing on the L. & N. Railroad.

The history of creosoted wood on the L. & N., or predecessor lines, is an interesting one and dates back to 1869 when the old New Orleans, Mobile & Chattanooga Railroad, which built the line between New Orleans and Mobile, erected a creosoting plant at Gautier, Miss., in order that the bridge timbers, which supported its line for a good many of the miles between the two cities mentioned, might be protected from the assaults of the teredo, a form of marine life which feeds upon untreated wood. At first, the creosoting of the timbers was done by boiling or soaking them in the creosote oil. This method did not sufficiently impregnate the piling and when the oil had been washed out the teredo blithely attacked its favorite dish, necessitating the rebuilding of much of the line within nine months' time of its construction. Thereafter, more careful thought was given to the matter and finally the N. O. M. & C. adopted a process which forced the creosote oil into the timber through heavy pressure. This thoroughly impregnated the wood and proved so satisfactory that when the L. & N. took over the line in 1880, it soon began to creosote the timber used elsewhere in bridges and trestles on the System in order to protect them from decay.

When it was decided to extend the creosoting treatment to crossties in 1912, it was found that the plant at Gautier did not have sufficient capacity for the job and the Company constructed a plant at Guthrie, Ky., devoted exclusively to treating ties for track. This plant was later leased to Bond Brothers, of Louisville, and still later to the Koppers Company.

Essentially, climate and traffic are the two factors which determine the size and kind of ties used on various parts of the System. Red oak and black gum, after being properly seasoned, were the two woods which were chiefly creosoted by the L. & N. for crosstie use.

The L. & N. has also made considerable use, on its southern divisions, in years past, of cypress ties, unseasoned and untreated. However, the cypress ties were never used in the track north of Montgomery because of climatic reasons.

The L. & N. learned many things about track construction and the maintenance of its roadbed in the well-attended school of experience. Thus, it soon learned that the life of its crosstie wood was materially lessened by the rail which gouged deep shoulders in it, resulting in rough-riding track. This was overcome by the use of the tie plates before mentioned. Then, it found, as traffic increased, that the rail had a tendency to creep forward, under the pounding of the wheels, in the direction of the heaviest traffic. This tendency was discouraged, at first by the use of tie plates, and still later by the use of rail anchors, which are applied to the rail, adjacent to the tie, some types being driven. They thus bind the rail and if it starts to run, the rail anchor strikes the crosstie and prevents farther progress. In similar manner, gauge rods keep the parallel rails at the proper distance from each other.

The L. & N. also learned that it was more economical to fence considerable portions of its right-of-way than to pay the damages on unavoidably killed livestock, which had strayed upon the track. It learned that proper drainage of the roadbed would not only help keep its track smooth and level, but would lengthen its life as well.

Reinforced concrete section at south end of Hagans Tunnel on the C. C. & O. Connection as it appeared in 1929 before completion.

All these lessons, of course, were not learned at once, but extended over a number of decades. As a matter of fact new things about track maintenance and construction are still being learned every day. Many of these are admittedly still in the experimental stage. (For example, in May 1932, the Company experimented with the GEO type of track construction on about two miles of its Cincinnati Division, near Visalia, Ky. This proved very satisfactory, but as it is so much more expensive than L. & N. standard track construction, it had never been felt that its additional advantages justified this increased cost. In GEO track construction each rail is more securely fastened to the crosstie by an elaborate set-up consisting of a double-shouldered tie plate, four screw spikes, bolts and nuts and wood shim. The last is placed between tie plate and rail and acts as a cushion. Advantages claimed for the GEO track are reduction of noise, elimination of spreading and creeping of rails and pumping of track and longer life for ties and rails.)

The use of welded rail, however, has done much to obviate the need for GEO track.

There were a number of other developments involving the railroad track which occurred during the closing decades of the 19th Century. These developments came within the province of the signal department

The old and the new in bridge construction. At the left is the former L. & N. bridge across the Ohio River at Henderson, Ky., and at the right is the present-day bridge. This picture was taken in the latter part of 1932 when the new bridge was nearing completion. The old bridge was torn down shortly thereafter.

and included such things as interlocking plants, pipe-operated derails, spring switches, automatically-operated crossing gates, automatic block signals and other automatic signals of one sort or another. In comparatively recent years automatic train control, car retarders, centralized traffic control and hotbox detectors have also made their appearance upon L. & N. track.

The L. & N.'s track and right-of-way are also the location of a number of items essential to railroad operation, which have not been previously mentioned. There are the various sign posts of one sort or another which decorate the right-of-way and which mean many things to many people. Some of the principal types of sign posts, or markers, are those which define the limits of the right-of-way; indicate the distance from some principal terminal; show the permissable time table speed; indicate where whistles are to be sounded as required by rules or law, or show the distance to nearest water station, etc.

Dangling pieces of rope, popularly known as "ticklers," suspended from a wire hung high above the track, which warn the trainmen riding on top of cars of the approach of a tunnel, bridge or some other structure with a low clearance; bumping posts, switch stands, cattle-guards, and hand-operated derails are also found on the railroad right-of-way.

Some mention has already been made of some of the structures peculiar to the railroad right-of-way, such as section houses, stock chutes, water tanks, freight and passenger stations, track scales, coaling stations, sand houses, tool houses, cinder pits, turn-tables and the like. Most of these have understandably been a part of the L. & N.'s physical plant from the very beginning, but all of them have undergone a considerable evolution which in each case has increased their effectiveness as a part of the railroad. In nearly every case the impetus behind such evolution has been a constantly-increasing traffic, which has impartially rendered obsolescent facilities once considered quite adequate. This march of progress has also brought to the Railroad's right-of-way some entirely new types of structures. Outstanding are the railroad's overhead bridges and underpasses, which eliminate grade crossings, and thus make travel safer, both for the traveler on the highway and the passenger on the train. The L. & N.'s first grade elimination project, which was undertaken primarily for that purpose, involved the Breckinridge Street crossing at Louisville and was completed in 1883. The Pope Street crossing, also at Louisville, was completed in 1891.

Following the advent of the automobile more and more grade crossings were eliminated, either by the construction of overhead bridges or underpasses. Since 1937, work of this sort has greatly increased, as the L. & N. has carried out a far-reaching program in cooperation with the federal government. At the end of 1962 here's how the grade crossing situation on the L. & N. looked:

Grade Crossings
(Railroad with Railroad)

There are 93 such crossings on which the L. & N. performs the maintenance, as reported to the I. C. C.

(Railroad with Highway)

Crossings protected by gates, watchmen, or audible or visible signals..1,010
Protected by fixed signs or barriers....................4,398
Not protected 382
Total crossings at grade...................... 5,790

In addition to the highway grade crossings of the railroad there are also some crossings of the L. & N.'s line with that of other railroads, electric interurbans, street railways or with its own line.

While it is true that the Railroad's first grade separation project was not completed until 1883, it is a fact that prior to that time there were a number of "incidental" grade separations on its line, which resulted from the building of a tunnel through a hill, atop of which ran a road, the bridging of a stream which was closely paralleled by a highway or the construction of a trestle across a hollow traversed by a country road.

As the L. & N.'s track and roadbed changed with the times so too did its methods of maintenance. In the old days track maintenance, like nearly everything else, was a leisurely-conducted affair. Section crews at first poled their way to and from work on flat-bottom cars which were propelled forward by the impetus received from a good, hearty push on the ground with a pole, and when the hand car made its appearance it was regarded as a great step forward. Prior to the turn of the century most track work was done manually with pick and shovel, or spike maul and crow-bar, and machinery, except for such bulky items as steam shovels and pile drivers, was unknown. These latter were chiefly used in construction work. In 1905, the L. & N. obtained a steam-powered ditcher and in the following decade experimented tentatively with such items as a derrick car, a wrecking crane, a Lidgerwood unloader, ballast spreaders and locomotive cranes. The first motor car made its appearance upon L. & N. track shortly after the close of World War I and was not long in completely replacing the hand cars of grandfather's era.

Today, the L. & N. has 660 motor cars in service. These cars are continually being replaced with vehicles and, at present, there are 486 vehicles operating over highways only, and 112 vehicles that can operate on highway and rail. It has been in comparatively recent years, however, that mechanization has come into its own on the L. & N.'s track. As of December 31, 1963, there was a total of 2904 units of equipment. Major units include: 20 multiple tampers, 5 spot tampers, 29 ballast regulators, 13 spike drivers, 31 spike pullers, 10 tie bed scarifiers, 13 track liners, 9 tie removers, 10 tie inserters, 39 burro cranes, 15 crawler cranes, 16 locomotive cranes, 7 truck cranes, 2 hi-rail truck cranes, 7 pile drivers, 7 ditcher spreaders and 39 bull graders. The maintenance of way work has also been facilitated in recent years by the timely acquisition of such useful items as weed mowers, track cleaners, adzing machines, air compressors and many other items of power equipment.

Thanks to a vigorous program of research, modification and refinement which extended throughout 1963, the L. & N.'s present-day mechanized track gangs can do the jobs to be done easier, faster, better and safer. In addition to the tools and machinery previously mentioned, recent innovations in track maintenance have included the automatic raising device on multiple tamper, the rail bond grinder, the automatic rail hook attachment, the hydraulic boom attachment, the switch point roller, the portable machine unloader, assorted set-offs, the remote controlled tie inserter, the automatic wire carrier and special cars for unloading crossties. Today, using assembly-line, mass-production techniques, many machines and tools speed the work of tie-renewal, rail replacement and track resurfacing.

That part of the L. & N.'s physical plant, at the end of the year 1963, which was represented by its 5,656 miles of first main track, its 455 miles of second-main track and its 3,146 miles of passing and yard tracks was a thing of truly impressive dimensions. It consisted in part of some 1,650,000 tons of steel rail, 575,000 tons of rail fastenings, 23,059,851 treated crossties, about 77,000,000 board feet of lumber in switch ties, bridge ties, etc., and about 23,500,000 cubic yards of ballast. The other items in the track or roadbed and along the right-of-way, such as switches and frogs, guard rails and clamps, switch stands, signals, bridges and buildings, and tunnels, etc., also represented a truly stupendous amount of work, thought, materials and money.

As of December 31, 1963, there were 4,332 bridges and trestles on the L. & N., with a total length of 104 miles, representing 1,249 steel bridges, with a total length of 37.5 miles and with 175,004 tons of steel in them; 2,741 timber trestles with a total length of 58.3 miles, and 342 concrete trestles with a total length of 8.2 miles.

Bridge across the Cumberland River at Nashville during the latter years of the Civil War. Note flanking block houses for protection of bridge. Man at extreme right is supposed to be Albert Fink, famous L. & N. official and bridge builder.

The L. & N. had 106 tunnels with a total length of 18.22 miles. Of these, 50, or 9.2 miles, were concrete lined, 18, or 2.48 miles, were lined with brick or timber, and 38, or 6.54 miles, were not lined, having been dug through solid rock.

Much of the L. & N.'s right-of-way was fenced with woven or barbed wire and the supporting posts were of black locust, juniper, concrete or steel.

The L. & N.'s total investment in its track, roadbed, right-of-way and structures, as of December 31, 1963, amounted to $479,882,211. In 1963, it spent $10,868,998 for additions to and betterments of that portion of its physical plant, and another $30,275,352 was expended for normal maintenance and repair. It cost the L. & N. about $4,000 in 1963 to maintain each mile of main track.

Keeping the L. & N.'s "railroad" in tip-top condition is thus a big job, an expensive one and one, moreover, that never ends. The average life of a treated crosstie is about 20 years, that of the average new steel rail laid in main track about 15 years and each stretch of track has to be re-ballasted about once every two or three years. The Company is constantly improving its track and that, too, results in change and reconstruction.

For instance, in the 1950s, the L. & N. laid several miles of "frozen-joint" rail track, notably on the Birmingham and Knoxville and Atlanta divisions (more or less experimentally); and in 1958 placed its first welded rail in the track. This consisted of some 15 miles on the M. N. O. & P. Division and involved the installation of 120 "strings" of welded rail, each about one-quarter of a mile long, which had been welded at Mobile. At the end of 1963, the L. & N. had **150** miles of 132 lb. welded rail in its track.

Commencing in 1929, each mile of the more important main-line track has been inspected by a Sperry Detector Car, which detects inner defects in the rails which are hidden from the eye, and the track generally is constantly under the close scrutiny of the section forces. Despite the mechanization of track work, the "human element" continues to be an important one. Many skills are necessary to keep track and roadbed in tip-top condition and to supplement the work of the machines. The operators of the equipment, mechanics, welders, motor car maintainers, foremen, supervisors and higher officials of the L. & N. are all members of a team whose goal has remained unchanged throughout the years – a "railroad" as good as the best.

Presidents of the L. & N. Railroad

From	To	President
September 27, 1851	October 2, 1854	Shreve, L. L.
October 2, 1854	October 2, 1860	Helm, John L.
October 2, 1860	June 11, 1868	Guthrie, James
June 11, 1868	October 8, 1868	Houston, Russell
October 8, 1868	August 18, 1874	Newcomb, H. D.
August 26, 1874	October 6, 1875	Martin, Thomas J.
October 6, 1875	March 24, 1880	Standiford, E. D.
March 24, 1880	December 1, 1880	Newcomb, H. V.
December 1, 1880	February 26, 1881	Green, E. H.
February 26, 1881	May 19, 1884	Baldwin, C. C.
May 19, 1884	June 11, 1884	Rogers, J. S.
June 11, 1884	October 6, 1886	Smith, Milton H.
October 6, 1886	March 9, 1891	Norton, Eckstein
March 9, 1891	February 22, 1921	Smith, Milton H.
March 17, 1921	February 3, 1926	Mapother, Wible L.
March 23, 1926	November 17, 1934	Cole, Whitefoord R.
November 27, 1934	July 1, 1950	Hill, James B.
July 1, 1950	April 1, 1959	Tilford, John E.
April 1, 1959	—	Kendall, William H.

(Presidents' photographs on pages 386-387)

WILLIAM H. KENDALL
April 1, 1959

JOHN E. TILFORD
July 1, 1950 - April 1, 1959

JAMES B. HILL
November 17, 1934 - July 1, 1950

WHITEFOORD R. COLE
March 23, 1926 - November 17, 1934

WIBLE L. MAPOTHER
March 17, 1921 - February 3, 1926

MILTON H. SMITH
June 11, 1884 - October 6, 1886
March 9, 1891 - February 22, 19.

ECKSTEIN NORTON
October 6, 1886 - March 9, 1891

J. S. ROGERS
May 19, 1884 - June 11, 1884

C. C. BALDWIN
February 26, 1881 - May 19, 188

E. H. GREEN
December 1, 1880 – February 26, 1881

H. V. NEWCOMB
March 24, 1880 – December 1, 1880

E. D. STANDIFORD
October 6, 1875 – March 24, 1880

H. D. NEWCOMB
October 8, 1868 – August 18, 1874

RUSSELL HOUSTON
June 11, 1868 – October 8, 1868

JAMES GUTHRIE
October 2, 1860 – June 11, 1868

JOHN L. HELM
October 2, 1854 – October 2, 1860

L. L. SHREVE
September 27, 1851 – October 2, 1854

Presidents
Of the
L & N
Railroad
1851-1963

(A photograph of the sixth president, **Thomas J. Martin**, could not be located.)

387

Railroads Acquired, Leased or Constructed to Form Louisville & Nashville System

ALABAMA AND FLORIDA RAILROAD – 1899†
ALABAMA MINERAL RAILROAD – 1891
ATHENS AND TELLICO RAILWAY – 1911
ATLANTA, KNOXVILLE AND NORTHERN RAILWAY – 1905
BARDSTOWN AND LOUISVILLE RAILROAD – 1860
BAY MINETTE AND FORT MORGAN RAILROAD – 1905
BIRMINGHAM AND TUSCALOOSA RAILROAD – 1915
BIRMINGHAM MINERAL RAILROAD – 1887
BIRMINGHAM, SELMA AND NEW ORLEANS RAILWAY – 1901
BLACK MOUNTAIN RAILROAD – 1923
CHESAPEAKE AND NASHVILLE RAILWAY – 1906
CINCINNATI INTER-TERMINAL RAILROAD – 1904
CUMBERLAND AND MANCHESTER RAILROAD – 1927
CUMBERLAND AND OHIO RAILROAD
  (Northern and Southern Divisions – 1881 and 1878
CUMBERLAND RIVER AND TENNESSEE RAILROAD – 1901
DECATUR BELT AND TERMINAL RAILROAD – 1892
GALLATIN AND SCOTTSVILLE RAILWAY – 1906
HARRIMAN, KNOXVILLE AND EASTERN RAILROAD – 1912
HENDERSON BRIDGE AND RAILROAD – 1885
JELLICO, BIRDEYE AND NORTHERN RAILWAY – 1902
KENTUCKY AND VIRGINIA RAILROAD – 1915
KENTUCKY CENTRAL RAILWAY – 1891
KENTUCKY HIGHLANDS RAILROAD – 1908
KNOXVILLE, LaFOLLETTE AND JELLICO RAILROAD – 1905
LEWISBURG AND NORTHERN RAILROAD – 1915
LEXINGTON AND EASTERN RAILWAY – 1913
LOUISVILLE AND ATLANTIC RAILROAD – 1909
LOUISVILLE, CINCINNATI AND LEXINGTON RAILWAY – 1881
LOUISVILLE HARRODS CREEK AND WESTPORT RAILROAD – 1881
LOUISVILLE, HENDERSON AND ST. LOUIS RAILWAY – 1929
MADISONVILLE, HARTFORD AND EASTERN RAILROAD – 1910
MEMPHIS AND OHIO RAILROAD – 1867
MEMPHIS, CLARKSVILLE AND LOUISVILLE RAILROAD – 1868
MIDDLE AND EAST TENNESSEE CENTRAL RAILROAD – 1906
MIDDLESBOROUGH BELT RAILROAD – 1896
MIDDLESBOROUGH RAILROAD – 1896
MOBILE AND MONTGOMERY RAILWAY – 1881
NASHVILLE AND DECATUR RAILROAD – 1871
NASHVILLE, CHATTANOOGA AND ST. LOUIS RAILWAY – 1957
NASVHILLE, FLORENCE AND SHEFFIELD RAILWAY – 1887
NEW ORLEANS, MOBILE AND TEXAS RAILROAD – 1880
OWENSBORO AND NASHVILLE RAILWAY – 1881
PENSACOLA AND ATLANTIC RAILROAD – 1891
PENSACOLA AND SELMA RAILROAD – 1880
PENSACOLA RAILROAD – 1880
PINE MOUNTAIN RAILROAD – 1905
ST. LOUIS AND SOUTHEASTERN RAILWAY – 1879
SHEFFIELD AND TUSCUMBIA RAILROAD – 1896
SHELBY RAILROAD – 1881
SHELBY, BLOOMFIELD AND OHIO RAILWAY – 1901
SOUTH AND NORTH ALABAMA RAILROAD – 1871
SOUTHEAST AND ST. LOUIS RAILWAY – 1881
SOUTHERN ALABAMA RAILROAD – 1899
SWAN CREEK RAILWAY – 1908
WASIOTO AND BLACK MOUNTAIN RAILROAD – 1911
YELLOW RIVER RAILROAD – 1906

*Listing includes only names of railroads as designated when acquired. Numerous very small roads acquired to form some of the branch line trackage are not included.

†Year first operated by L. & N.

In Grateful Acknowledgment

The author wishes to gratefully acknowledge his debt and to express his appreciation to the many officials and other employes of the L. & N. Railroad whose kind cooperation lightened his work of research. A by no means complete list of those who helped on the first edition would certainly include (with titles shown as of 1942): J. J. Elder, executive assistant; J. L. James, assistant editor, L. & N. Magazine; M. K. Gilbert, assistant secretary; R. O. Kessack, chief clerk and freight car distributor, superintendent of transportation's office; F. A. Russell, advertising agent; G. T. Tate, principal assistant engineer; C. H. Blackman, chief engineer; D. P. Bibb, accounting engineer; I. D. Behen, special engineer, superintendent of machinery's office, L. J. Kleinman, supervisor of mails; James Killoran, chief clerk to engineer-maintenance of way, and I. W. Newman, assistant engineer, chief engineer's office, all of Louisville, and J. E. White, Hazard, Ky.; V. D. Howard, Nashville, Tenn.; Miss Mossie Heninger, Knoxville, Tenn., and J. E. McShane, Middlesboro, Ky., division editors for the L. & N. Magazine at the points mentioned.

Some of those listed in the preceding paragraph also assisted in the publication of subsequent editions of the L. & N. History. Particular valuable assistance in the compilation and publishing of this fifth edition of the history was received from Warren A. McNeill, director of public relations, Louisville; Norman F. Hurt, public relations representative, Louisville; Edison H. Thomas, manager, news bureau, Louisville; Charles B. Castner, assistant manager, news bureau, Louisville; William R. Heffren, assistant editor, L. & N. Magazine, Louisville; C. N. Beasley, chief photographer, Louisville; P. A. Wagner, then-superintendent of dining cars, Louisville; James B. Clark, chief engineer, Louisville; Mr. Kleinman; Grady R. Sproles, Jr., assistant chief engineer, Louisville; and N. C. Kieffer, manager of industrial development, Louisville.

The author throughout has leaned heavily upon such sources as "The Historical Development of the Louisville & Nashville Railroad System," by J. G. Kerr; "The Corporate History of the L. & N. Railroad Company and Roads in Its System," by E. W. Hines; "The Beginning of the L. & N.," by Thos. D. Clark, Ph.D.; "The Story of Coal and Iron in Alabama," by Ethel M. Armes; "American Railroads – Government Control and Reconstruction Policies," by William J. Cunningham, A. M.; "The Louisville & Nashville Railroad – An Outline History," by John Leeds Kerr; "The L. & N. Railroad – 1850-1868," an unpublished thesis by James F. Tanner; "Locomotives of the L. & N." by Paul T. Warner; the Company's Annual Reports, 1850-1963, old files in the president's and general manager's offices, past issues of the L. & N. Magazine, old files of newspapers published along the line, the minute books of the Company, and various documents, contracts, etc., in the secretary's office. Many persons generously contributed pictures and items of interest for inclusion in the history and many conversations had with veteran employes were also of valuable assistance in forging a link between the present and the past.

Index

A

"A" Street Cut-off, Louisville 108
Abandonment of branch lines 256, 307
Aber, R. A. 148
Adairville Branch 256
Adams, B. J. 26
Adams Express Company 343
Adams, George 196
Air brakes, applied 54, 142, 143
Air brakes, evolution of 333
Air conditioning 258
"Airline" Route. 7
Air lines 229
Airplanes, competition 272
Alabama & Chattanooga Railroad 48
Alabama & Florida R. R. 58, 62, 141
Alabama Courier 52
Alabama Great Southern R. R. . . 48, 128, 240
Alabama State Docks 244
Alabama Steel & Shipbuilding Co. 122
Aldrian Mine 206
Aldrich, Truman H. 85, 105
Alice Furnace 120
Ambler, C. E. 217
Amendments to charter. 11, 39
American Association. 124, 199
American Car and Foundry Co. 343
American Cyanamid Plant, Pensacola . . . 305
American Express Company 344
American Locomotive Company 358
American Railway Association 124
American Railway Express Company . . . 343
Anderson, General 31
Anderson, John B. & Co. 347
Andrews Raid 321
Annex to general office building 244
Anniston & Atlantic R. R. 88
Anniston & Cincinnati R. R. 88
"Arbuckles" 148
Armes, Miss Ethel, "Story of Coal
  and Iron in Alabama" 50, 157
Arthur, Alexander A. 94
Asher Coal Mining Co. 250
Asher, T. J. 199
Association of American
  Railroads 260, 270
Association of Ry. Executives 260
Atchison, Topeka & Santa Fe R. R. 221
Athens & Tellico Ry. 155
Atkinson Yard, New 311
Atlanta & West Point R. R. 67
Atlanta & West Point Ry. 254
Atlanta Journal 161
Atlanta, Knoxville & Northern Ry. 144
Atlantic Coast Line Railroad . . . 161, 204, 319
Atmore, C. P. 52
"August Belmont" (steamship) 107
Automatic air brakes, evolution of 333
Automatic block signals, installation
  of, 1912, and thereafter. 225
Automatic couplers applied 143
Automatic couplers, evolution of 332
Automatic telephone system, general
  office building 209
Automatic train control, first
  installation of 236
Automobiles via piggyback 308
Auto Vans, fast freight trains 319

B

Baggage service, history of 343
Baird & Co., locomotives 53
Bald Mountain, early obstacle. 147
Baldwin, C. C. 73
Baldwin County, penetration of by
  railroad; development of, etc. 151
Baldwin, M. W. 349
Ballast 373
Baltimore & Ohio 1, 3, 353
Baltimore & Ohio S. W. Ry. 135
Banditry on trains . . . . 111, et seq.
Bardstown Branch 16
Baring Brothers 93
"Barocoa," steamship 106
Barrage Balloon Training Center 277
Barren County Railroad 16
Basic iron produced in Alabama . . . 120, 121
Bay Minette and Fort Morgan
  Railroad, construction of 159
Beam truss 371
Belmont, August & Co. 161
Belmont, Major August 161, 231
Belpaire fire-box 356
Bessemer, beginning of 84
Bessemer, Henry 374
Bethlehem Iron Company 376
Big Four Route. 3
Birmingham and Northwestern Railroad . . 217
Birmingham, beginning of 48
Birmingham Mineral R. R. 84, 86
Birmingham Rolling Mills Co. 122
Birmingham, Selma & New Orleans
  Railway, purchase of 156
Birmingham Southern R. R. 141
Birmingham & Tuscaloosa Railroad 182
Birmingham underpasses 239, 240
"Black Satchel" the 148
Blair Fork Branch 198, 286
Blue Creek Extension 87
Board of Trade Building, Louisville 245
Boeing, Company, New Orleans 305
Bond Brothers 379
Bowaters Southern Paper Corporation . . . 306
Bowling Green & Tennessee Railroad . . . 9, 10
Boyd, General James F. 52
Boyles Shops, construction of 167
Boyles Yard constructed 291
Bragg, Gen. Braxton 35, 36
Brest-Litovsk, treaty of 213

BRIDGES –

  C. & O. 114
  Covington & Cincinnati Elevated
    Railroad & Transfer & Bridge Co. 114

Danville	253
Green River, rebuilt	239
Henderson	64, 252
Mobile River	239
N. & C. (Newport, Ky.)	69
Number of Miles on System	383
Pearl River	296
Raising and Strengthening	313
Brierfield, Blocton & Birmingham Ry.	105
Broadcast from Pan-American	259
Broaddus, Andrew	72
Brooks, T. E.	252
Bruce, Judge H. W.	173
Buckner, Gen. Simon Bolivar	31, 32
Buell, Gen. Don Carlos	35, 36, 37
Buffalo Creek Spur, completion of	198
Bullitt, Joshua	6
Burnside, Gen. Ambrose E.	39
Bus and truck competition, origin of	228

C

Cabooses, New	316
Cafeteria cars, operation of by Co.	214, 338
Cahaba coal fields	105
Cahaba Coal Mining Co.	85
Cain Creek Branch, construction of	158
Callahan Construction Company	201
Callahan, John	152
Camden Branch, completion of	156
Cammack, Addison	162
Camp Branch	286
Cannel coal	174
Capitalization complete, original	8, 9
Capital stock, increase in	66, 102, 181, 236
Carnegie, Andrew, interests	120
Carnegie Bros. Co. Ltd.	376
Carolina, Clinchfield and Ohio Railway	204
Carolina, Clinchfield and Ohio Connection, building of	204, 249
Carr's Fork Branch, completion of	198
Carriers Taxing Act of 1937	261
Carrollton Railroad	365
Carter & Thomas, stages	22
Catron's Creek Branch, building of	202
Cecilian Branch	55
Centennial celebration on L. & N.	288
Centralized hiring of employes	300
Centralized traffic control	274, 276, 285, 291
Central of Georgia R. R.	86, 134
Central Southern R. R.	46
Century Branch	306
Chadwell, I. L.	182
"Chairs" (for support of rail)	374
Change of gauge	78, et seq.
CHARTER –	
Granting of	2
Description of	4
Chatsworth, Ga., naming of	149
Chavies Coal Company	198
Chef Menteur Bridge	236
Chenoa Branch, building of	205
C. & O. Bridge	247
Chesapeake and Nashville Railway Company, origin of	178

Chesapeake & Ohio Ry.	114
Chesapeake, Ohio & Southwestern R.R.	129
Chesapeake & Ohio Southwestern Railway	56
Chicago & Alton R. R.	345
Chicago & Eastern Illinois Ry.	133, 339
Chicago, Indianapolis & Louisville Ry.	163
Chicago, St. Louis & New Orleans Ry.	56
Chicago Times-Herald	133
Cholera epidemic	13
Christian, John L., new director	324
Chrysler Corporation, New Orleans	305
Cincinnati, Green River and Nashville R.R.	178
Cincinnati, Hamilton & Dayton R.R.	248
Cincinnati Inter-Terminal R. R.	241, 248
Cincinnati Southern	178
Cincinnati Union Terminal	240
City of Louisville stock purchase	16
"City of Miami," inauguration of	272
Civil War	29, et seq.
Clark, Edgar E.	210
Clarksville & Princeton Branch	256
Clarksville Mineral Branch	118, 256
Clear Fork Branch	201
Clear Fork Tunnel Branch	201
Clinton Engineering Works	277
Clover Fork Extension commenced	205, 277
Cloverport and Victoria Railroad	174
Coach 665, General's museum car	323
COAL	
And iron in Alabama	84, 85
As engine fuel, first use of	53
Fields of Eastern Kentucky	182, et seq.
Fields of Western Kentucky	74
From Alabama	66
Traffic	309
Coaling plant, Pensacola	240
Coal traffic – C. V. Division, brief history of	206
Coal traffic – E. K. Division, brief history of	206
Coke furnaces	65
Cole, Whitefoord R.	260
Colonization of territories served	151
Colston, William A.	217
Combustion Engineering, Chattanooga	319
Communications Systems, L. & N.'s	313, 314
Congressional Medals of Honor, First	322
Conservation of material	275, 276
Consolidated Aluminum's new plant	305
Consolidated Coal Company	198
Consolidation of divisions	259
Consolidation type locomotives	355
Cooper, J. Crossan, Jr., new director	324
Copper Basin of Tennessee	145, 146
Copperhill, Tenn.	145
Corbin Yard, completion of northbound yard	226
Cottier, Alonzo E.	215
Courier-Journal	77, 193
Courtenay, W. H.	252
Courtesy rallies	266
Covington & Cincinnati Elevated R. R. & Transfer & Bridge Co.	114
Covington & Lexington R. R.	115, 116

Cow Creek Branch 153
Craig, G. W. 44
Crawford, Ky., yard 227
Creosote treatment 61, 379
Crescent City Sleeping Car Company . . . 348
Crescent, The, New equipment
   ordered for 283
Criminals, activities on trains . . . . . 111, et seq.
Crist, James F., new director 324
Crosstie, evolution of 378
Crossties, number of 372
Cullman, Ala. 52
Cullman, John S. 52
Cumberland & Manchester Railroad . 205, 238
Cumberland & Ohio R. R. 56, 72, 178
Cumberland Gap Tunnel 98, 99
Cumberland Valley Branch 91
Cutchins, W. S., new director 324

D

Dalton Boys, the 110
Danger Fork Branch, completion of 198
Danville, Tenn., bridge 253
Data Processing 314
"Davidson" (locomotive) 349
Davidson Branch Spur, completion of . . . 198
Day, H. G. 217
DeBardeleben Coal & Iron Co. 85
DeBardeleben, H. F. 85
Decatur shops built 90
DeCoursey Yard, New automated 311
Delano, Lyman 252
Delano, Warren, Jr. 199
"Depression, The" 250
Diamond buttons 234, 235
Dickens, Charles 19
Diesel electric
   locomotives . . . . 269, 290, 315, 364, et seq.
Dining car, evolution of 337
Dining car service – World War II 279
D'Invilliers, E. V. 91
Divisions consolidated 259
Dixie Flagler 272
Dixie Hummer 133
Dixie Jets, fast freight trains 318
Dixieland, The 273
Doe Run Spur 292
"Doodle-Bug, The" 241
DOUBLE-TRACKING –
   C. V. Division 1924-26 227
   Covington and Winchester 193
   E. K. Division in 1920-1926 227
   Gentilly and Higgins, La. 276
   Harlan and Corbin 206
   Hazard and Perritt 206
   Lebanon Jct. and Shepherdsville 172
   Lebanon Jct. to Parkston 238
   Livingston to Corbin 180
   Patio to Sinks 227
   Ravenna and Pryse 206
Dudley Branch 105
Duke, Gen. Basil 37
Duncan, Alexander E. 324
duPont, New Plant in Tennessee 305

Dutch stockholders 73
Dynamometer car 262

E

Eads Bridge, St. Louis 63
Eager, George R. 146
Earlington Cut-off, construction of 175
Earnings, World War I 209
East End Station, Cincinnati 249
Eastern Ky. coal fields . . . . 178, et seq.
East Tennessee, Virginia & Georgia R. R. . . . 67
Edgefield & Kentucky R. R. Co. 64
Educational program for
   supervisory personnel 300
Elder, J. J. 232
Electro-Motive Division 362
Elizabethtown, first train to 22
Elizabethtown, Lexington and
   Big Sandy Railroad 134
Elkhorn coal field 185
Elkhorn Collieries Company 198
Elkins Act of 1903 110
Elkton & Guthrie R. R. 100, 119
Ellijay R. R. 144
Elliott, Howard 210
Elliott, Major R. H. 184
Elyton Land Co. 48
Emergency R. R. Transportation
   Act – 1933 258
Employe advantages in 1963 325
Engines – (See Illustrations)
English investments 73
Ensley, Col. Enoch 75, 85
"E. O. Saltmarsh" (steamer) 107
Epidemics, cholera, yellow fever,
   etc. 13, 53, 56, 124, 125
Erie R. R. 248
Ernest, Mr. & Mrs. G. W. 57
Etowah Shops, construction of 154, 167
Eureka Co., at Oxmoor, Ala. 65
Eureka Furnace Co. 85
European bond market explored 12
Evans automobile loading device 262
Evans, George E. 132, 251
Evansville & Southern Illinois R. R. 63
Evansville & Terre Haute R. R. 133
Evansville, Carmi & Paducah Railroad . . . 63
Evansville, Henderson & Nashville R. R. . 64, 74
Exchange Hotel, dispute at 49
Export Coal Company 105
Express Service, evolution of 343

F

Fairbanks Locomotive Works 349
Family Rallies 266
Fast freight lines 40
Fast freight service 267, 268, 318
Fawcett, Colonel J. C. 173
FEDERAL CONTROL –
   Inception of 216
   Act of March 21, 1918 216
   Cost of 221
   Settlement payment to L. & N. by Govt. . . 223

During World War II . . . . 214, et seq.
Federal Safety Appliance Act 332
Feminine personnel, increase in
 During World War I 215
Feminine personnel, increase in
 During World War II 279, 280
Fies Spur 286
Financial Inspection Tours,
 1954 and 1962 . . . . 298, 299
Fink, Albert
 . . . . . . 18, 42, 51, 52, 53, 131, 239, 371
FIRST –
 Accidents on L. & N. 17
 Basic iron produced in Alabama 120
 Coke pig iron, Oxmoor 65
 Grade Separation Project 382
 Railroad completed west of
  Alleghenies 69
 Steel produced in Alabama 86
 Steel rail placed in L. & N. track 54
 Track laid 12
 Train, Louisville to Knoxville 67
 Train, Louisville to Nashville 25
 Train over L. & N. 25
 Train to Elizabethtown 22
 Train to Harlan 202
 Woman L. & N. employe 72
First Creek Branch, completion of 197
Flood in Ohio Valley 264
Floods in Eastern Kentucky and Tenn. . . . 320
Floods on divisions 245
Foley Branch – Construction of 159
Ford Motor Company, Nashville . . . 292, 305
Fordsville Branch, completion of 175
Fort Wayne and Southern Railroad 3
Four Mile Branch – building of 205
Fox, James W. 185
Frankfort and Cincinnati Railway –
 acquisition of, etc. 179
Franklin Route, early surveys 7
Freight cars, new and rebuilt 317
Friendly Service movement 266
Fruit Growers Express 317
Frozen-Joint Rail 384
Fuller, William A. 321
Fulton, John 185

G

Gadsden Ordnance Plant 270
Gallatin and Scottsville Railway 178
Galt House 49
Gap Associates 94
Garvin, William 26
Gate City Branch 256
Gates-Hawley pool 160
Gates, John W. "Bet-a-million" 160
Gates Sleeping Car Company 347
Gauge, change of
 (See change of gauge)
Gaulbert St. Cut-off, Louisville . . . 108, 377
Geddes, Major James 6, 173
General Electric spur at Louisville,
 serves G.E., Ford and others 292
General goes on commemorative campaign 321

General Motors, Electro-Motive
 Division 362
General Office Building,
 2nd & Main 55, 56
General office building annex 244
General offices at Louisville, history of . . . 164
General Order 27 221
General Time Convention 83
GEO type of track 380
"George MacLeod" (locomotive) 349
"George Rogers Clark" (Pullman) 346
Georgia Railroad 119, 134
Georgian, The 283
Gibbs-Inman Building, Louisville 245
Gilmer, Frank 49
Gilmer, J. N. 48
Gilmore, Jim 152
Glasgow Railway 16, 119
Glasgow Route 7
Gonzalez Spur serves Chemstrand
 near Pensacola, Fla. 292
Good will tours 232
Gould, Jay 73
Gould, John V. 6, 7
Government ownership, agitation for
 – 1921 232
Group insurance, inception of 234
Grade crossings 382
Grade separation, Birmingham 239, 240
Grade separations, East Louisville 263
Grade separations, 4th and G and
 3rd and K, Louisville 239
Grade separations, Greater Cincinnati . . . 240
Green, Col. Edward H. 73, 162, 353
Green, Hetty 73, 162, 353
"Green Line," fast freight 40
Green River 7, 14
Green River Bridge 14, 23
Gross ton miles handled per freight
 train hour 291
Gulf Coast storms 176, 210, 240
Gulf ports 45
Gulf Transit Co. 106
Gulf Wind, The, inaugurated 284
Guthrie, James . . . 8, 18, 26, 28, 31, 41, 50, 131

H

Hall, Bolling 49
Harahan, J. T. 132
Hardin, Ben 8
Harlan Coal Land Company 199
Harlan, J. B. 111
Harlan, Ky., first train to 202
Harlan, Marion B. 111
Harriman, Knoxville & Eastern R. R. 155
Harris, Gov. Isham G. 31
Harrison, Fairfax 210
Harp, Green 152
Hawley, Edwin 160
Hawley-Gates combination 160
Haydon, J. D. 93
Haydon Mountain Tunnel 180

Hays, Will S. 355
Hazard Herald (Building of North
  Fork Extension) 194, 195
Hazard, Ky., completion of railroad
  to 195, 196
Helena & Blocton Branch 105
Helm, John L. 2, 15, 19, 23, 26
Henderson & Nashville R. R. 22
Henderson Bridge 64, 76, 252
Henderson Bridge Co. 64, 76
Henderson Steel & Mfg. Co. 86
Hepburn Act 110
Highcliff, Tennessee, train
  wreck at 279
Hill, James B. 260, 266, 286, 288
Hill, L. M. 337
Hillman, T. T. 85
Hines, Walker D. 132, 221
Hiwassee Loop 148
Hobbs, R. R. 246
Holden, Hale 210
Homestead Spur 286
"Hook and Eye," The 148
Horne, C. M. 196
Hotbox Detectors 314
Houston, Judge Russell 50, 130
Howe Truss 371
Howell Shops built 90
Hubbard, Elbert 104
Humming Bird, The, placed in
  service 283
Huntington, Collis P. 114, 129
Huntsville Branch No. 1 87
Huntsville Branch No. 2 .... 88, 155
Hyatt, Gus. 111

I

Illinois Central R. R. 56, 102, 129, 174
"Industrial parks" created 299, 306
Industrialization in the South 304
Industry expansion on L. & N.,
  1949-58 286
Industry, new on L. & N. 305
Inspection of watches 83
Institutional advertising 1921-1926 232
International Harvester Company 199
Interstate Commerce Commission
  .... 109, 110, 236, 247, 257
Interstate Railroad 204
Iron, basic, produced in Alabama 120
Iron in track
  (change to steel) 367

J

Jake's Branch Spur 198
"James Guthrie" (locomotive) 349
"James Guthrie" (Pullman) 346
James, Jesse 110
Janney type couplers 333
Jeffersonville & Columbus Railroad 3
"John James Audubon" (Pullman) 346
Johnston, Gen. Joseph E. 150
Joseph, David J. Co. 256

Jouett, E. S. 189
Justin, Edsall & Hawley 12, 368

K

Kayne Avenue yards 135
Keen, J. D. 219
Keesler Field 277
Kendall, President William H. 301
Kenmont Coal Company 198
Kennedy, W. F. 217
Kentenia Corporation 199
Kentucky and Mississippi Railroad 4
Kentucky and Virginia Railroad 200
Kentucky Central (railroad or rail-
  way) 69, 114, 248
Kentucky Locomotive Works 165, 353
Kentucky Union Railway Co. 183
"Kiddie Specials" 284
Knight Cars 347
Knoxville, Cumberland Gap &
  Louisville (railroad or railway) ... 97, 161
Knoxville Daily Journal 201
Knoxville, LaFollette and Jellico
  Railroad 144, 151, 201
Knoxville Southern R. R. 146
Krug, Frank 252
Kruttschnitt, Julius 210, 211

L

Lackawanna Iron & Coal Company ... 376
Lady Ensley Coal, Iron & R. R. Co. 75
Lamb, A. J. 93
Land grants 68, 271
Lane Commission 220
Laying of crossties, first 12
Laying of rail, first 12
Lay-offs, two-day 251
Leatherwood Creek Branch built ... 198, 277
Lebanon Branch 39, 67
Leeds, Pulaski 86
Leewood Yard expanded 312
Left Fork Branch 205, 250
LeGros, A. F. 239
Lehigh and New England Railroad 316
Lester, Harry 111
Lewis, Maj. E. C. 137, 173
Lewisburg and Northern Railroad 182
Lexington and Eastern Railway
  .... 184, 186, 188, et seq.
Lexington & Frankfort R. R. 71
Lexington & Ohio Railroad .. 2, 3, 69, 70, 349
Lick Branch Spur, building of. 205
Licking & Lexington R. R. 116
Lighting in coaches (evolution of) 328
Lincoln, Abraham 30
Lincoln Memorial University 95
Link-and-pin coupler 143, 332
Little Belle Furnace 120
Little Miami R. R. 248, 249
Lively, H. T. 233
Lively Lines 233
Locke, E. S. 217
Locomotive classification chart 353

LOCOMOTIVES –
(See illustrations "engines")
Longest non-stop coal-powered run
  in U. S. 273
Loomis, Daniel P. 322
Lot's Creek Branch 198
Louisville and Atlantic
  Railroad .... 187 et seq., 256
Louisville & Bardstown Railroad 16
Louisville & Cleveland Straight Line
  Railroad 3
Louisville & Frankfort R. R. 71
Louisville & Nashville and Great
  Southern 52
L. & N. Cooperative Club 232, 300
L. & N. Credit Union 232
L. & N. Employes' Magazine 233, 282
L. & N. Fishing Club 300
L. & N. Golf Club 232, 300
L. & N. Veterans Club 300
L. & N. Railway Operating
  Battalion 281
Louisville & Nashville Terminal Co. ... 135
Louisville & Sandusky Railroad 3
Louisville Bridge Co. 41
Louisville, Cincinnati & Lexington
  (railroad or railway) 69, 72, 247
Louisville Courier 6, 20, 21, 22
Louisville Courier-Journal 219
Louisville Democrat 6
Louisville & Gulf Line (fast freight) ... 40
Louisville, Hardinsburg & Western 175
Louisville, Harrods Creek &
  Westport R. R. 72, 102
Louisville, Henderson & St. Louis
  Railway 173
Louisville Journal 6
Louisville, Paducah & Southwestern
  R. R. 55
Louisville, St. Louis and Texas
  Railway 108
Louisville Southern 187
Loyall Yard 226
Lynch, Ky. (U. S. Steel) 204
Lynn Camp, Ky. 119

M

Madisonville, Hartford and Eastern R.R. ... 175
Magoffin, Governor 30
Mail handling, electronic 315
Maloney Branch 274
Mammoth Cave National Park 105
Mammoth Cave Railroad 103
Mann Boudoir Car Company 347
Mann, Col. E. H. 133
Mapother, Wible L. 217, 235
Marietta & North Georgia R. R. .. 144, 145, 149
Marietta, Canton & Ellijay R. R. 144
Marigold Spur 286
Markham, C. H. 219
Martin, Thomas J. 53
Martin's Fork Branch 204
Maryville Branch 155

Master Car Builders' Association 333
Maxine Spur 282
Mayo, John C. C. 192
Maysville & Lexington R. R. 115
McAdoo, William G. 220
"McAdoos" (freight engines) 359
McAllister, Ward 95
McBride, Mrs. Charles E. 72
McCallum Truss 371
McCracken, A. M. 174
McCracken, C. W. 174
McCracken, H. M. 174
McCracken, J. K. 174
McCracken, W. V. 173
McCreath, Andrew S. 91, 185
McDonald, W. J. 217, 324
McDowell, W. A. 196
McHarg, Henry K. 148
McKee & Swigert 70
McKinney, J. I. 125
Memphis & Charleston R. R. 22, 75
Memphis & Grenada R. R. 22
Memphis & Little Rock R. R. 22
Memphis & Ohio
  Railroad 18, 26, 27, 43 371
Memphis Branch 17, 20, 23, 26, 42
Memphis, Clarksville & Louisville
  R. R. 18, 26, 27, 43
Memphis Union Station 209
Mengel, C. C. & Bros. Co. 107
Merger with N. C. & St. L. Ry.,
  Aug. 30, 1957 298
Meridian and Bigbee River Railway ... 157
Middle and East Tennessee Central
  Railroad 178
Middlesboro News-Record 201
Middlesborough Belt R. R. 99
Middlesborough R. R. 98, 99
Middlesborough's name 93
Mikado type freight locomotives 358
Milan Ordnance Center 276
Milan, Tenn. 282
Military establishments served by
  L. & N. (World War II) 270, 276, 277
Milner, John T. 48, 49, 85
"Milton H. Smith" (Pullman) 346
Missouri Pacific R. R. 79
Mitchell, E. K. 49
Mobile & Great Northern R. R. 58
Mobile and Montgomery Railway 58
Mobile & Ohio R. R. 22
Mobray, F. W. 109
Mogul type engines 355
Monarch Sleeping Car Company 347
Monon Route 3, 163
Montfort, ... 217
Montgomery & Prattville R. R. 134
Moore & Richardson Locomotive
  Works 349, 351
Morgan, Gen. John
  Hunt 33, 34, 37, 239
Morgan, J. P. & Co. 161
Morganfield Branch 268
Morton-Atkinson Cut-off 175
Morton, Seymour & Co. 11, 16, 367

395

Morton, W. S. Jr. ... 197
Moses, A. J. ... 324
Motor cars ... 383
Mountain Eagle (newspaper) ... 194
Mountain type locomotives ... 360
Mt. Vernon R. R. ... 63
Muir, Judge ... 31
Muldraugh's Hill ... 7, 14, 15, 18, 238, 368
Murphy, Sallie Curtis, first woman employe ... 72
Muscogee Wharf coaling plant ... 240

N

Napier Branch ... 256
Nashville American (newspaper) ... 138, 139
Nashville & Chattanooga Railroad ... 3, 25, 49
Nashville & Decatur R. R. ... 45, 46, 75, 134
Nashville & Florence R. R. ... 75
Nashville & Memphis R. R. ... 26
Nashville & Northwestern R. R. ... 22, 43
Nashville, Chattanooga & St. Louis Ry. ... 62, 67, 85, 118, 119, 135, 290, 298
Nashville Daily Sun ... 138
Nashville, Florence & Sheffield (Railroad or Railway) ... 75, 119
Nashville Terminals ... 135 et seq.
Nashville Union Station ... 138 et seq.
National Railway Historical Society ... 322
National Railway Publication Co. ... 124
New Albany and Salem Railroad ... 3
Newcomb, H. D. ... 50, 53
Newcomen Society of North America honors L. & N. ... 289
New Orleans, Mobile & Chattanooga R. R. ... 59, 379
New Orleans, Mobile & Texas R. R. ... 58, 59, 60
Newport & Cincinnati Bridge ... 69, 172, 241, 247, 249
Newport News and Mississippi Valley Railroad ... 174
New York Central Sleeping Car Company ... 347
New York Rapid Transit Transportation Co. ... 162
Nicknames applied to railroads ... 134
Niles and Company ... 349
Noble, Samuel ... 88
Norfolk & Western Ry. ... 183
North & South, publication ... 151
Northern Coal and Coke Co. ... 186
North Fork Extension ... 189, et seq. 208
Norton, Eckstein ... 73, 99
"No. 29" (Song) ... 355

O

O'Brien, R. E. ... 92
O'Fallon Branch, abandonment of ... 274
Official Guide ... 124
Ohio River flood ... 264, et seq.
Ohio Valley Railway ... 102

"Old Kentucky Home" ... 102
Old Wallins Creek Coal Company ... 206
"Old Reliable" (origin of nickname) ... 52
Oliver, Lucien, E., new director ... 324
Oliver Springs Branch ... 201
Organizational Set-up Revised ... 324
Owensboro & Nashville (Railroad or Railway) ... 64, 74

P

Pacific type passenger locomotives ... 360
Paducah, Tennessee & Alabama R. R. ... 129
Paine, E. H. & Company ... 348
Paine Harris & Company ... 347
Paine Wang & Company ... 348
Paine, Wang and Shelton Sleeping Car Company ... 348
Pan-American Broadcast ... 259
Pan-American, The ... 235
Panics of 1873, 1893 and 1907 ... 51, 55, 176
Paris, Tenn., Shops ... 168
Pascagoula, grain elevator at ... 305
Passenger fares, reduced ... 253, et seq.
Passengers carried, 1950-58 ... 293
Pay cuts ... 251
Pearl Harbor ... 274, 275
Pecos River bridge ... 193
Pee Vee Spur ... 286
Pennsylvania R. R. ... 3, 248
Pensacola & Atlantic R. R. ... 68, 141
Pensacola & Louisville R. R. ... 62
Pensacola & Selma R. R. ... 62
Pensacola coaling plant ... 240
Pensacola R. R. ... 62
Pensions ... 170, et seq.
Pennsylvania Railroad ... 3, 69, 79
Perkins, Thatcher ... 53, 353
Pick-up & Delivery Service ... 254
Pierce, R. R. ... 173
Piggyback Operations ... 296, 307
Pine Mountain R. R. ... 155
Pioneer Mining & Mfg. Co. ... 85
Pipe lines ... 278
Plum St. yard ... 249
Pontchartrain Railroad ... 58
Poor Valley Route ... 91
Portland Railroad ... 70
Port Royal R. R. ... 67
Potters Fork Spur ... 198
Powell, J. R. ... 48
Powell's Valley R. R. ... 97
Powers, Col. J. D. ... 173
Prattville Branch ... 256
Pratt Coal & Coke Co. ... 66, 85
Pratt Coal Company ... 158
Pratt, Daniel ... 85
Prudential Insurance Company ... 234
Puckett's Creek Branch ... 205
Pullman's Palace Car Company ... 348
Pullman Southern Car Company ... 348
Pullman car (evolution of) ... 344
Pullman cars, named on L. & N. ... 346
Pullman cars, 57 acquired on July 1, 1949 ... 283

Pullman Company 344
Pullman, George M. 345

Q

Quarles, Wm. A. 28

R

Radio, Two-way for end-to-end
   communication for freight trains 295
Radio, Pan-American broadcast 259
Radnor, Tenn., yards 182, 291

RAIL –
   Evolution of 367
   Rail, 132-pound, installed 378
Rail records broken (run of "Dixie
   Hummer") 133
"Railroad Bill" (Morris Slater) 111
Railroad Credit Corp. 253
Railroad Retirement Act 171, 261
Railroad War Board 210
Railroad Y.M.C.A. (history of on
   L. & N.) . . . . 169, et seq., 206
Railway Battalion (728th) Engineer
   Reserve 281
Railway Express Agency 344
Railway Mail Service 340
Railway Post Office 340
Railway Transfer, Louisville 72, 108
Rallies, Family 266
Rawls, R. M. 52
REA Leasing Corporation 308
Recapture Clause 233, 258
Red Mountain 84
Refrigerator cars 335
Relay Depot, E. St. Louis 63
Re-numbering of locomotives 351
Republic Iron & Steel Co. 85, 120
Richmond Branch 42, 256
Richmond Locomotive Company 359
Richmond, Nicholasville, Irvine and
   Beattyville Railroad 187
Riddle, Colonel Wm. 6
Rigolets Bridge 236
Rip Van Winkle Sleeping Car
   Company 348
Roadway machinery 383
Robbery, first train 43, 44
Robertson, J. W. 51
Robinson, James P. 6
Robinson, L. L. 6, 367
Rockhouse Creek Branch 198, 286
Rogers & Company 355
Rogers, J. S. 73
Rome Railroad of Georgia 67
Roosevelt, Franklin D. 199
Rowe, "Billy" 133
Rowland shop facilities 119
Rowland, D. W. C. 83
Ruffner Mine No. 2 256
Rutland Railway 316
Ryan, Thomas Fortune 73

S

Safety Appliance Act 122
Sage, Russell 48, 49, 73
St. Louis & Southeastern Ry. 63, 64, 77
St. Louis-San Francisco Ry. 86
Saturday Evening Post 282
Schenectady Locomotive Works 351
Schumpp, George 52
Scrip – issuance of during money
   panic of 1907 176
Segal, Adolph 188
Selective Service Act 269
Selma & Gulf R. R. 62
Service buttons 232, 234
Shawneetown & Eldorado R. R. 63
Sheffield & Tuscumbia Railway 75
Sheffield Iron & Steel Co. 75
Shelby Railroad 72
Sherman, Frank 334
Sherman, Gen. W. T. 32, 150
Shippers' Advisory Boards 270
Shopmen's strike of 1922 228
Shops at Decatur built 90, 167
Shops at Howell built 90
Short Line 71, 108
Shreve, L. L. 2, 7, 15
Sibert Shops and Yard 244
"Sidney Lanier" (Pullman) 346
Silver Bullet 267
Slater, Morris 111
Slaughter, Thomas 73
Sleeping car service 283
Sleeping cars, lightweight, placed in
   service in 1953 294
Slemp, C. Bascom 192
Sloss Furnace Co. 85
Sloss, Col. J. W. 49
Sloss, James H. 85
Smith, General Kirby 35, 117
Smith, Milton H. 52, 53, 65, 73, 84,
91, 128, 131, 164, 173, 185, 217, 218, 230
Smithers, E. L. 217
Snowball Special 320
South & North Alabama
   R. R. . . . . 45, 46, 48, et seq. 65, 84, 86, 179
South Atlantic & Ohio R. R. 99
South Branch 256
South Carolina Ry. 129
South Louisville Shops . . . . . 165, et seq., 358
South Wind 272, 361
Southeastern Army Air Depot 270
Southeastern Presidents' Conference 260
Southern Alabama R. R. Co. 140
"Southern Belle" 351
Southern Express Company 343
Southern Railway 3, 67, 75, 86, 98, 105,
                            117, 122, 240, 265
Southern Railway & Steamship
   Association 79
Southland, The (magazine) 151
Sparhawk, John, Jr. 188
Spencer, Samuel 128
Sperry Detector Car 384

Standard Oil of Kentucky, New Plant	305
Standard Return guaranteed	223
Standard Time Act	220
Standard Time, creation of	82
Standiford, E. D.	53
Stanton, John C.	48, 49
State Docks, Alabama	244
Station at Birmingham	296
Station at Mobile	296
Station at New Orleans	296
Stations abandoned at Cincinnati	241
Steamboats, purchased by L. & N.	54, 107
Steel, first, produced in Alabama	86
"Stephen Collins Foster" (Pullman)	346
Stevenson, V. K.	25, 48
Stone, Henry L.	217
Stone, Isaac	8
Storms on Gulf Coast	176, 210, 240

STOCK –

Of L. & N. as originally chartered	4
Purchases by City of Louisville	8
100% dividend	66
Straight Creek Branch	202, 205
Strawberry Yard re-opened	277
Strike on the L. & N., 1955	296
Strikes and strike threats	288
Suggestion System	266
"Sumner" (locomotive)	349
Swan Creek Railway	182, 268
Sycamore Powder Mills	137
Symbol freight trains	277
Synott, T. W.	188

T

Talking Rock, Ga. (naming of)	149
Tampa-Sutton Fine Coal Case	309
Tank car	335
Tate, Sam	48
Tate, Sam & Associates	47, 48
Taylor, Camp Zachary	214
Tennessee, Alabama & Texas R. R.	101
Tennessee & Alabama R. R.	3, 46, 75
Tennessee & Alabama Central R. R.	46, 47
Tennessee and Western Railroad	208
Tennessee Centennial Exposition	133
Tennessee Coal Iron & R. R. Co.	85, 120
Tennessee Copper Co.	146
Tennessee Midland Ry.	129
Tennessee Ridge	7, 15
Tennessee Western R. R.	209, 268
Tensas River bridge	239
Teredo Navalis	60, 61
Terminal Railroad Association of St. Louis	172
Terminal Railroad of St. Louis	172
"Texas" (origin of)	173
Thomas, S. B.	6
Tie-treating plant at Gautier, Miss.	379
Tie-treating plant at Guthrie, Ky.	379
Tilford, John E.	289, 301
Tilford Yard (Hills Park)	291
Time, Standard, beginning of	82
Tod, E. Kennedy	185
Toledo, Saginaw and Michigan Railroad	174
Toonigh, Ga.	149
Track (evolution of)	367
Track and roadbed (physical construction of)	367
Trade-mark, L. & N., adopted	52
Trailer Train Company	308
Train, first over L. & N.	25
Train-naming contest attracts 300,000 entries	283
Train robbers	44, 110, 111
Train robbery, first	44
Train wreckers	112, 113
Transportation Act (1940)	271
Transportation Act (1920)	232
Troop trains, World War II	277
Truck and bus competition (origin of)	228
Truman, President Harry S.	288
Tunnel Clearance Project	313
Tuscaloosa Mineral Railroad	182
T.V.A. steam plants, coal for	310
Tyler, A. L.	88

U

Underwood, Oscar W.	85
Underwood, William T.	85, 127, 155
Unified Collateral Trust Bonds (1940)	269
Unified Mortgage issued	102, 103
Union Railway and Transit Co.	172
United States Coal and Coke Co.	204
United States Railroad Administration	359
United States Railroad Labor Board	226
United States Steel Corporation	204
Unitized coal train	310
Urban Building, Louisville	245
Uz, Ky. (origin of name)	197

V

Valuation – Company's properties	257
van der Berg, Y.	106
Vandiver, Gov. Ernest	322
Vaughan, F. W.	77
Vice presidents, resident, appointed	324
Virginia and Tennessee Railroad	183
Virginia Locomotive Works	355
Vogue Zeigler Spur	286
Vultee Air Corporation	270

W

Wage increase of 1937	267
Wagner Palace Car Company	347
Wagner, R. J.	217
Walker Survey	190
Walters, Henry	162, 185, 251
Walschaerts valve gear	357
War Between the States	29, et seq.
War Bonds purchased through payroll deductions	280
"Warren County" (locomotive)	349

Washington, George (V. P. of L. & N.)	67
Wasioto and Black Mountain Railroad Company	199, et seq.
Watts Steel & Iron Syndicate	93, 94
Wauhatchie Yard, Chattanooga	291, 312
Welded rail laid in 1958	380
Wells-Fargo & Company	343
Wells, Reuben	79
Western & Atlantic R. R.	154
Western Ky., coal fields	74
Western Railway of Alabama	62
Western Union suit	245, 246
Westinghouse air brake instruction car	333
Westinghouse, George	54
Westinghouse Naval Gun Mount Plant	270
West Point Branch	75, 256
Wetumpka Branch	56
Wickersham, G. W.	217
Wiggins, A. L. M., chairman of board	288, 323
Willard, Daniel	210
Williams, Nels	113
Willoughby, J. E.	153, 186, 197
Winchester and Beattyville Railroad	187
Wisconsin Steel Company	199
Wolf Creek Ordnance Plant	270
Woman, first one employed	72
Women employes	279, 280
Woodruff Sleeping and Parlor Coach Co.	347
Woodward Iron Co.	85
World War I	210, et seq.
World War II	274, et seq.
Wrecks	56

Y

Yates, C. R., elected director	324
Yellow Fever epidemics	56, 124, 125
Yellow River R. R.	141
Yonts Fork Spur	198
Young, H. Lane	324
Y.M.C.A. (Railroad)	169

Illustrations

A

Adairville Branch, abandonment of	257
Advertisement of the L. & N. appearing in Edwards' Louisville Directory for 1866-1867	41
America's heaviest rail shipment	321
Armistice Day parade float of L. & N.	218
"August Belmont" (steamer)	101
Auto-rack trains on L. & N.	308
Automatic block signaling (lower and upper quadrant methods)	224

B

Baggage coach of old train	341
Baker, F. N.	132
Baker's Hill	131
Baldwin, C. C.	386
Bells, donated to churches	292
Blast furnaces at Ensley in 1900	123
Blast furnaces at Middlesboro, Ky., in 1890	92
Bowaters Southern Paper Corporation	306
Bowling Green Shops in 1879	89
Boyles Yard (air view)	302
Breckinridge Street underpass, Louisville	261
BRIDGES -	
Bacon Creek after destruction by Confederates	36
Barren River, Bowling Green, Ky.	89
C. & O. across Ohio at Cincinnati	248
Cumberland River (early day)	369
Danville, Tenn.	248
Demolition at Irvine, Ky.	278
Fourteenth Street, Louisville, Ky. at time of completion	43
Green River, after partial destruction by Confederates	29
Green River, in 1859	21
Henderson (old and new)	248, 381
Henderson (original)	79
Henderson (erection of in 1884)	77, 78
Nashville, during Civil War	384
Rigolets	235
Bulkhead flat car	331

C

Caboose (L. & A.) at Irvine, Ky., in 1907	181
Caboose, newest on the L. & N.	316
Car hoist at Louisville prior to change of gauge	124
Car retarders, DeCoursey, Ky.	271
Centralized Traffic Control - control board	303
Charter, signing of	2
Cincinnati Union Terminal (air view)	243
Clover Fork Branch, surfacing of	203
Cloverport, Ky., Shops	172
Coach travel during War Between States	332
Coal hopper, 50-ton	317
Coal hopper, 100-ton	331
Coal (lump of Alabama coal on L. & N. flat-car)	87
Coal moved by unitized trains	310
Coal movement on L. & N.	311
Coaling plant, Muscogee Wharf, Pensacola, Fla.	240
Coke container gondola	335
Cole, Whiteford R.	386
Construction camp on Clear Fork Branch	153
Construction - New Lines, Eastern Kentucky	191

399

Corbin, Ky., yard in 1900 115
Coupler, modern day 333
Covered hopper, Boca Grande, 70-
   ton capacity 320
Cumberland Avenue in Middlesboro,
   Ky. in 'nineties 93
Cumberland Furnace in 1929 118
Cushioned Cargo Car 330

D

Data-Processing Center, Louisville 314
Day coach interior in Gay Nineties 332
Day coach travel –1950s 332
DeCoursey, Ky., car repair track and
   east yard during 1937 flood 262
DeCoursey Yard completed in 1963 312
Diesel electric switch engines Nos.
   10 and 11 270
Diner-lounge car 337
Dining car in the 1920s (interior view) . . . 337
Dixie Flagler 266, 329
Dixie Hummer's record run 132
Double track construction near Langford,
   Ky. 227
Double tunnel near Fountain Head,
   Tenn., in 1859 27
Draftees off to camp (World War I) 208

E

East Louisville grade separation 377
Employe benefits on L. & N. 325
ENGINES –
   No. 7 . . . . 116, 341
   No. 8 350
   No. 10 . . . . 180, 270, 362
   No. 11 270
   No. 20 350
   No. 25 352
   No. 35 136
   No. 38 350
   No. 77 350
   No. 102 352
   No. 133 352
   No. 151 354
   No. 266 359
   No. 269 352
   No. 282 352
   No. 295 362
   No. 409 360
   No. 450 363
   No. 500 . . . . 354, 365
   No. 501 352
   No. 801 364
   No. 989 354
   No. 1015 366
   No. 1200 354
   No. 1281 354
   No. 1480 359
   No. 1600 365
   No. 1882 – Last scheduled run of
      steam-powered train on L. & N. 291
   No. 1906 358
   No. 1960 361
   No. 2101 359
   No. 2500 364
Etowah in 1905 154
Evacuation of refugees by train from
   Louisville during 1937 flood 264

F

Family Rally, Louisville, July 10, 1935 . . . 267
Federal Control, 1943-1944 (Army
   Officers) 280
Financial Inspection Tour 296
Fire department, L. & N. Shops,
   10th and Ky., Louisville, in 1898 168
FIRST –
   Engine through Yellow Rock Tunnel . . . 193
   Locomotive of L. & O. R. R. 73
   L. & N. time table 24
   Passenger car of L. & O. R. R. 74
   Passenger station at Louisville, Ky. 109
   Passenger train into Harlan, Ky. 205
   Passenger train out of Hazard, Ky. 188
   Train through Hagan's Tunnel 252
Flood at East St. Louis, Ill., in 1903 137
"Four Seasons" Hotel at Harrogate,
   Tenn., in 1891 96
Freight cars, rebuilding of at South
   Louisville 269
Freight cars at Nashville during War
   Between States 330
Freight equipment evolution 330

G

General office building – Air conditioning
   and modernization 297
General office buildings (past and
   present 64, 158
General, The, greeted by 10,000 persons
   at Big Shanty, Ga. 324
General, The, receives excellent press 322
Green, E. H. 387
Guthrie, James 387

H

Hack line between Hazard and
   Jackson, Ky. 184
Hagan's Tunnel 252, 380
Hazard, Ky., street scene 179
Helm, John L. 387
"Hercules" at Mammoth Cave, Ky. 105
Hewing ties for railroad track 117
Hill, J. B. 386
Hiwassee Loop 146
Horse-and-buggy days at Altoona, Ala. . . . 129
Hospital car (interior), Civil War 32
Hospital train – Civil War 31
Hotbox Detectors on the L. & N. 315
Houston, Russell 387
Howell, Ind., right-of-way south of,
   after 1937 flood 263
Humming Bird, The, modern passenger
   train 329
Hurricane, Gulf Coast, Sept. 1947 287

I

Industrial District, Derby City at
  Louisville 307
Industrial expansion on L. & N. (plant)...301
Institutional advertisement 234

K

Kendall, William H. 386
"Kiddie Special" - Operation between
  Louisville and Lebanon Junction, Ky. . . 293
Kinzel's Patent Rail Straightener 375
Knoxville, LaFollette and Jellico
  Railroad (laying of last rail) 149
Knoxville, LaFollette and Jellico
  Railroad (construction of) 147

L

L. & A. Caboose at Irvine, Ky. in
  1907 181
L. & E. freight train on Lollegrod
  Bridge in October 1909 183
L. & N. Magazine - March 1925 (re-
  production of cover) 233
L. & N. time table (first) 24
Lebanon Junction during Civil War 36
Line into Mobile prior to 1929 244
Link-and-pin method of coupling 333
Lively Lines - Dec., 1924 (reproduction
  of cover) 233
Locomotive classification chart 356
Locomotive repair section, machine
  shop, South Louisville 165
Locomotive undergoing repairs at
  South Louisville just after completion
  of shops 156
Louisville Chamber of Commerce -
  Tour of L. & N. lines 299
Louisville wharf during Civil War 34

M

Mapother, Wible L. 386
MAPS -
  Cincinnati-Atlanta line showing
    how formed 145
  Cumberland Valley Division 200
  Double track between Covington
    and Corbin 225
  L. & N. and the K. C. G. & L. Ry.,
    between Middlesboro and Cumberland
    Gap on November 4, 1896 98
  L. & N. in 1888. 71
  L. & N. lines in Alabama in 1890 85
  L. & N. in 1900 125
  Main Line trackage of the Eastern
    Kentucky Division 189
  Plum Street Produce Yard 250
  Rail and river connections of L. & N.
    in 1854 9
  Standard Time 81
Martin's Fork Branch, rail laying in 1911. . 200
Master mechanic's office at Etowah in 1907 152
McRoberts, Ky. (completion of railroad
  to) 197
Mechanization of office work 297
Mechanized equipment - South Louisville,
  Ky. 259
Middlesboro's "Big Fire" of 1890 97
Mobile Passenger Station 294
Monument to Mr. and Mrs. G. W.
  Ernest in Cave Hill Cemetery 57
Motion Picture - "The Old Reliable" -
  filming of scene. 299
Muldraugh's Hill in 1893. 239
Muldraugh's Hill after double-tracking . . . 242
Multiple tamper 379
Mundfordville, Ky., during Civil War ... 33
Muscogee Wharf at Pensacola around
  the turn of century 240

N

New Orleans Union Passenger Terminal
  (air view) 294
Newcomb, H. D. 387
Newcomb, H. V. 387
"Niggerhead" Rock 99
Norton, Eckstein 386

O

Oak Hill camp established by police
  department 174
Offices - Mechanization of 297
Ore train at Ensley, Ala., in 1900. 121

P

Pan-American broadcast -
  Advertisement of 258
Pascagoula, Miss., New refinery at 305
Pass - annual - Louisville and Nashville and
  Great Southern Railroad 50
Passenger equipment evolution 329
Personnel Development Program 286
Piggyback cars 295
Piggyback ramp, portable 309
Pine Sleepers 346
"Pioneer" (first Pullman), interior view . . . 345
Plum Street Produce Yard,
  Cincinnati 249
Pratt Coal & Coke Company mine
  in 1879 63
Prudential Insurance Company
  group insurance policy 233
Public Relations pamphlet issued by
  management 234
Pullman equipment, evolution of 345
Pullman parlor car (early day),
  interior of 347
Pullman (present day), interior of. 346
Push boat scene on North Fork of
  Kentucky River 187
Pusher-service diesels 284

R

Radio on Pan-American 231

Radio – two-way, providing end-to-end
   communication on freight trains 300
Radnor, Tenn., Freight House 298
Rail evolution 372
Railroad accident 370
Railroad Y. M. C. A. at 3rd and
   Central, Louisville 171
Railway Express Agency at Louisville . . . 342
Railway post office car 338, 339
Relay House – Birmingham 47
Retarder yard, DeCoursey, Ky. 271
Retarders – Automatic control of
   (VELAC) 303
Rockhouse Creek Branch, construction
   of 285
Rogers, J. S. 386
Rowe, J. W. 132

S

"E. O. Saltmarsh" – steamer 101
Samson, Ala., evolution of 148
Scrip issued to employes during panic
   of 1907 175
Section gang at Baker's Hill 131
Service buttons 232
Service stars, lobby, G. O. B. 280
Shops at Bowling Green, Ky., in
   1893, following storm 113
Shreve, L. L. 387
Sibert Yard 241
Silver Bullet 268
Sleeping car on New York Central
   in 1869 344
Smith, Milton H. 386
Soldiers moving to camp 272
Southern Belle 49
South Louisville Shops 155, 156
South Louisville Shops, $5 million
   mechanized car-repair shop at 319
South Wind 266
Special agents on Clear Fork Branch
   in 1903 153
Standard Oil Refinery at Pascagoula 305
Standard Oil Refinery reactor vessel 321
Standiford, E. D. 387
STATIONS –
   Altoona, Ala. 129
   Baxter Avenue 377
   Birmingham in 1873 46
   Birmingham, opening of 107
   Birmingham, in 1960 322
   Canal Street, New Orleans, in 1887 . . . 60
   Central Union at Cincinnati 243
   Church Street (N. C. & St. L. at
      Nashville) 141
   Cincinnati Union (air view) 243
   Louisville Union 111
   Memphis Union 211
   Mobile around turn of century 59
   Nashville Union 140
   Nashville Union (clock and figures) . . . 142
   Nashville Union (construction of) . . 138, 139
   New Orleans Canal Street in 1880s 60
   Pennsylvania, Cincinnati 243
   Peewee Valley (opening of) 68
   St. Louis Union 150
   Water St., Louisville, during flood 263
Steam's farewell – last regularly scheduled
   run on L. & N. 291
Stores department storage yard at
   South Louisville 260

T

Tarragona St. Wharf at Pensacola
   around turn of century 103
Tilford, John E. 386
Time Table (1859) 24
"Titania" (early-day Pullman), interior
   view 345
TOTE (Trailer-On-Train-Express) cars . . . 295
Track abandonment scene –
   Adairville Branch 257
Trade-mark 52
Train, Barrett Lightning Matinee 54
Trainside scene – World War I –
   Louisville Union Station 209
Troop train passing through Big Cut
   on L. & N. during Civil War 30
Tunnel clearance for bigger loads 313

U

Unitized coal trains 310
U. S. R. R. Administration letterhead
   used by L. & N. 215
VELAC – Automatic Retarder Control
   System 303

W

Water Street, Louisville, during
   1937 flood 263
Wauhatchie Yard completed in 1961 312
Webb, Dave L., coal mine near Seco, Ky. . . . 190
Welded rail 296
Whitesburg, Ky. group (attorneys,
   engineers, etc.) 191
Whitesburg, Ky., in 1912 194
Wiggins, A. L. M. 294
Wolf Creek Ordnance Plant – building
   of spur line to 273
Wood-chip car, Jumbo 100-ton type 317
Wood, E. L. 132
Work train on C. V. Division 95
World War I – coach 208
World War I – scene at Louisville
   Union Station 209
World War I – scene at Hawesville, Ky. . . 217
World War II – Tanks on flatcars 276
Wreck near Wilcox, Ala., in 1897 112

Y

Yellow Fever Epidemic refugee trains 55
Y. M. C. A. (railroad) at South
   Louisville 171

www.ingramcontent.com/pod-product-compliance
Lightning Source LLC
Chambersburg PA
CBHW080723230426
43665CB00020B/2590